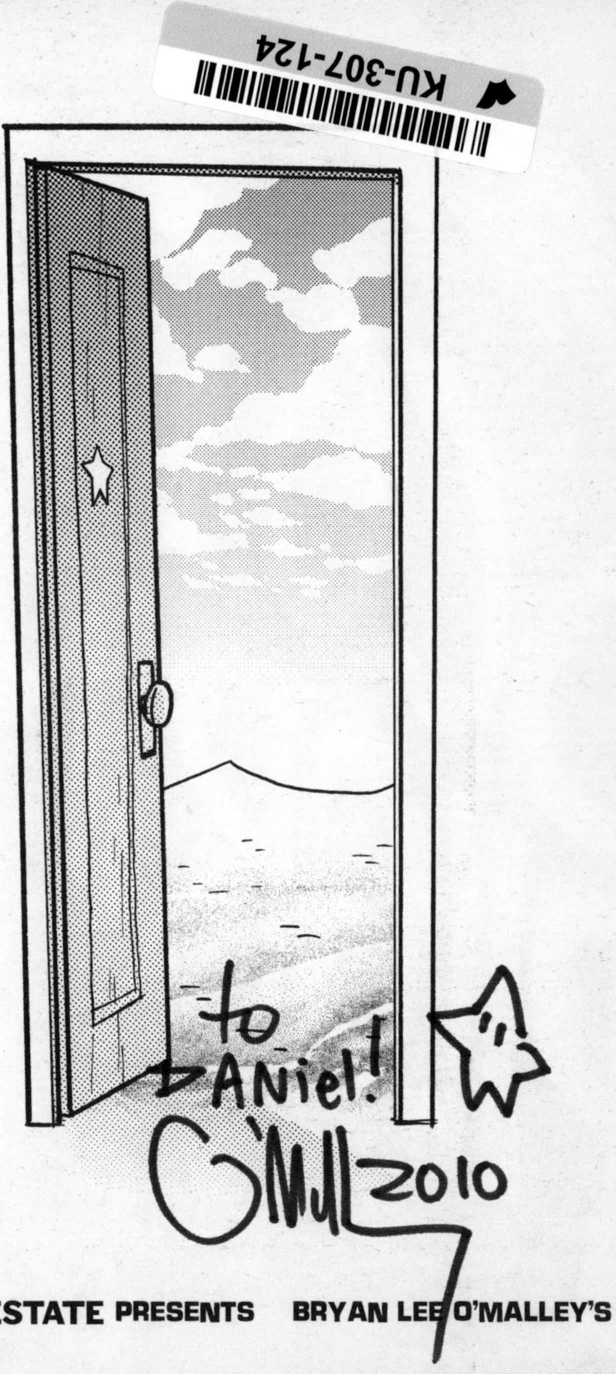
to
DANiel!
O'Mull 2010

FOURTH ESTATE PRESENTS BRYAN LEE O'MALLEY'S

SCOTT PILGRIM

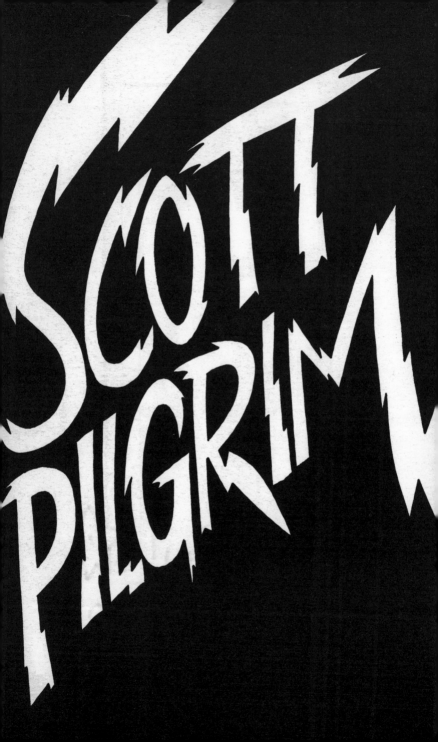

IN HIS
FINEST
HOUR

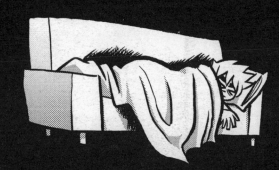

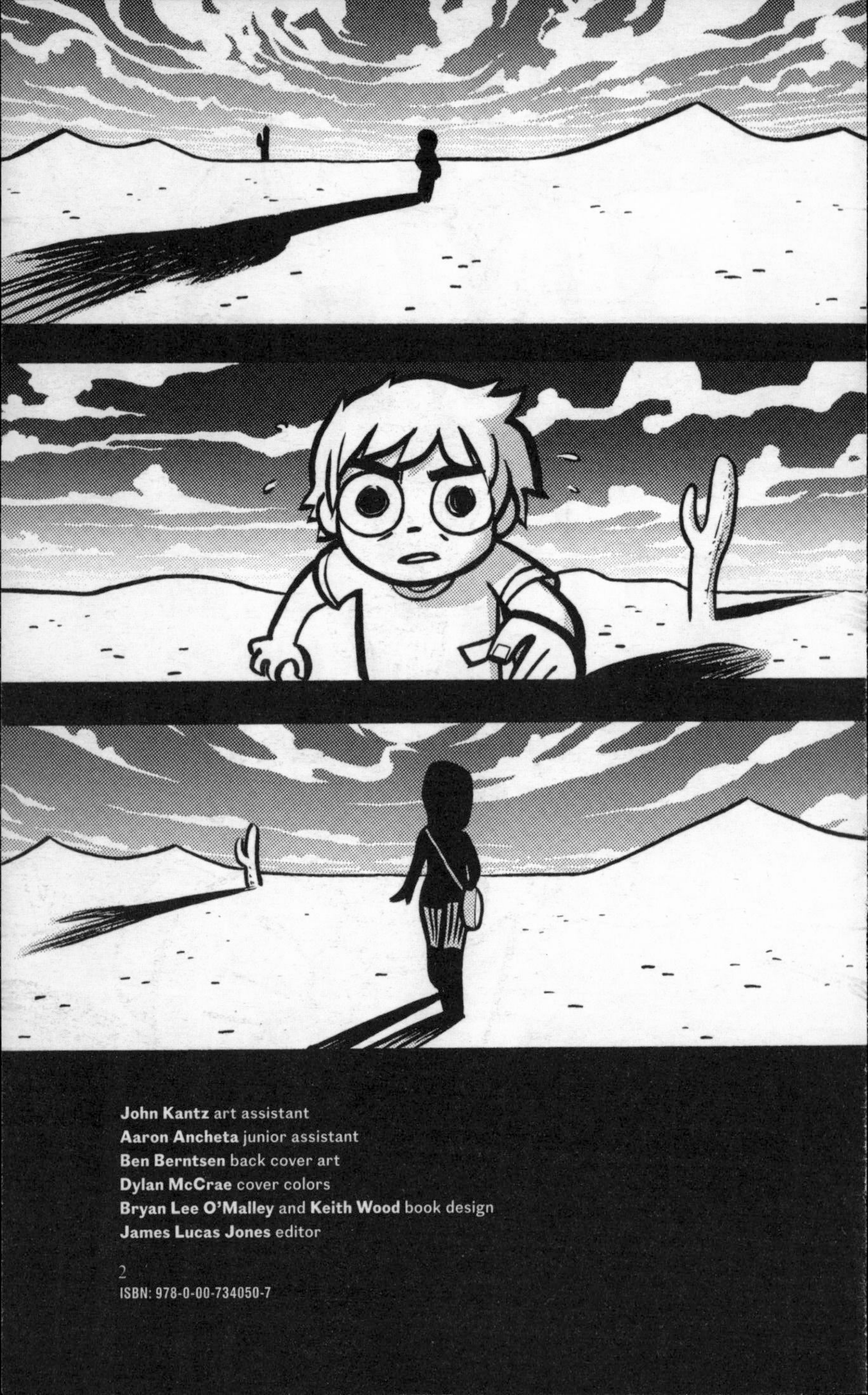

John Kantz art assistant
Aaron Ancheta junior assistant
Ben Berntsen back cover art
Dylan McCrae cover colors
Bryan Lee O'Malley and **Keith Wood** book design
James Lucas Jones editor

2
ISBN: 978-0-00-734050-7

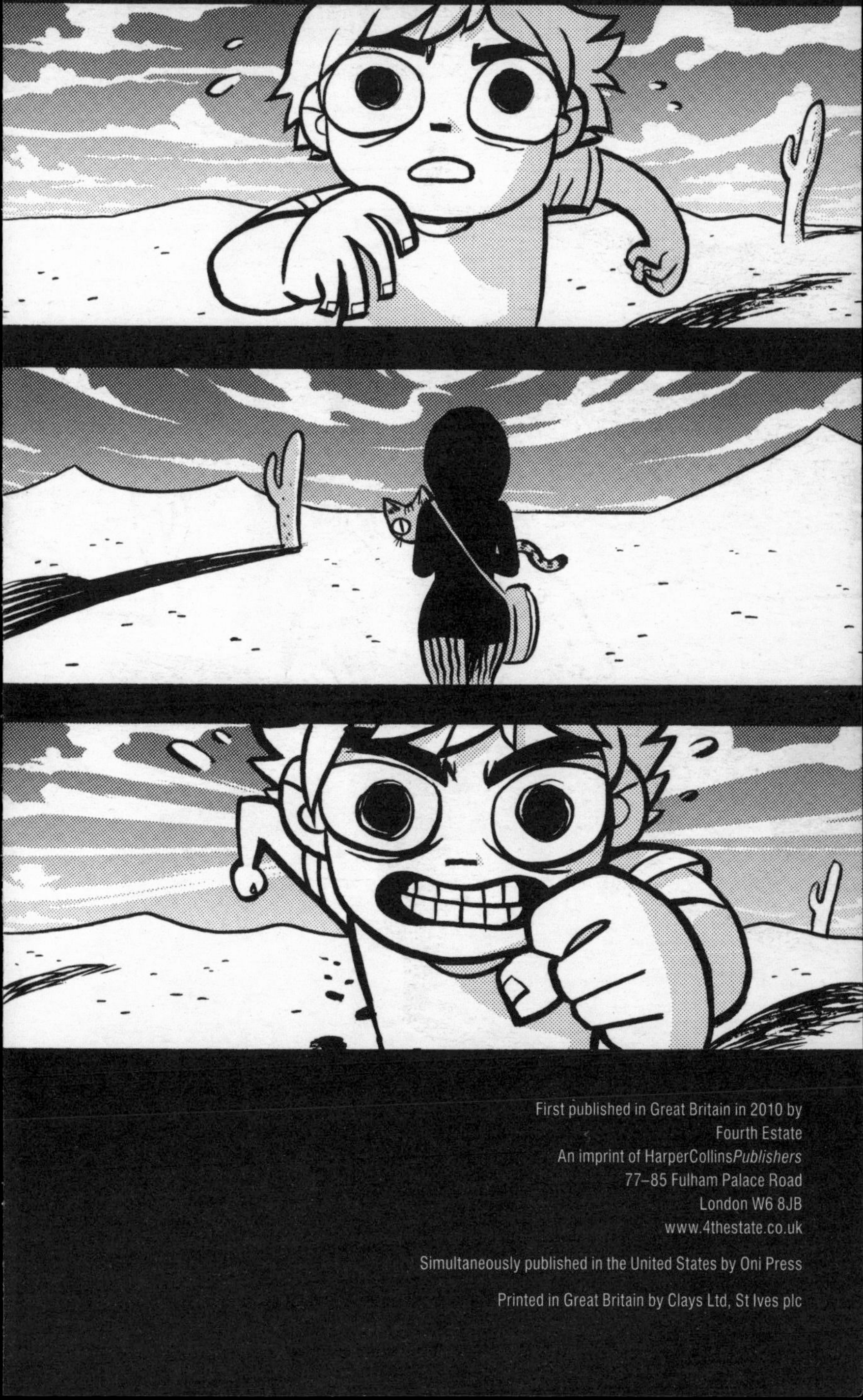

First published in Great Britain in 2010 by
Fourth Estate
An imprint of HarperCollins*Publishers*
77–85 Fulham Palace Road
London W6 8JB
www.4thestate.co.uk

Simultaneously published in the United States by Oni Press

Printed in Great Britain by Clays Ltd, St Ives plc

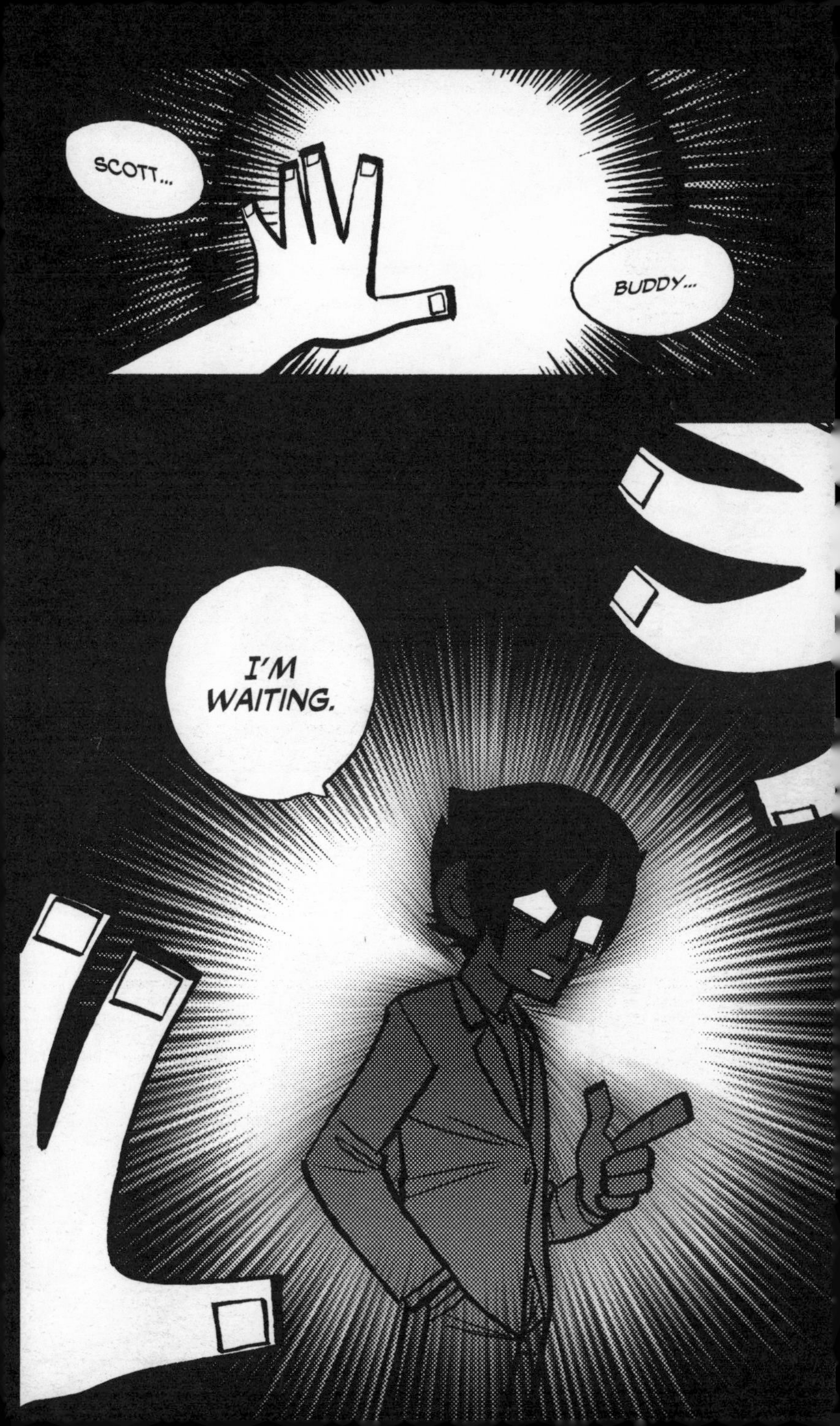
SCOTT...
BUDDY...
I'M WAITING.

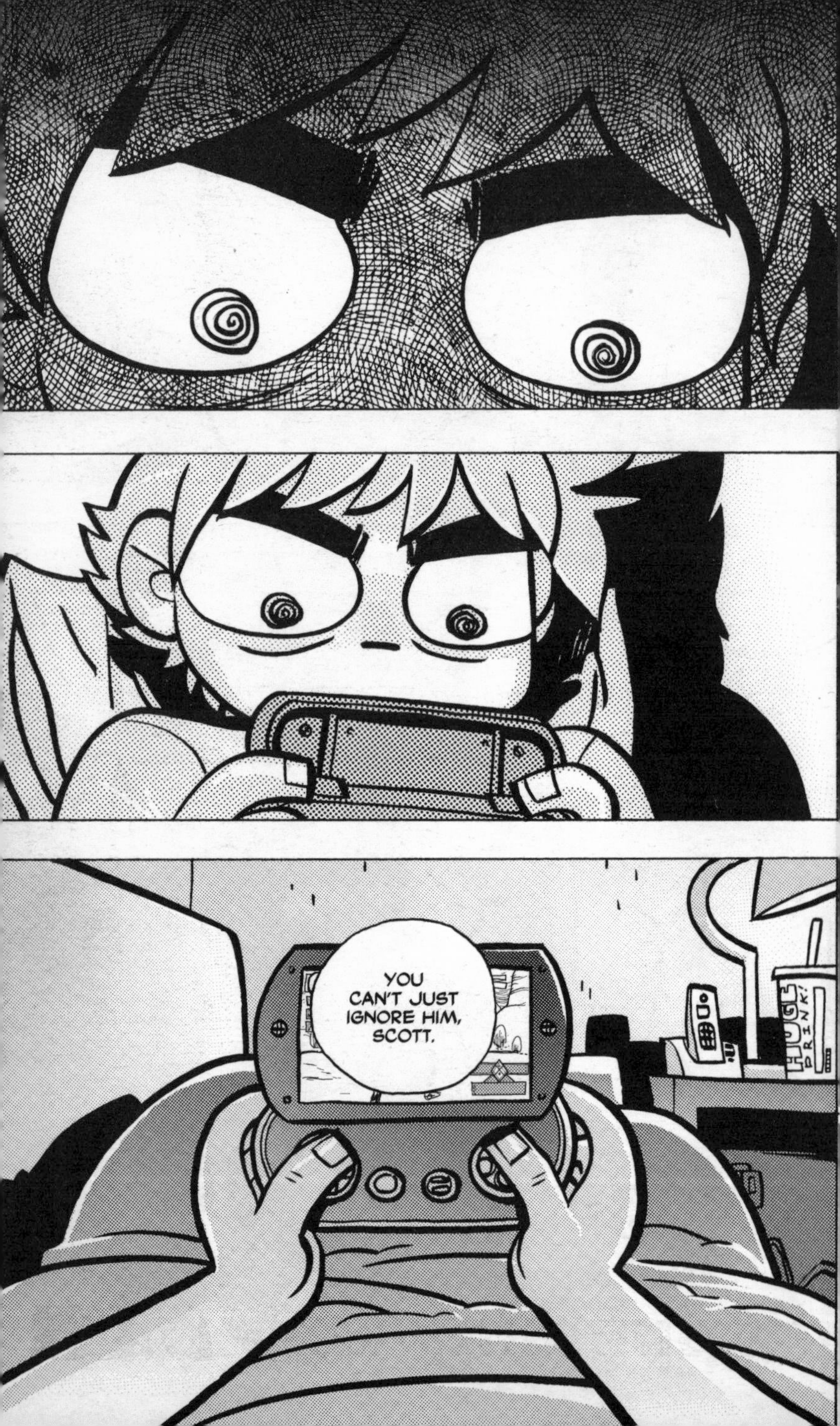
YOU CAN'T JUST IGNORE HIM, SCOTT.
HUGE DRINK!

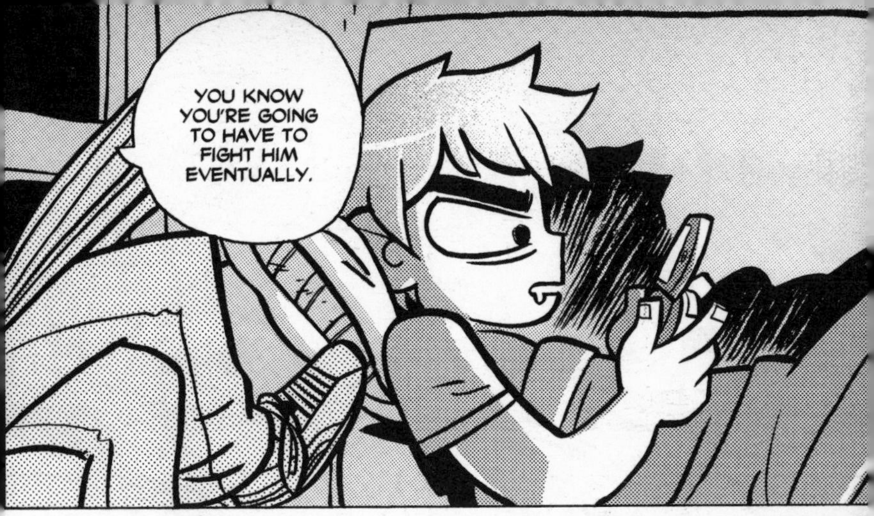
YOU KNOW YOU'RE GOING TO HAVE TO FIGHT HIM EVENTUALLY.

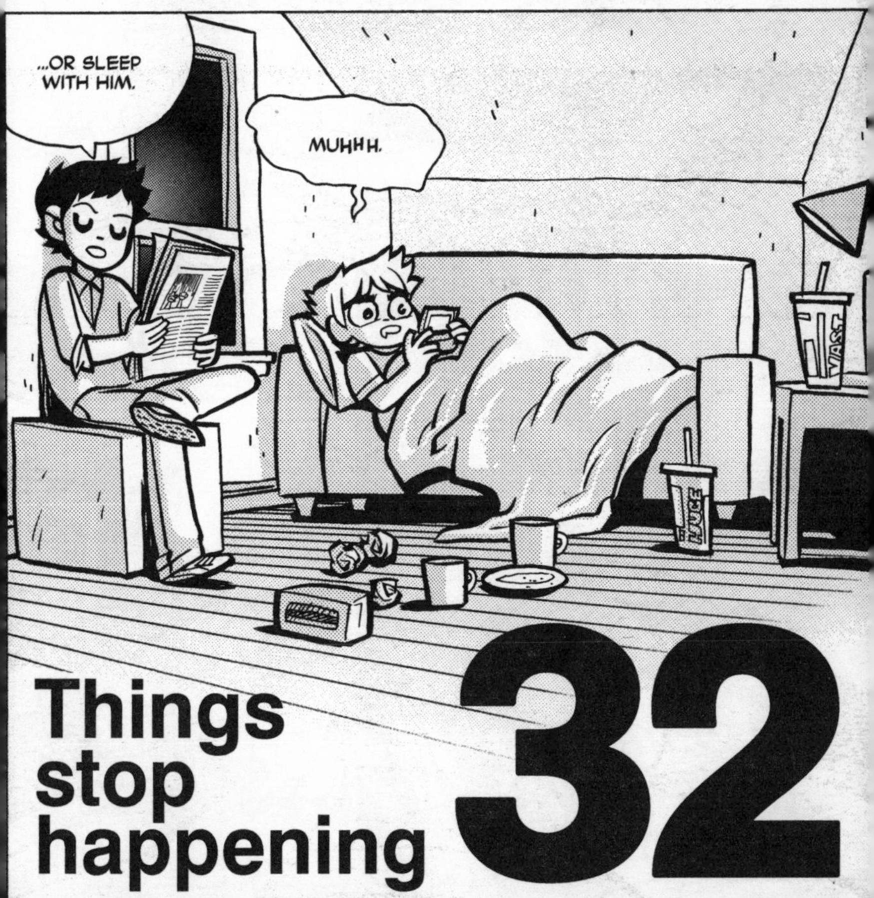
...OR SLEEP WITH HIM.
MUHHH.

Things stop happening 32

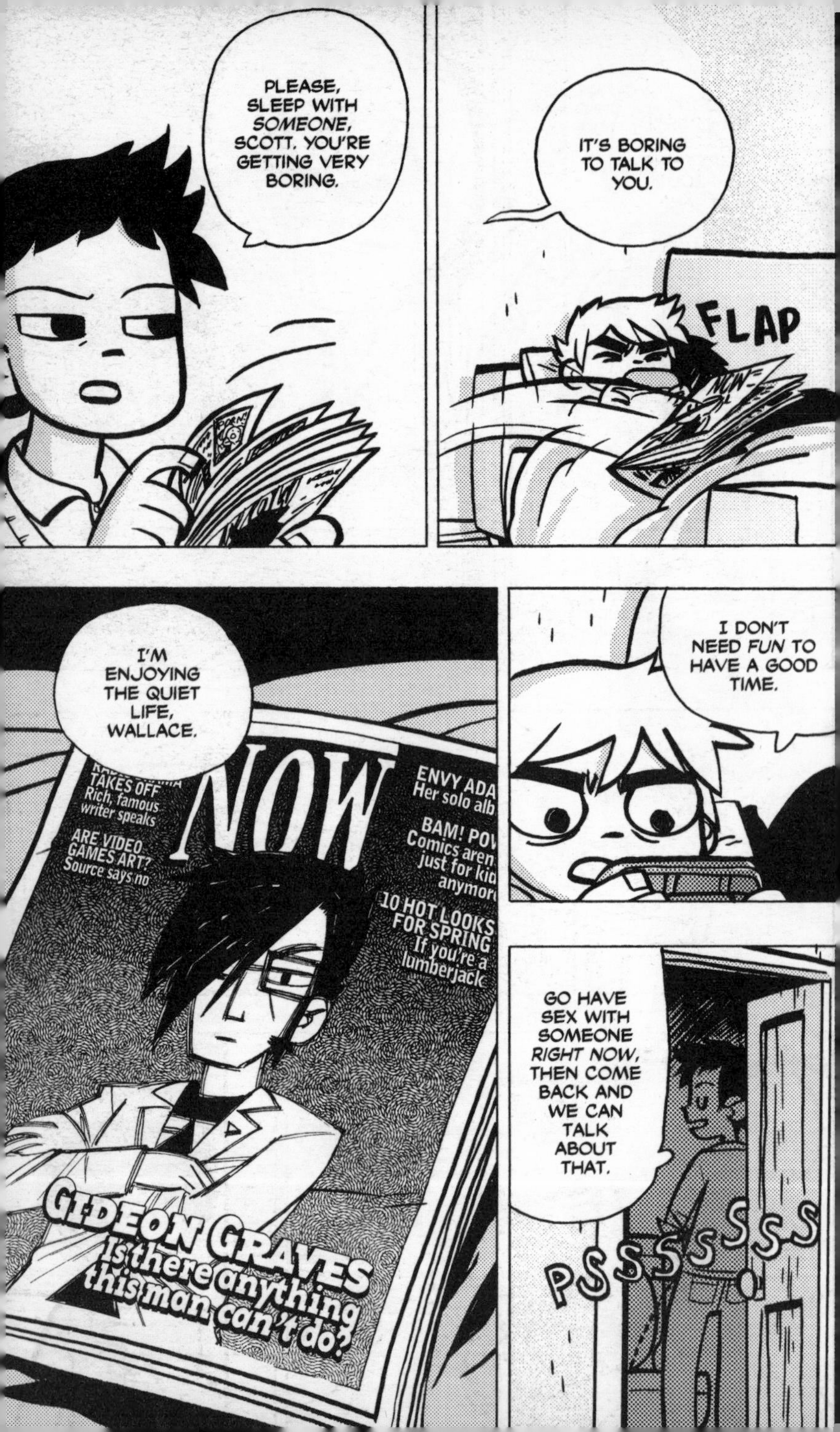

PLEASE, SLEEP WITH *SOMEONE*, SCOTT. YOU'RE GETTING VERY BORING.
IT'S BORING TO TALK TO YOU.
FLAP
I'M ENJOYING THE QUIET LIFE, WALLACE.
NOW
TAKES OFF
Rich, famous writer speaks
ARE VIDEO GAMES ART?
Source says no
ENVY ADA
Her solo alb
BAM! POV
Comics aren
just for kid
anymor
10 HOT LOOKS FOR SPRING
If you're a lumberjack
GIDEON GRAVES
Is there anything this man can't do?
I DON'T NEED *FUN* TO HAVE A GOOD TIME.
GO HAVE SEX WITH SOMEONE *RIGHT NOW*, THEN COME BACK AND WE CAN TALK ABOUT THAT.
PSSSSSSS

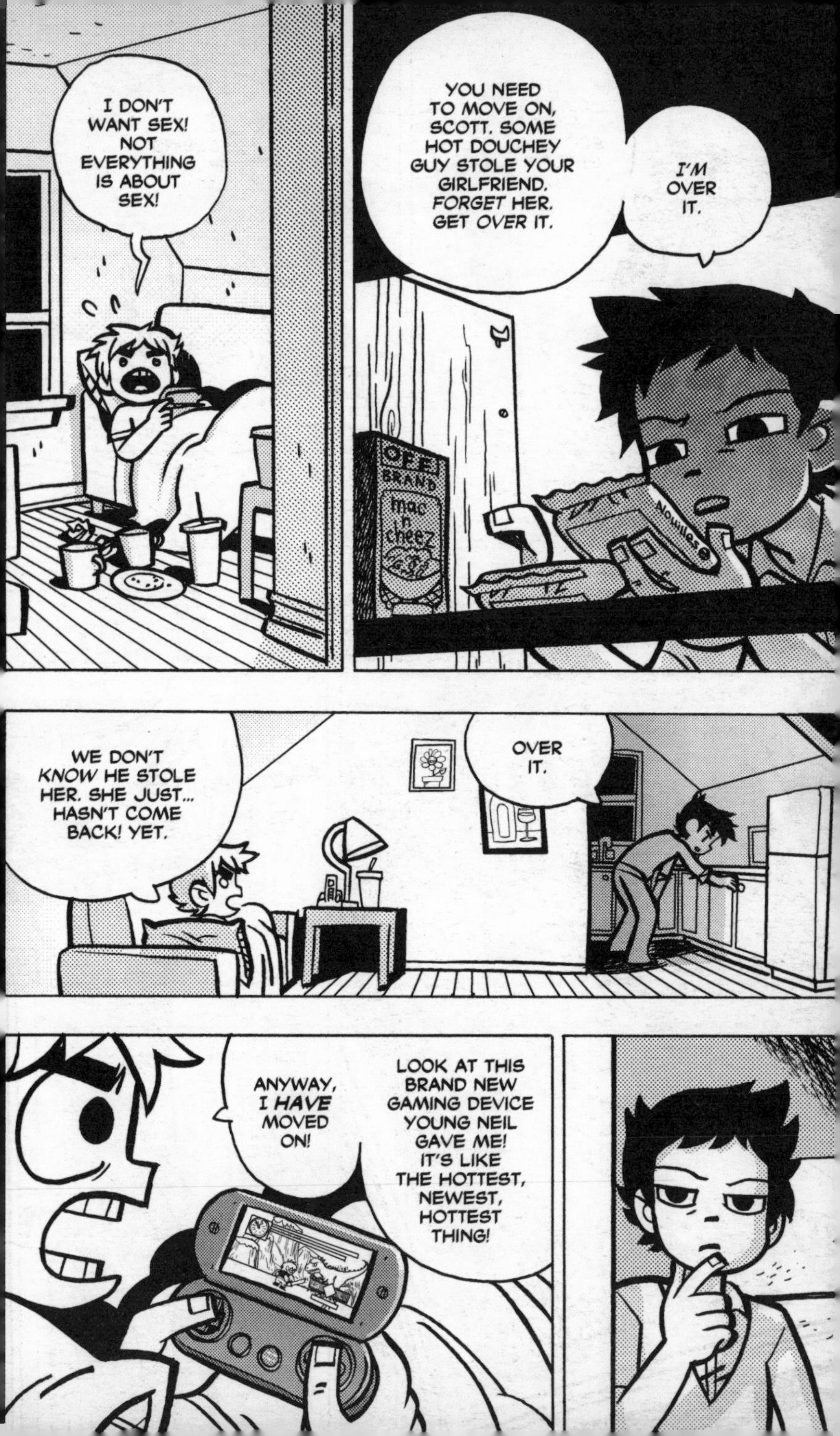
I DON'T WANT SEX! NOT EVERYTHING IS ABOUT SEX!
YOU NEED TO MOVE ON, SCOTT. SOME HOT DOUCHEY GUY STOLE YOUR GIRLFRIEND. *FORGET* HER. GET *OVER* IT.
I'M OVER IT.
OFF BRAND mac n cheez
Nouilles
WE DON'T *KNOW* HE STOLE HER. SHE JUST... HASN'T COME BACK! YET.
OVER IT.
ANYWAY, I ***HAVE*** MOVED ON!
LOOK AT THIS BRAND NEW GAMING DEVICE YOUNG NEIL GAVE ME! IT'S LIKE THE HOTTEST, NEWEST, HOTTEST THING!

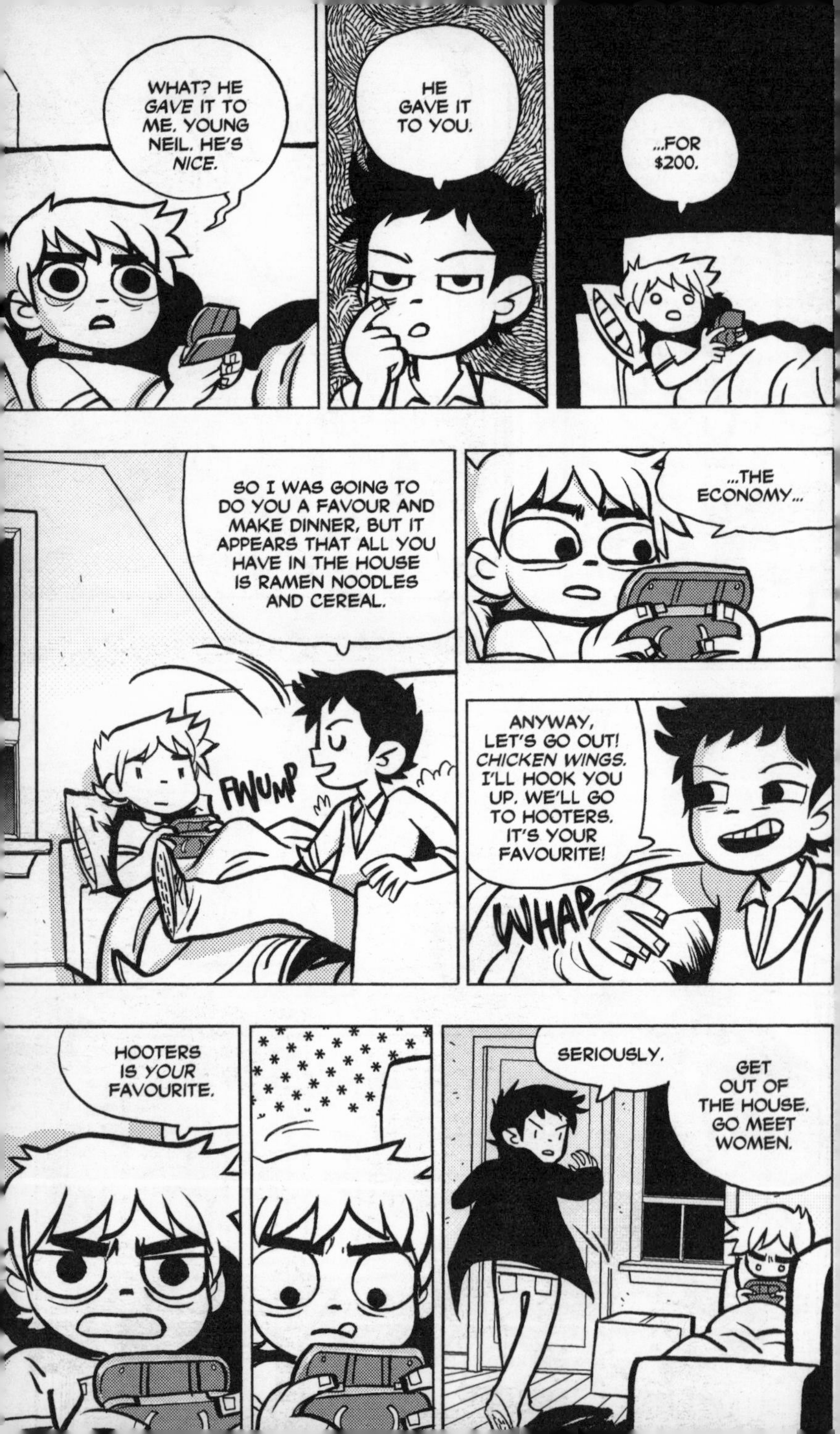
WHAT? HE *GAVE* IT TO ME. YOUNG NEIL. HE'S *NICE.*
HE GAVE IT TO YOU.
...FOR $200.
SO I WAS GOING TO DO YOU A FAVOUR AND MAKE DINNER, BUT IT APPEARS THAT ALL YOU HAVE IN THE HOUSE IS RAMEN NOODLES AND CEREAL.
FWUMP
...THE ECONOMY...
ANYWAY, LET'S GO OUT! *CHICKEN WINGS.* I'LL HOOK YOU UP. WE'LL GO TO HOOTERS. IT'S YOUR FAVOURITE!
WHAP
HOOTERS IS *YOUR* FAVOURITE.
SERIOUSLY.
GET OUT OF THE HOUSE. GO MEET WOMEN.

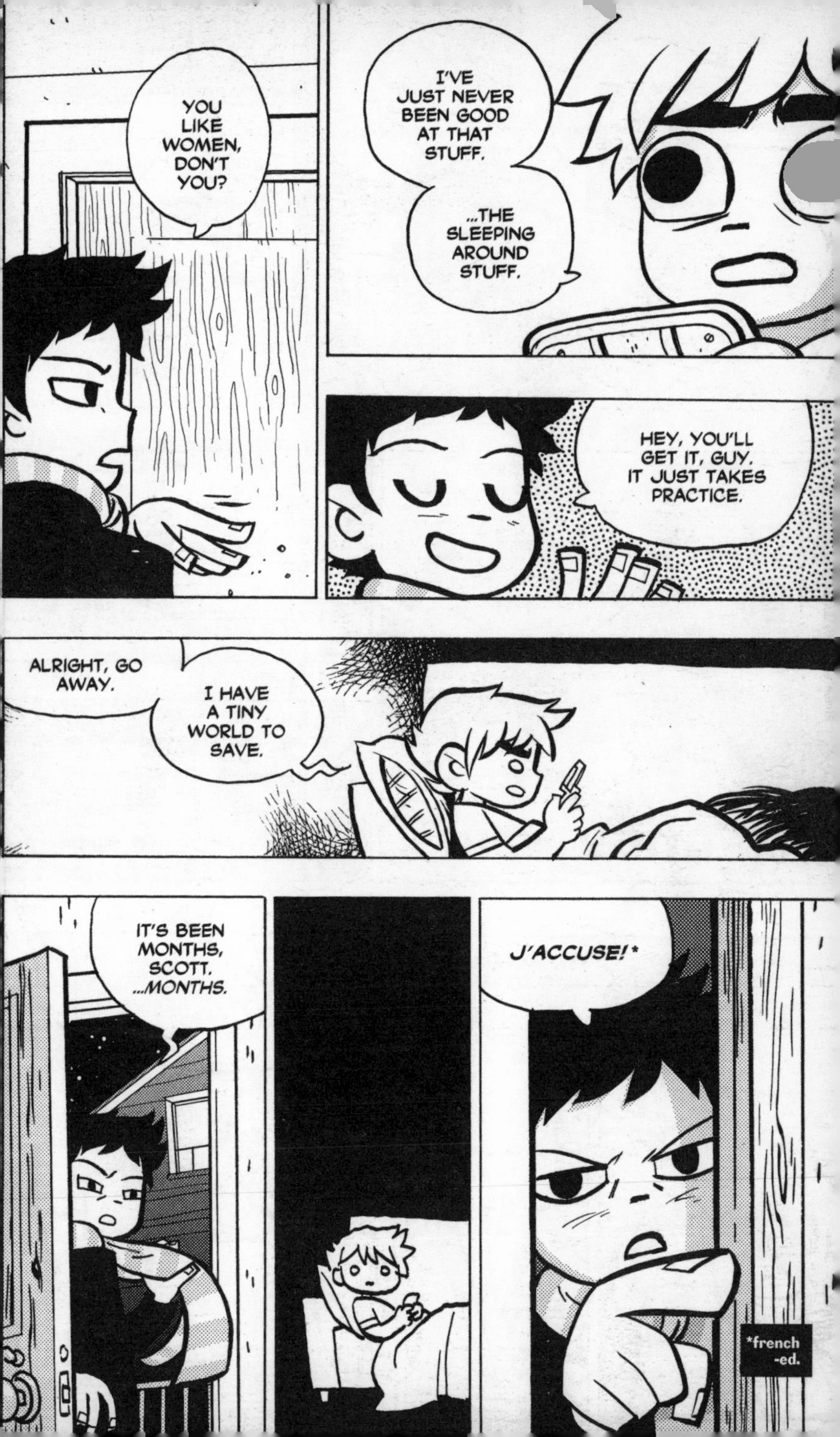
YOU LIKE WOMEN, DON'T YOU?
I'VE JUST NEVER BEEN GOOD AT THAT STUFF.
...THE SLEEPING AROUND STUFF.
HEY, YOU'LL GET IT, GUY. IT JUST TAKES PRACTICE.
ALRIGHT, GO AWAY.
I HAVE A TINY WORLD TO SAVE.
IT'S BEEN MONTHS, SCOTT. ...MONTHS.
J'ACCUSE! *
*french -ed.

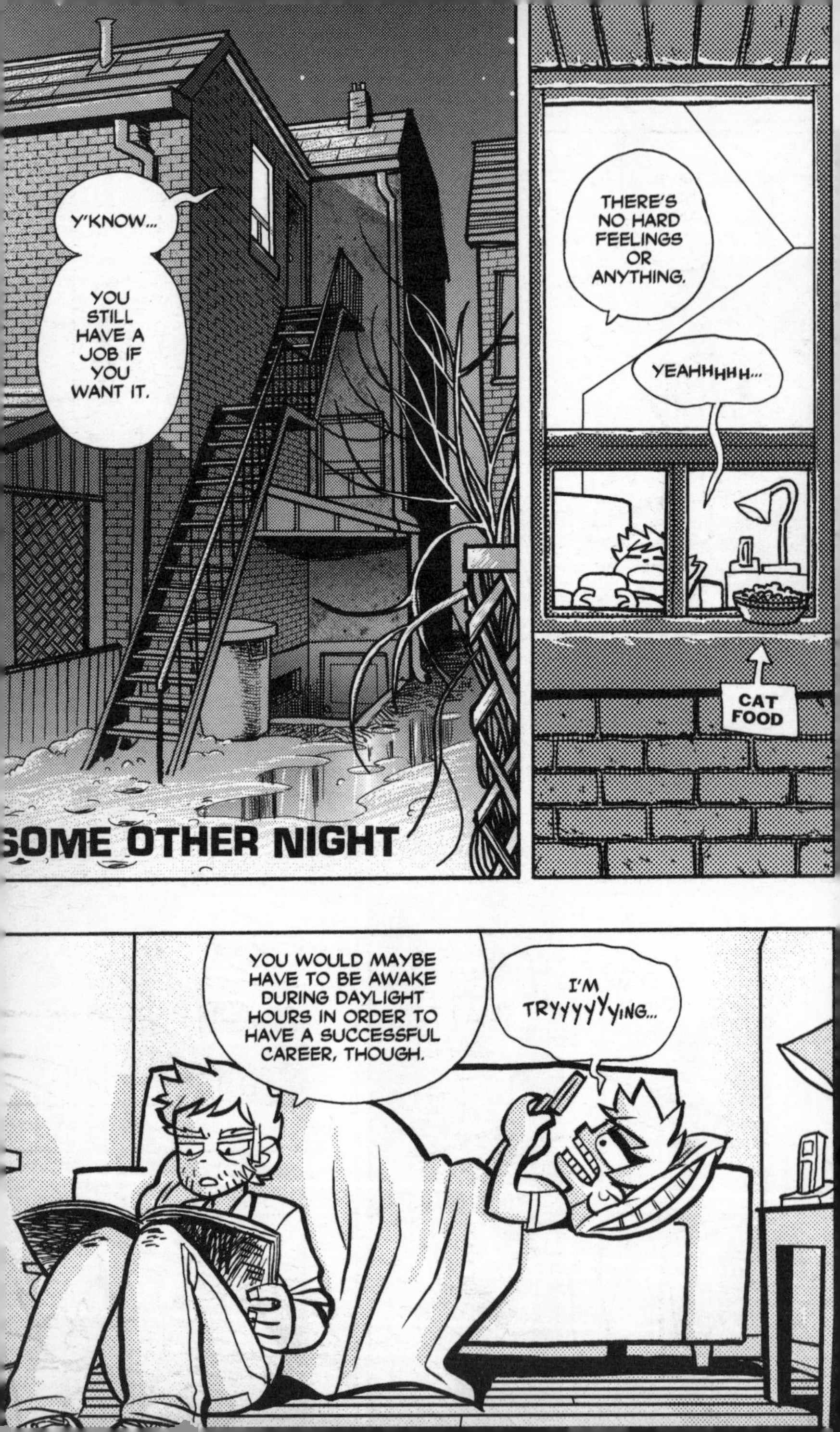
Y'KNOW...
YOU STILL HAVE A JOB IF YOU WANT IT.
SOME OTHER NIGHT
THERE'S NO HARD FEELINGS OR ANYTHING.
YEAHHHHHH...
CAT FOOD
YOU WOULD MAYBE HAVE TO BE AWAKE DURING DAYLIGHT HOURS IN ORDER TO HAVE A SUCCESSFUL CAREER, THOUGH.
I'M TRYYYYYYING...

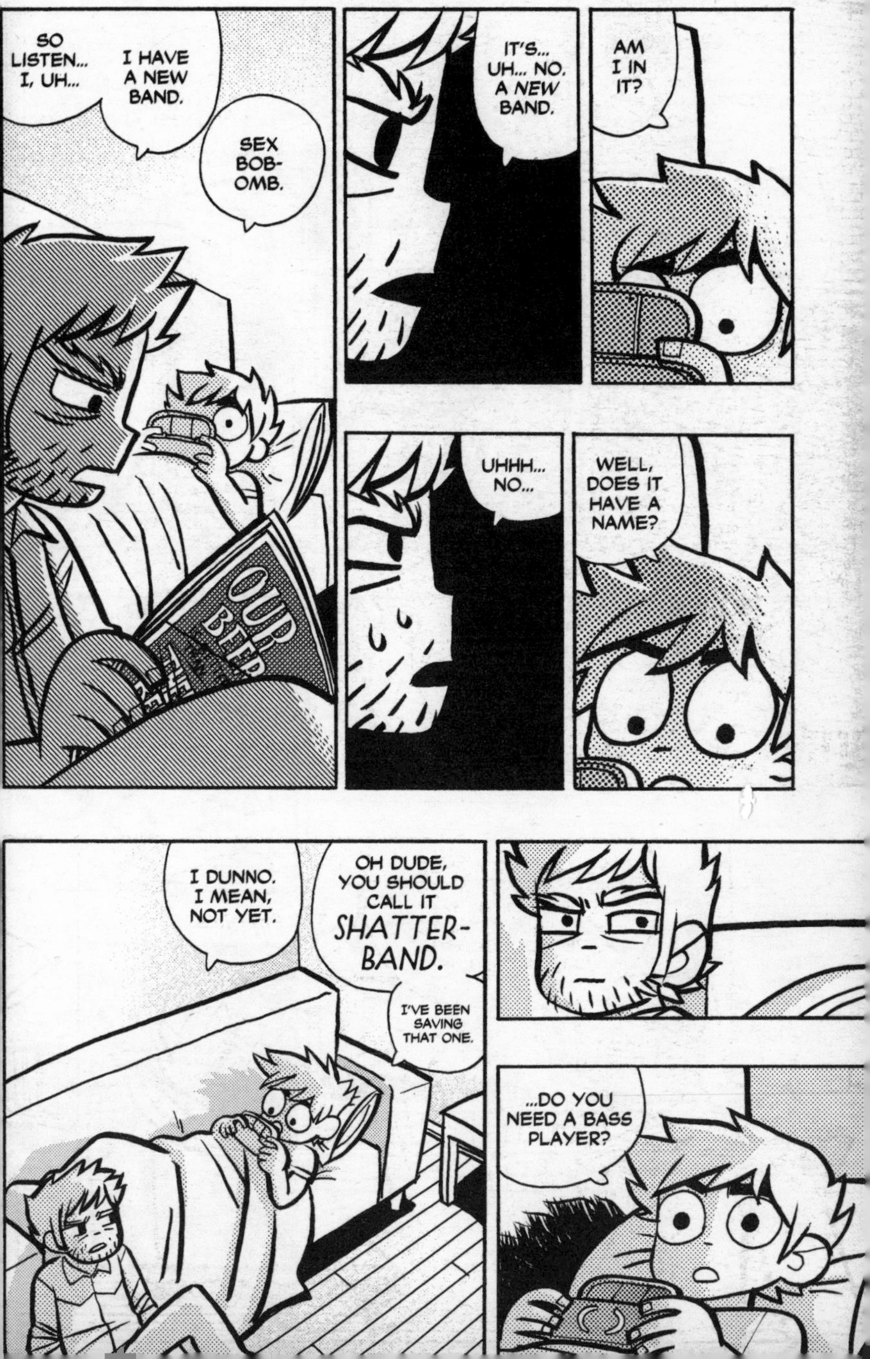
SO LISTEN... I, UH...
I HAVE A NEW BAND.
SEX BOB-OMB.
IT'S... UH... NO. A NEW BAND.
AM I IN IT?
UHHH... NO...
WELL, DOES IT HAVE A NAME?
I DUNNO. I MEAN, NOT YET.
OH DUDE, YOU SHOULD CALL IT SHATTER-BAND.
I'VE BEEN SAVING THAT ONE.
...DO YOU NEED A BASS PLAYER?

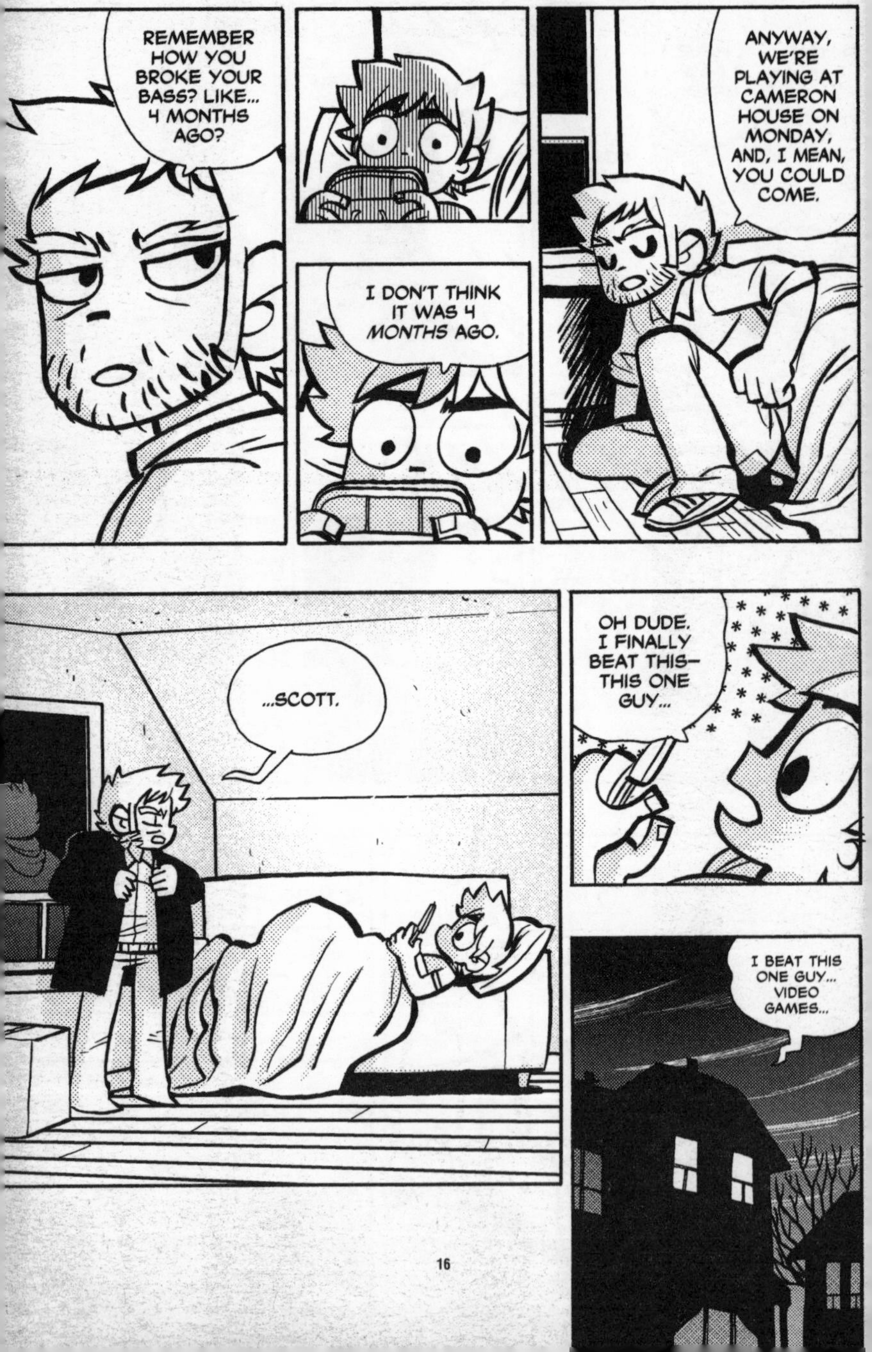
REMEMBER HOW YOU BROKE YOUR BASS? LIKE... 4 MONTHS AGO?
I DON'T THINK IT WAS 4 *MONTHS* AGO.
ANYWAY, WE'RE PLAYING AT CAMERON HOUSE ON MONDAY, AND, I MEAN, YOU COULD COME.
...SCOTT.
OH DUDE. I FINALLY BEAT THIS— THIS ONE GUY...
I BEAT THIS ONE GUY... VIDEO GAMES...

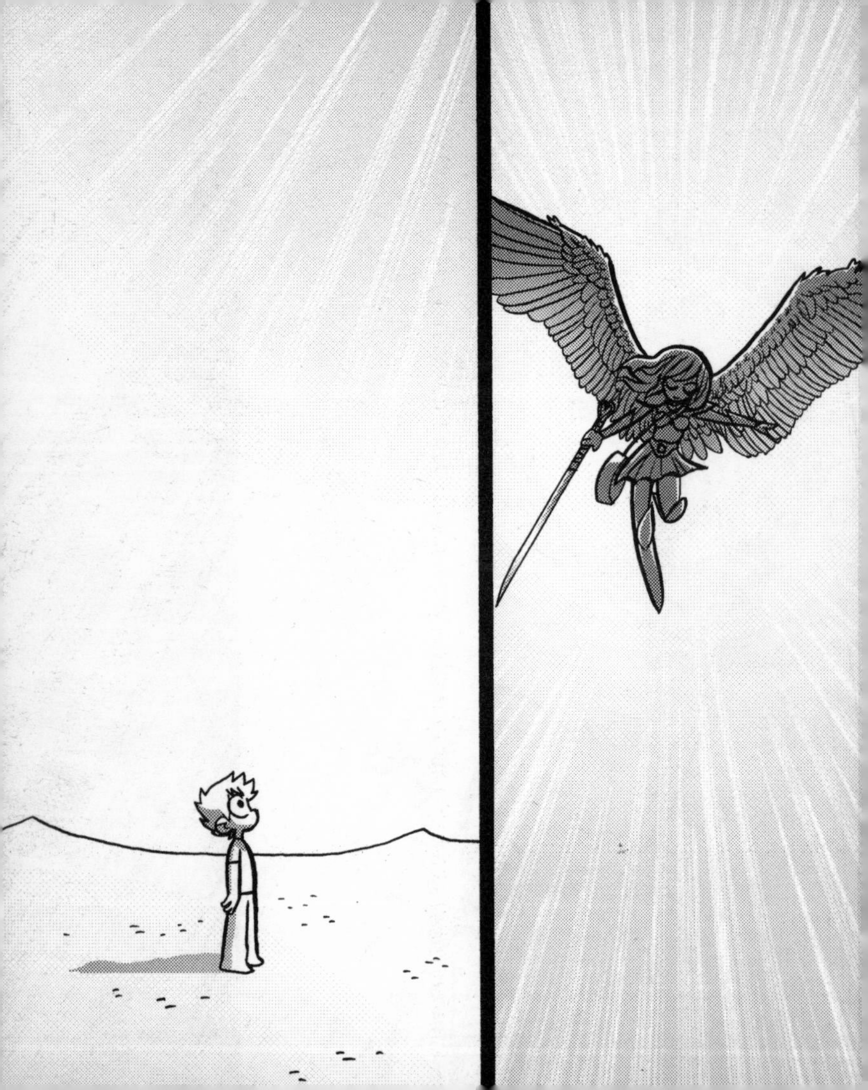

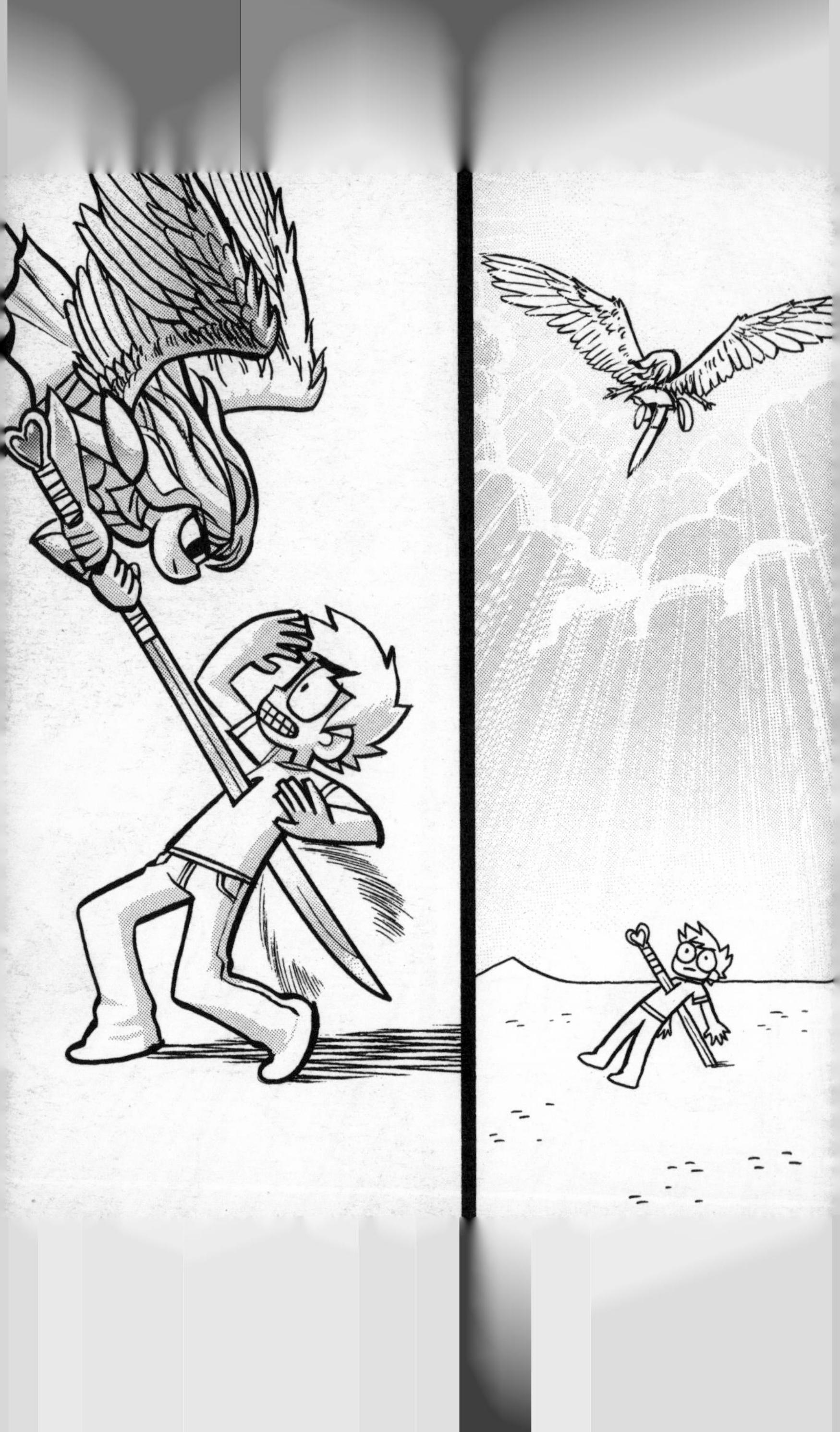

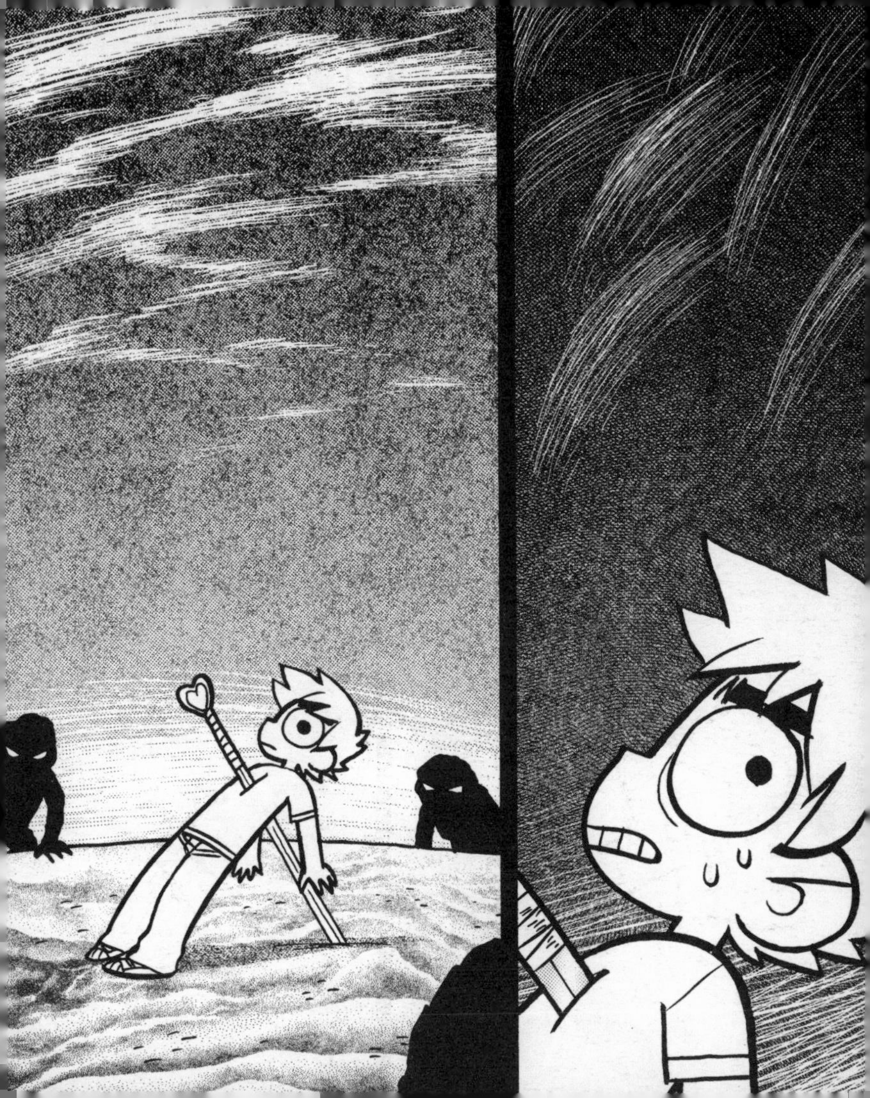

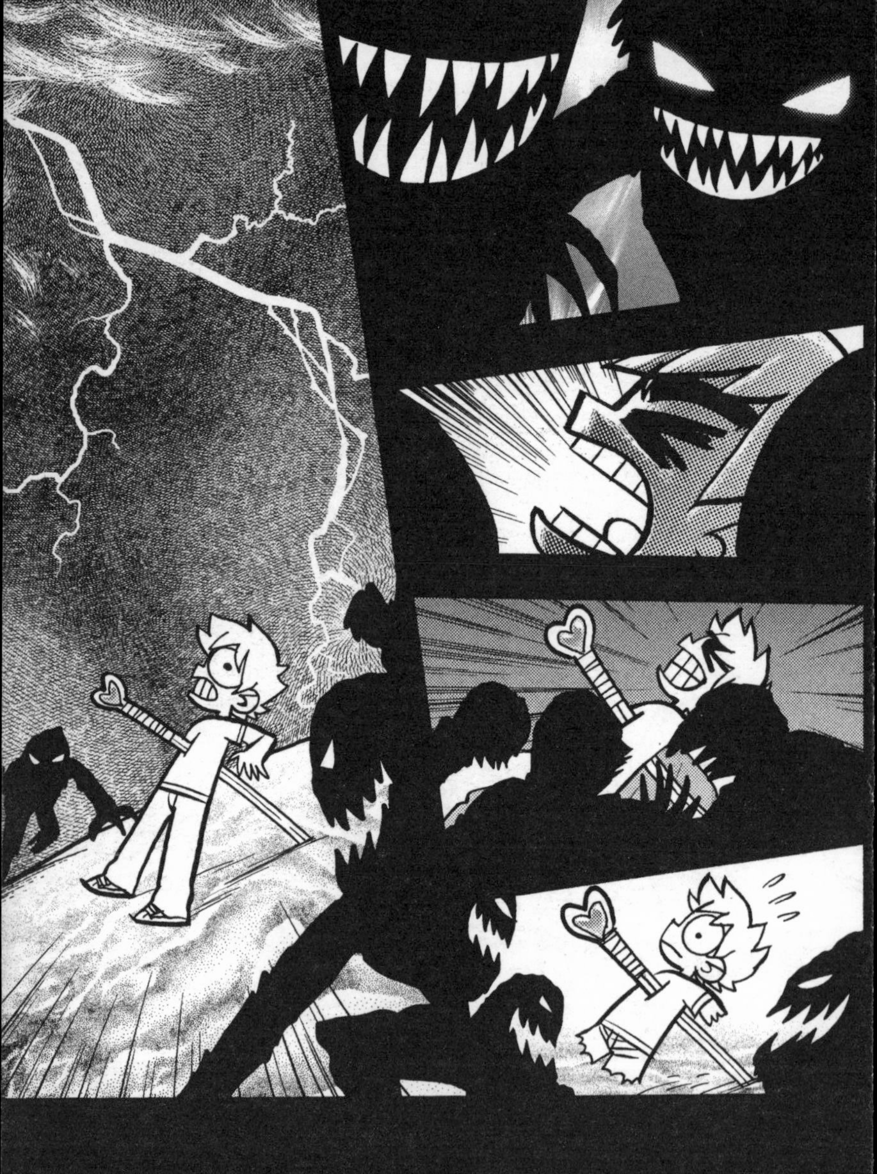

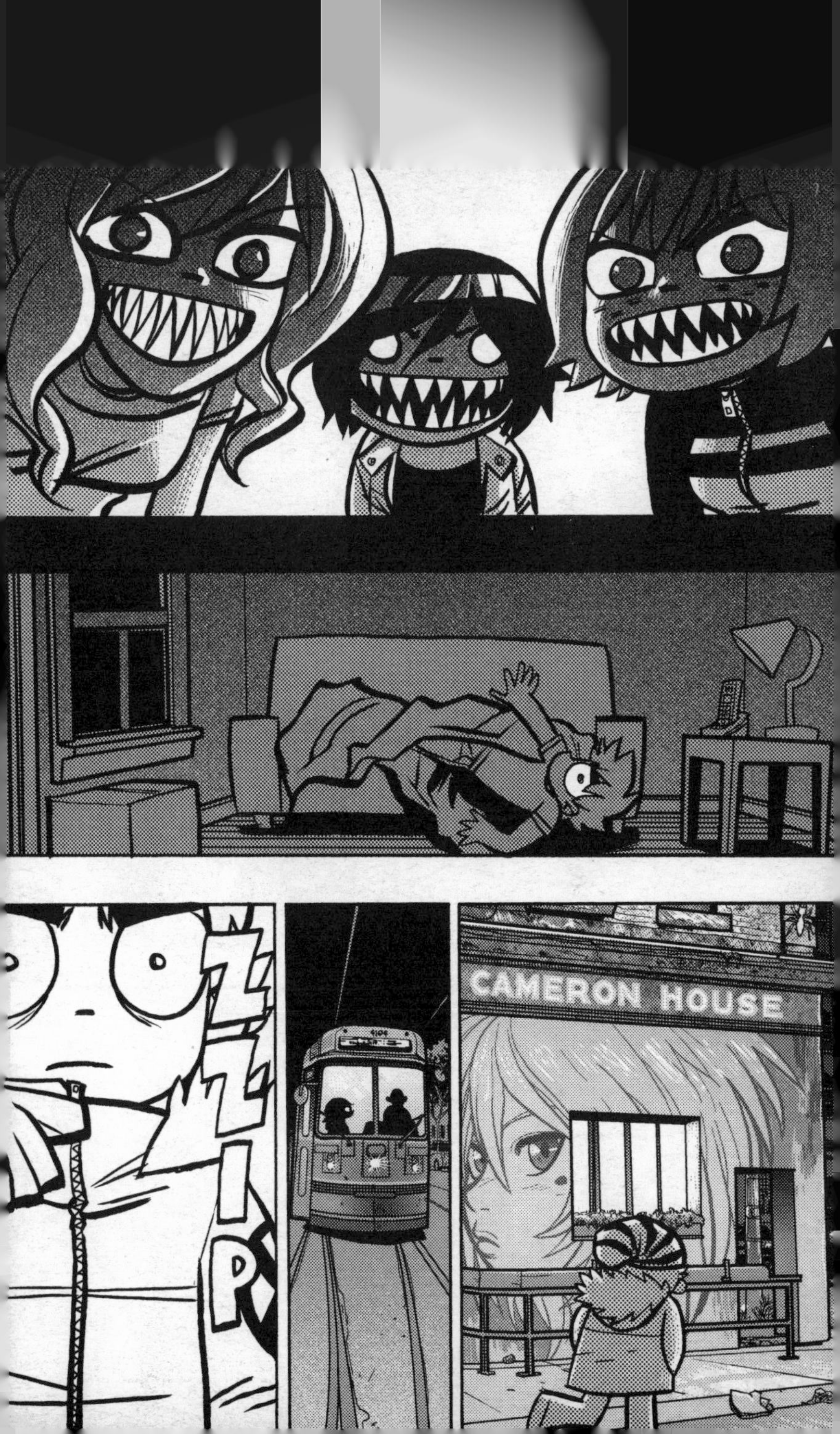
ZZIP
CAMERON HOUSE

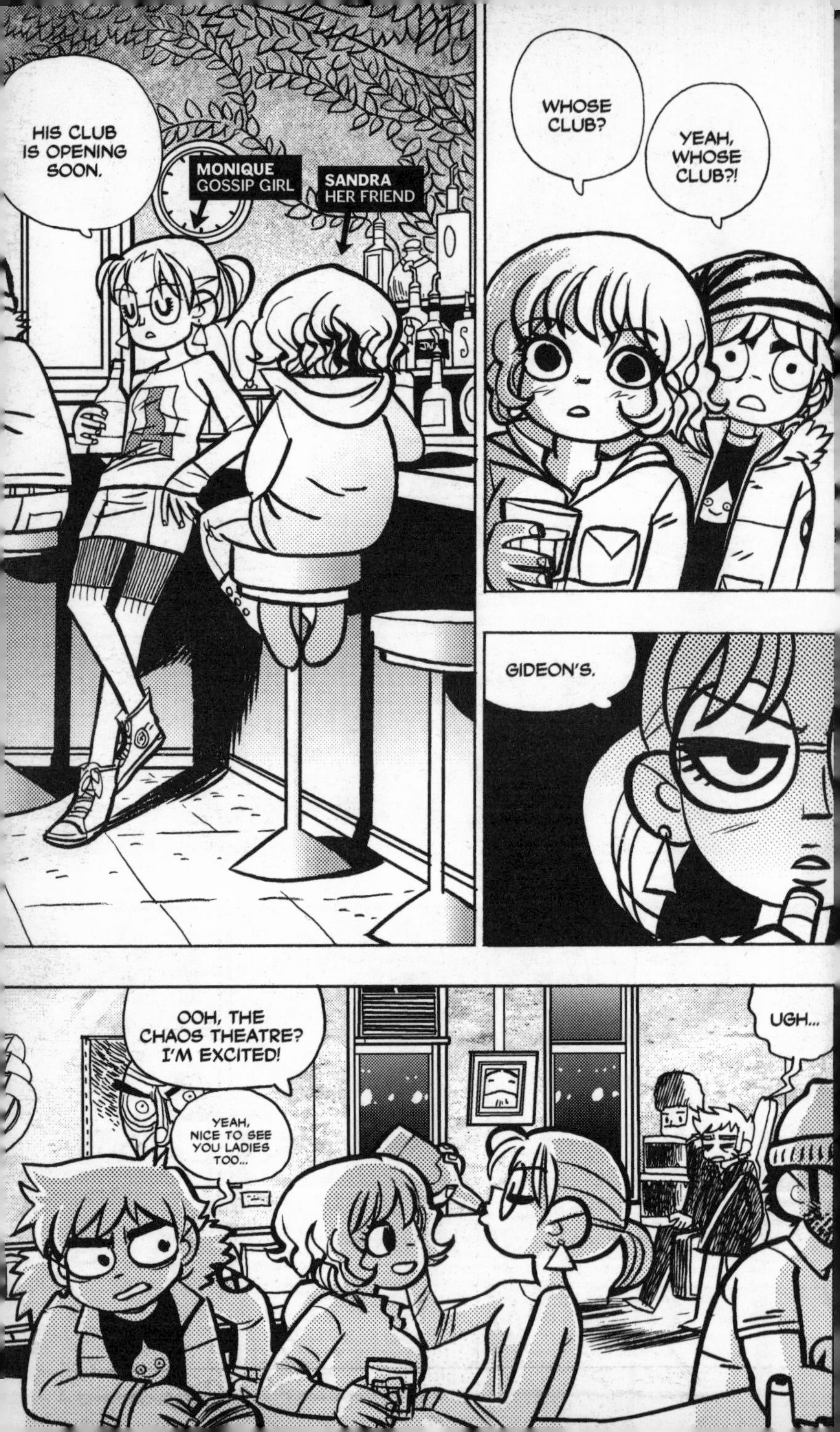

HIS CLUB IS OPENING SOON.
MONIQUE GOSSIP GIRL
SANDRA HER FRIEND
WHOSE CLUB?
YEAH, WHOSE CLUB?!
GIDEON'S.
OOH, THE CHAOS THEATRE? I'M EXCITED!
YEAH, NICE TO SEE YOU LADIES TOO...
UGH...

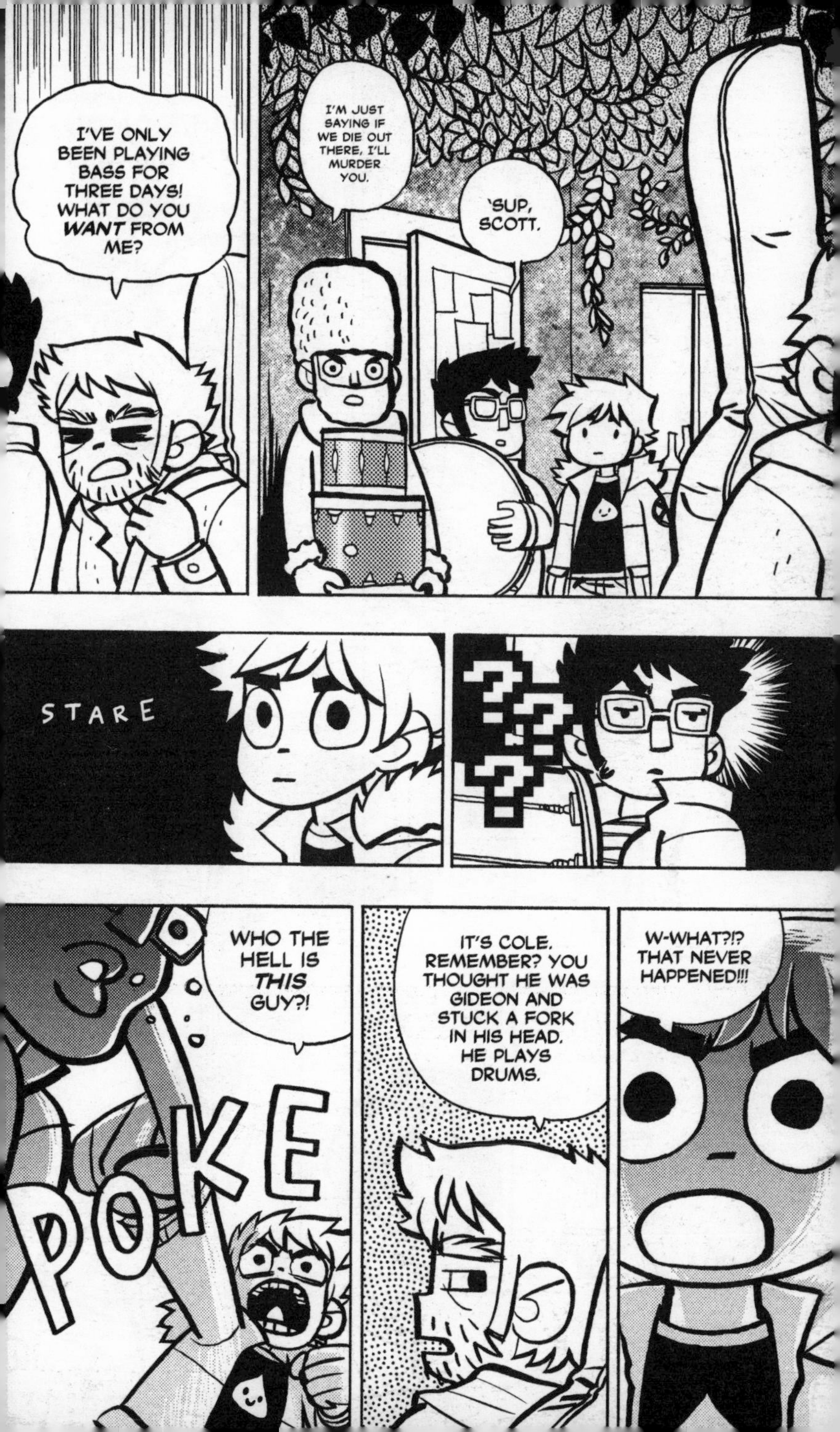
I'VE ONLY BEEN PLAYING BASS FOR THREE DAYS! WHAT DO YOU WANT FROM ME?
I'M JUST SAYING IF WE DIE OUT THERE, I'LL MURDER YOU.
'SUP, SCOTT.
STARE
WHO THE HELL IS THIS GUY?!
POKE
IT'S COLE. REMEMBER? YOU THOUGHT HE WAS GIDEON AND STUCK A FORK IN HIS HEAD. HE PLAYS DRUMS.
W-WHAT?!? THAT NEVER HAPPENED!!!

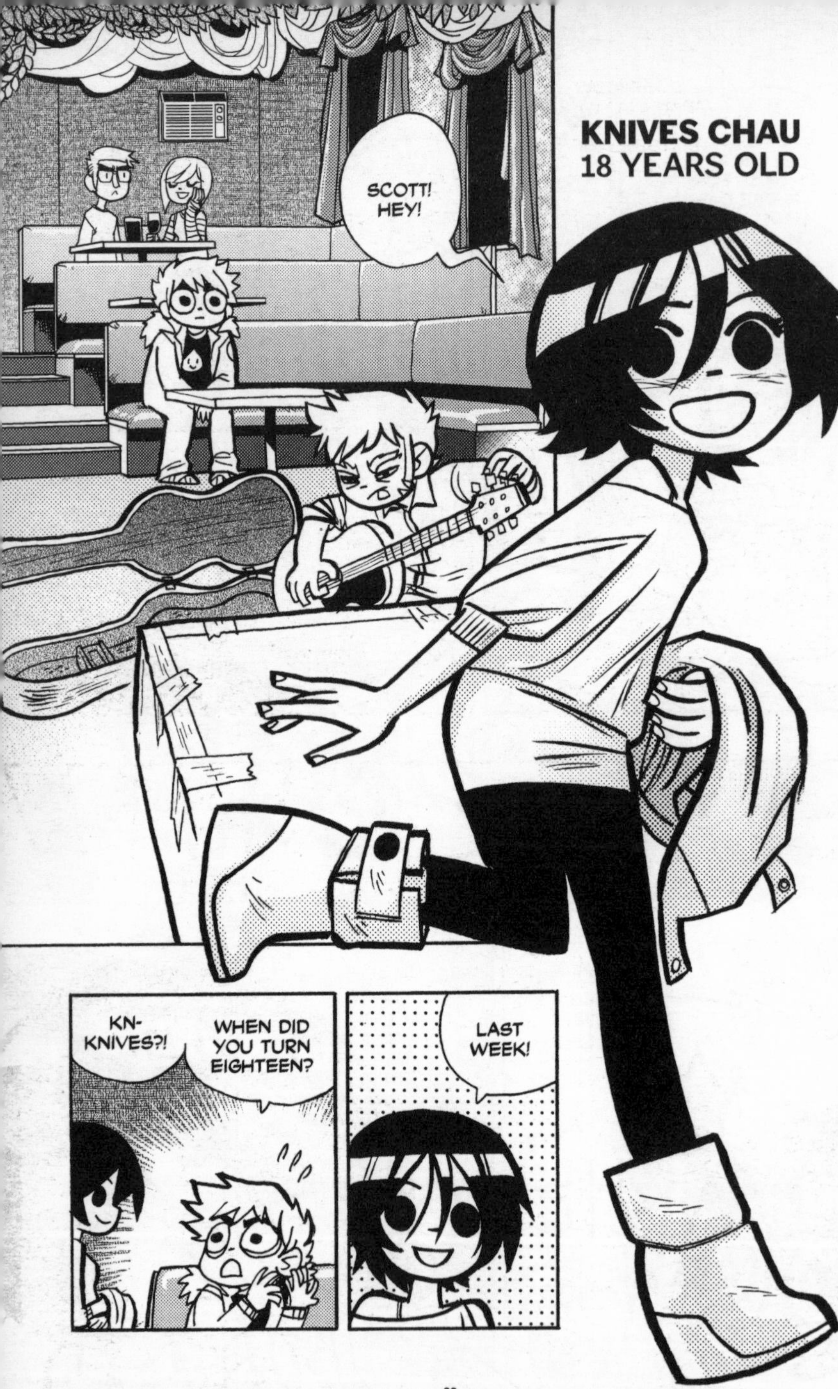
KNIVES CHAU
18 YEARS OLD
SCOTT! HEY!
KN- KNIVES?!
WHEN DID YOU TURN EIGHTEEN?
LAST WEEK!

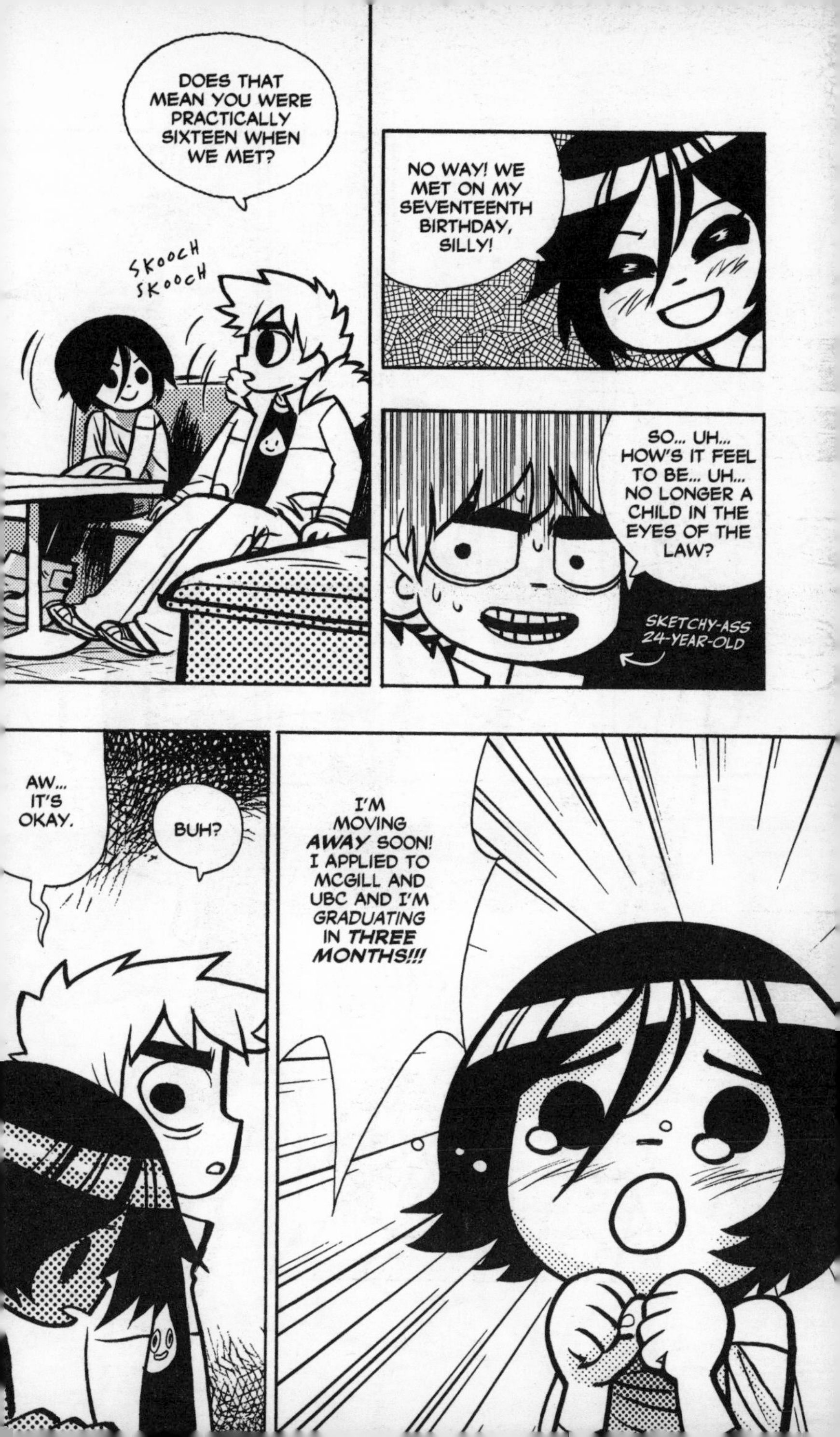
DOES THAT MEAN YOU WERE PRACTICALLY SIXTEEN WHEN WE MET?
SKOOCH SKOOCH
NO WAY! WE MET ON MY SEVENTEENTH BIRTHDAY, SILLY!
SO... UH... HOW'S IT FEEL TO BE... UH... NO LONGER A CHILD IN THE EYES OF THE LAW?
SKETCHY-ASS 24-YEAR-OLD
AW... IT'S OKAY.
BUH?
I'M MOVING AWAY SOON! I APPLIED TO MCGILL AND UBC AND I'M GRADUATING IN THREE MONTHS!!!

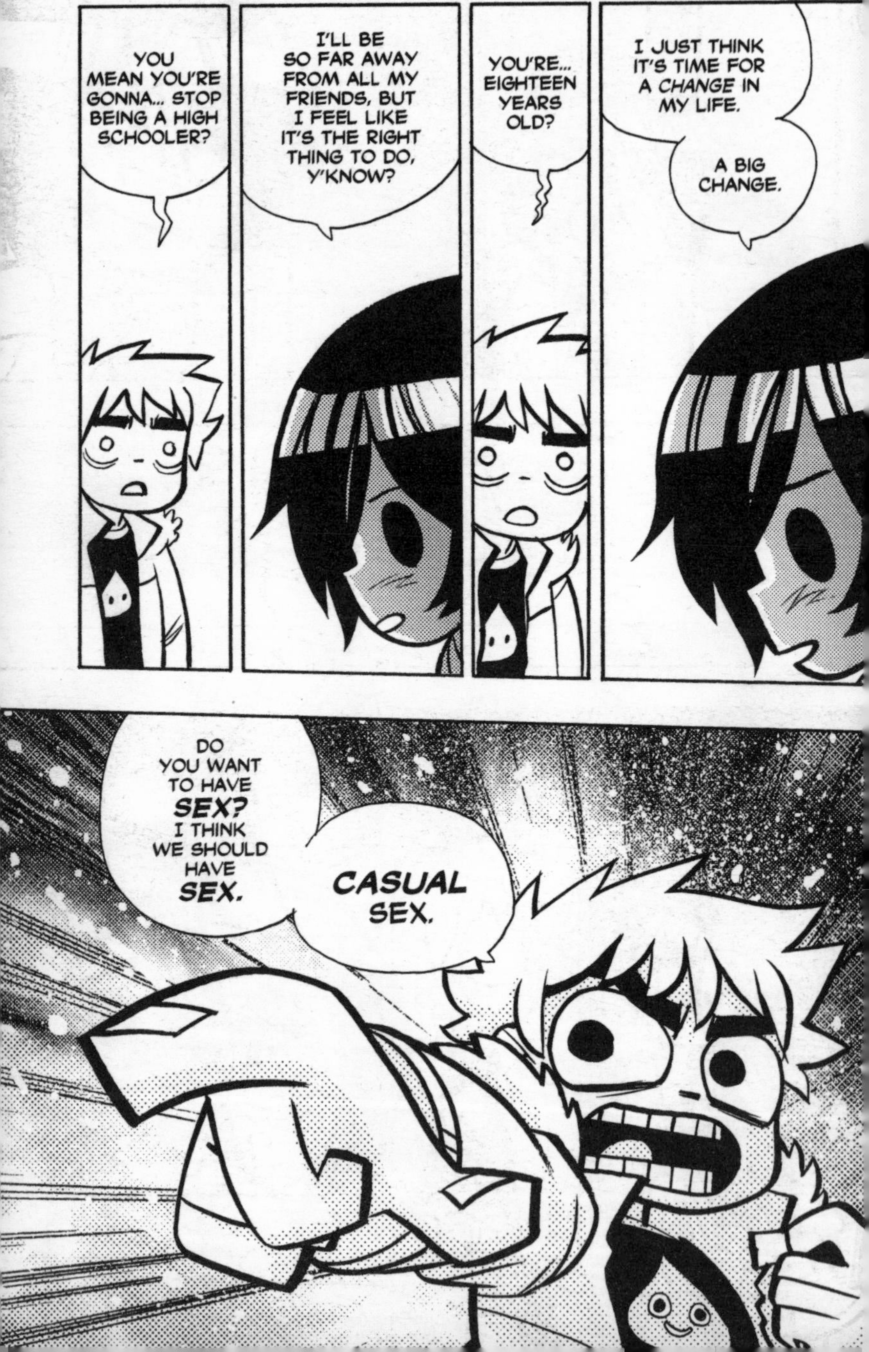
YOU MEAN YOU'RE GONNA... STOP BEING A HIGH SCHOOLER?
I'LL BE SO FAR AWAY FROM ALL MY FRIENDS, BUT I FEEL LIKE IT'S THE RIGHT THING TO DO, Y'KNOW?
YOU'RE... EIGHTEEN YEARS OLD?
I JUST THINK IT'S TIME FOR A *CHANGE* IN MY LIFE.
A BIG CHANGE.
DO YOU WANT TO HAVE **SEX?** I THINK WE SHOULD HAVE **SEX.**
CASUAL SEX.

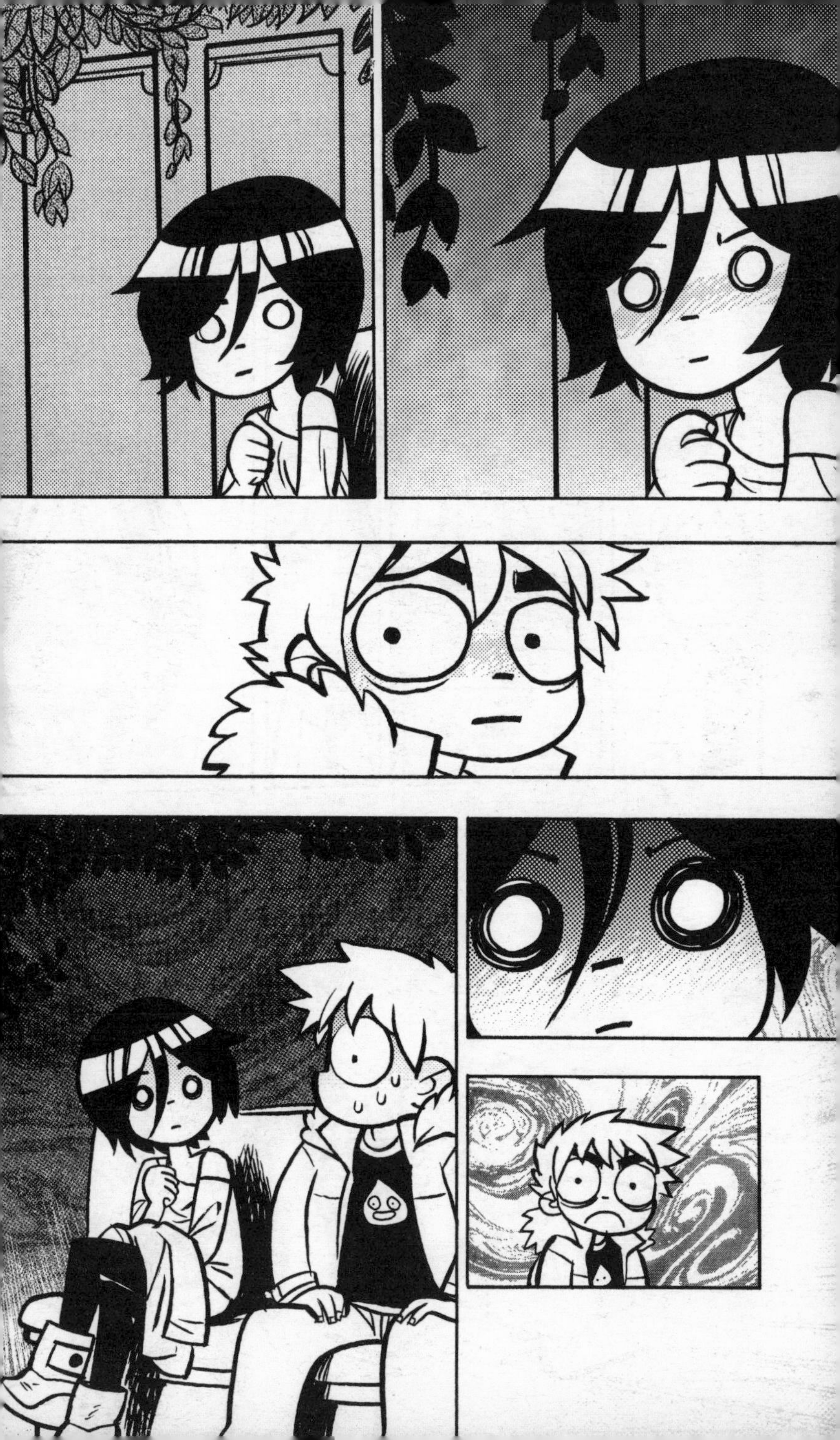

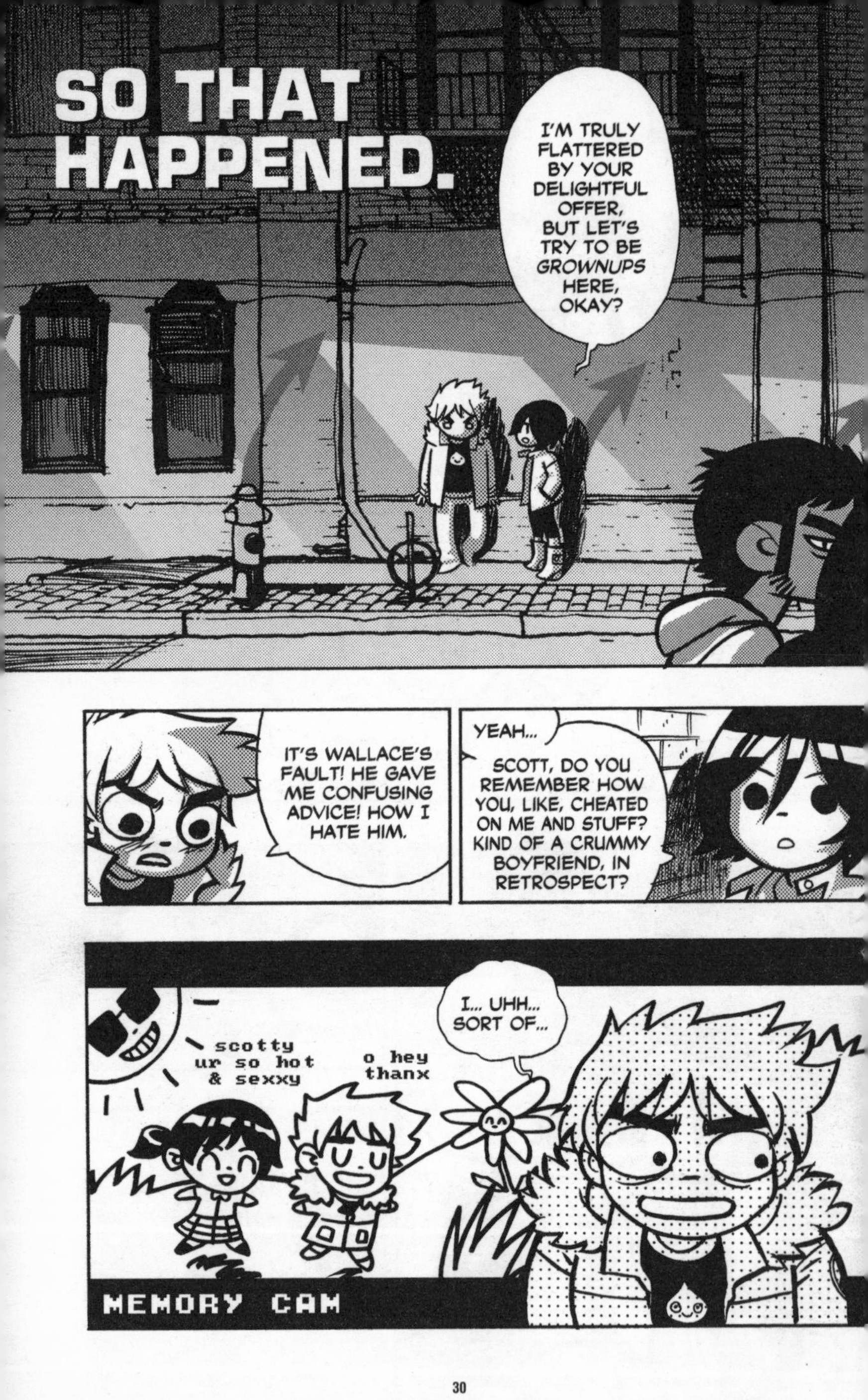
SO THAT HAPPENED.
I'M TRULY FLATTERED BY YOUR DELIGHTFUL OFFER, BUT LET'S TRY TO BE GROWNUPS HERE, OKAY?
IT'S WALLACE'S FAULT! HE GAVE ME CONFUSING ADVICE! HOW I HATE HIM.
YEAH...
SCOTT, DO YOU REMEMBER HOW YOU, LIKE, CHEATED ON ME AND STUFF? KIND OF A CRUMMY BOYFRIEND, IN RETROSPECT?
scotty ur so hot & sexxy
o hey thanx
I... UHH... SORT OF...
MEMORY CAM

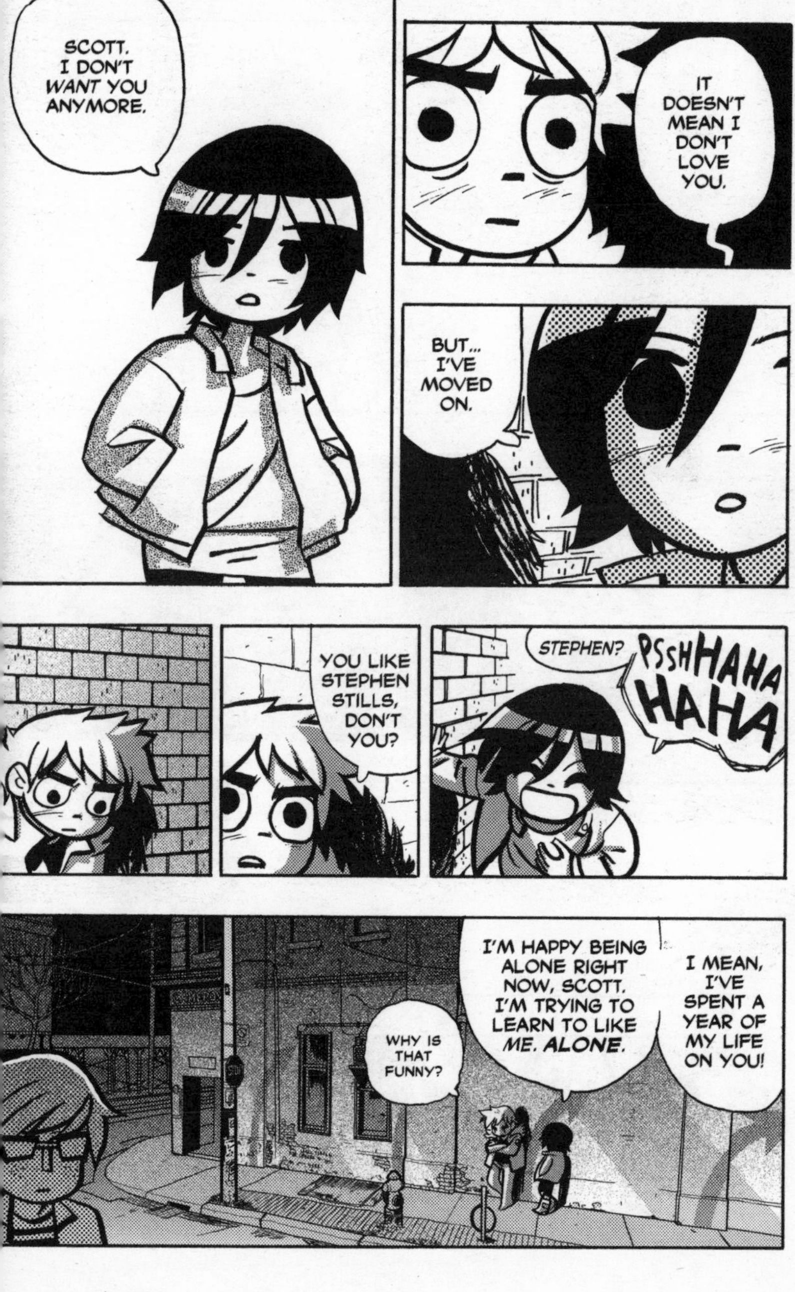
SCOTT. I DON'T WANT YOU ANYMORE.
IT DOESN'T MEAN I DON'T LOVE YOU.
BUT... I'VE MOVED ON.
YOU LIKE STEPHEN STILLS, DON'T YOU?
STEPHEN?
PSSHHAHA HAHA
WHY IS THAT FUNNY?
I'M HAPPY BEING ALONE RIGHT NOW, SCOTT. I'M TRYING TO LEARN TO LIKE ME. ALONE.
I MEAN, I'VE SPENT A YEAR OF MY LIFE ON YOU!

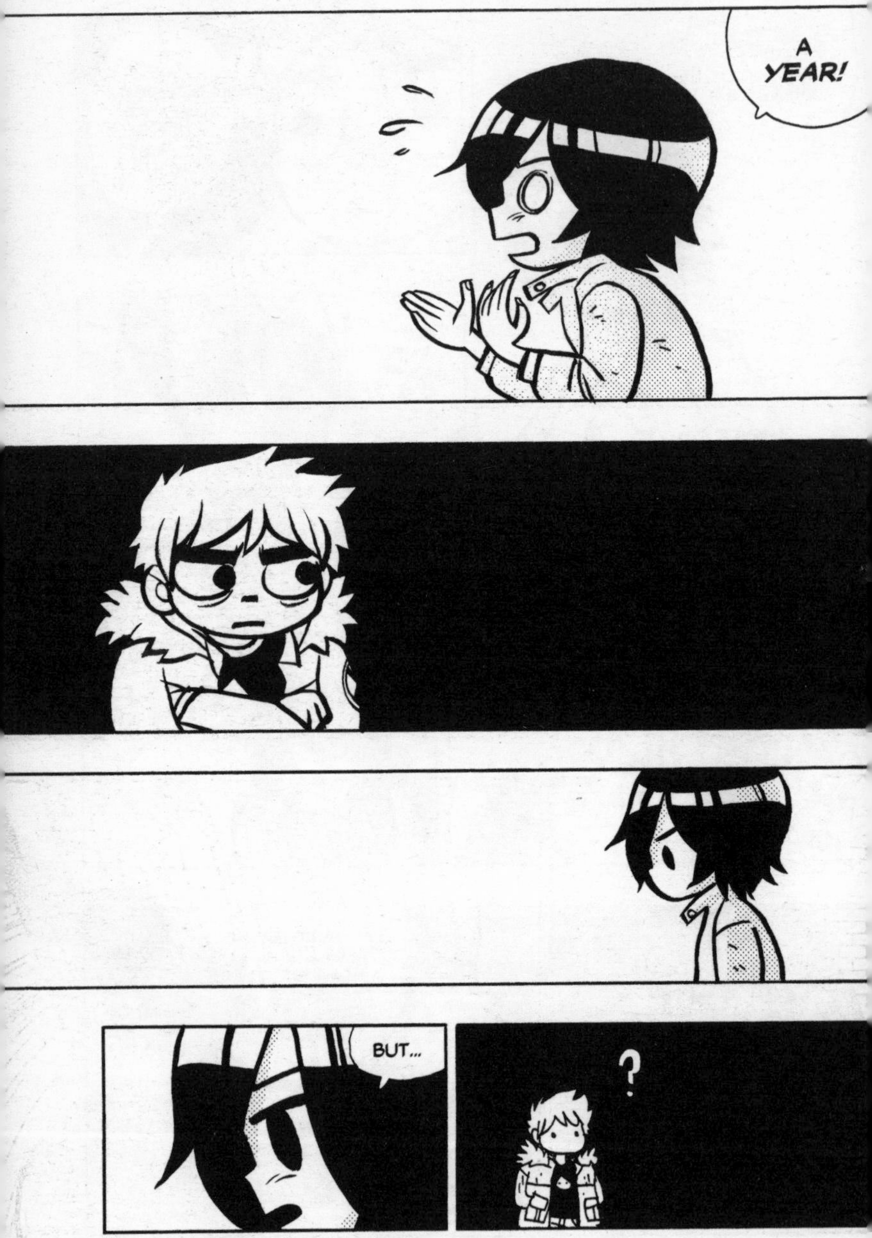
A YEAR!
BUT...
?

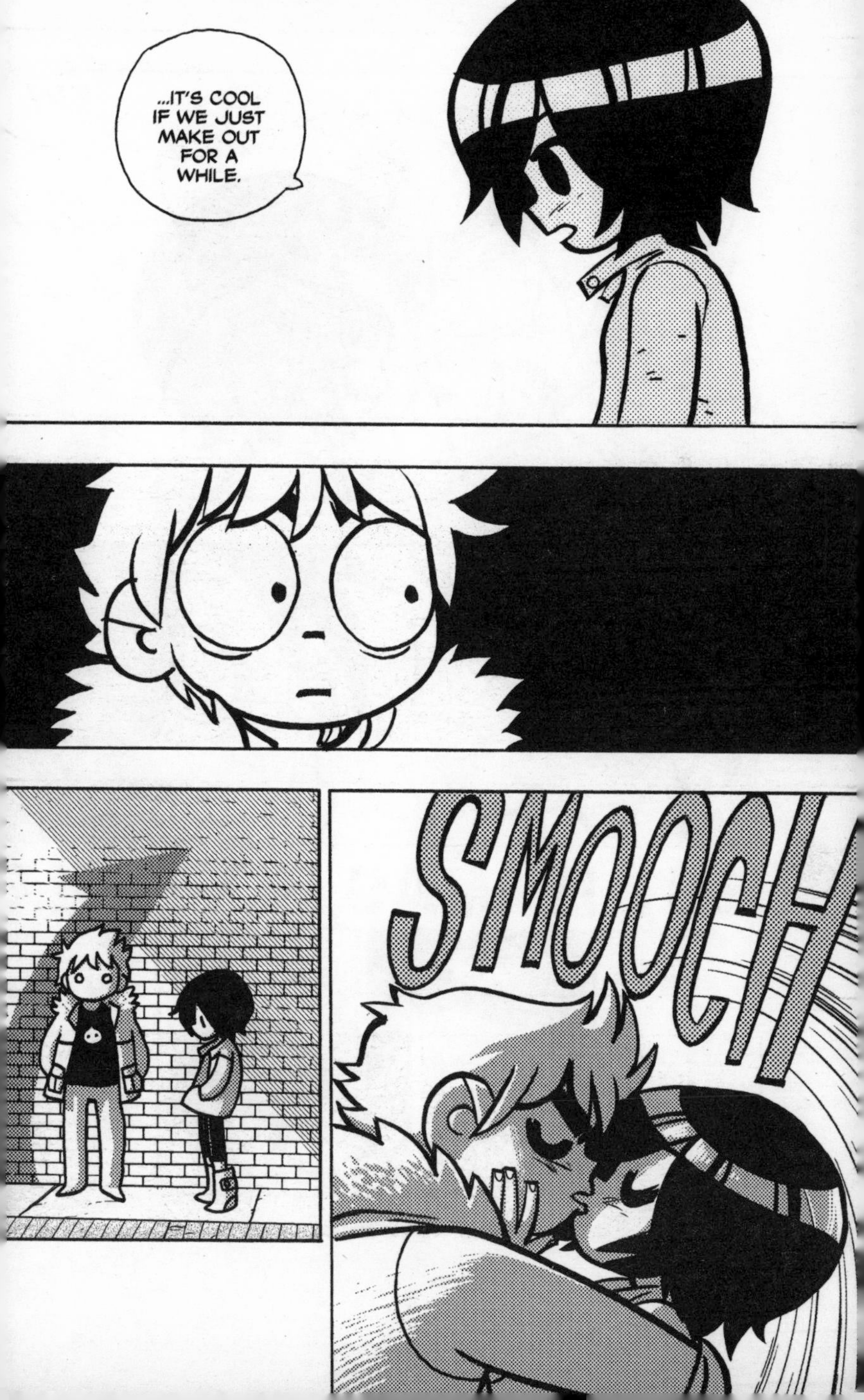
...IT'S COOL IF WE JUST MAKE OUT FOR A WHILE.
SMOOCH

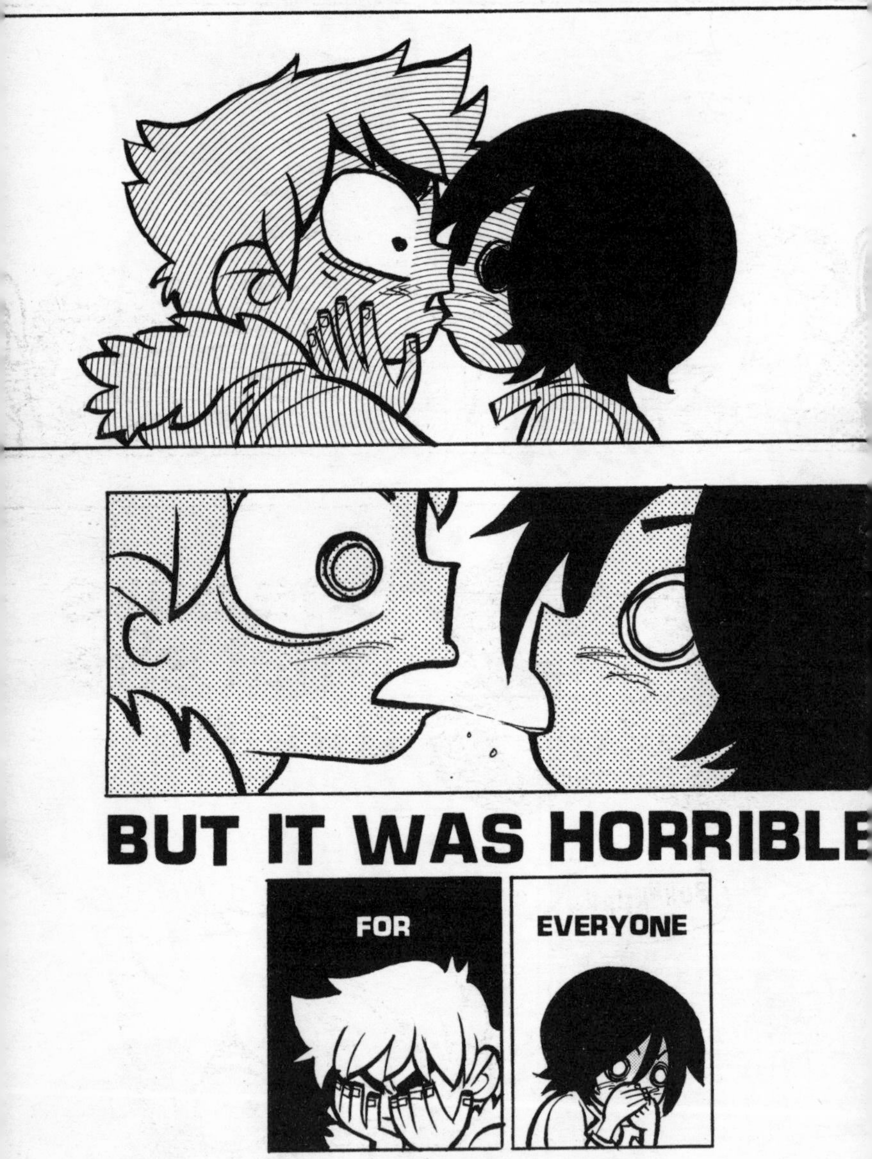
BUT IT WAS HORRIBLE
FOR
EVERYONE
AND THAT INCLUDES YOU

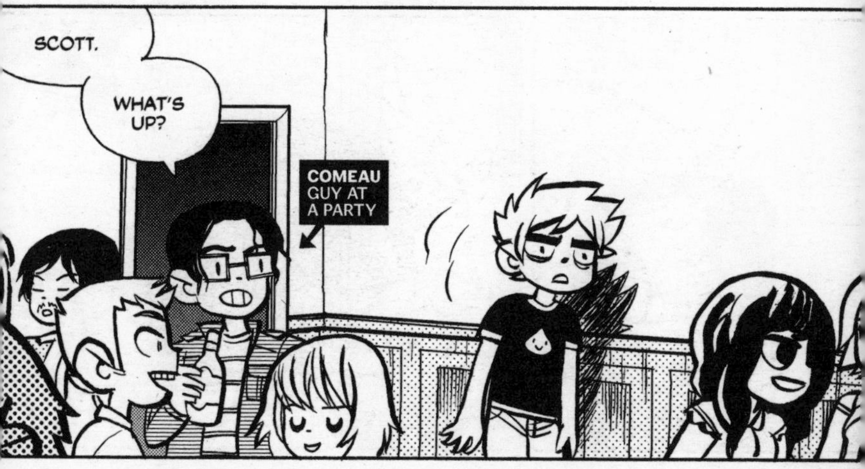
SCOTT.
WHAT'S UP?
COMEAU
GUY AT A PARTY

33 She says what she means

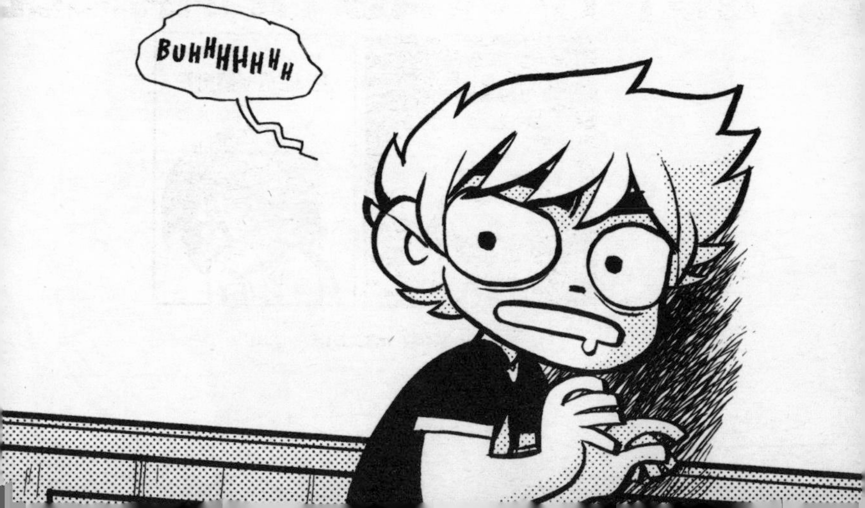
BUHHHHHHH

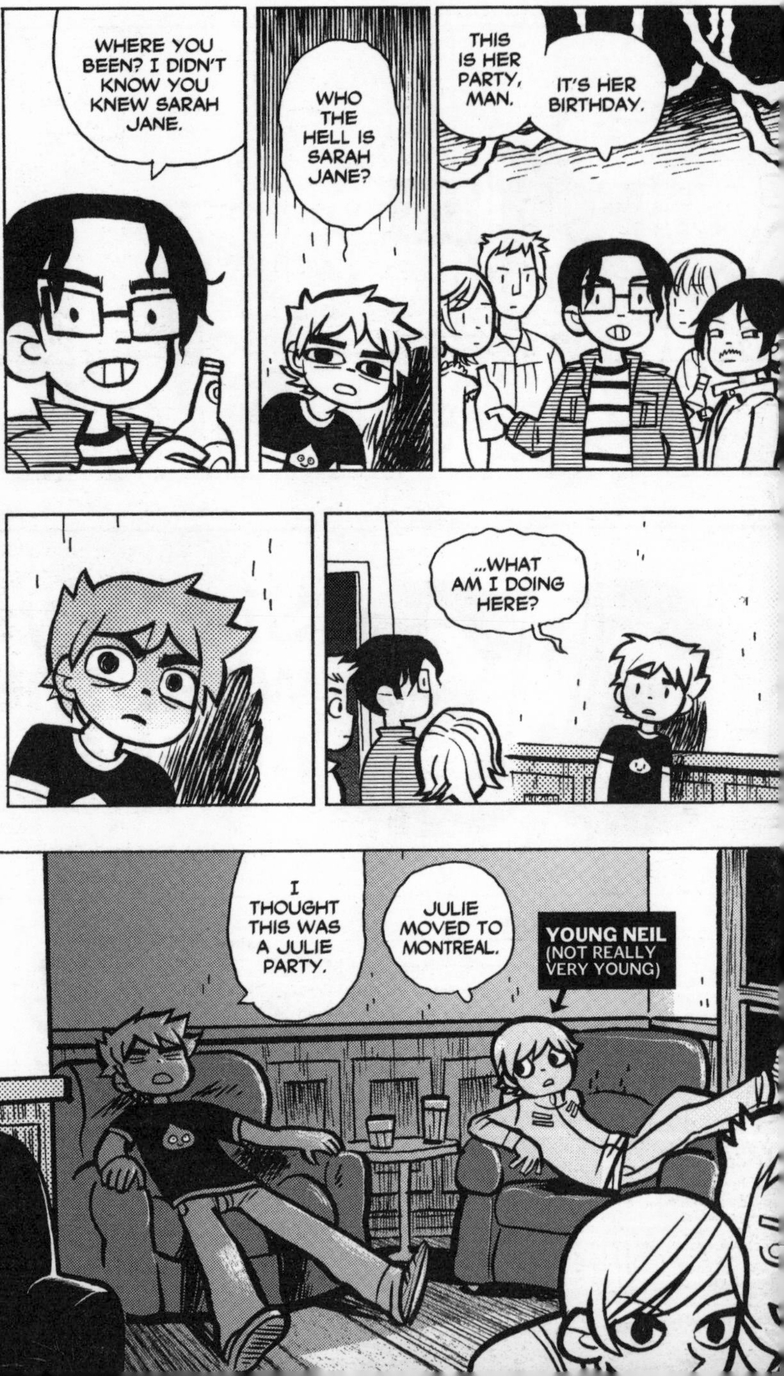
WHERE YOU BEEN? I DIDN'T KNOW YOU KNEW SARAH JANE.
WHO THE HELL IS SARAH JANE?
THIS IS HER PARTY, MAN.
IT'S HER BIRTHDAY.
...WHAT AM I DOING HERE?
I THOUGHT THIS WAS A JULIE PARTY.
JULIE MOVED TO MONTREAL.
YOUNG NEIL (NOT REALLY VERY YOUNG)

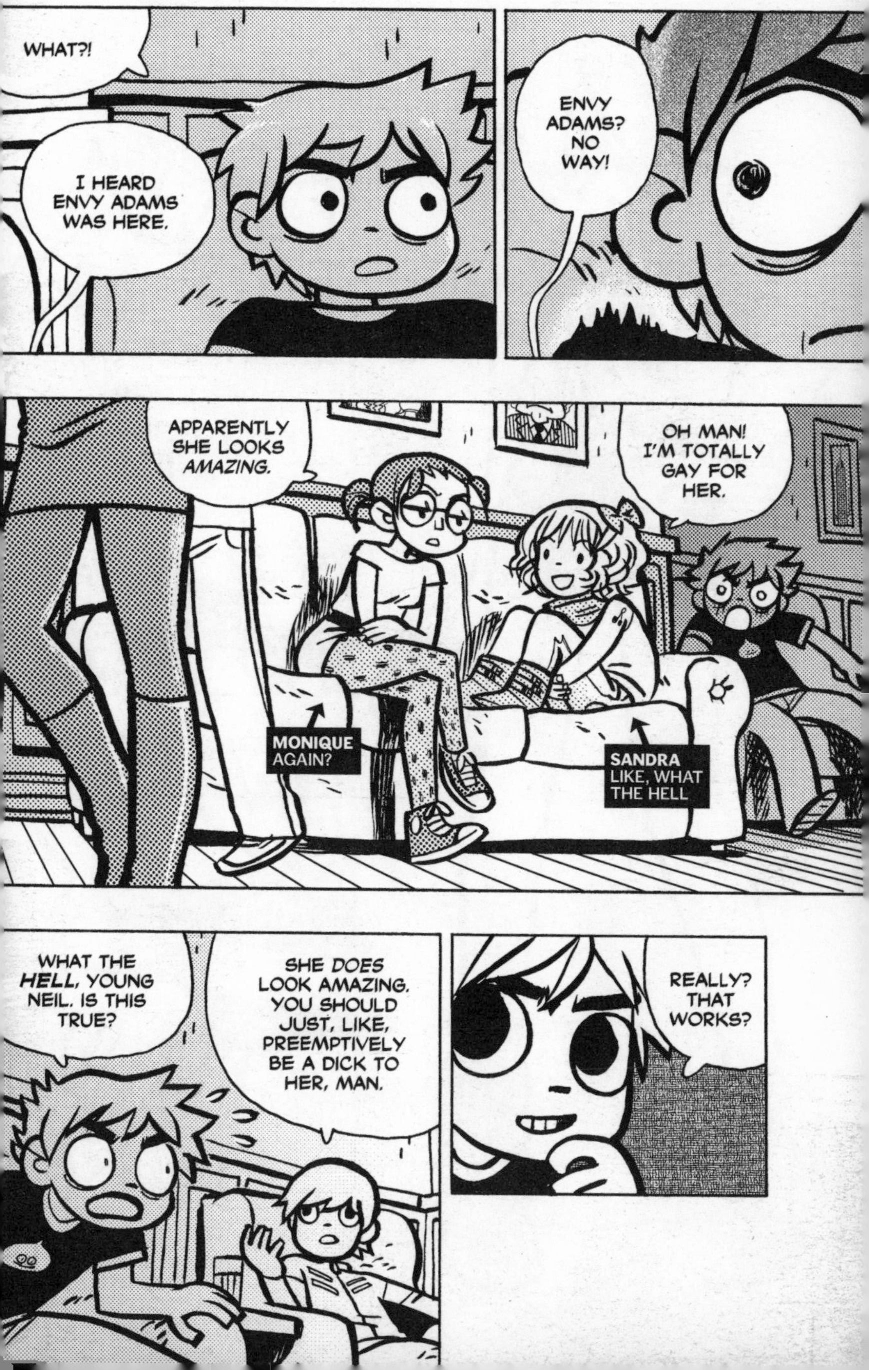
WHAT?!
I HEARD ENVY ADAMS WAS HERE.
ENVY ADAMS? NO WAY!
APPARENTLY SHE LOOKS *AMAZING.*
OH MAN! I'M TOTALLY GAY FOR HER.
MONIQUE AGAIN?
SANDRA LIKE, WHAT THE HELL
WHAT THE ***HELL***, YOUNG NEIL. IS THIS TRUE?
SHE *DOES* LOOK AMAZING. YOU SHOULD JUST, LIKE, PREEMPTIVELY BE A DICK TO HER, MAN.
REALLY? THAT WORKS?

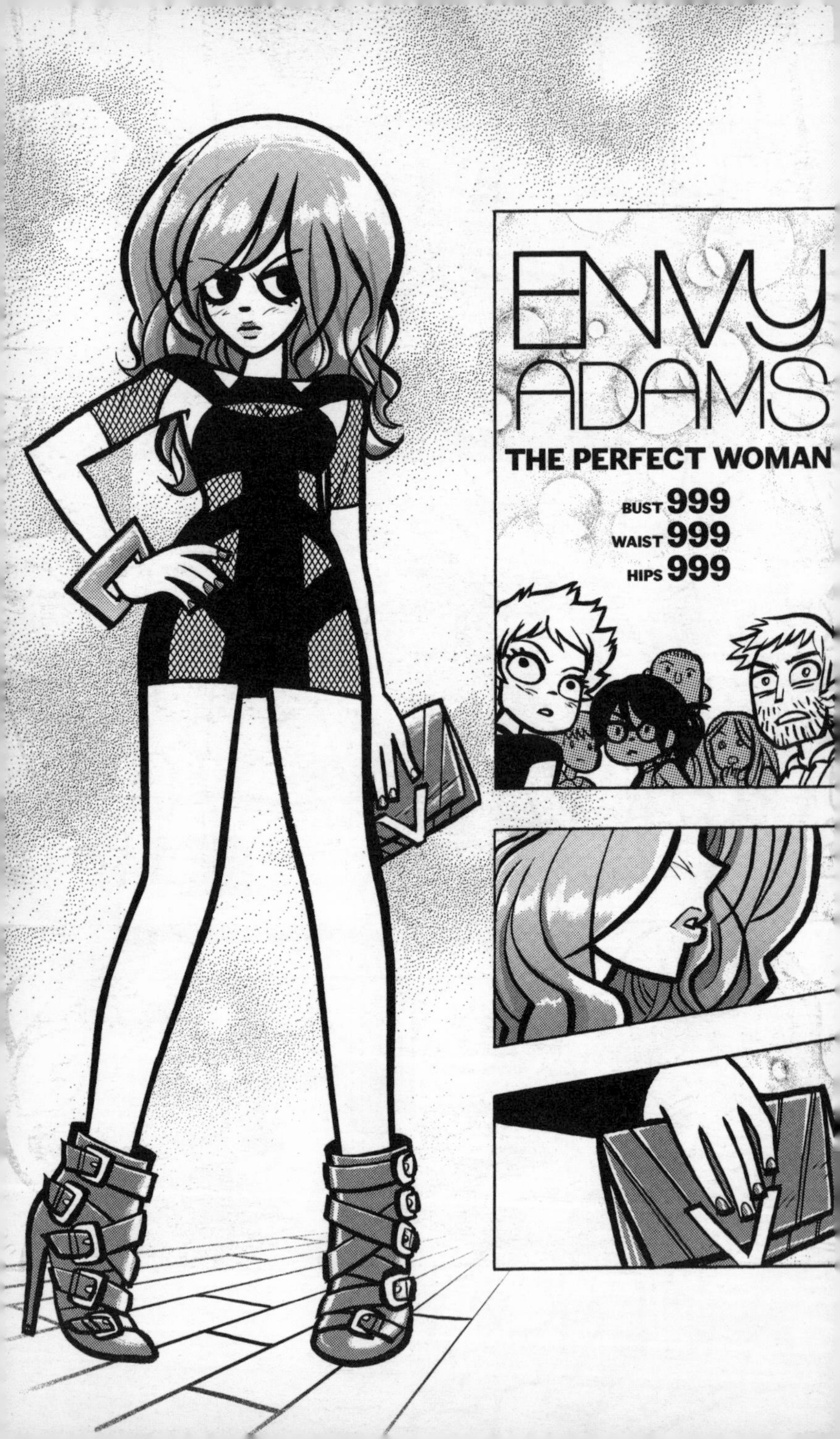
ENVY ADAMS
THE PERFECT WOMAN
BUST 999
WAIST 999
HIPS 999

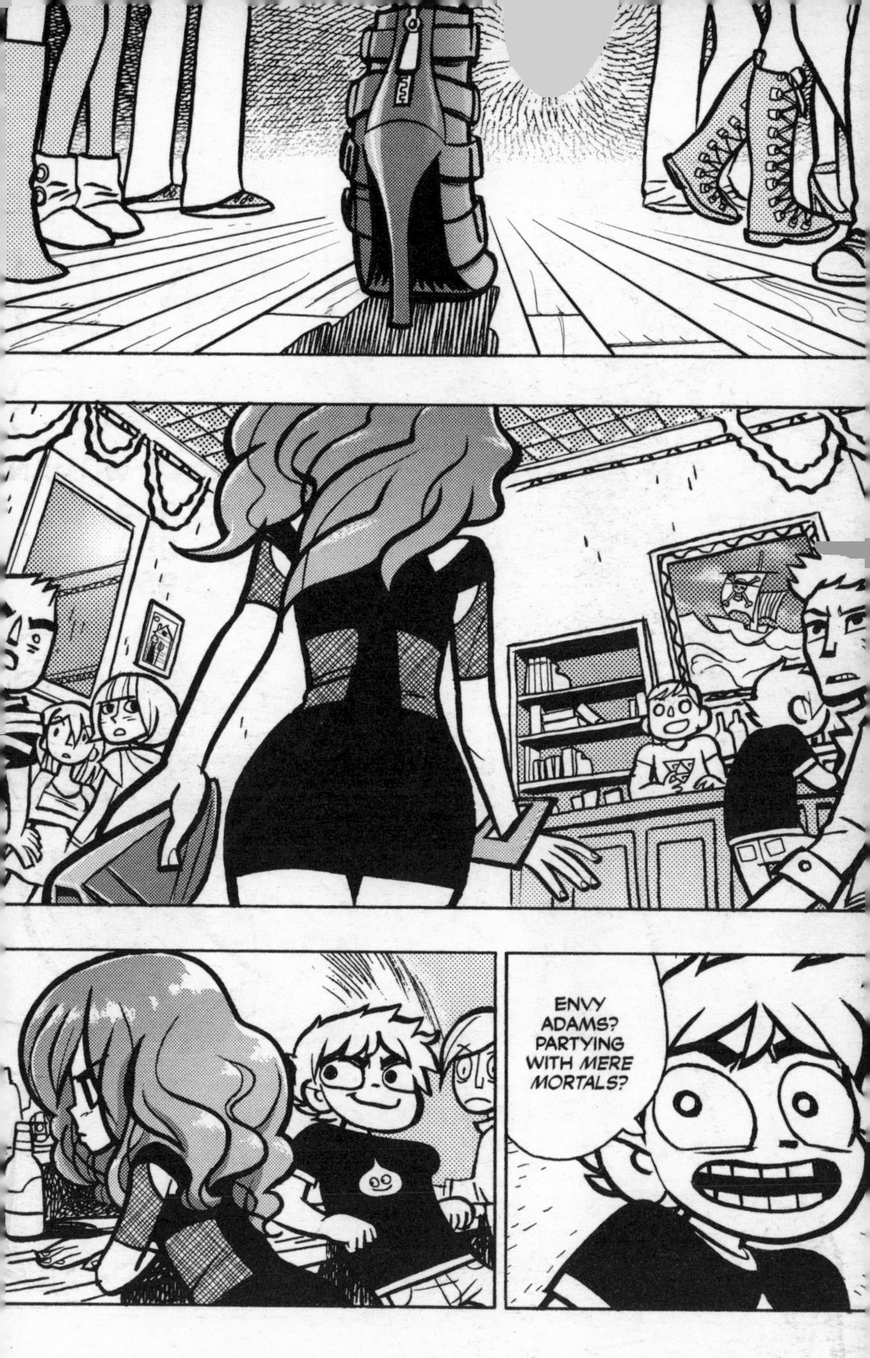
ENVY ADAMS? PARTYING WITH MERE MORTALS?

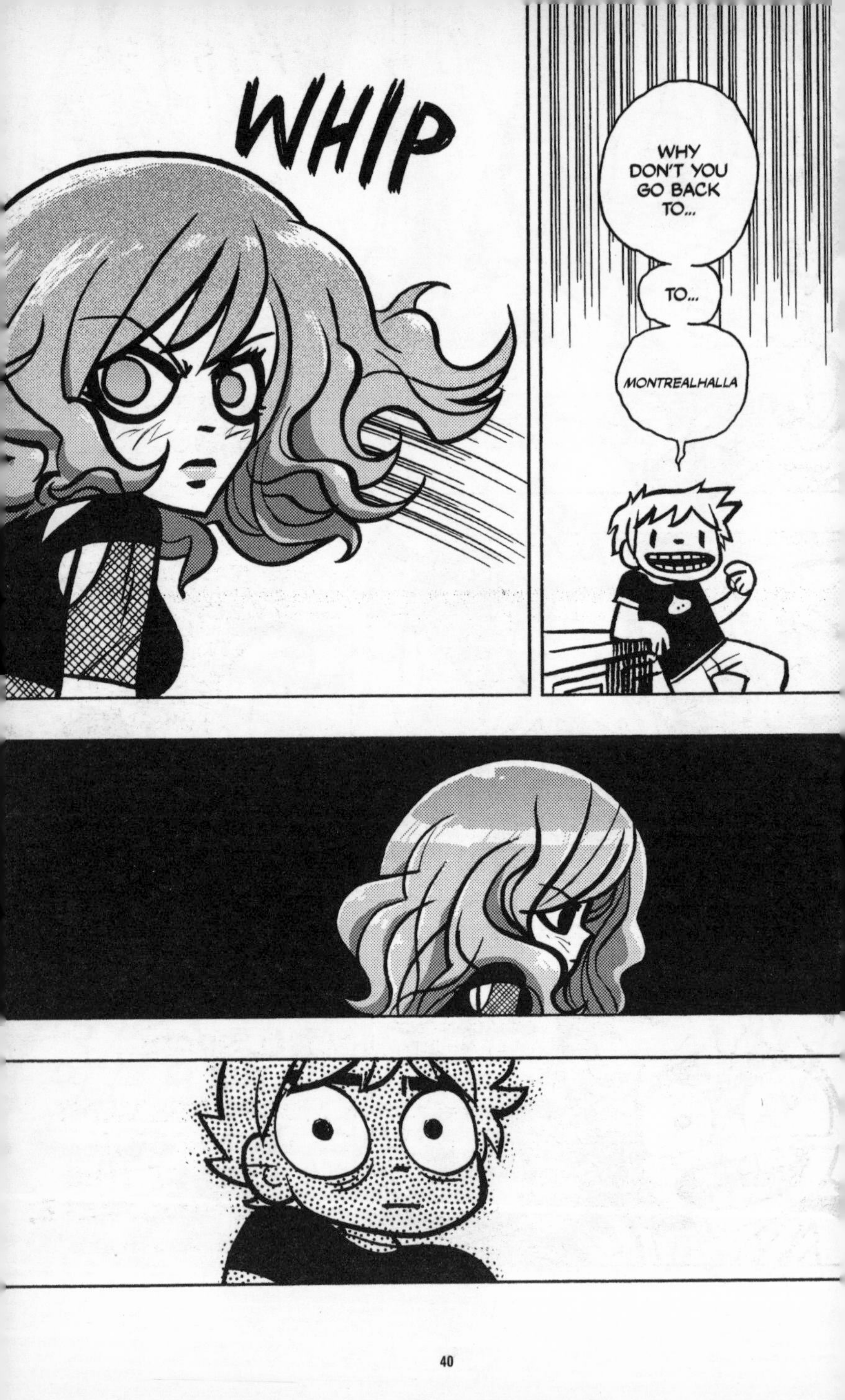
WHIP
WHY DON'T YOU GO BACK TO...
TO...
MONTREALHALLA

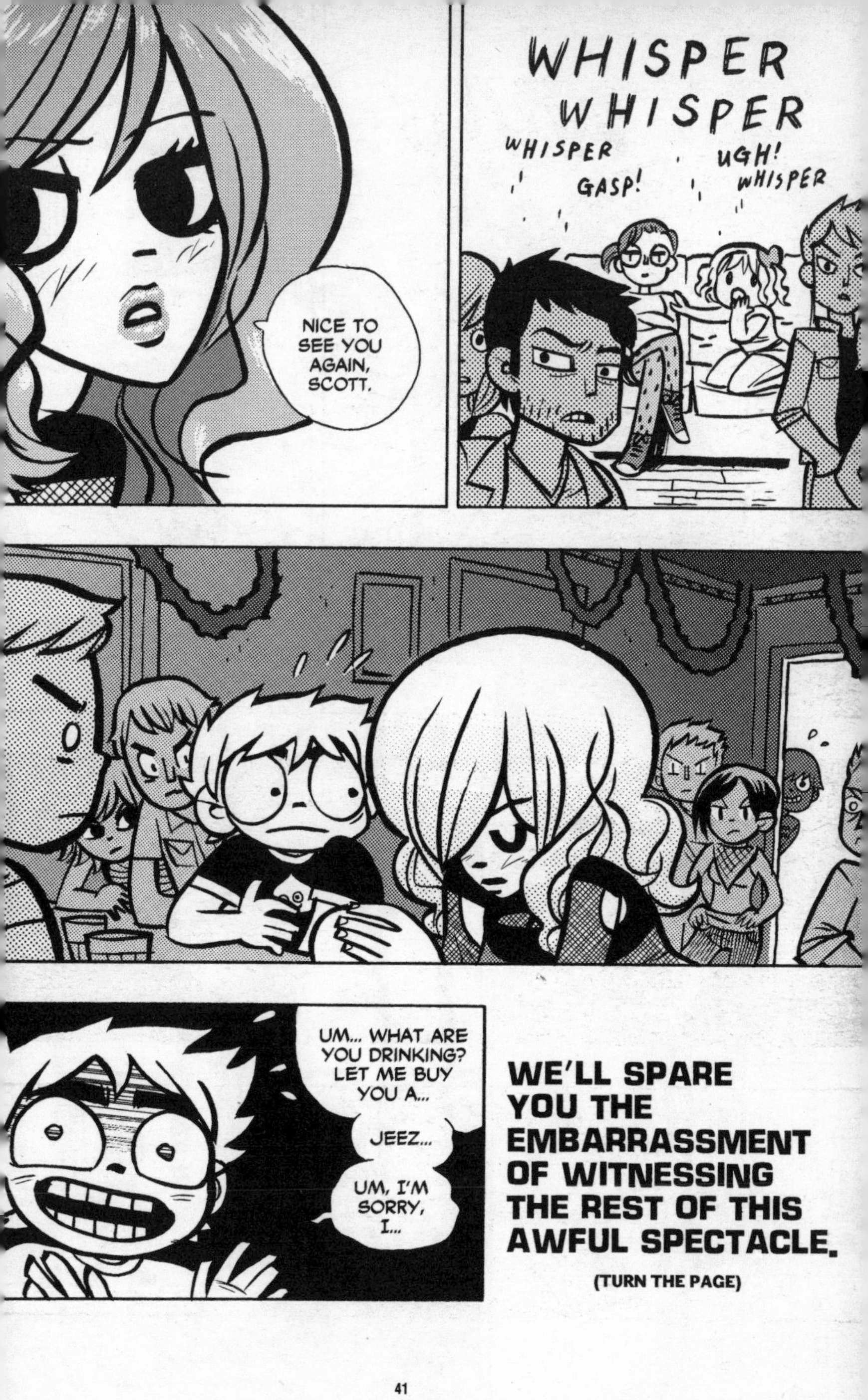
NICE TO SEE YOU AGAIN, SCOTT.
WHISPER
WHISPER
WHISPER
GASP!
UGH!
WHISPER
UM... WHAT ARE YOU DRINKING? LET ME BUY YOU A...
JEEZ...
UM, I'M SORRY, I...
WE'LL SPARE YOU THE EMBARRASSMENT OF WITNESSING THE REST OF THIS AWFUL SPECTACLE.
(TURN THE PAGE)

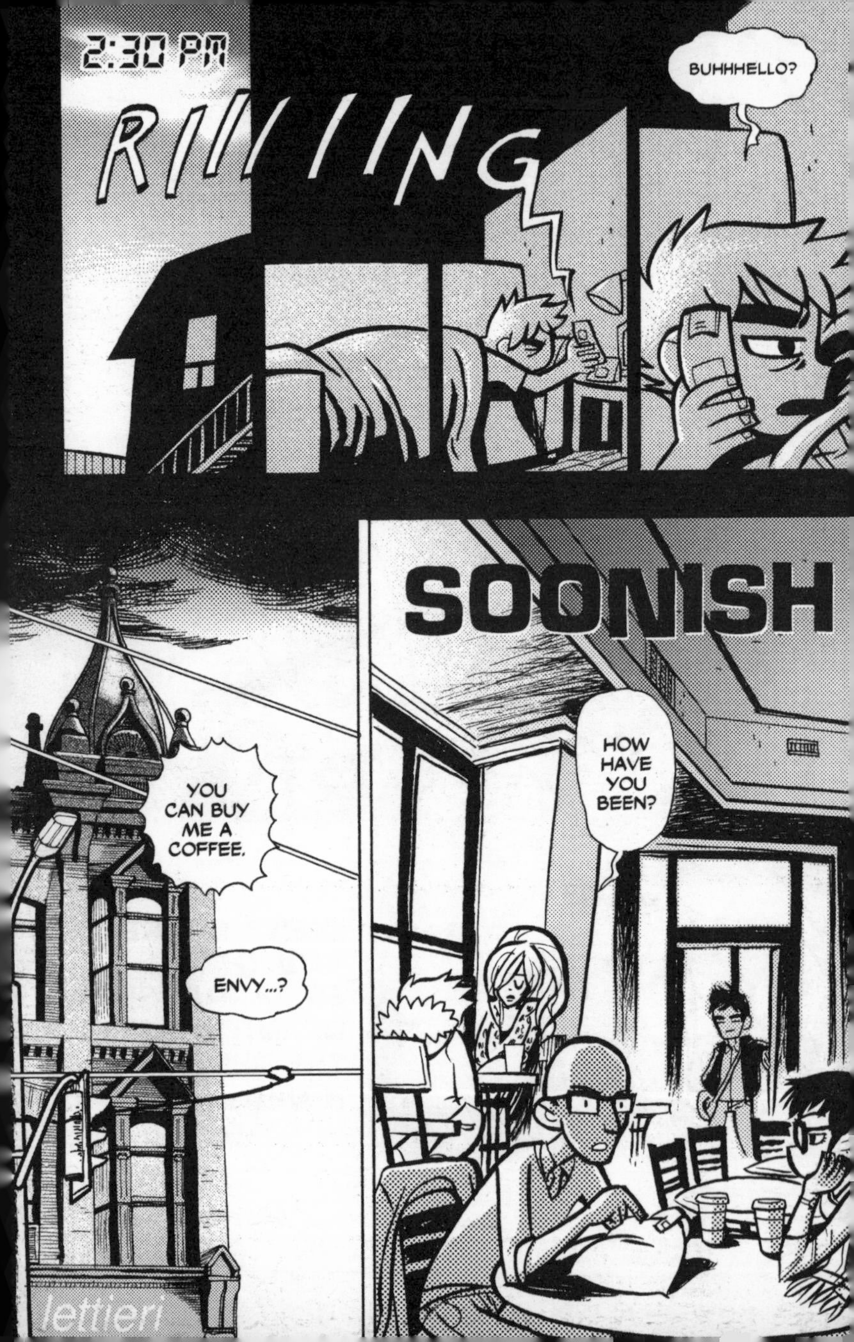
2:30 PM
RIIIIING
BUHHHELLO?
SOONISH
YOU CAN BUY ME A COFFEE.
ENVY...?
HOW HAVE YOU BEEN?
lettieri

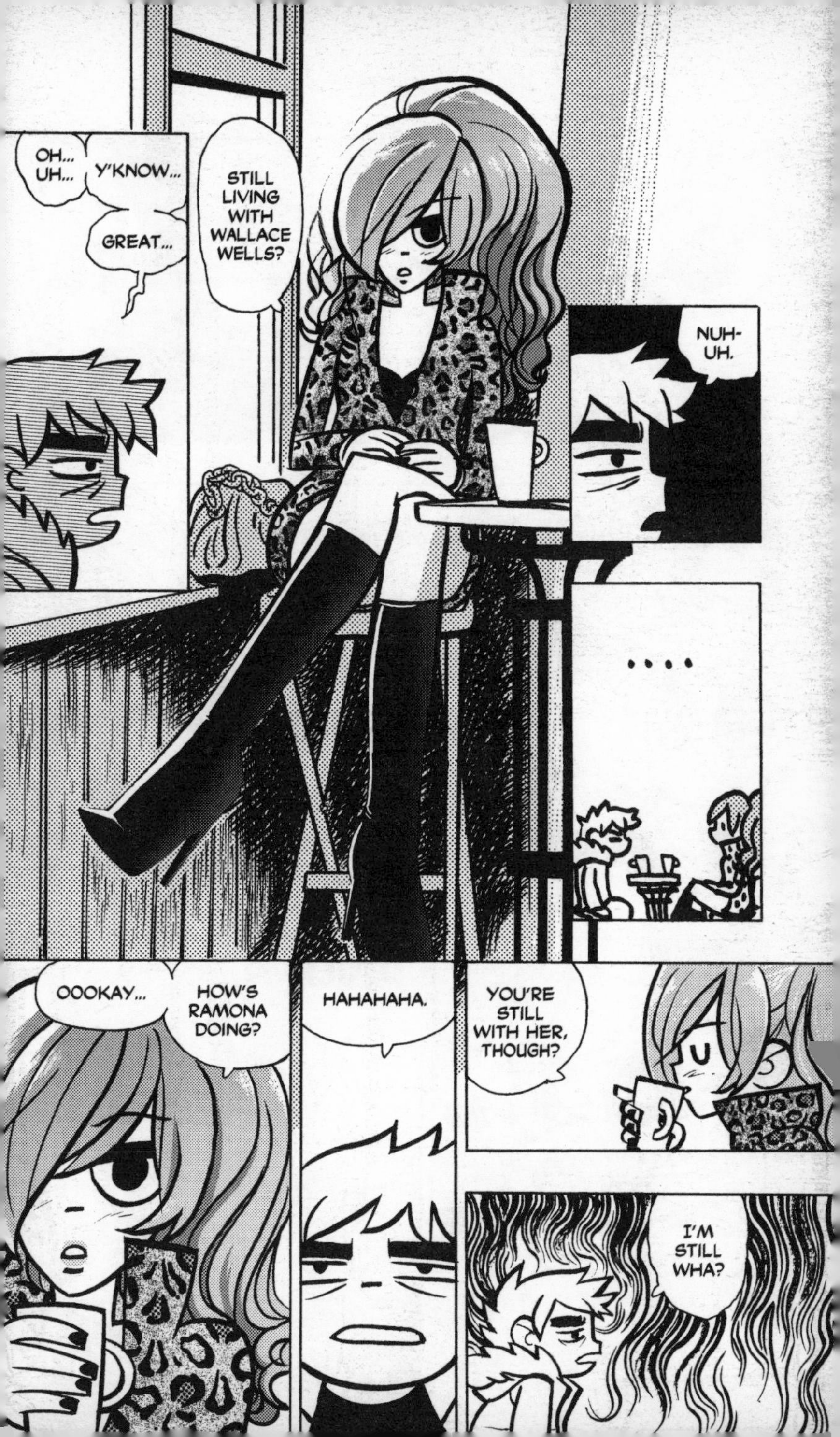

STILL LIVING WITH WALLACE WELLS?
OH... UH...
Y'KNOW...
GREAT...
NUH-UH.
....
OOOKAY...
HOW'S RAMONA DOING?
HAHAHAHA.
YOU'RE STILL WITH HER, THOUGH?
I'M STILL WHA?

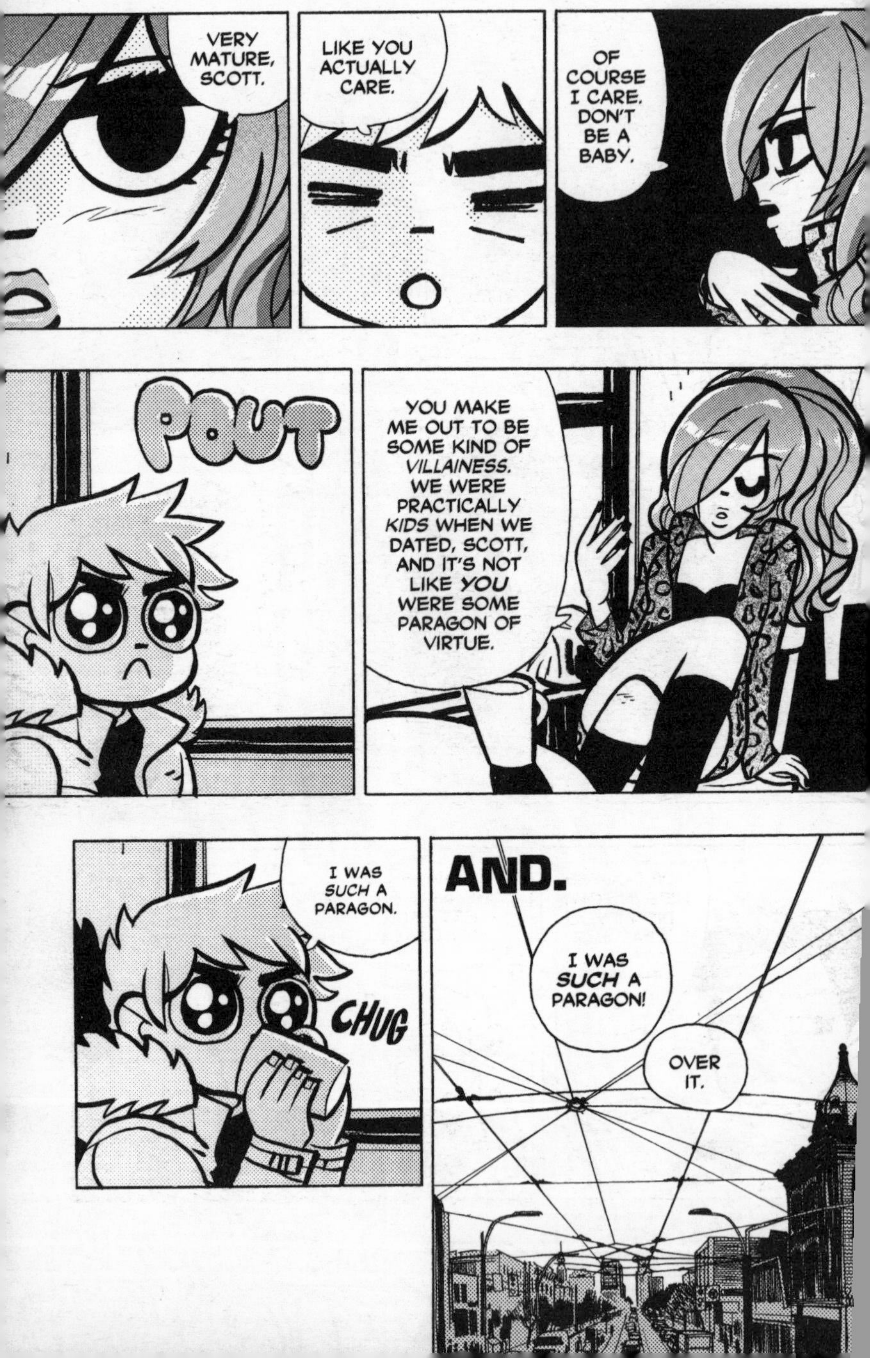
VERY MATURE, SCOTT.
LIKE YOU ACTUALLY CARE.
OF COURSE I CARE. DON'T BE A BABY.
POUT
YOU MAKE ME OUT TO BE SOME KIND OF *VILLAINESS.* WE WERE PRACTICALLY *KIDS* WHEN WE DATED, SCOTT, AND IT'S NOT LIKE *YOU* WERE SOME PARAGON OF VIRTUE.
I WAS *SUCH* A PARAGON.
CHUG
AND.
I WAS *SUCH* A PARAGON!
OVER IT.

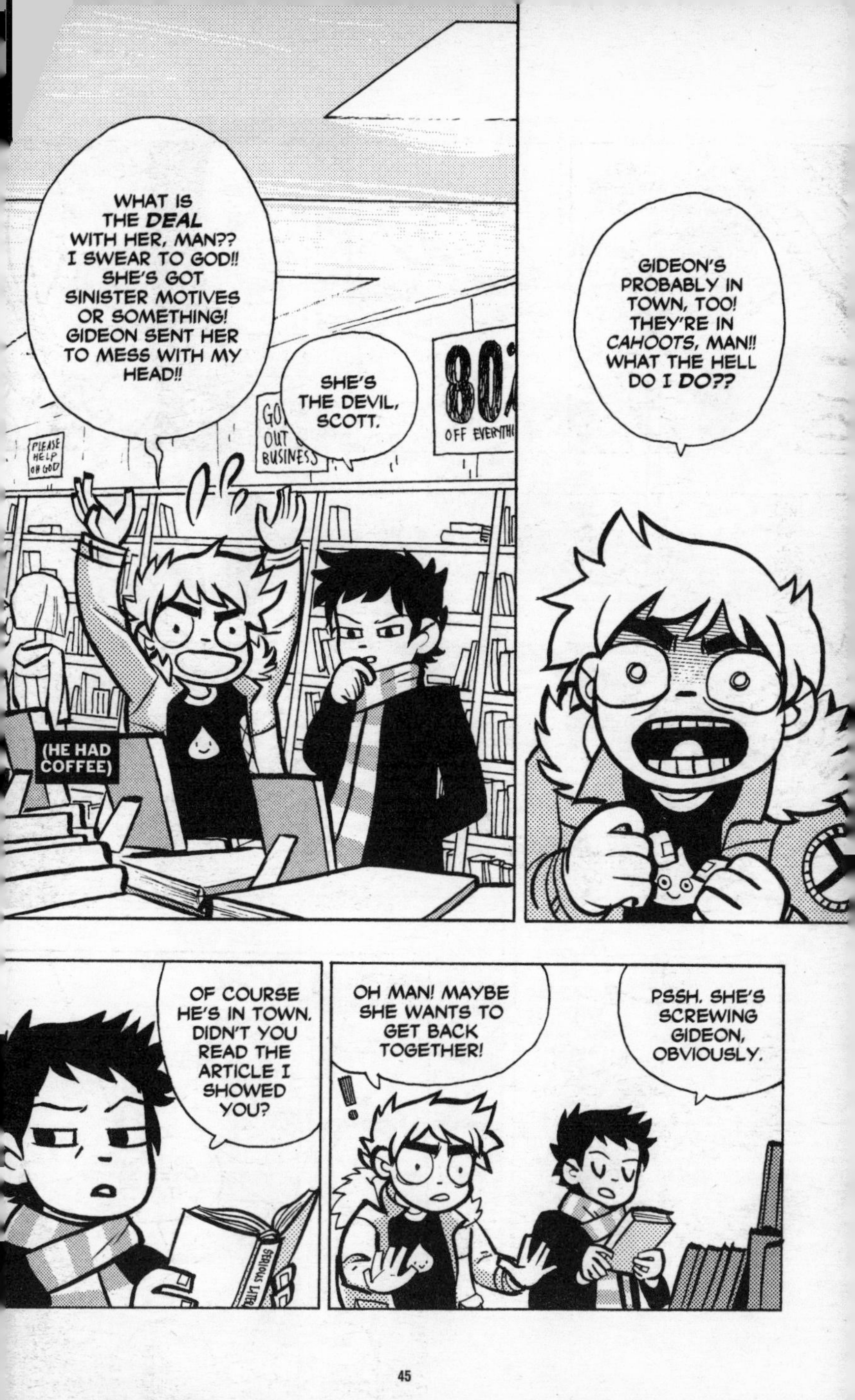
WHAT IS THE DEAL WITH HER, MAN?? I SWEAR TO GOD!! SHE'S GOT SINISTER MOTIVES OR SOMETHING! GIDEON SENT HER TO MESS WITH MY HEAD!!
SHE'S THE DEVIL, SCOTT.
PLEASE HELP OH GOD
GO... OUT ... BUSINESS
80 ... OFF EVERYTH...
(HE HAD COFFEE)
GIDEON'S PROBABLY IN TOWN, TOO! THEY'RE IN CAHOOTS, MAN!! WHAT THE HELL DO I DO??
OF COURSE HE'S IN TOWN. DIDN'T YOU READ THE ARTICLE I SHOWED YOU?
SERIOUS LITE...
OH MAN! MAYBE SHE WANTS TO GET BACK TOGETHER!
!
PSSH. SHE'S SCREWING GIDEON, OBVIOUSLY.

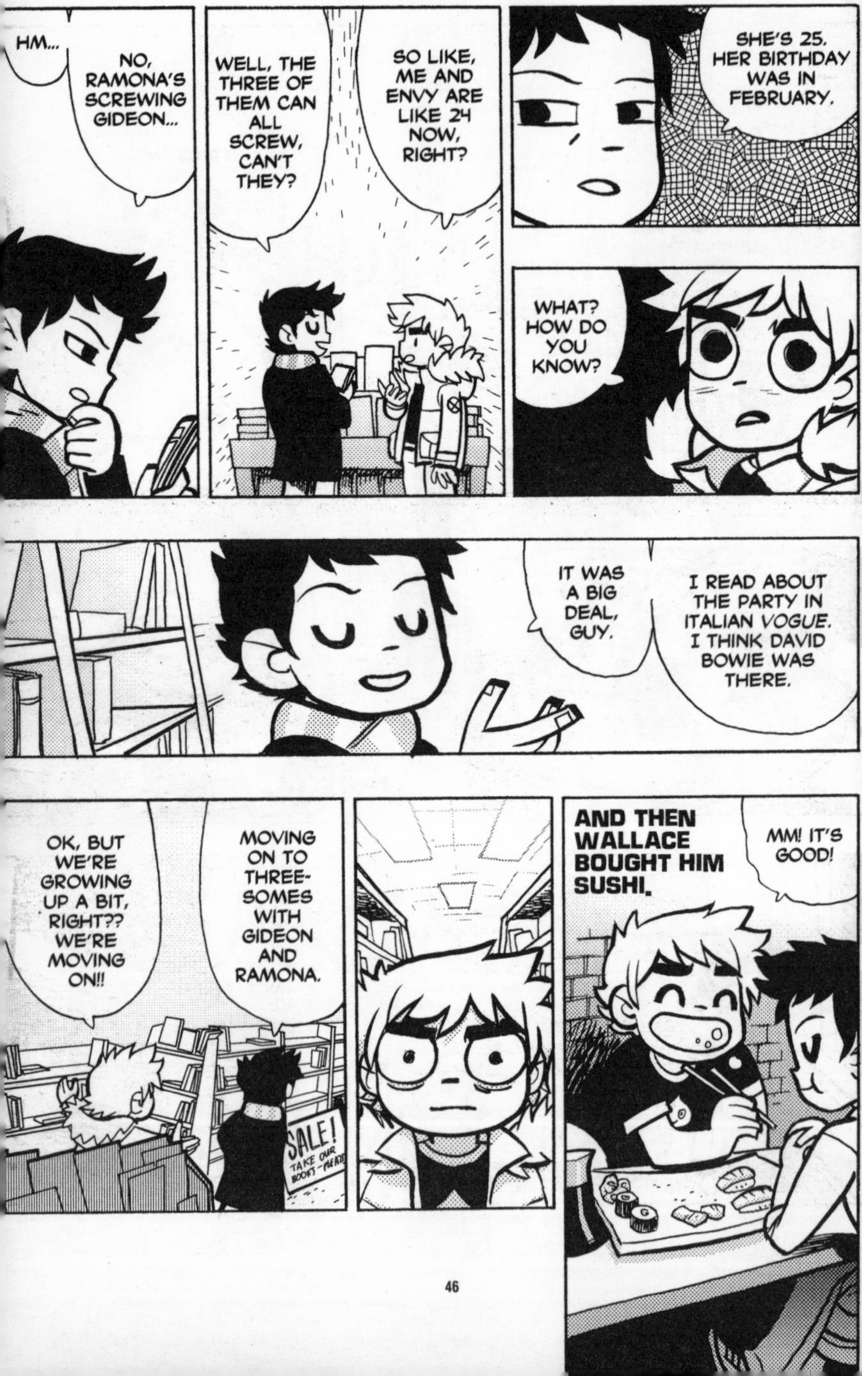
HM...
NO, RAMONA'S SCREWING GIDEON...
WELL, THE THREE OF THEM CAN ALL SCREW, CAN'T THEY?
SO LIKE, ME AND ENVY ARE LIKE 24 NOW, RIGHT?
SHE'S 25. HER BIRTHDAY WAS IN FEBRUARY.
WHAT? HOW DO YOU KNOW?
IT WAS A BIG DEAL, GUY.
I READ ABOUT THE PARTY IN ITALIAN *VOGUE*. I THINK DAVID BOWIE WAS THERE.
OK, BUT WE'RE GROWING UP A BIT, RIGHT?? WE'RE MOVING ON!!
MOVING ON TO THREE-SOMES WITH GIDEON AND RAMONA.
SALE!
AND THEN WALLACE BOUGHT HIM SUSHI.
MM! IT'S GOOD!

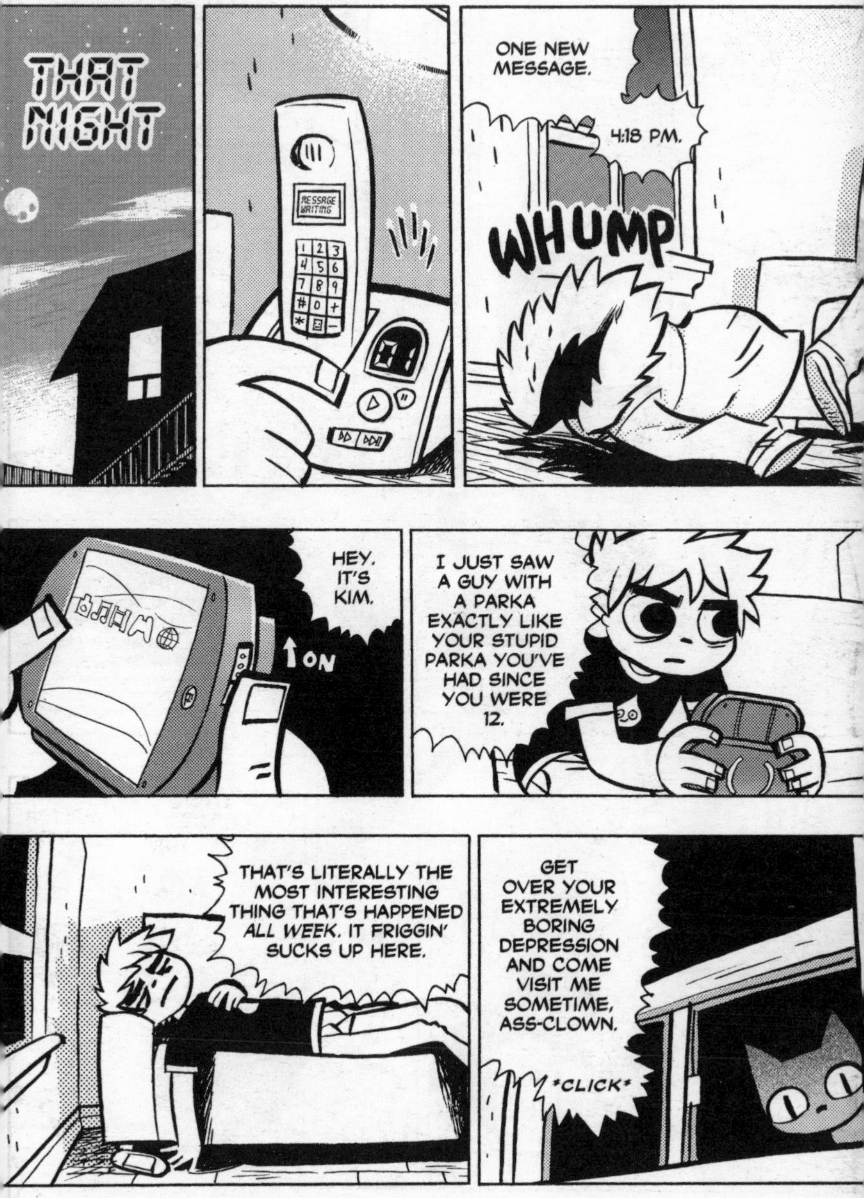
THAT NIGHT
MESSAGE WAITING
ONE NEW MESSAGE.
4:18 PM.
WHUMP
ON
HEY. IT'S KIM.
I JUST SAW A GUY WITH A PARKA EXACTLY LIKE YOUR STUPID PARKA YOU'VE HAD SINCE YOU WERE 12.
THAT'S LITERALLY THE MOST INTERESTING THING THAT'S HAPPENED ALL WEEK. IT FRIGGIN' SUCKS UP HERE.
GET OVER YOUR EXTREMELY BORING DEPRESSION AND COME VISIT ME SOMETIME, ASS-CLOWN.
CLICK

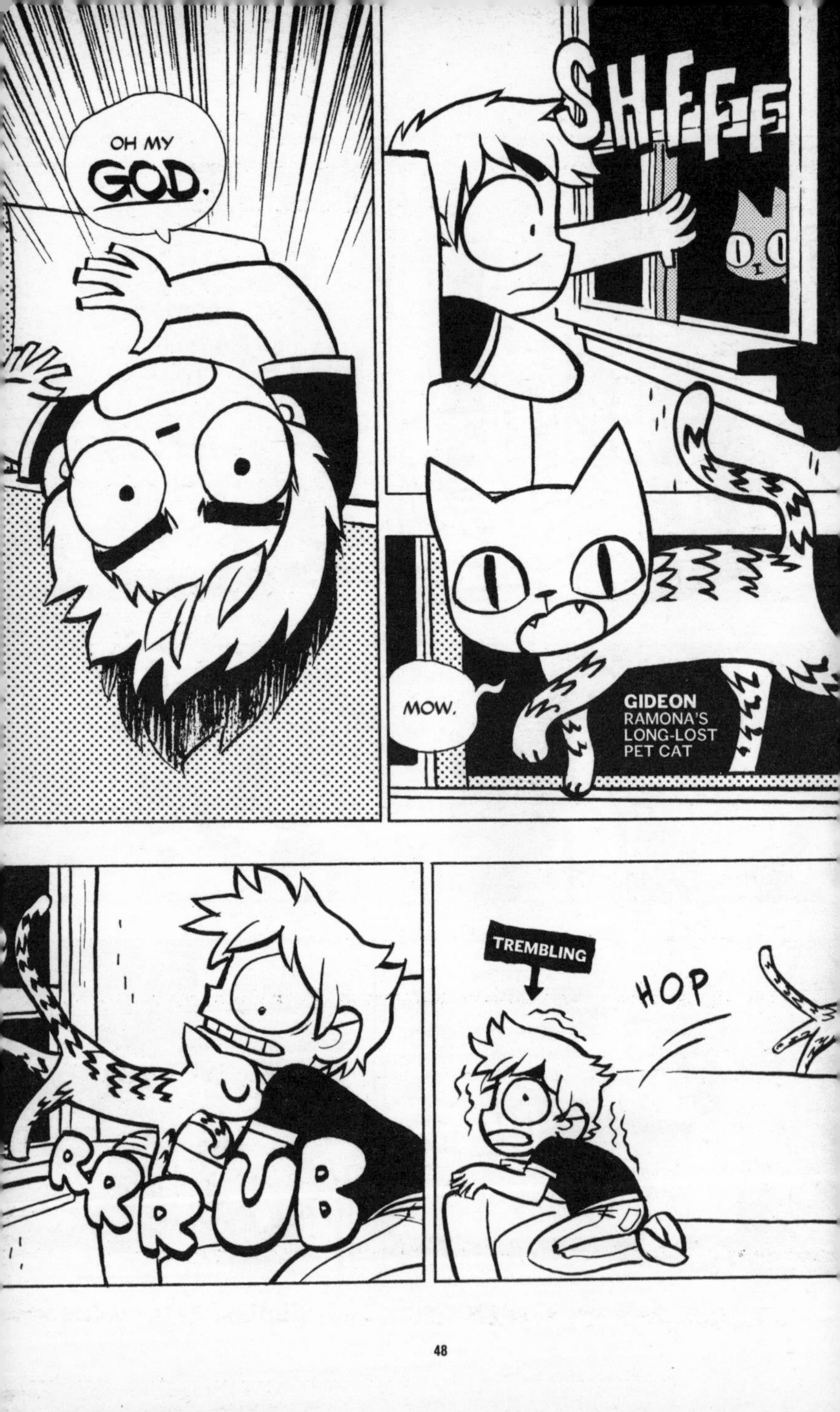
OH MY GOD.
SHFFFF
MOW.
GIDEON
RAMONA'S LONG-LOST PET CAT
RRRUB
TREMBLING
HOP

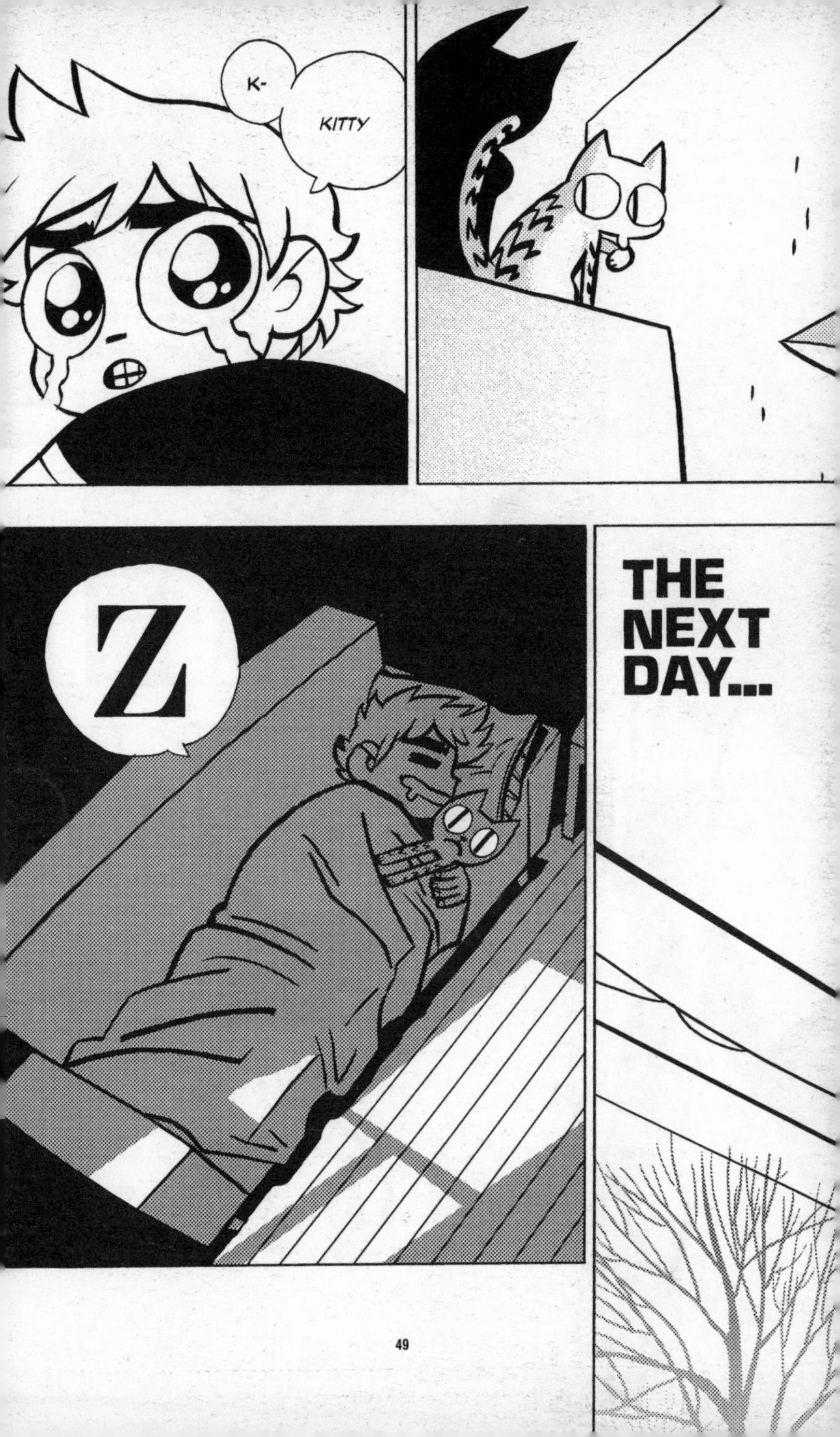
K-
KITTY
Z
THE NEXT DAY...

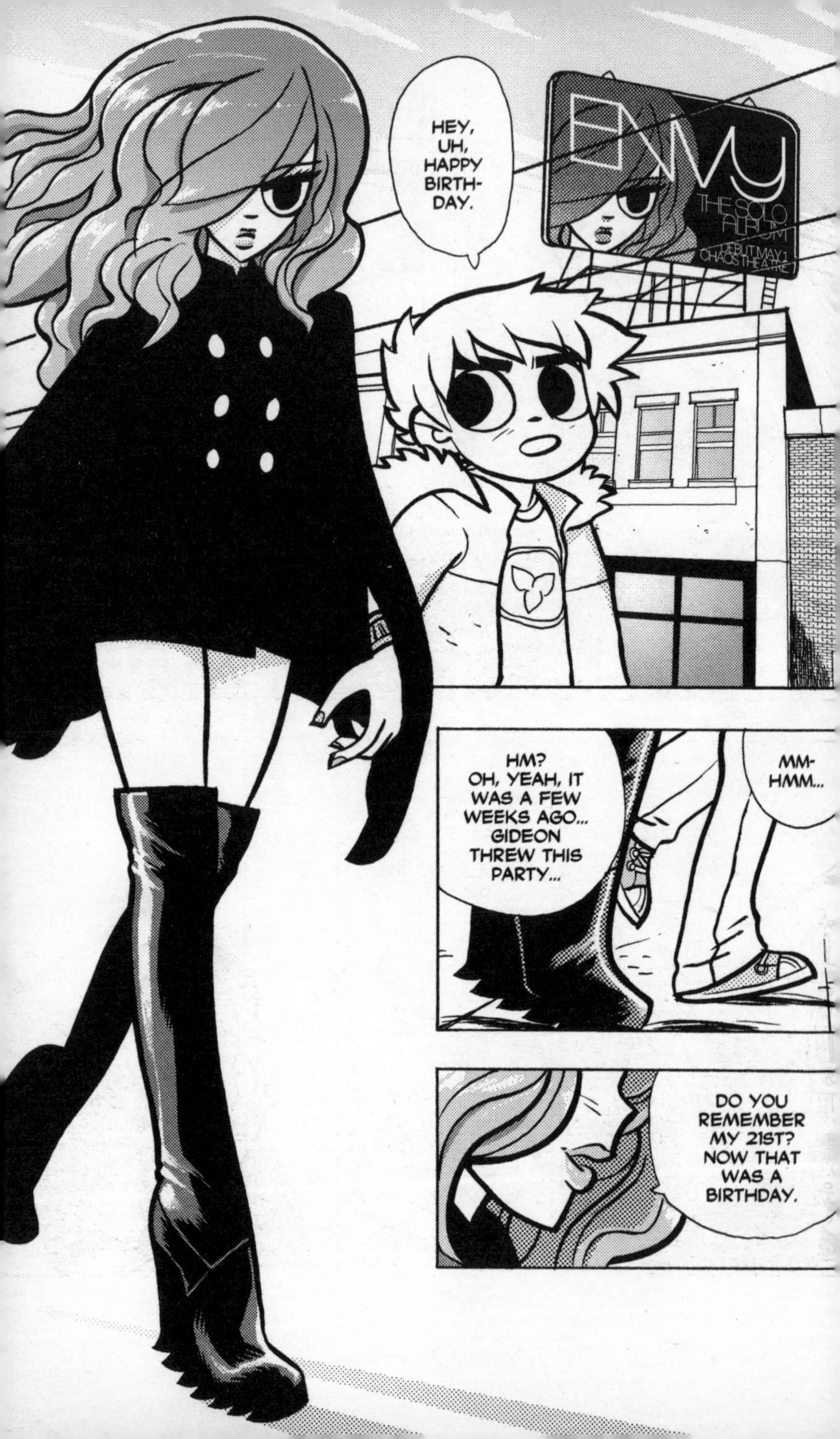
HEY, UH, HAPPY BIRTH-DAY.
ENVY THE SOLO ALBUM DEBUT MAY 1 CHAOS THEATRE
HM? OH, YEAH, IT WAS A FEW WEEKS AGO... GIDEON THREW THIS PARTY...
MM-HMM...
DO YOU REMEMBER MY 21ST? NOW THAT WAS A BIRTHDAY.

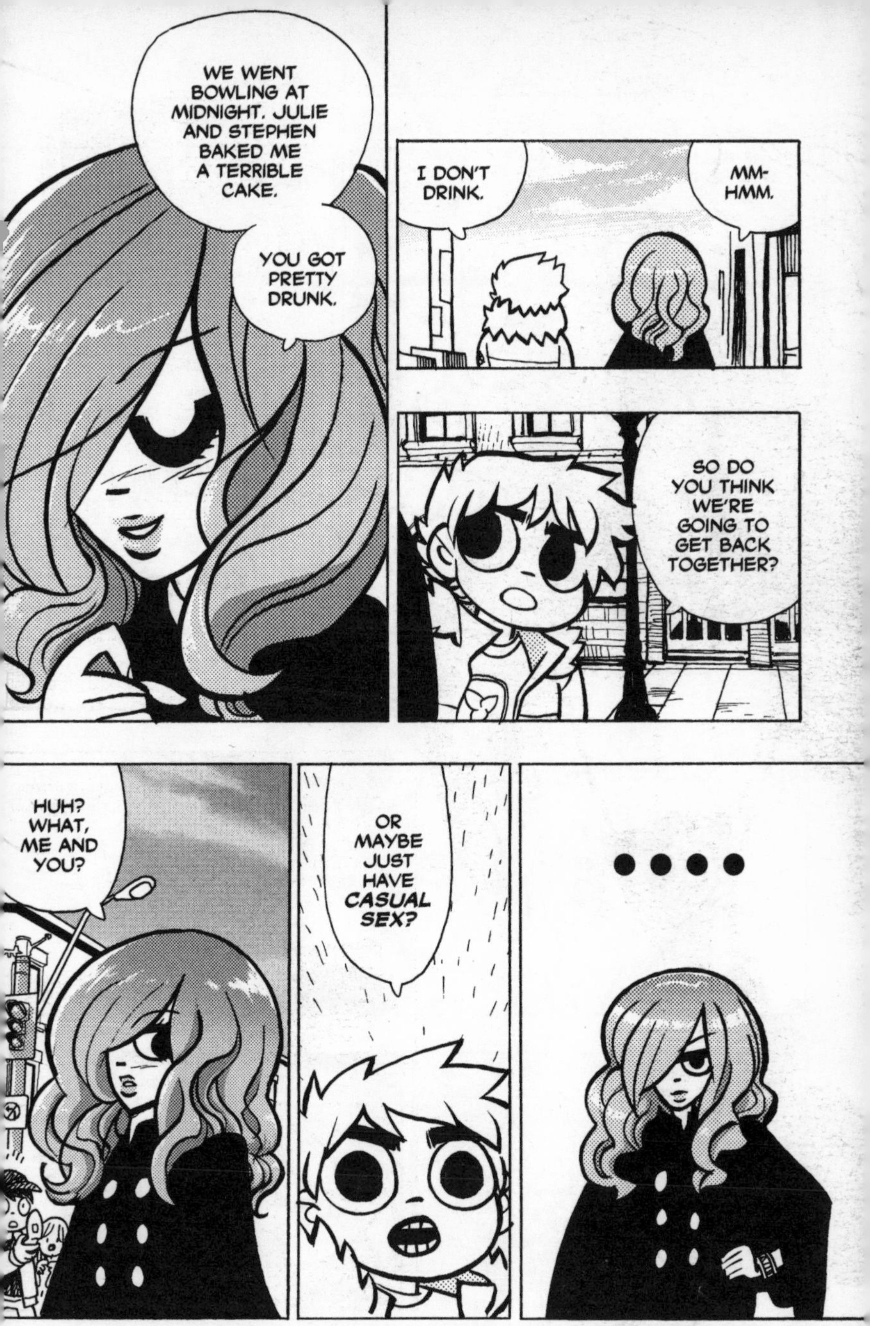

WE WENT BOWLING AT MIDNIGHT. JULIE AND STEPHEN BAKED ME A TERRIBLE CAKE.
YOU GOT PRETTY DRUNK.
I DON'T DRINK.
MM-HMM.
SO DO YOU THINK WE'RE GOING TO GET BACK TOGETHER?
HUH? WHAT, ME AND YOU?
OR MAYBE JUST HAVE *CASUAL SEX?*
• • • •

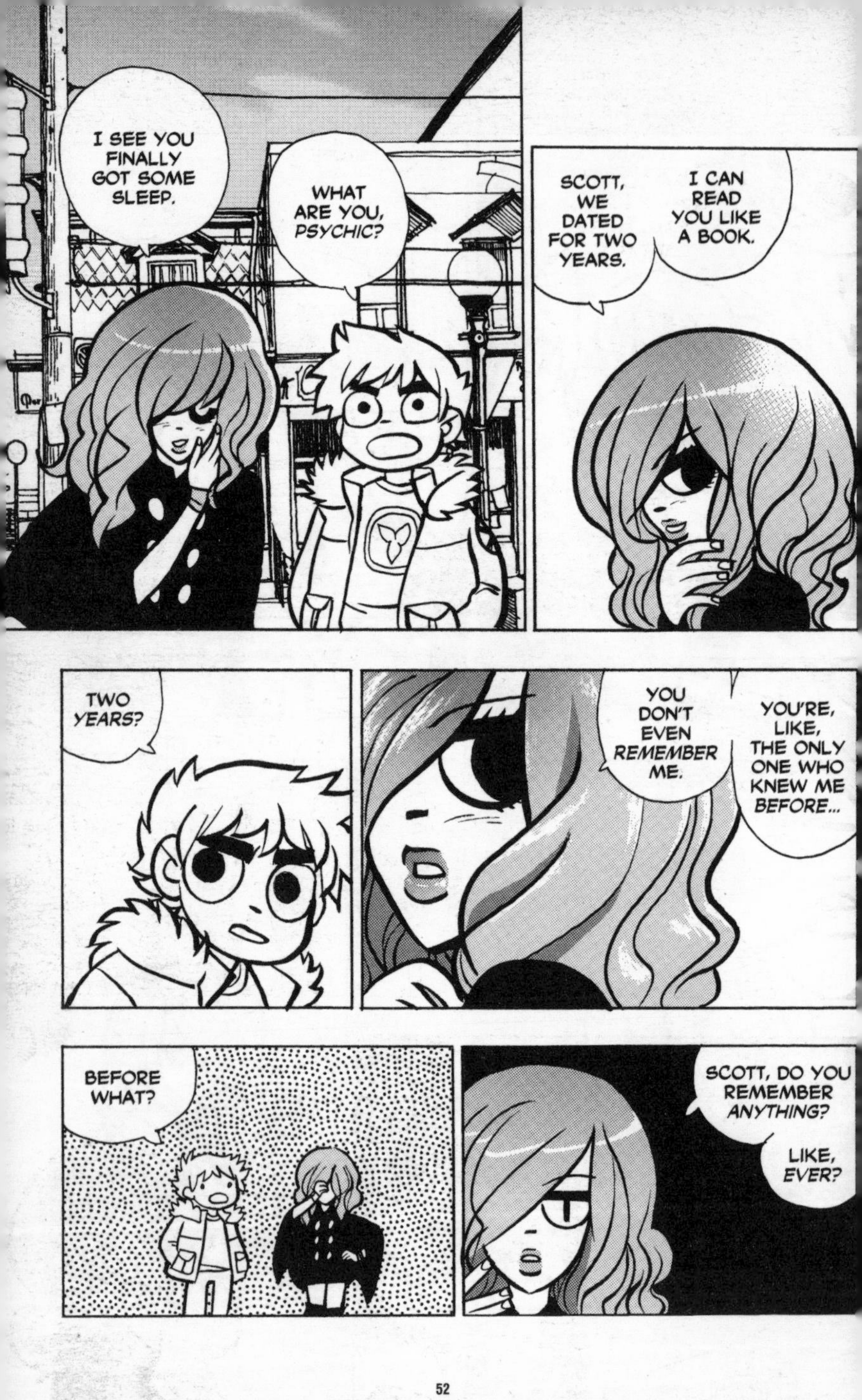
I SEE YOU FINALLY GOT SOME SLEEP.
WHAT ARE YOU, *PSYCHIC?*
SCOTT, WE DATED FOR TWO YEARS.
I CAN READ YOU LIKE A BOOK.
TWO *YEARS?*
YOU DON'T EVEN *REMEMBER* ME.
YOU'RE, LIKE, THE ONLY ONE WHO KNEW ME *BEFORE...*
BEFORE WHAT?
SCOTT, DO YOU REMEMBER *ANYTHING?*
LIKE, *EVER?*

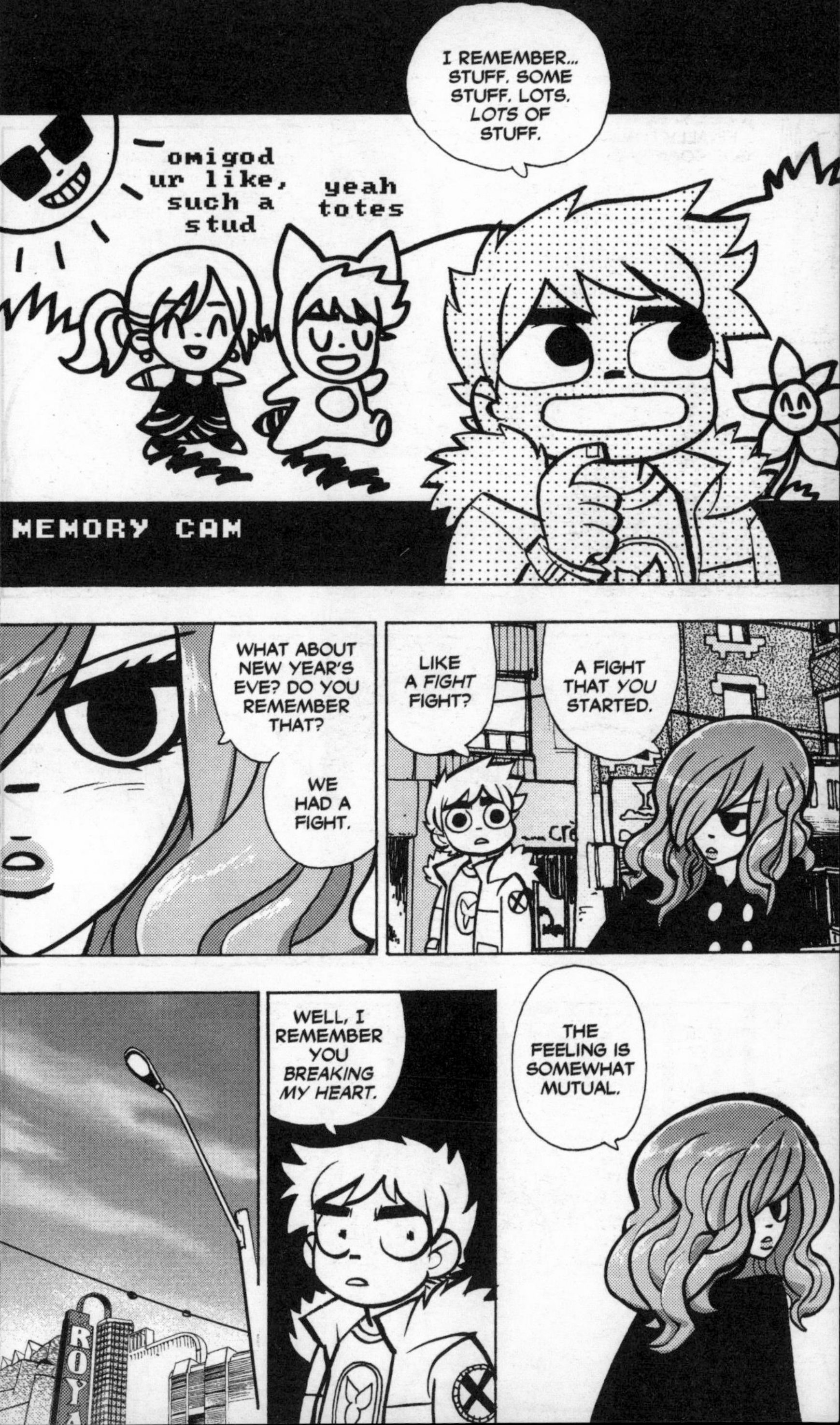
I REMEMBER... STUFF. SOME STUFF. LOTS. LOTS OF STUFF.
omigod ur like, such a stud
yeah totes
MEMORY CAM
WHAT ABOUT NEW YEAR'S EVE? DO YOU REMEMBER THAT?
WE HAD A FIGHT.
LIKE A FIGHT FIGHT?
A FIGHT THAT YOU STARTED.
WELL, I REMEMBER YOU BREAKING MY HEART.
THE FEELING IS SOMEWHAT MUTUAL.

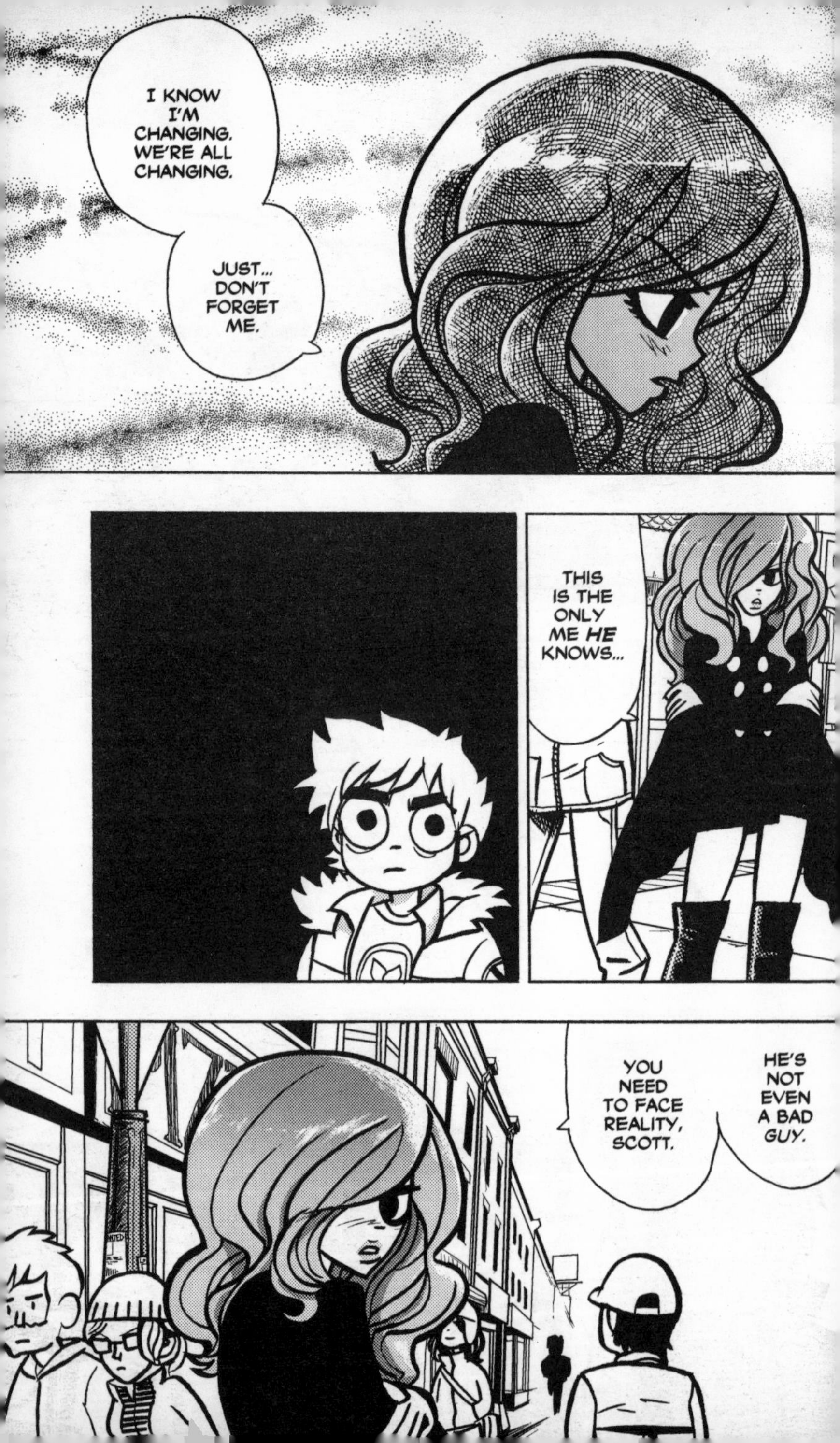
I KNOW I'M CHANGING. WE'RE ALL CHANGING.
JUST... DON'T FORGET ME.
THIS IS THE ONLY ME *HE* KNOWS...
YOU NEED TO FACE REALITY, SCOTT.
HE'S NOT EVEN A BAD *GUY*.

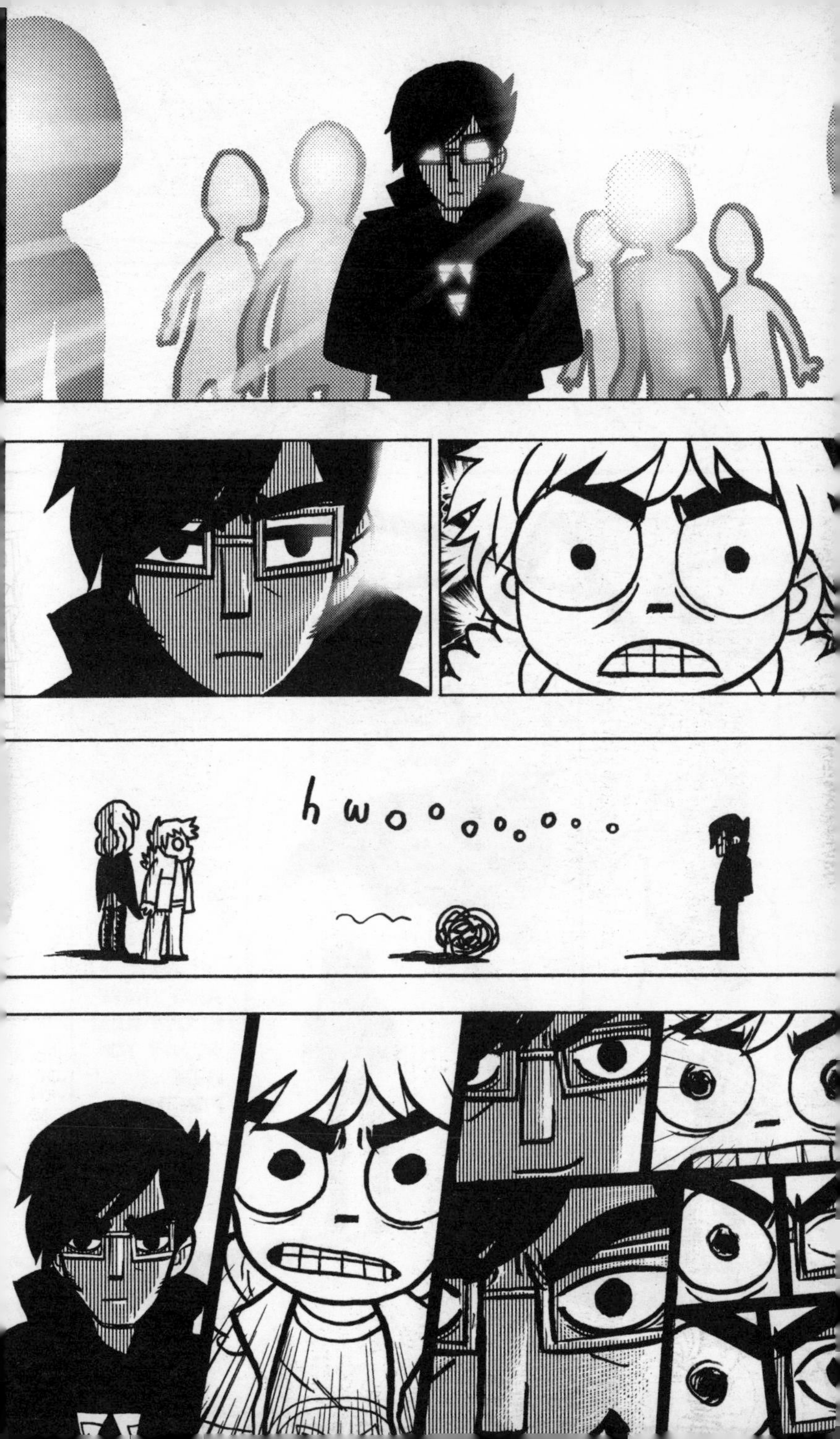
hwoooooooo

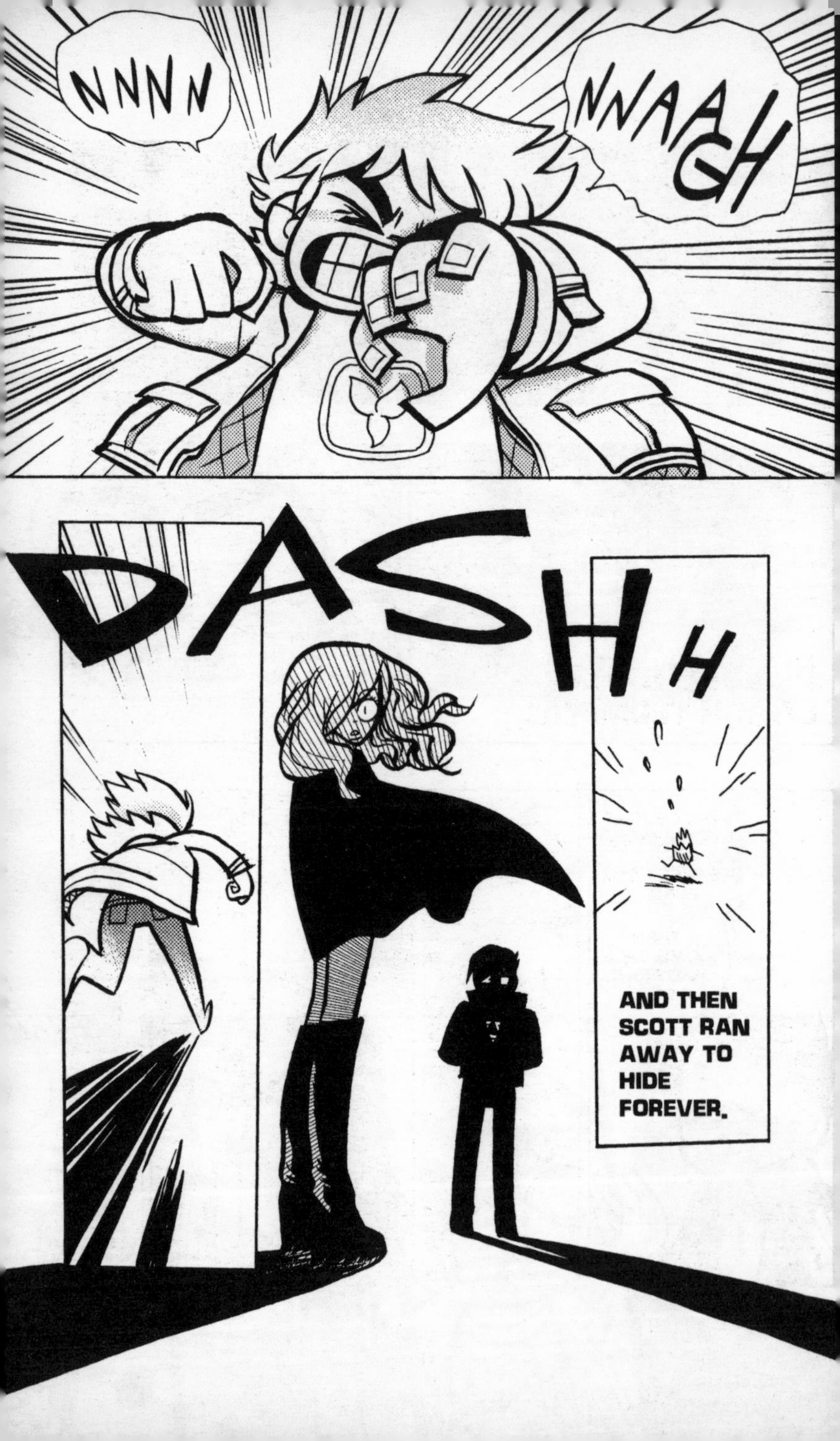
NNNN
NNAAGH
DASHH
AND THEN SCOTT RAN AWAY TO HIDE FOREVER.

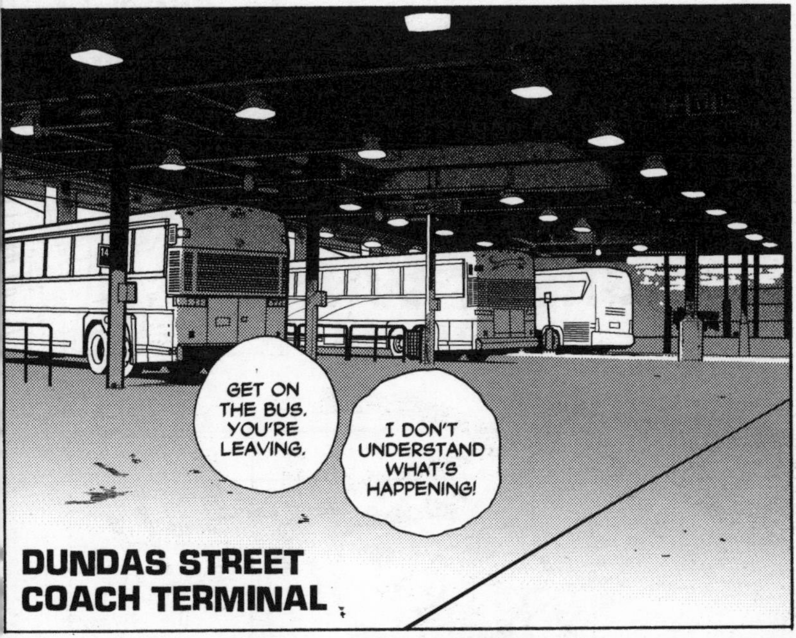
GET ON THE BUS. YOU'RE LEAVING.
I DON'T UNDERSTAND WHAT'S HAPPENING!
DUNDAS STREET COACH TERMINAL

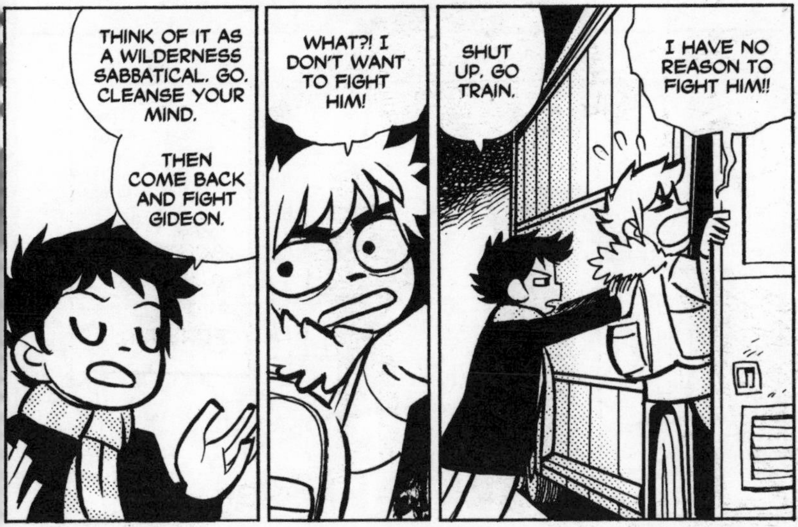
THINK OF IT AS A WILDERNESS SABBATICAL. GO. CLEANSE YOUR MIND.
THEN COME BACK AND FIGHT GIDEON.
WHAT?! I DON'T WANT TO FIGHT HIM!
SHUT UP. GO TRAIN.
I HAVE NO REASON TO FIGHT HIM!!

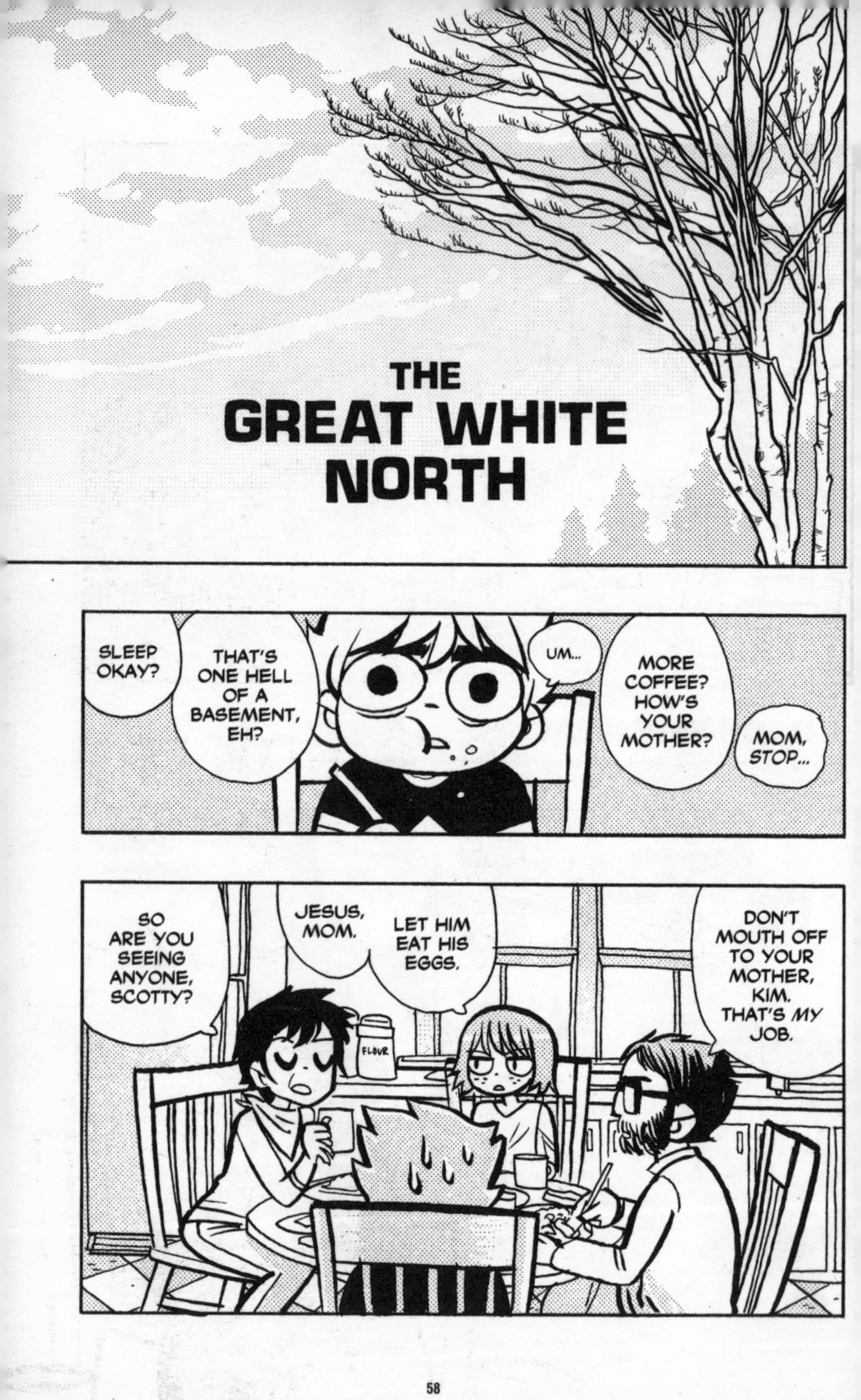
THE GREAT WHITE NORTH
SLEEP OKAY?
THAT'S ONE HELL OF A BASEMENT, EH?
UM...
MORE COFFEE? HOW'S YOUR MOTHER?
MOM, STOP...
SO ARE YOU SEEING ANYONE, SCOTTY?
JESUS, MOM.
LET HIM EAT HIS EGGS.
DON'T MOUTH OFF TO YOUR MOTHER, KIM. THAT'S MY JOB.
FLOUR

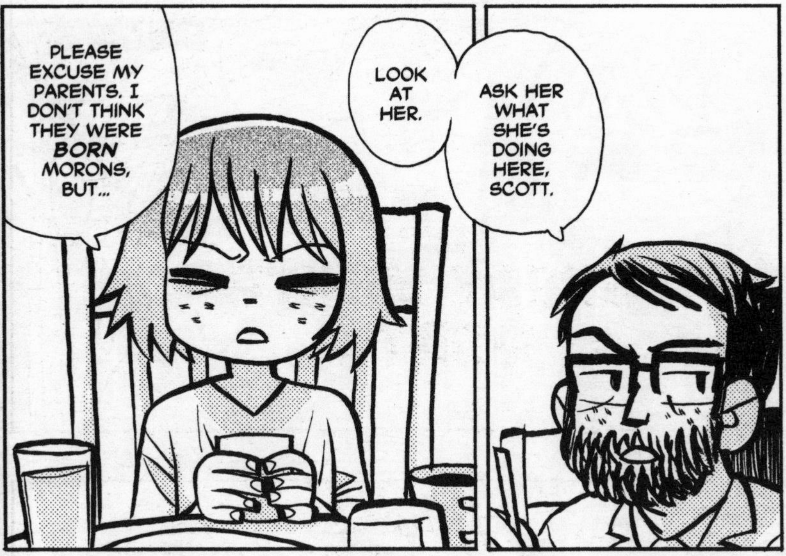
PLEASE EXCUSE MY PARENTS. I DON'T THINK THEY WERE *BORN* MORONS, BUT...
LOOK AT HER.
ASK HER WHAT SHE'S DOING HERE, SCOTT.

34 A link to the past

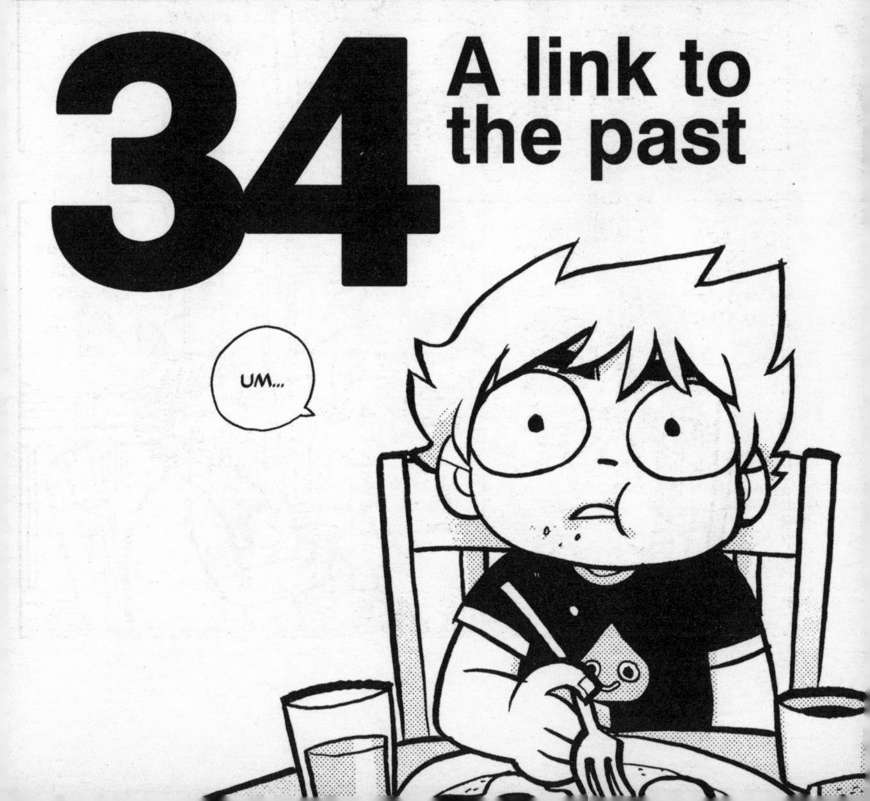
UM...

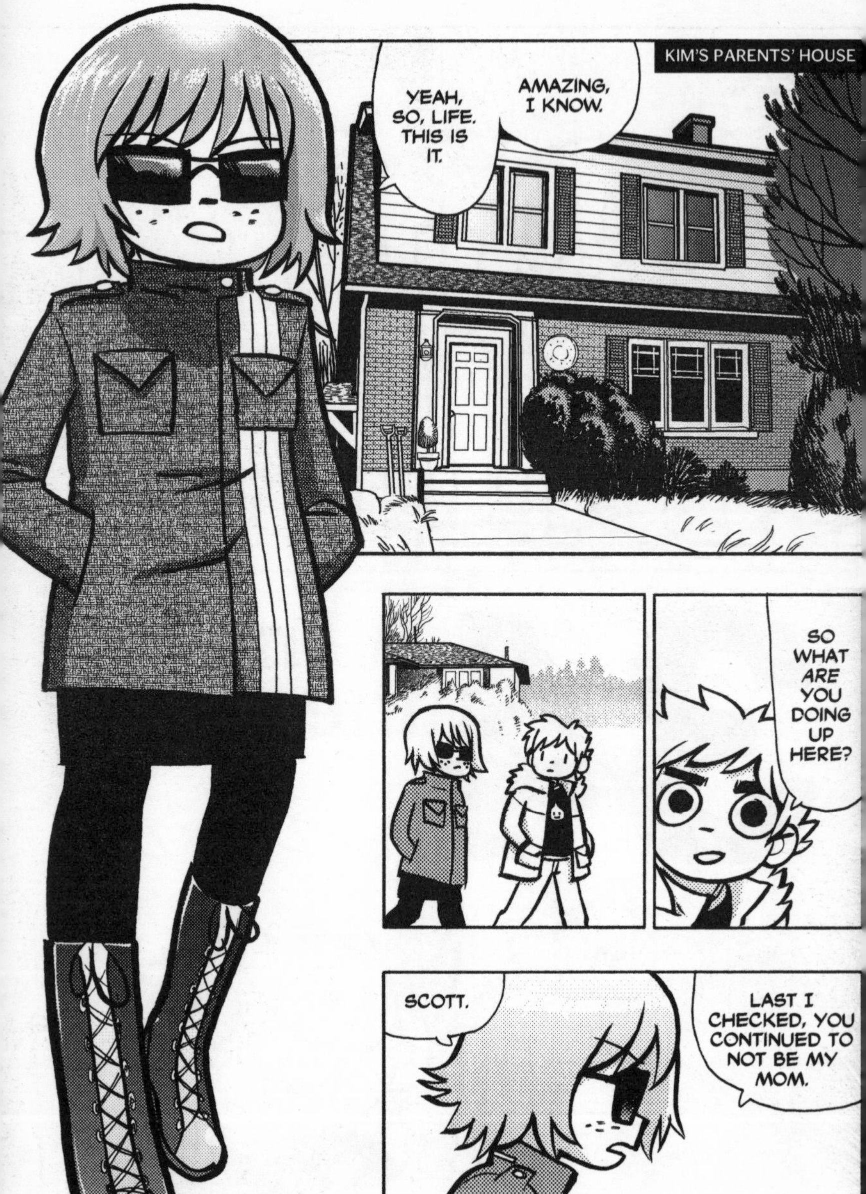
KIM'S PARENTS' HOUSE
YEAH, SO, LIFE. THIS IS IT.
AMAZING, I KNOW.
SO WHAT *ARE* YOU DOING UP HERE?
SCOTT.
LAST I CHECKED, YOU CONTINUED TO NOT BE MY MOM.

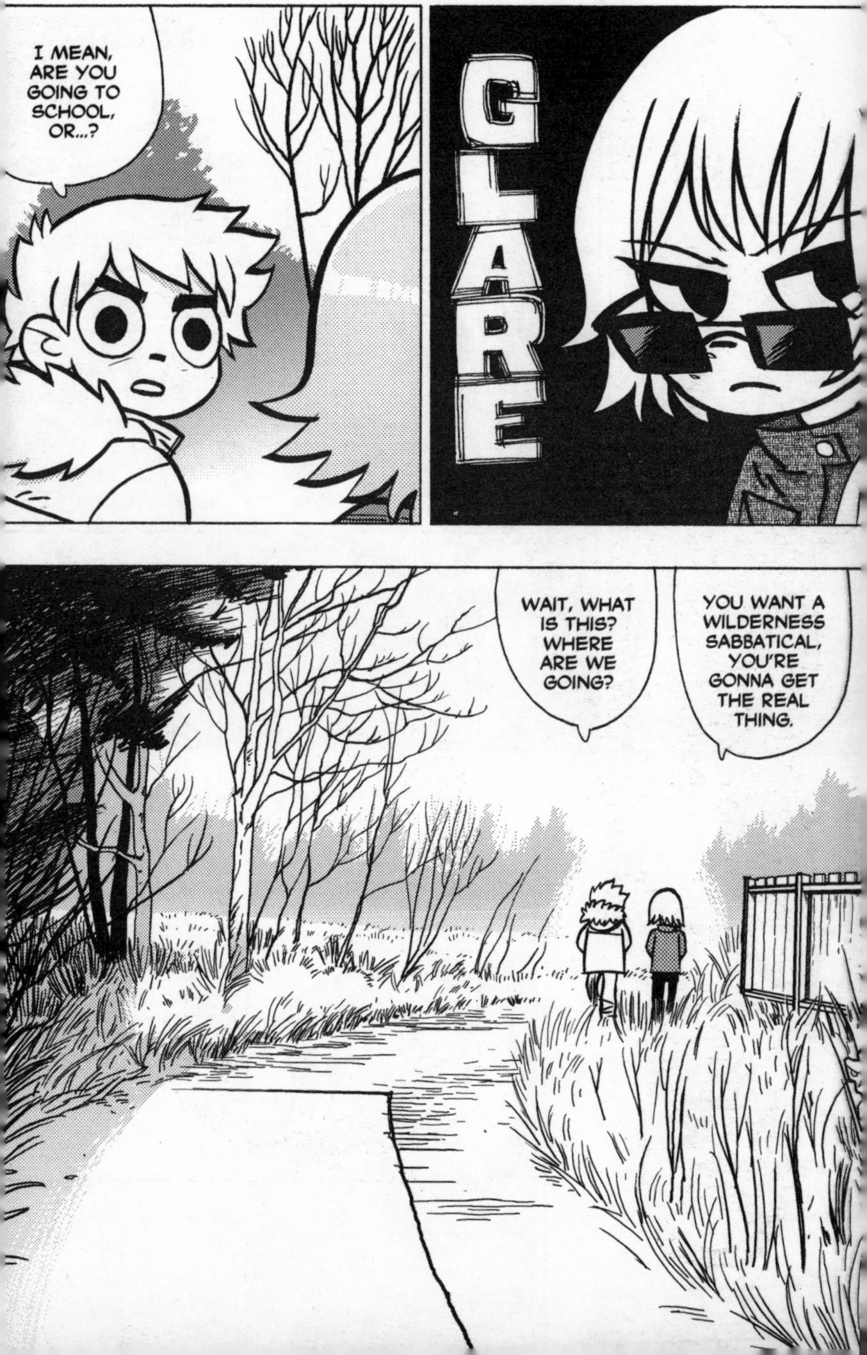
I MEAN, ARE YOU GOING TO SCHOOL, OR...?
GLARE
WAIT, WHAT IS THIS? WHERE ARE WE GOING?
YOU WANT A WILDERNESS SABBATICAL, YOU'RE GONNA GET THE REAL THING.

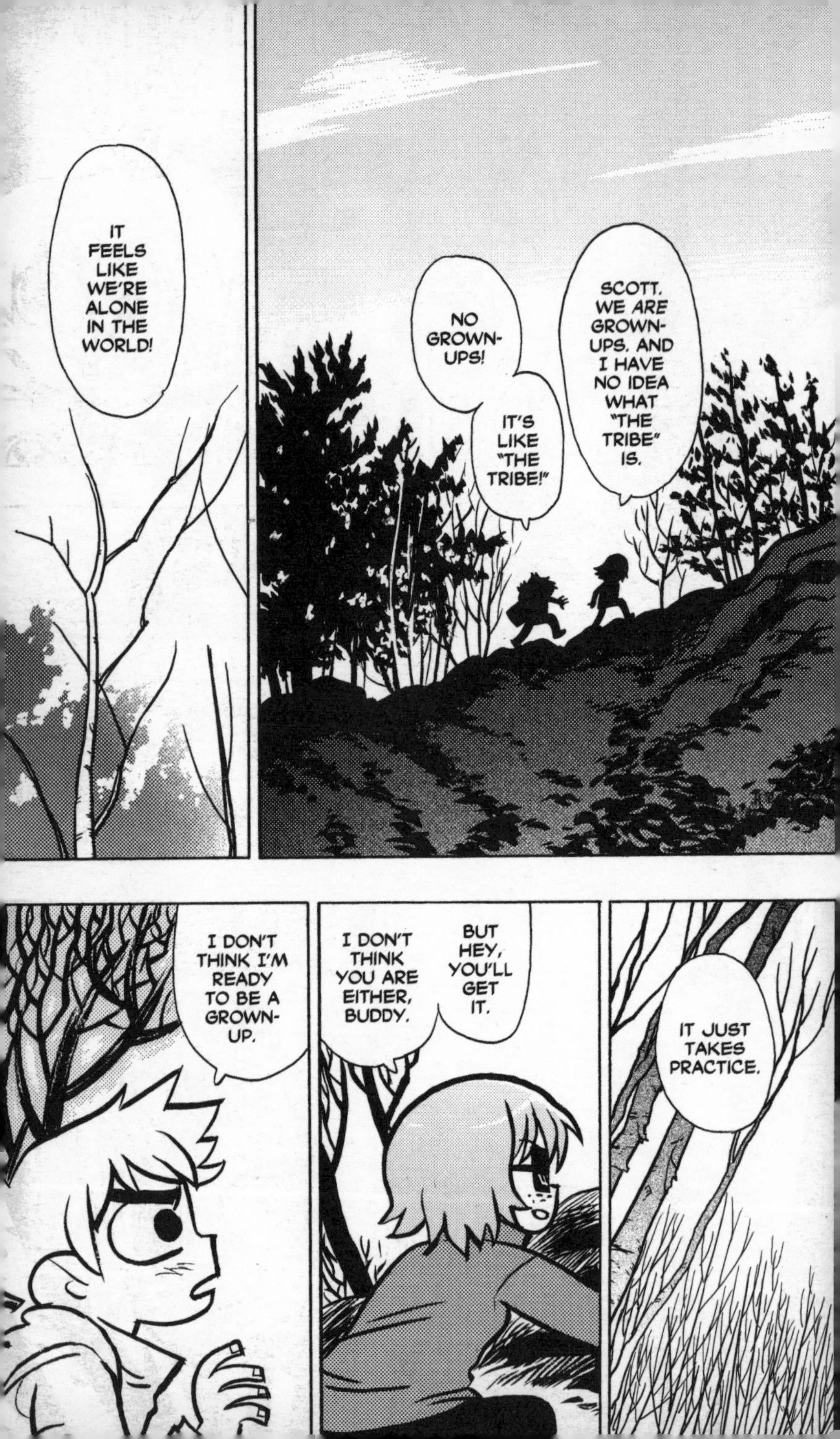
IT FEELS LIKE WE'RE ALONE IN THE WORLD!
NO GROWN-UPS!
IT'S LIKE "THE TRIBE!"
SCOTT. WE *ARE* GROWN-UPS. AND I HAVE NO IDEA WHAT "THE TRIBE" IS.
I DON'T THINK I'M READY TO BE A GROWN-UP.
I DON'T THINK YOU ARE EITHER, BUDDY.
BUT HEY, YOU'LL GET IT.
IT JUST TAKES PRACTICE.

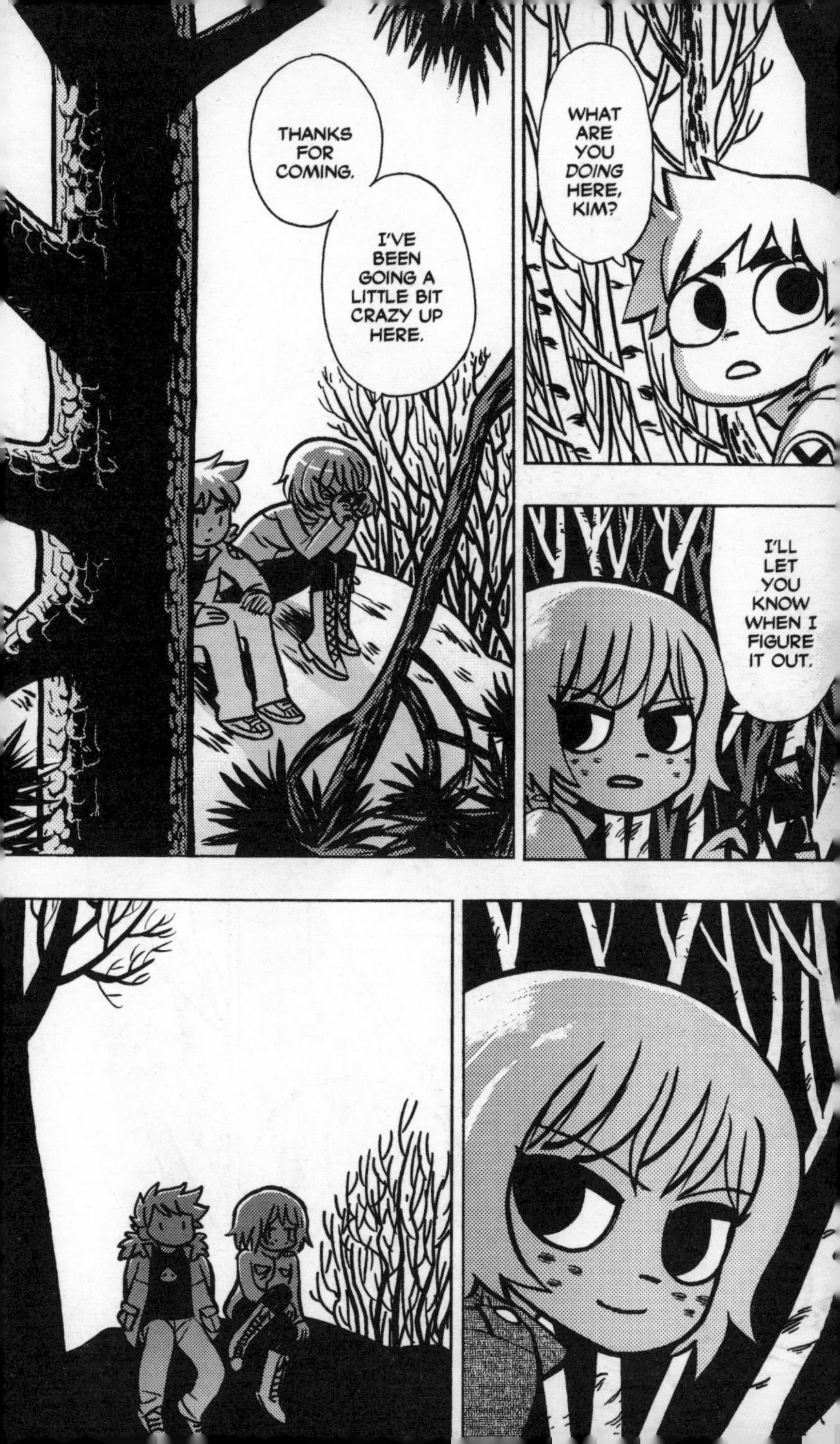
THANKS FOR COMING.
I'VE BEEN GOING A LITTLE BIT CRAZY UP HERE.
WHAT ARE YOU *DOING* HERE, KIM?
I'LL LET YOU KNOW WHEN I FIGURE IT OUT.

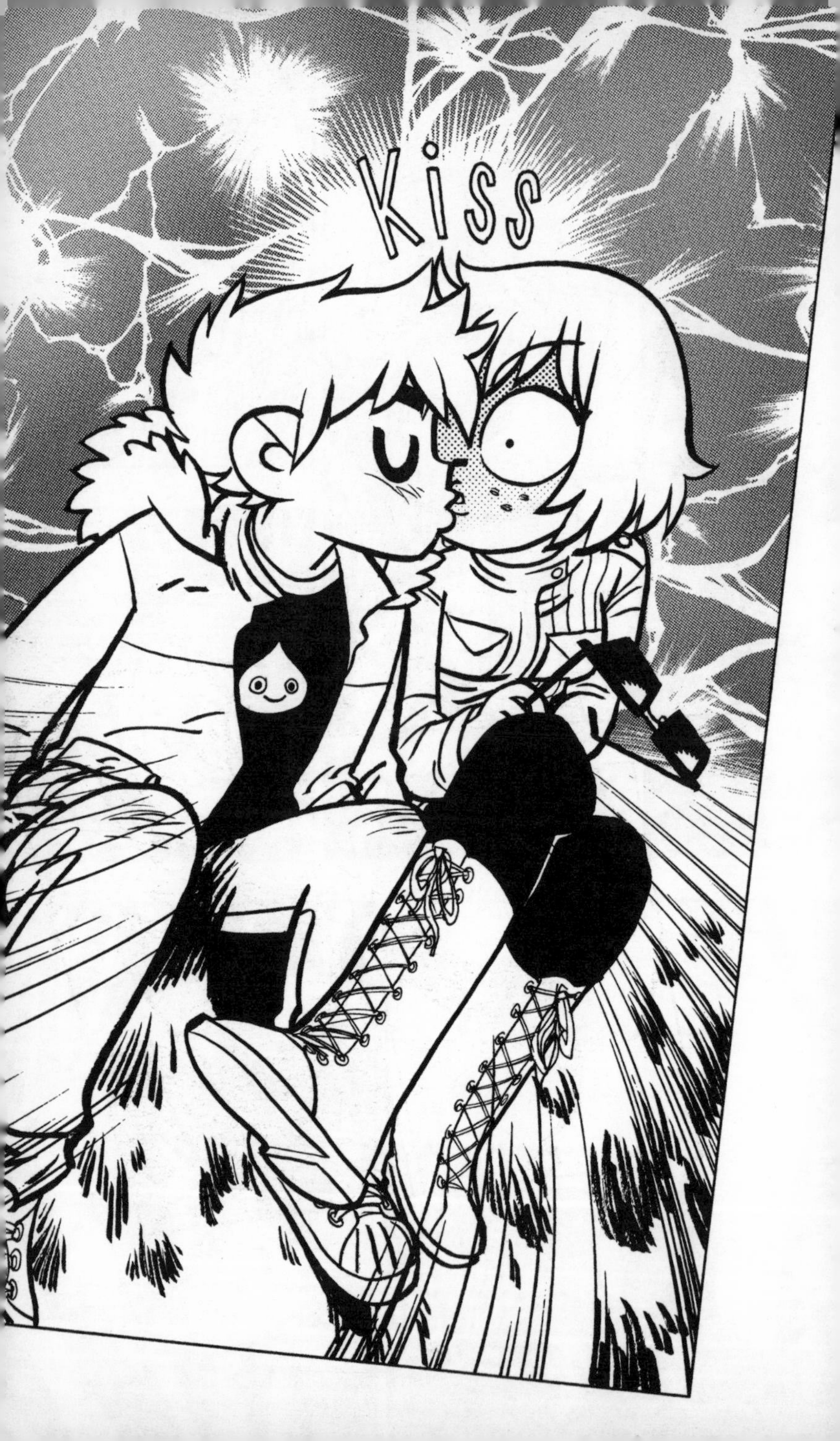
Kiss

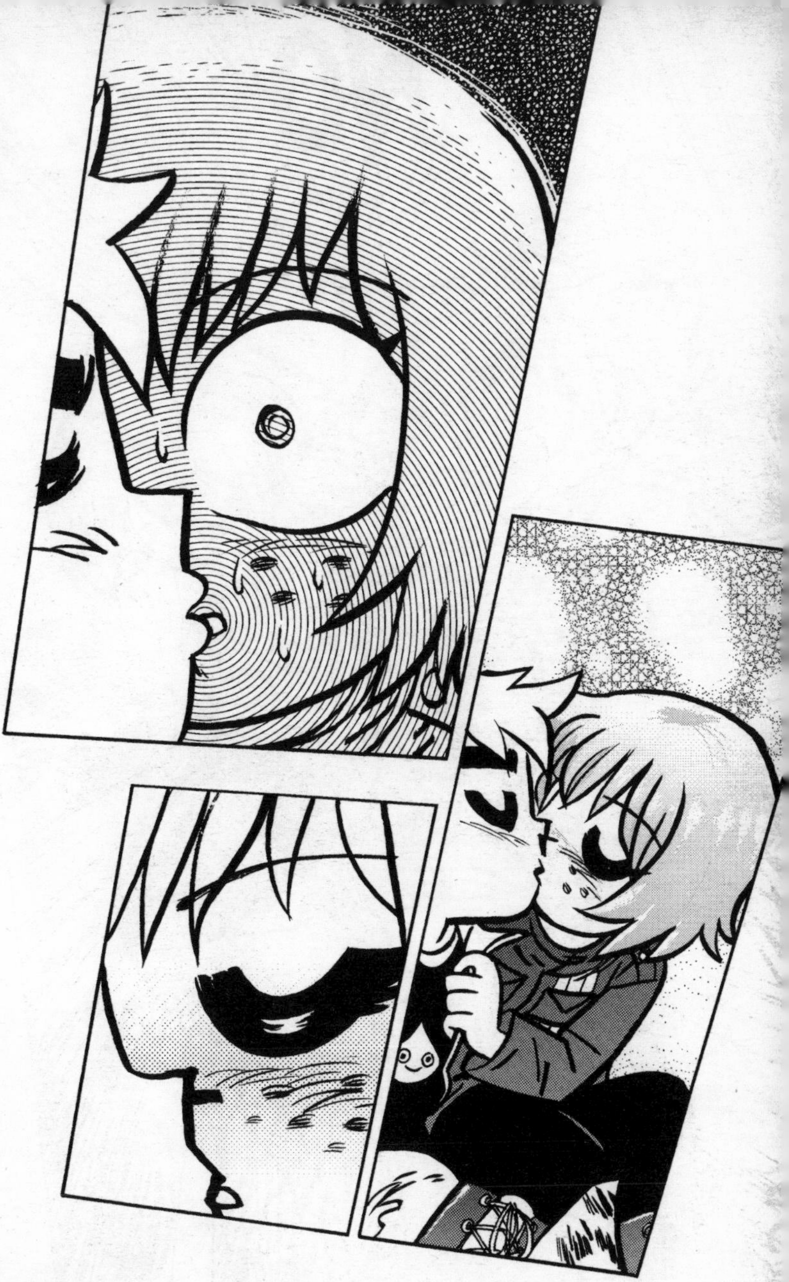

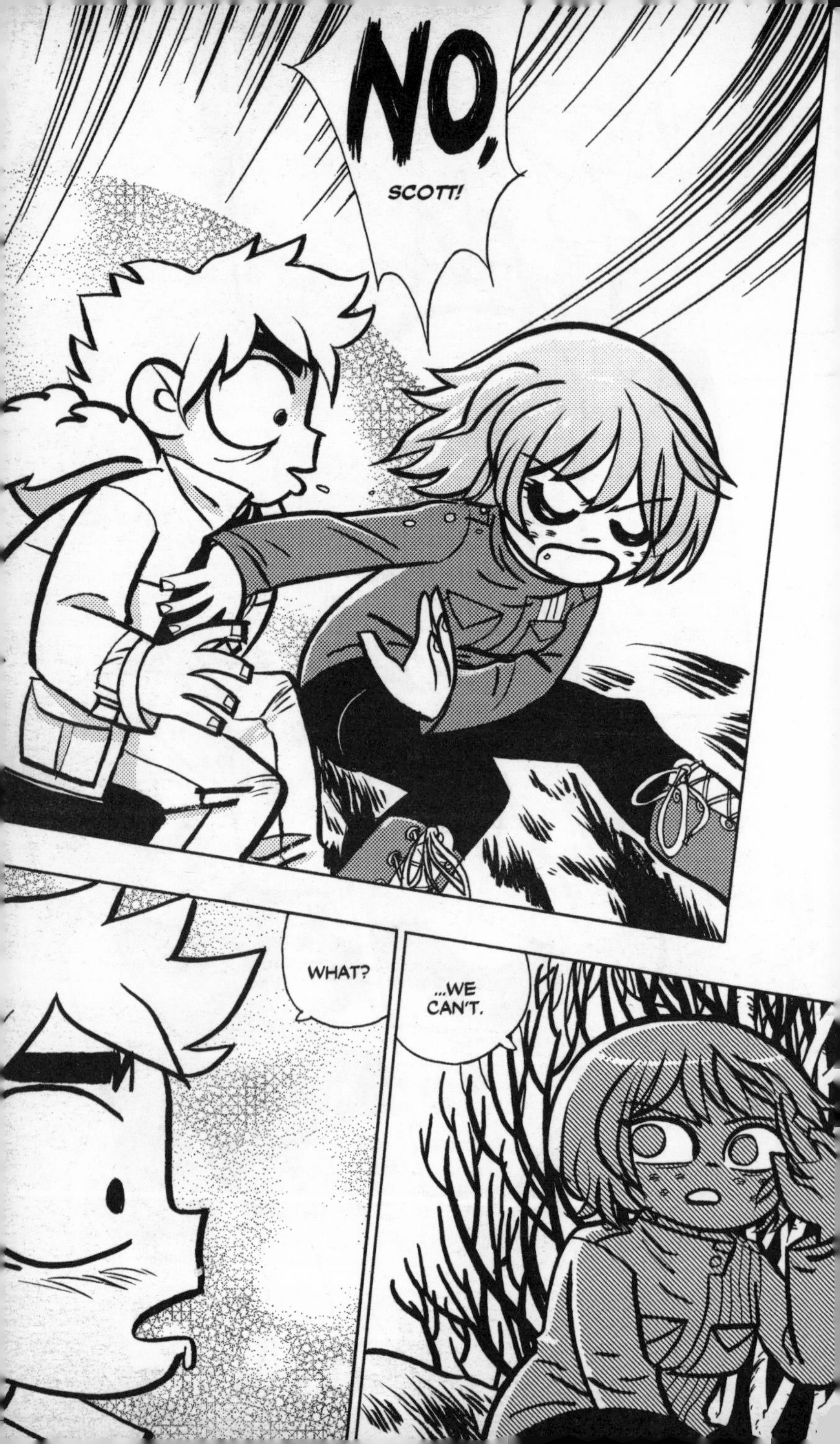
NO, SCOTT!
WHAT?
...WE CAN'T.

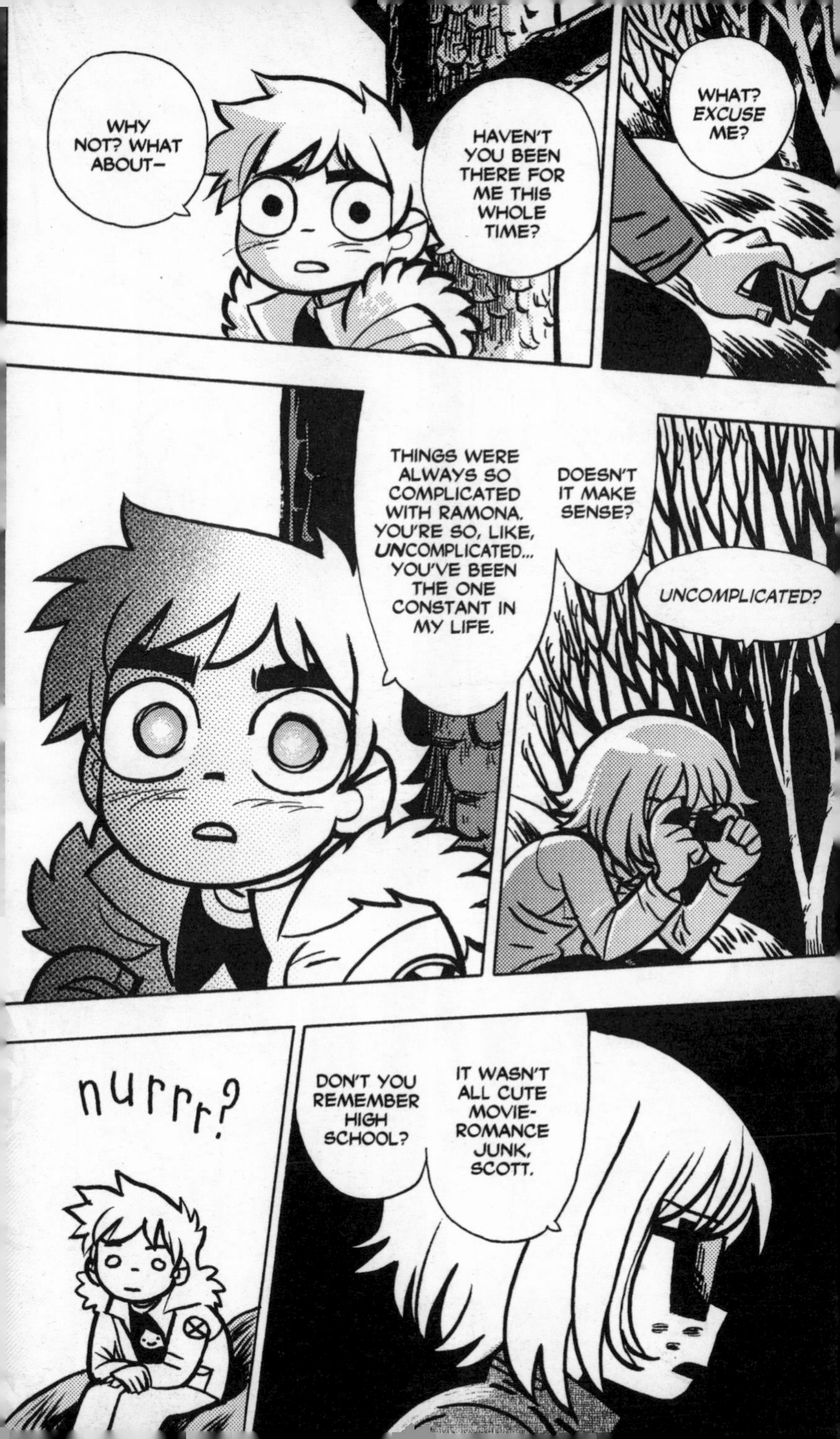
WHY NOT? WHAT ABOUT–
HAVEN'T YOU BEEN THERE FOR ME THIS WHOLE TIME?
WHAT? *EXCUSE* ME?
THINGS WERE ALWAYS SO COMPLICATED WITH RAMONA. YOU'RE SO, LIKE, ***UN***COMPLICATED... YOU'VE BEEN THE ONE CONSTANT IN MY LIFE.
DOESN'T IT MAKE SENSE?
UNCOMPLICATED?
nurrr?
DON'T YOU REMEMBER HIGH SCHOOL?
IT WASN'T ALL CUTE MOVIE-ROMANCE JUNK, SCOTT.

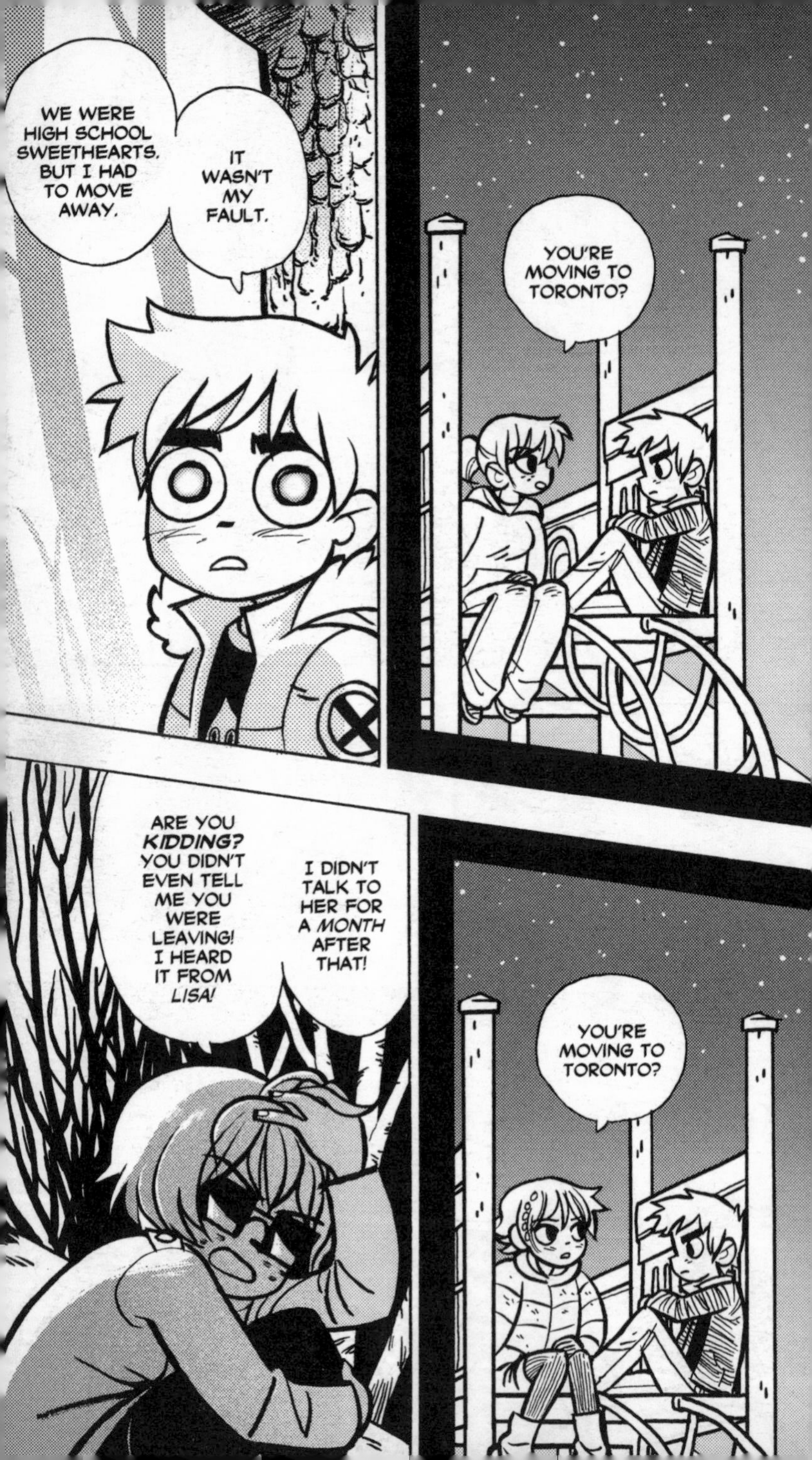

WE WERE HIGH SCHOOL SWEETHEARTS. BUT I HAD TO MOVE AWAY.
IT WASN'T MY FAULT.
YOU'RE MOVING TO TORONTO?
ARE YOU *KIDDING?* YOU DIDN'T EVEN TELL ME YOU WERE LEAVING! I HEARD IT FROM *LISA!*
I DIDN'T TALK TO HER FOR A *MONTH* AFTER THAT!
YOU'RE MOVING TO TORONTO?

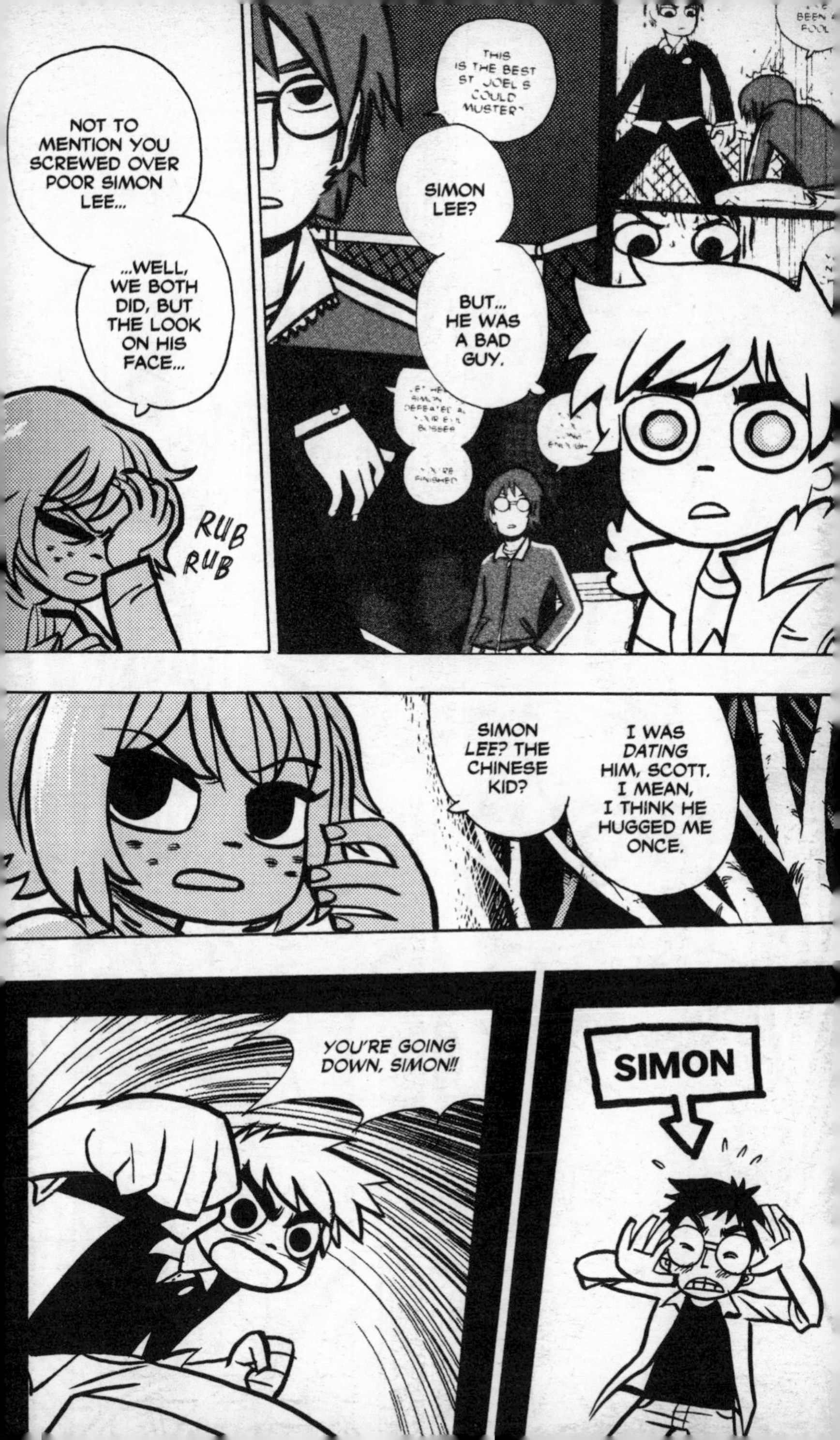
NOT TO MENTION YOU SCREWED OVER POOR SIMON LEE...
...WELL, WE BOTH DID, BUT THE LOOK ON HIS FACE...
THIS IS THE BEST ST. JOEL'S COULD MUSTER?
SIMON LEE?
BUT... HE WAS A BAD GUY.
RUB RUB
SIMON LEE? THE CHINESE KID?
I WAS DATING HIM, SCOTT. I MEAN, I THINK HE HUGGED ME ONCE.
YOU'RE GOING DOWN, SIMON!!
SIMON

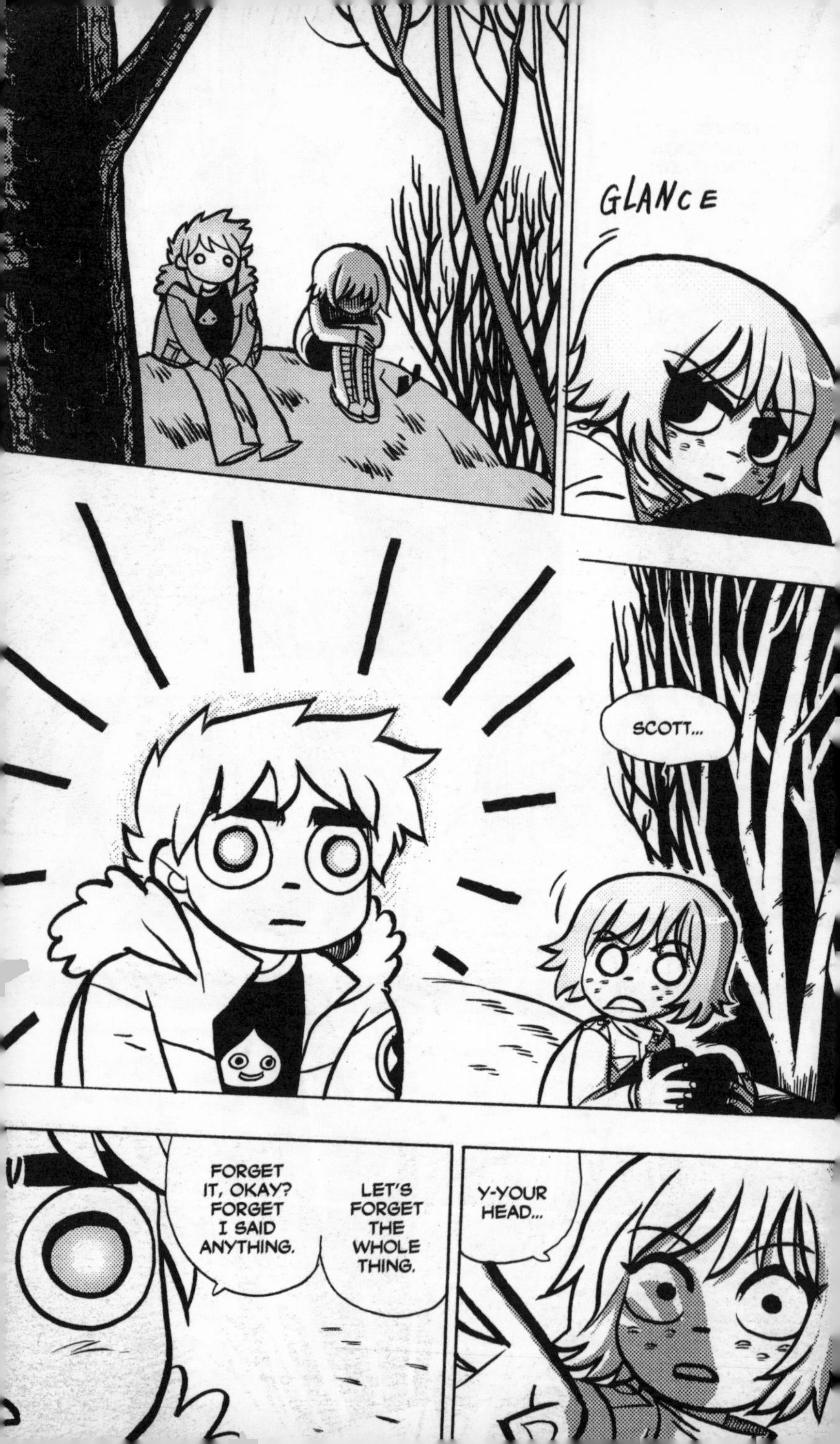
GLANCE
SCOTT...
FORGET IT, OKAY? FORGET I SAID ANYTHING.
LET'S FORGET THE WHOLE THING.
Y-YOUR HEAD...

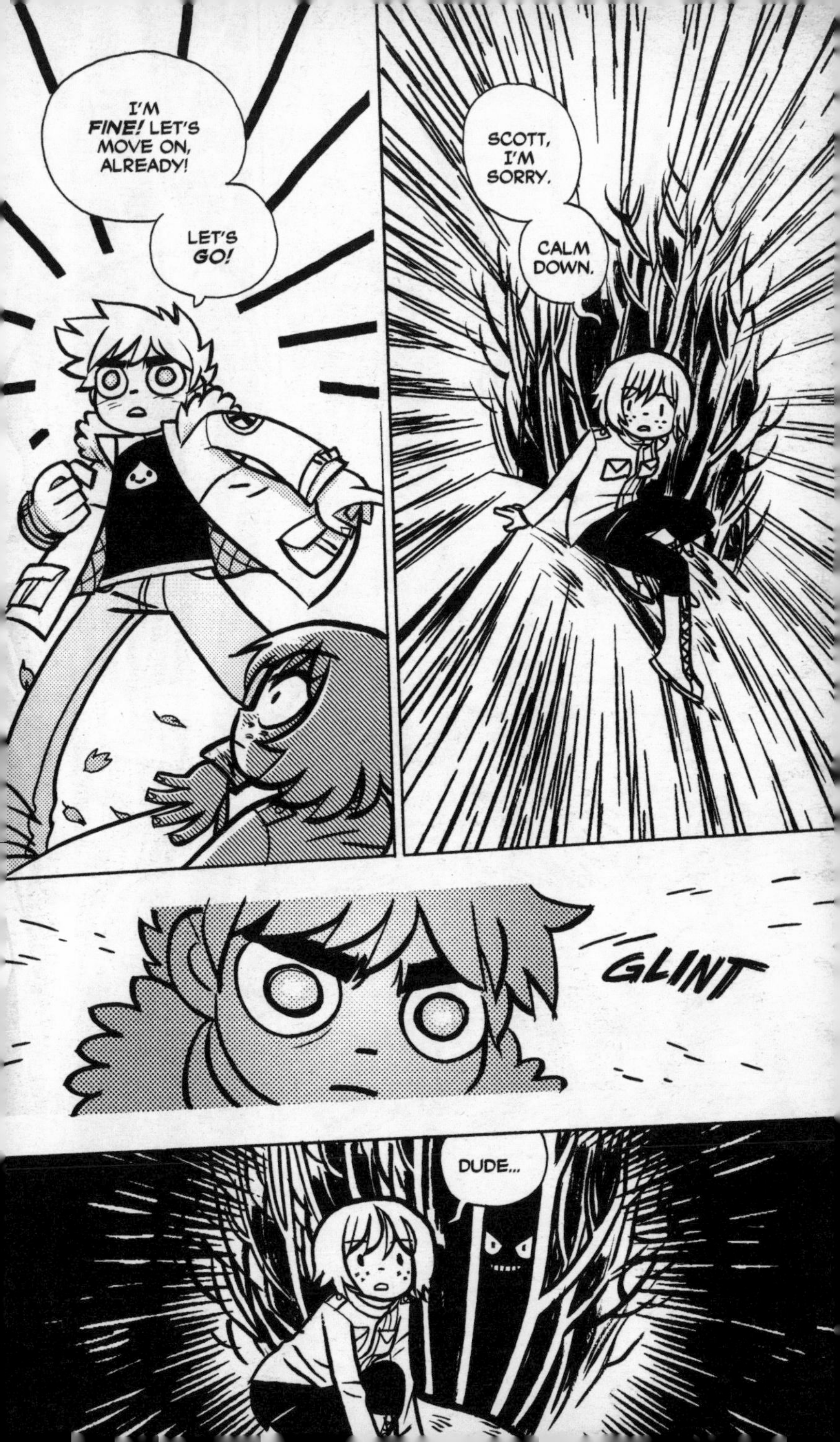
I'M FINE! LET'S MOVE ON, ALREADY!
LET'S GO!
SCOTT, I'M SORRY.
CALM DOWN.
GLINT
DUDE...

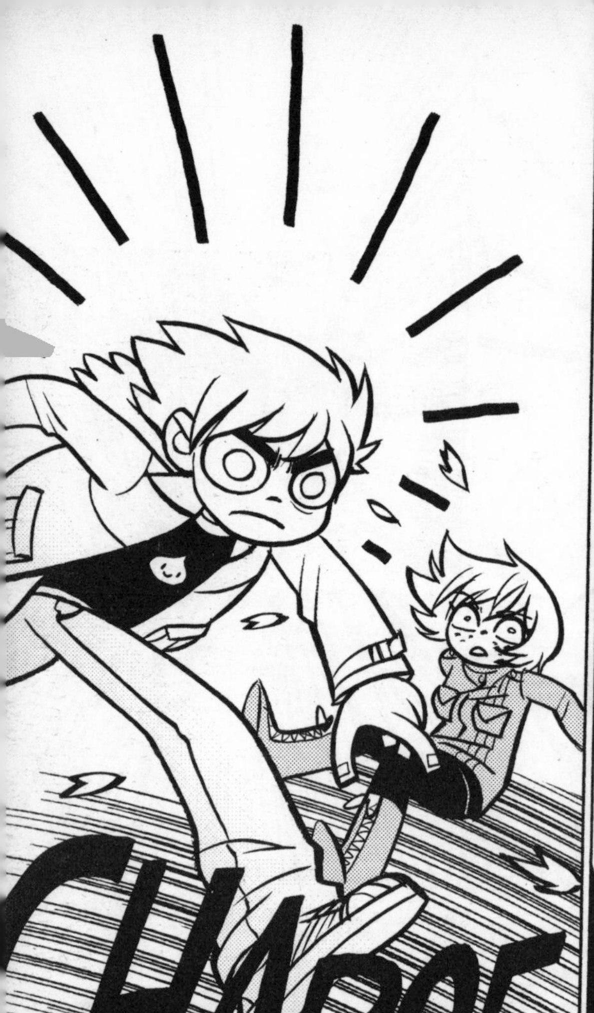
CHARGE
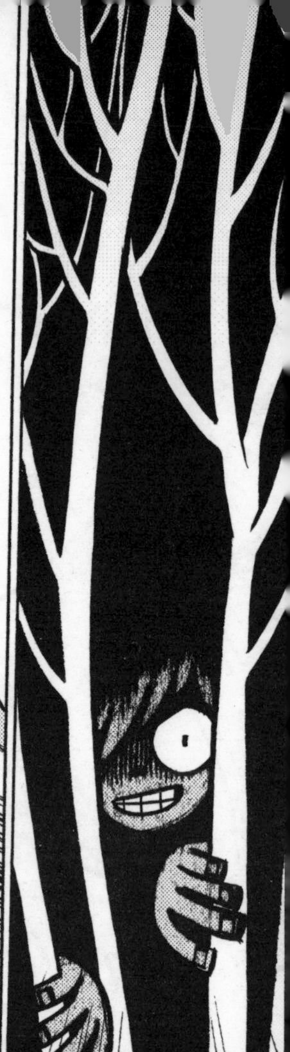

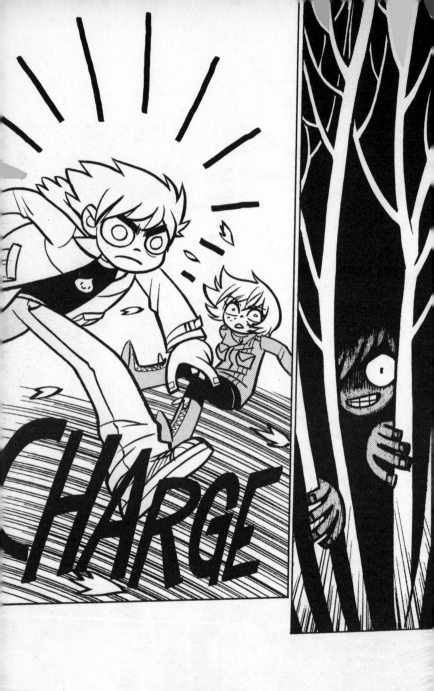

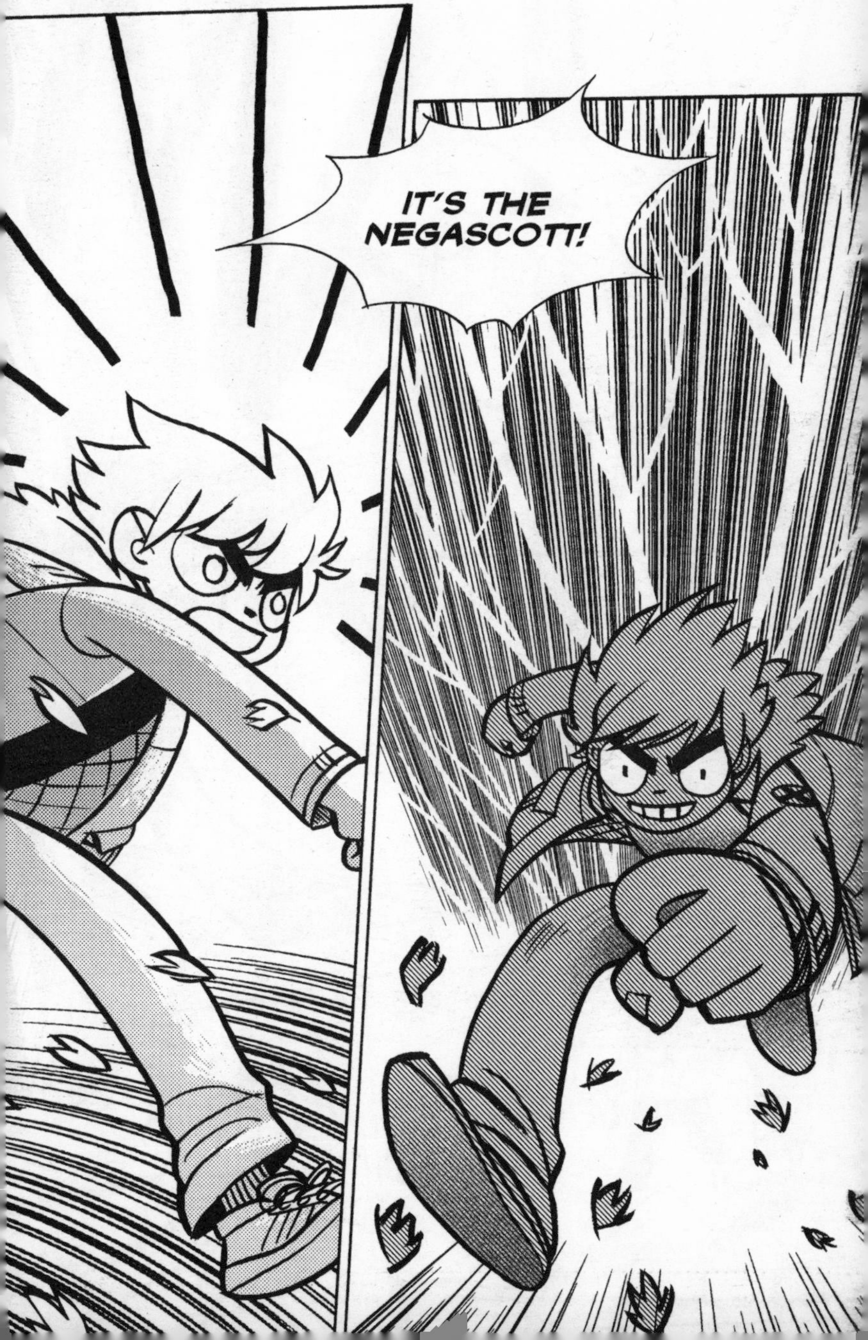
IT'S THE NEGASCOTT!

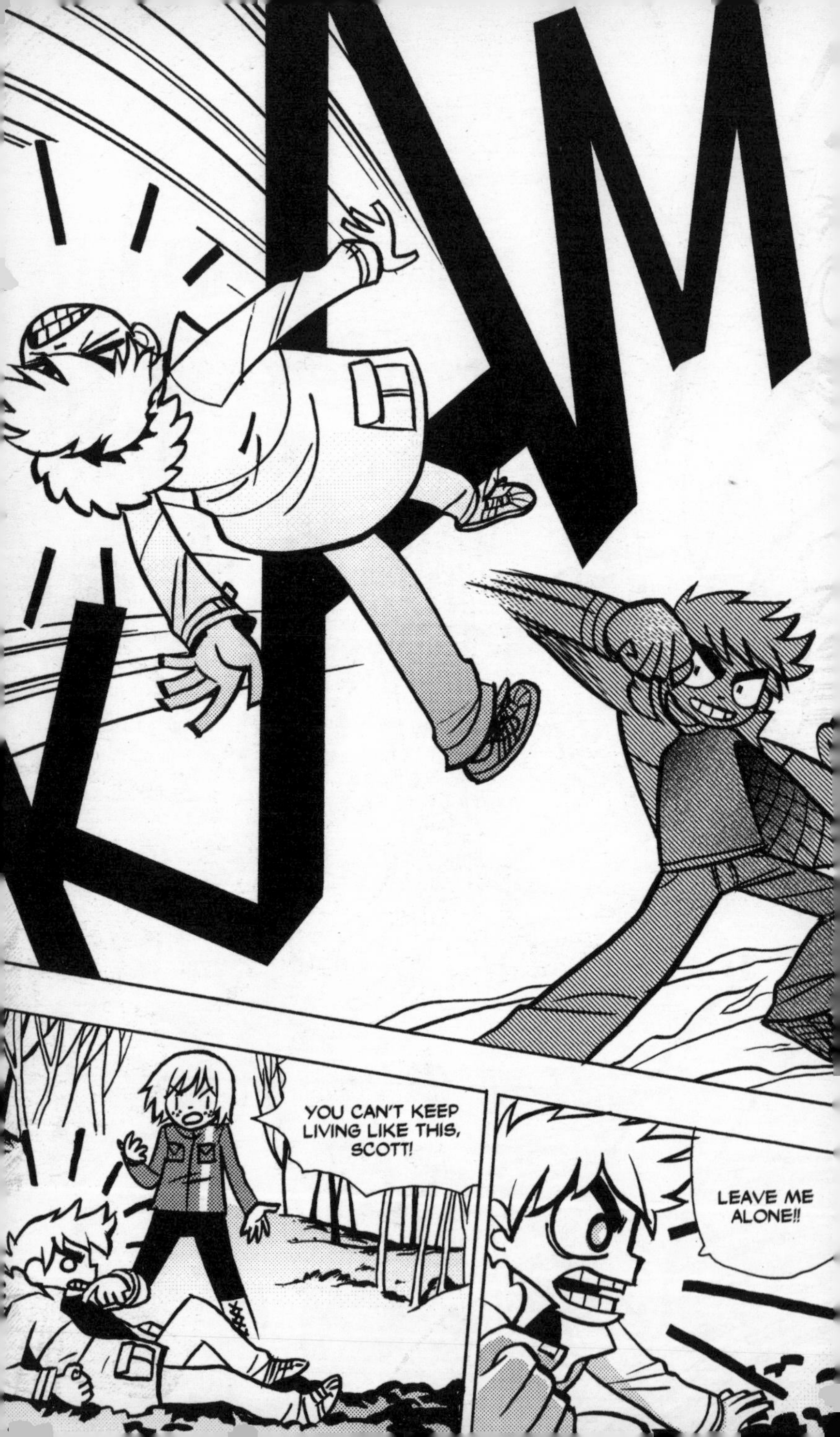
YOU CAN'T KEEP LIVING LIKE THIS, SCOTT!
LEAVE ME ALONE!!

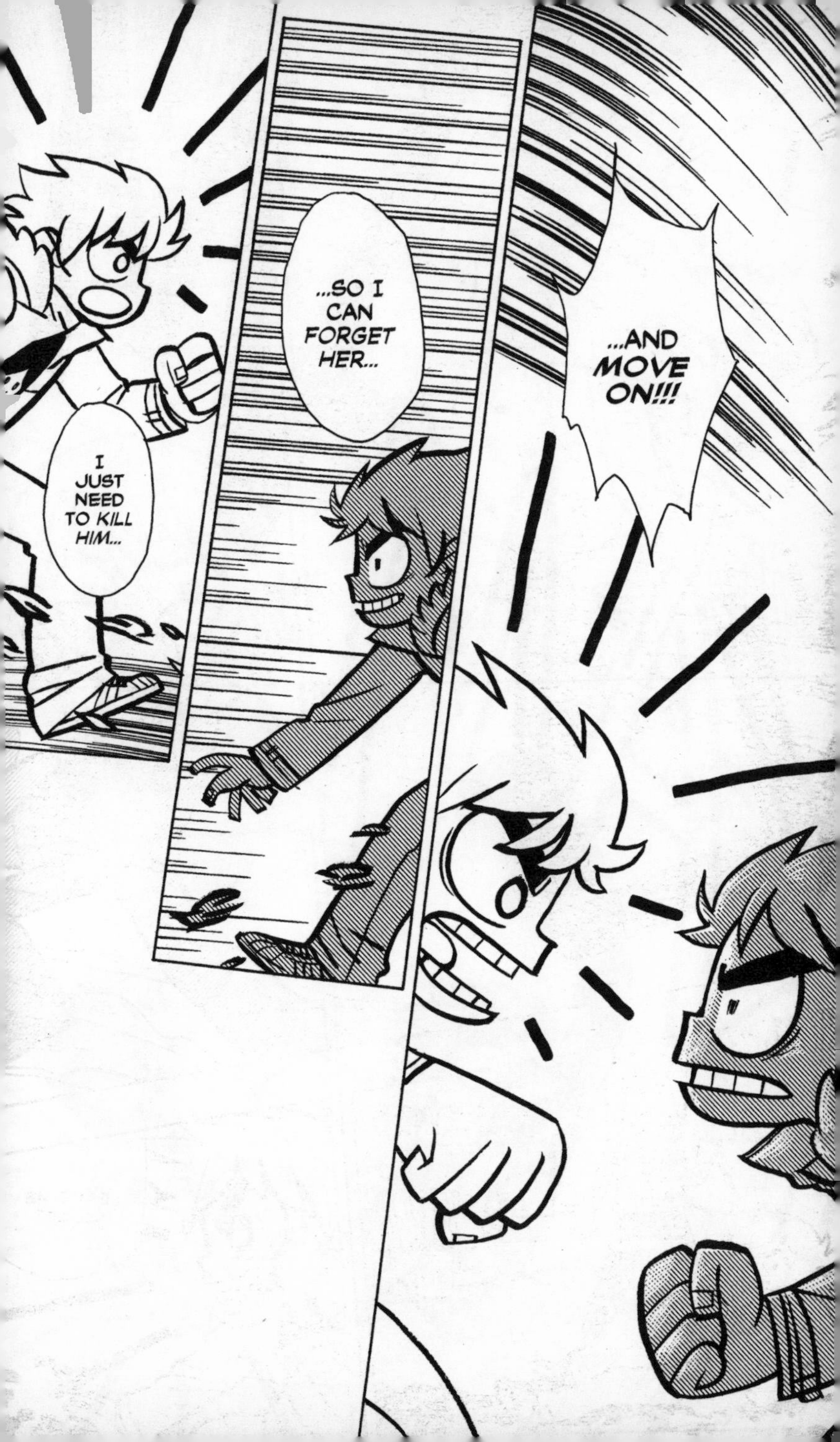
I JUST NEED TO KILL HIM...
...SO I CAN FORGET HER...
...AND MOVE ON!!!

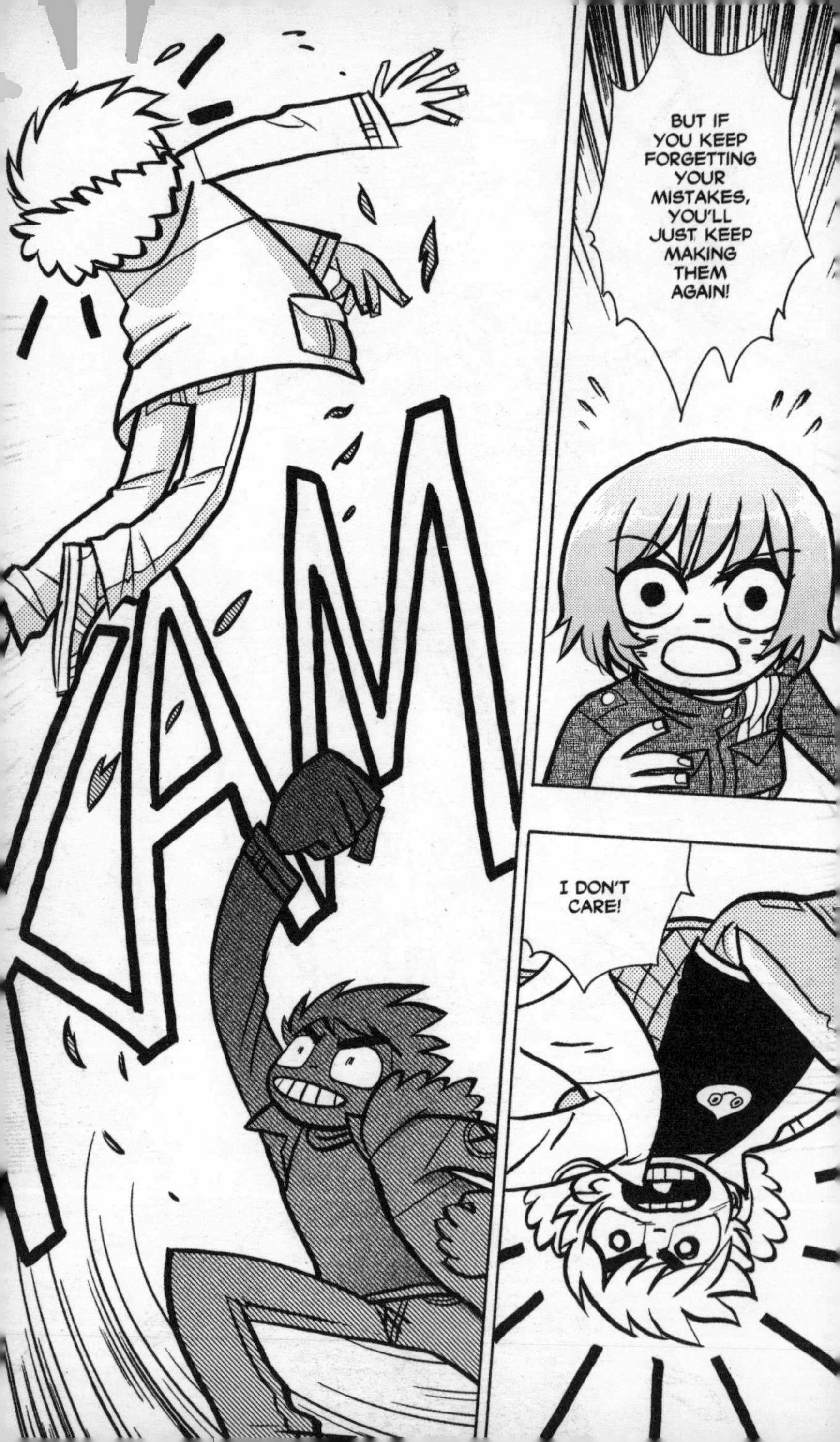
WHAM
BUT IF YOU KEEP FORGETTING YOUR MISTAKES, YOU'LL JUST KEEP MAKING THEM AGAIN!
I DON'T CARE!

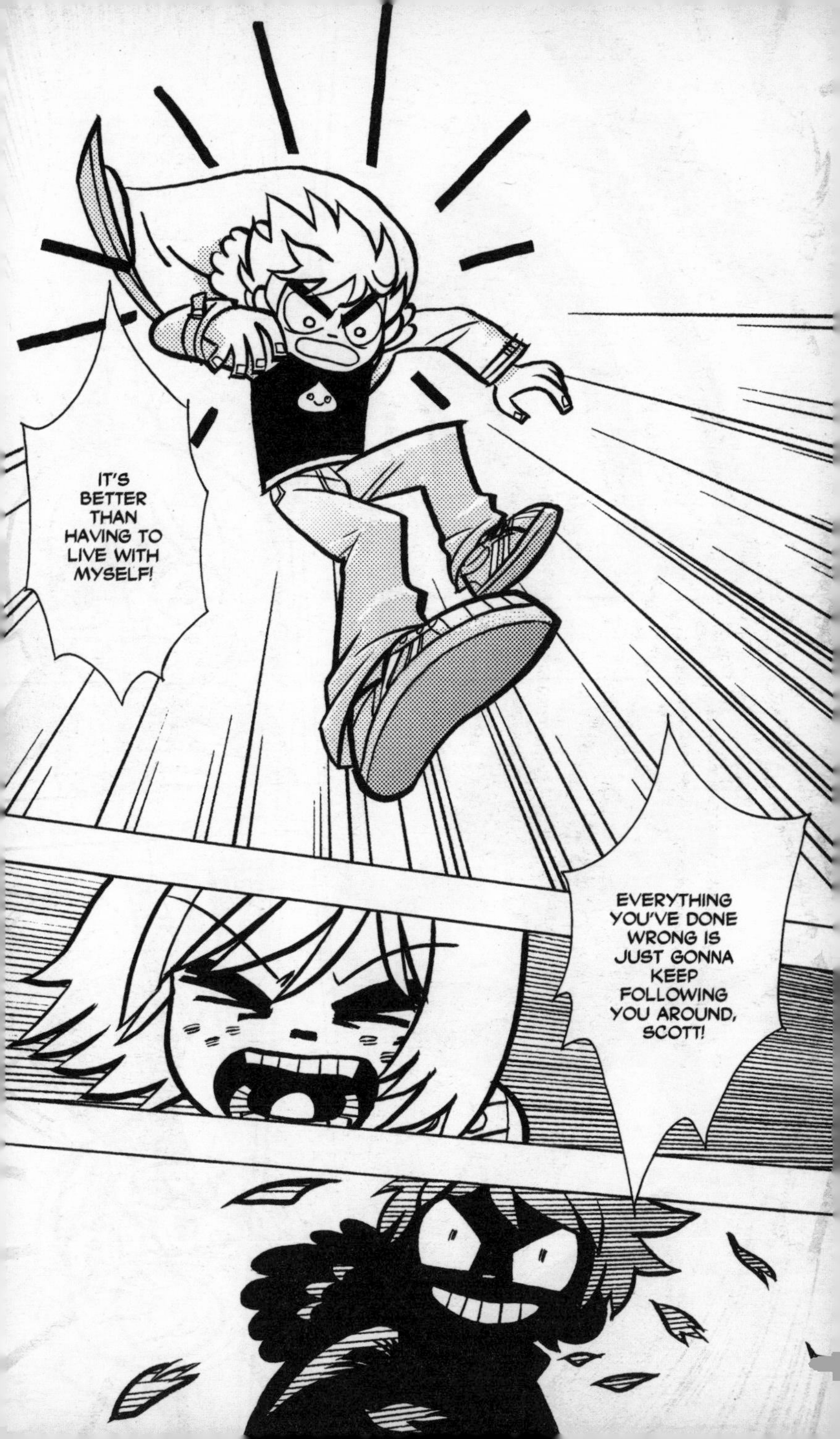
IT'S BETTER THAN HAVING TO LIVE WITH MYSELF!
EVERYTHING YOU'VE DONE WRONG IS JUST GONNA KEEP FOLLOWING YOU AROUND, SCOTT!

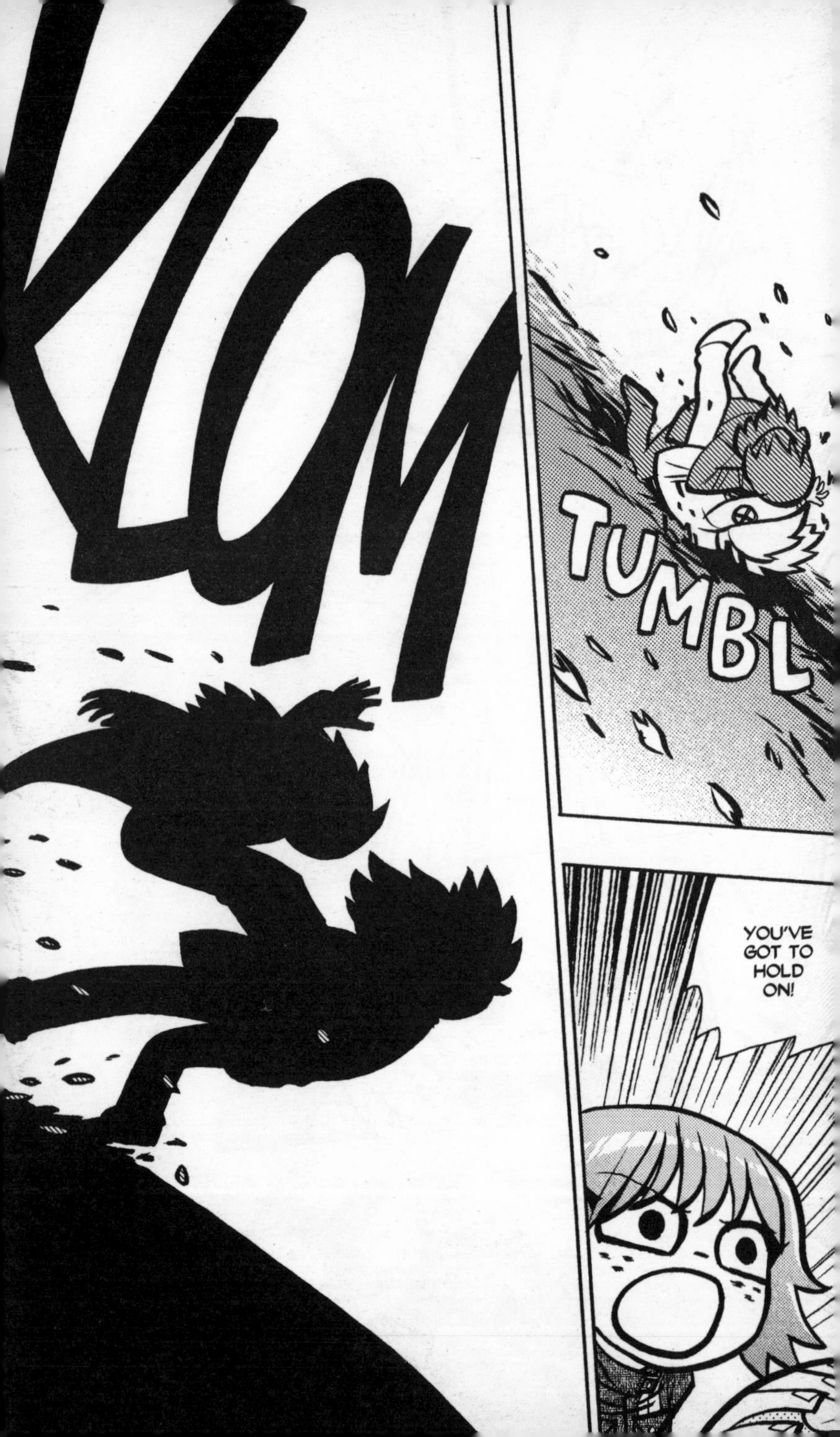
TUMBL
YOU'VE GOT TO HOLD ON!

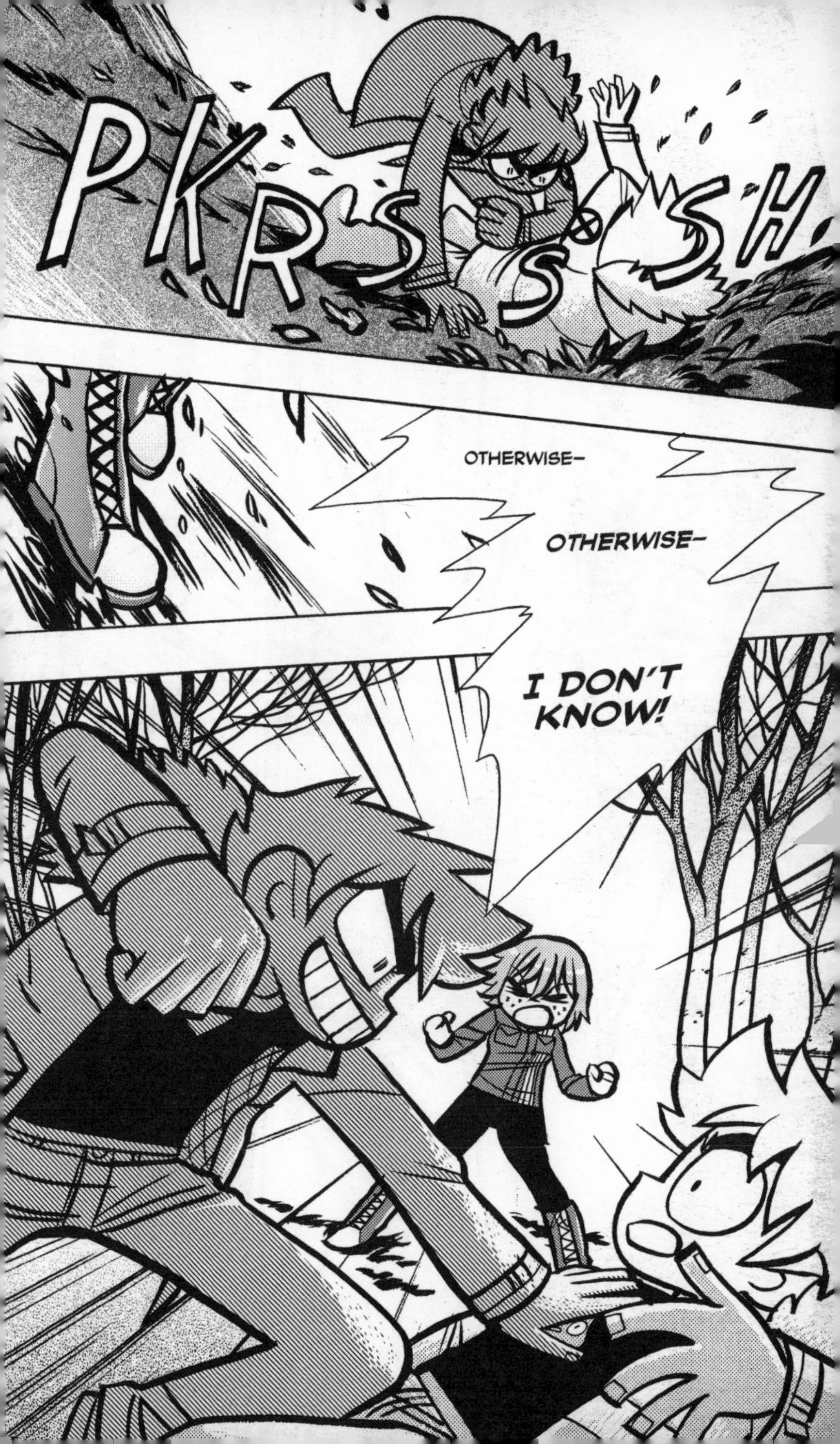
PKRSSSH.
OTHERWISE-
OTHERWISE-
I DON'T KNOW!

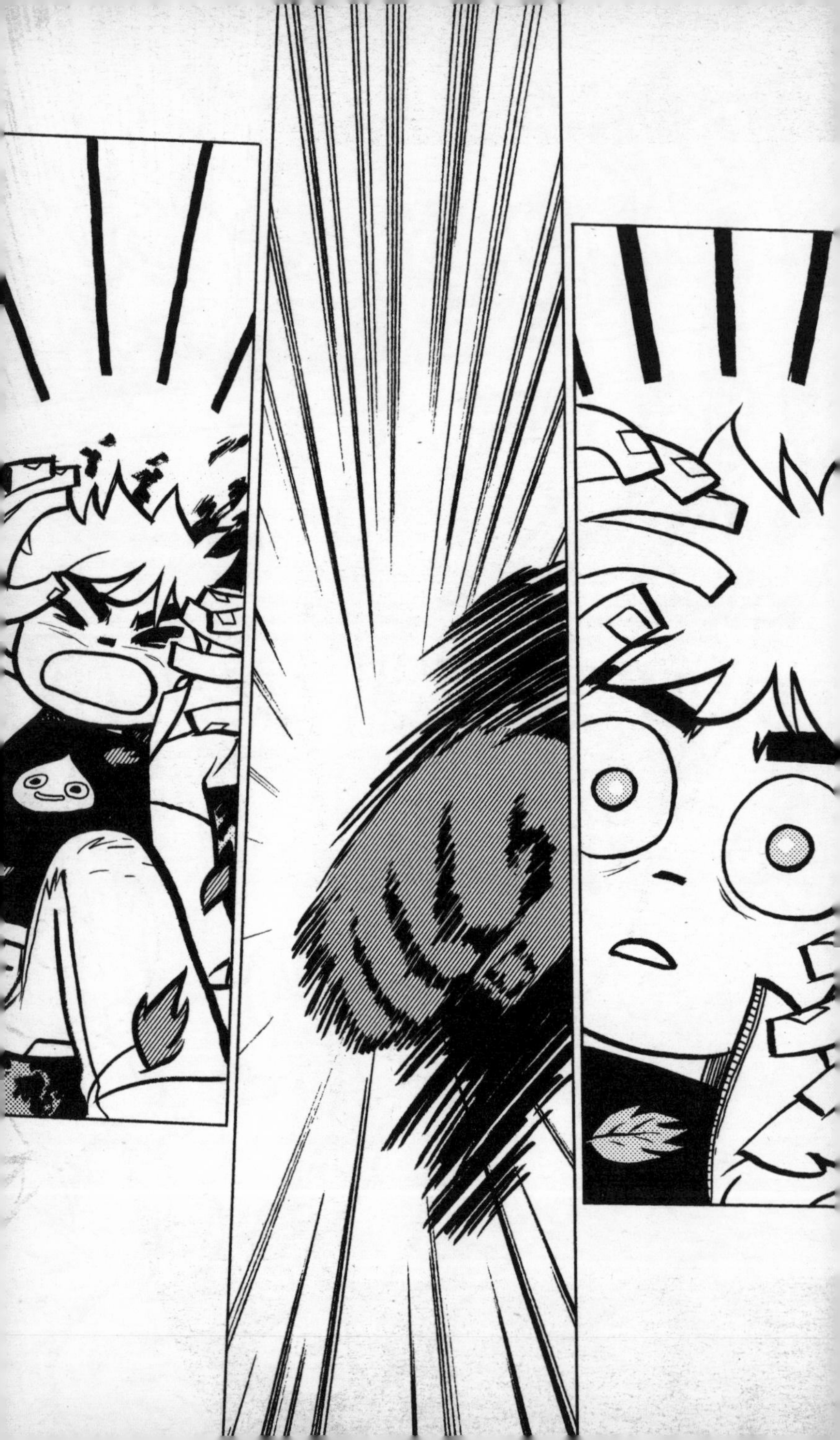

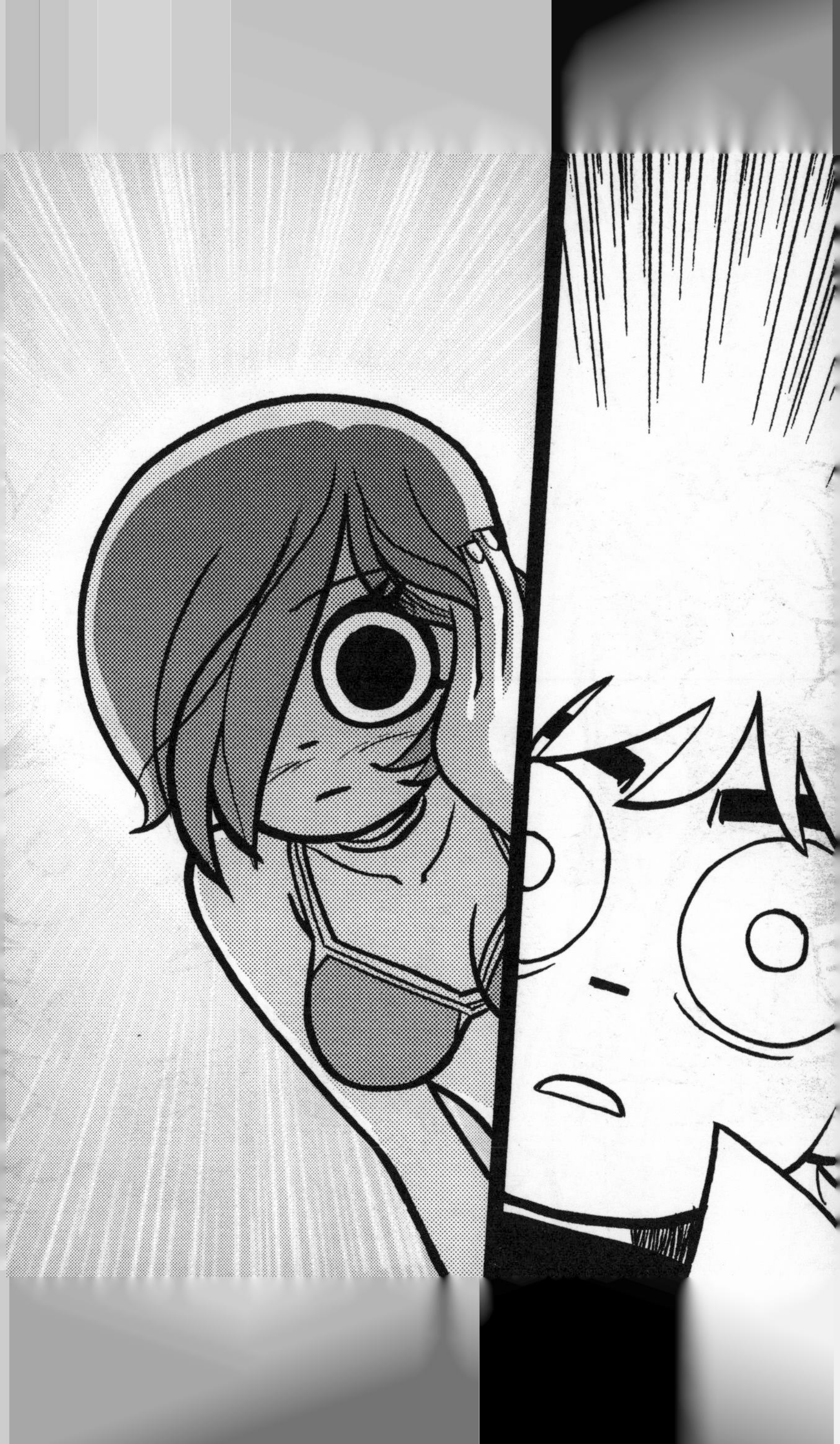

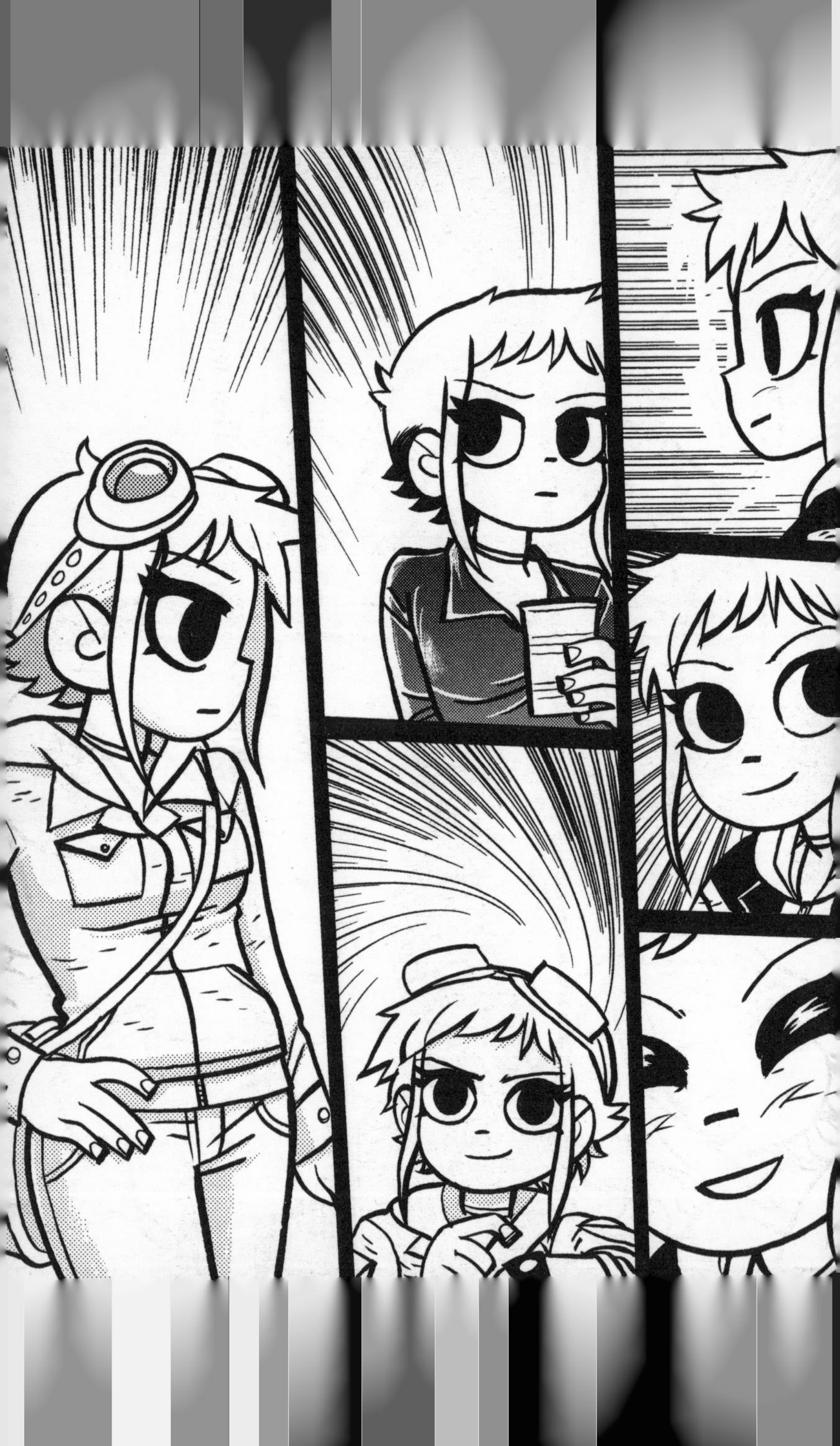

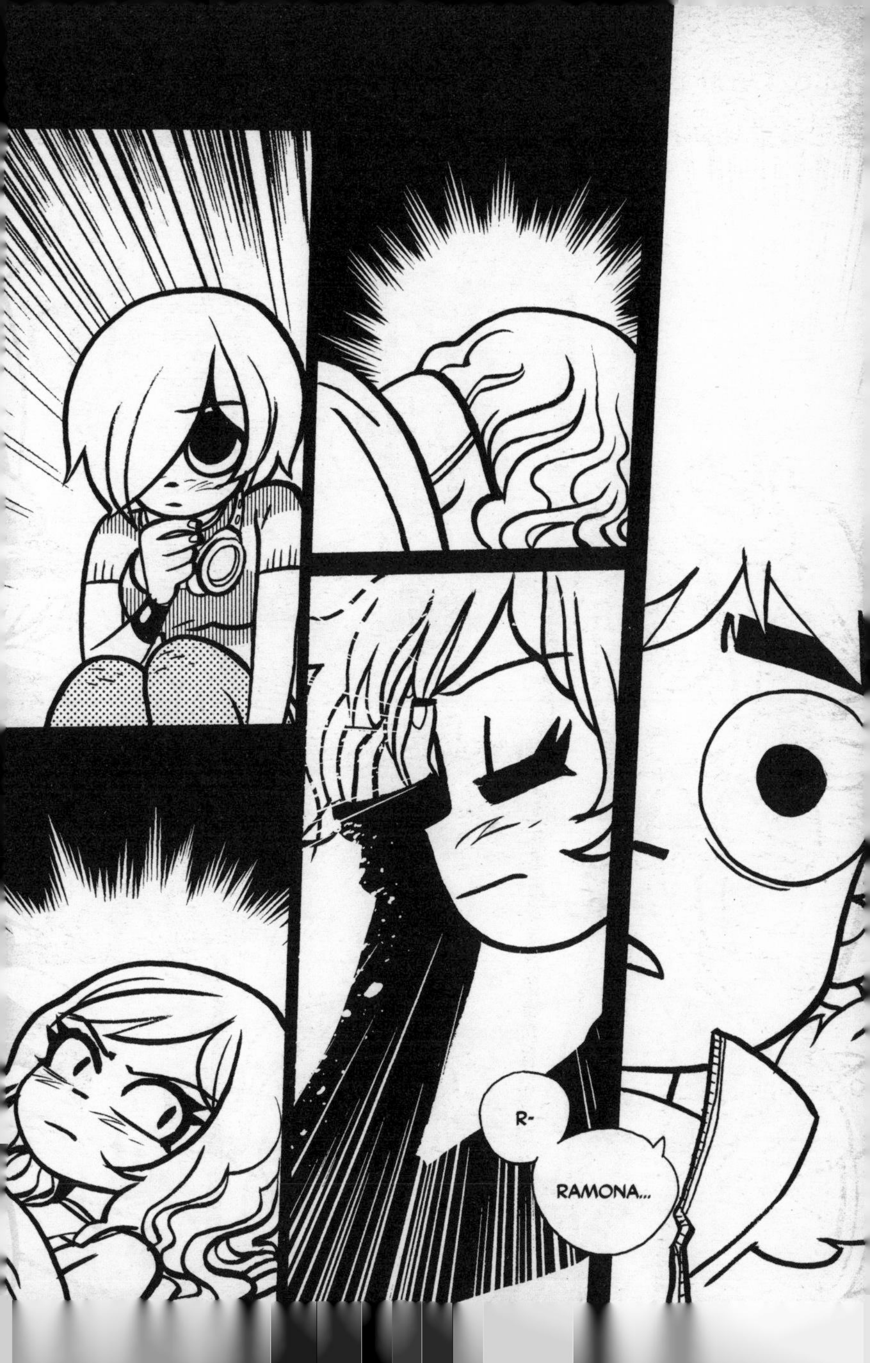
R-
RAMONA...

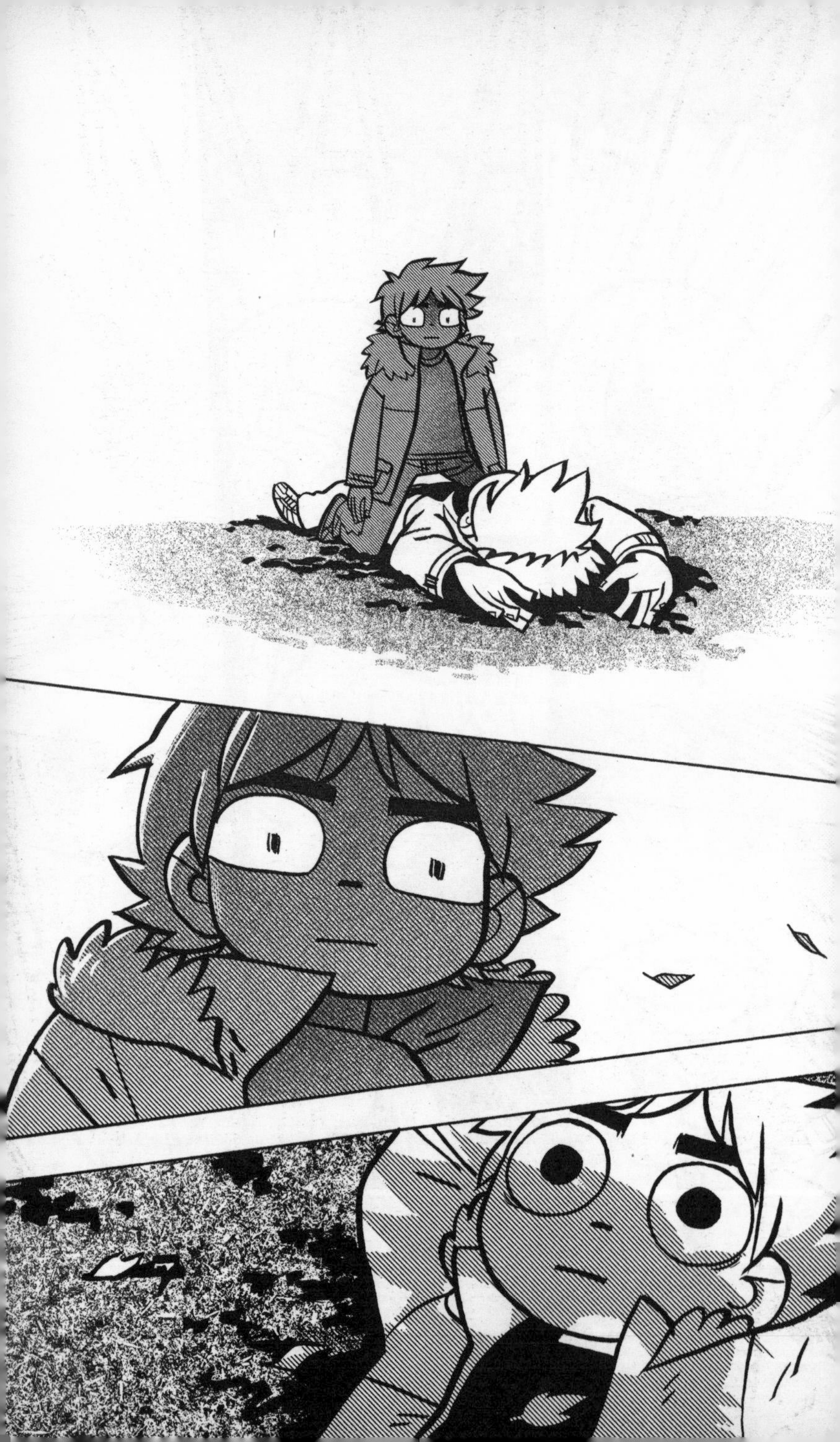

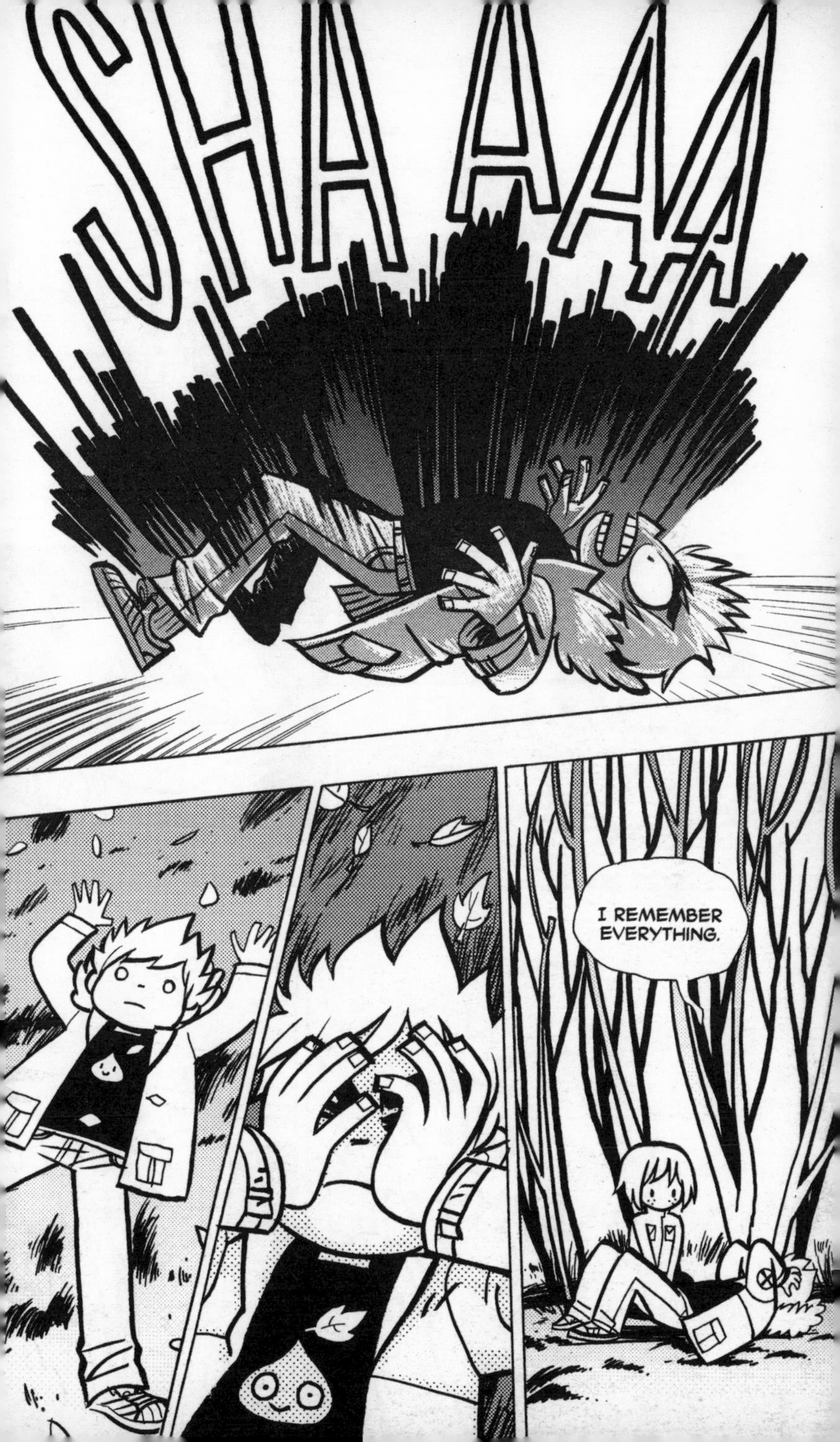
SHAAAA
I REMEMBER EVERYTHING.

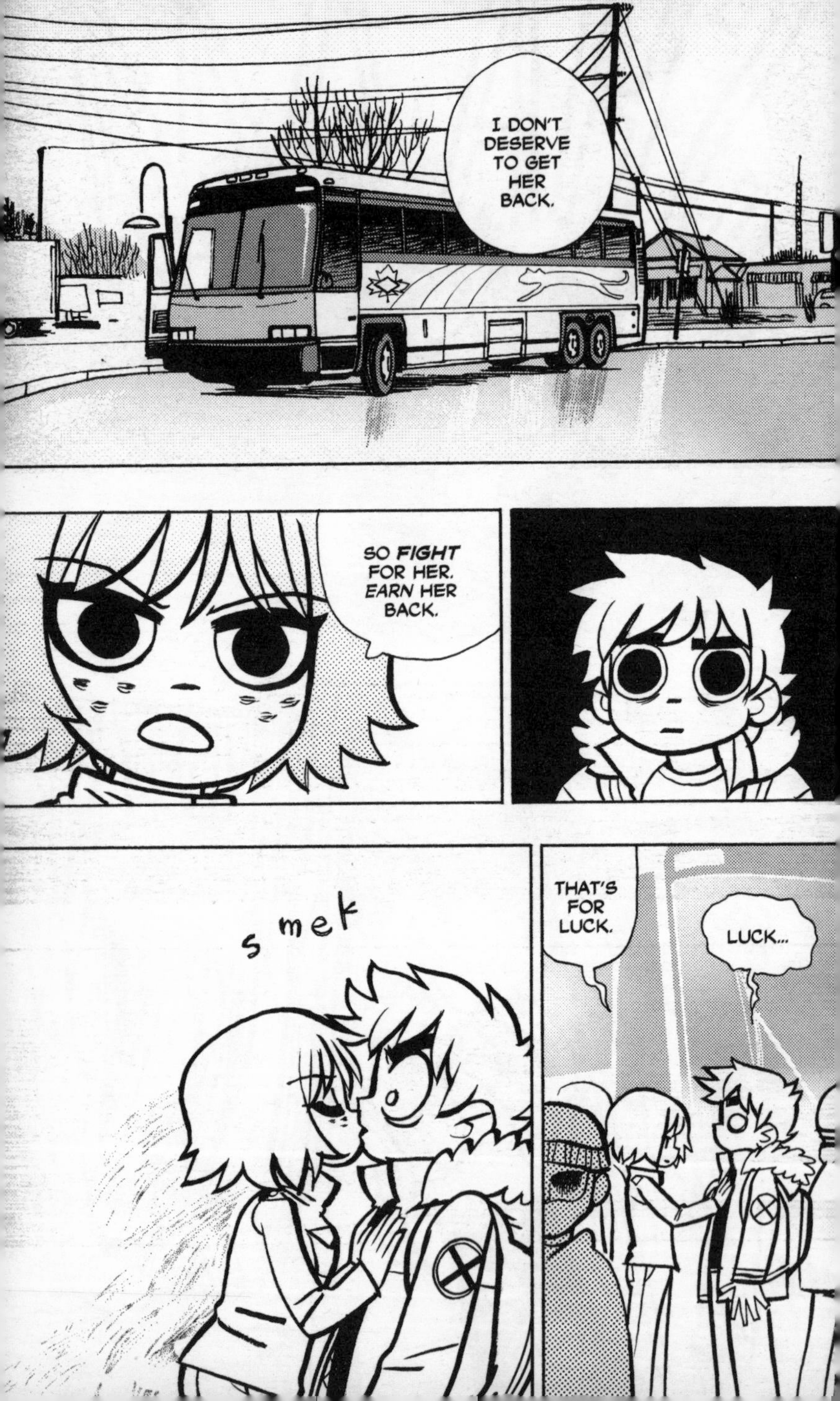
I DON'T DESERVE TO GET HER BACK.
SO *FIGHT* FOR HER. *EARN* HER BACK.
s mek
THAT'S FOR LUCK.
LUCK...

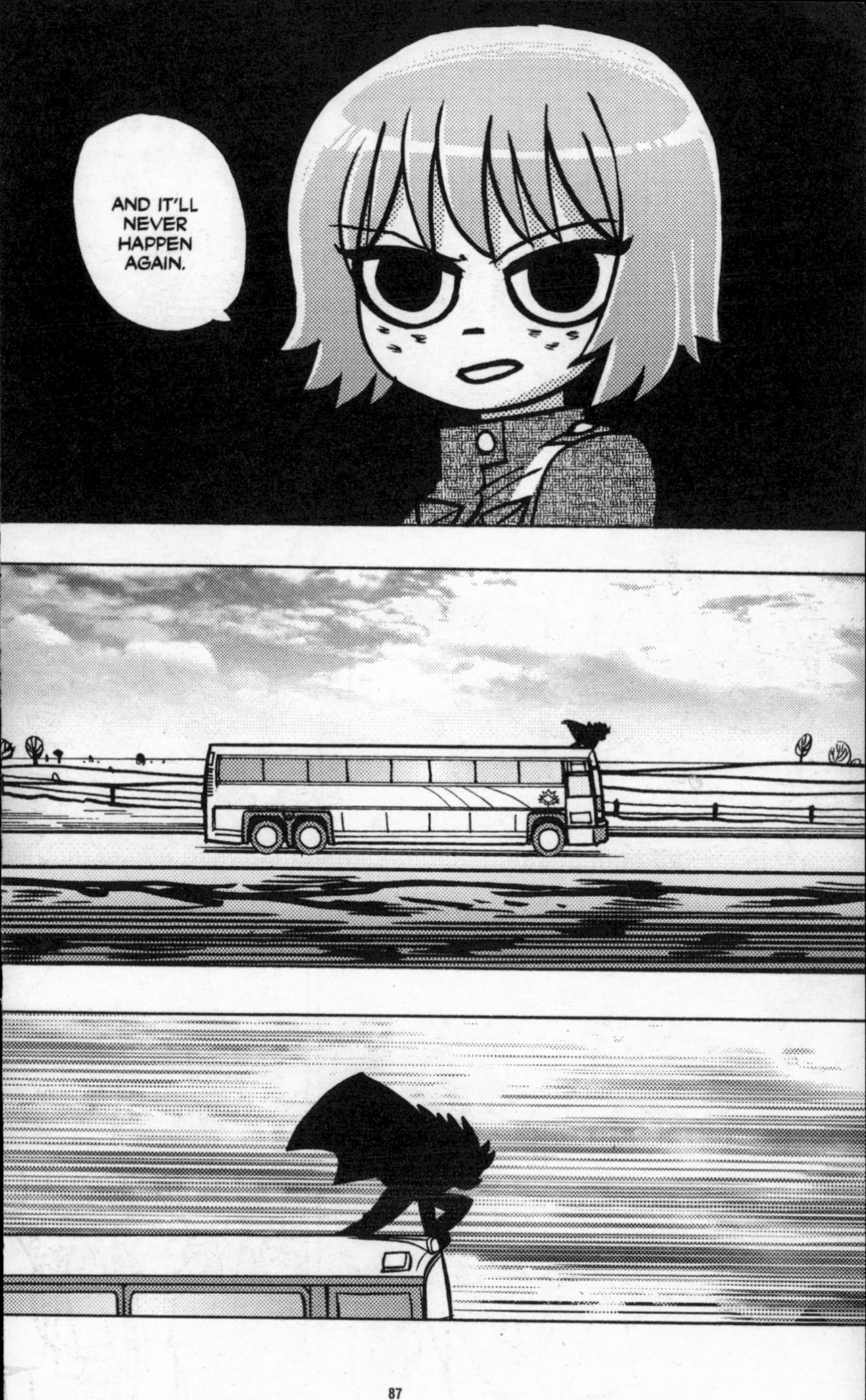
AND IT'LL NEVER HAPPEN AGAIN.

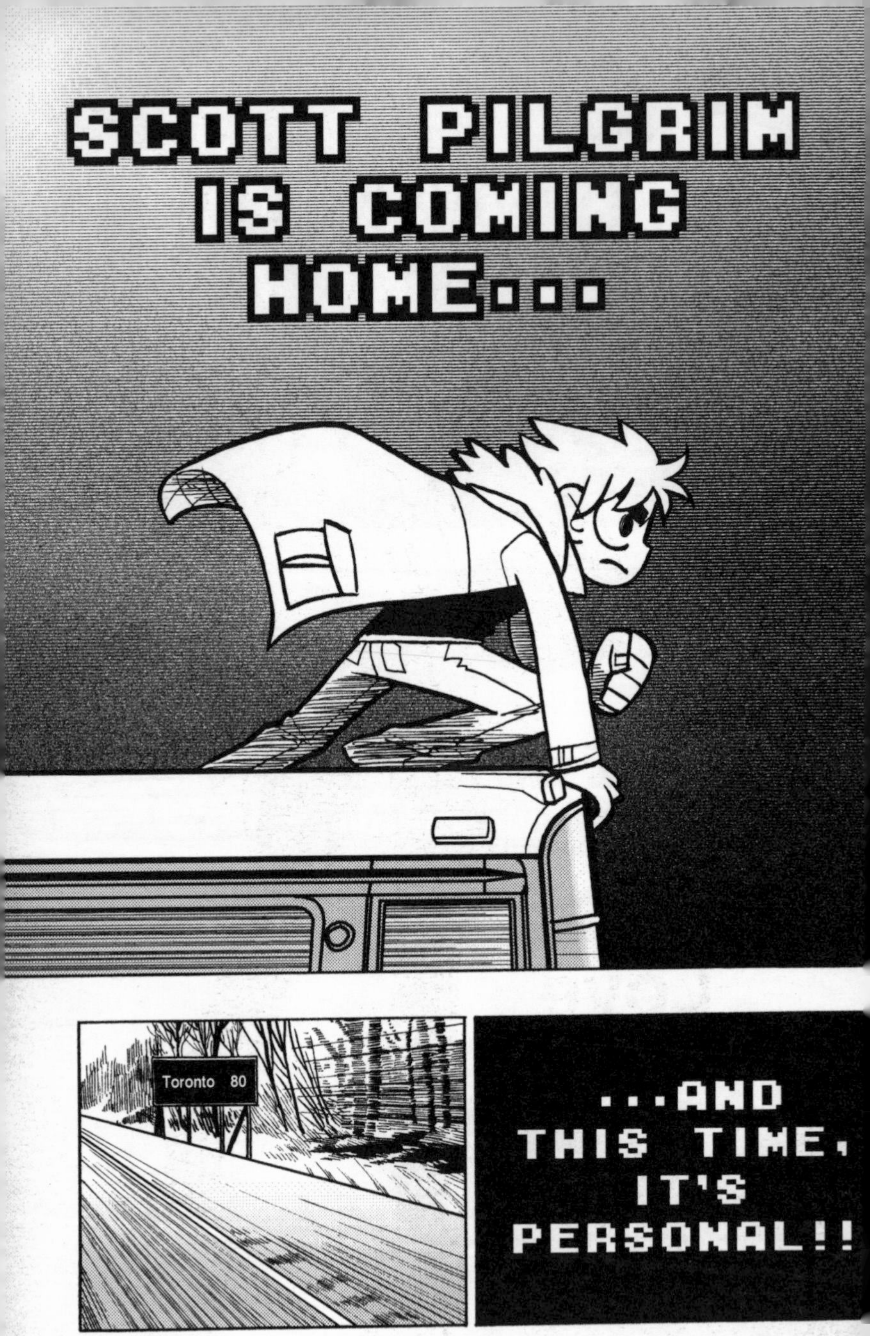
SCOTT PILGRIM IS COMING HOME...
Toronto 80
...AND THIS TIME, IT'S PERSONAL!!

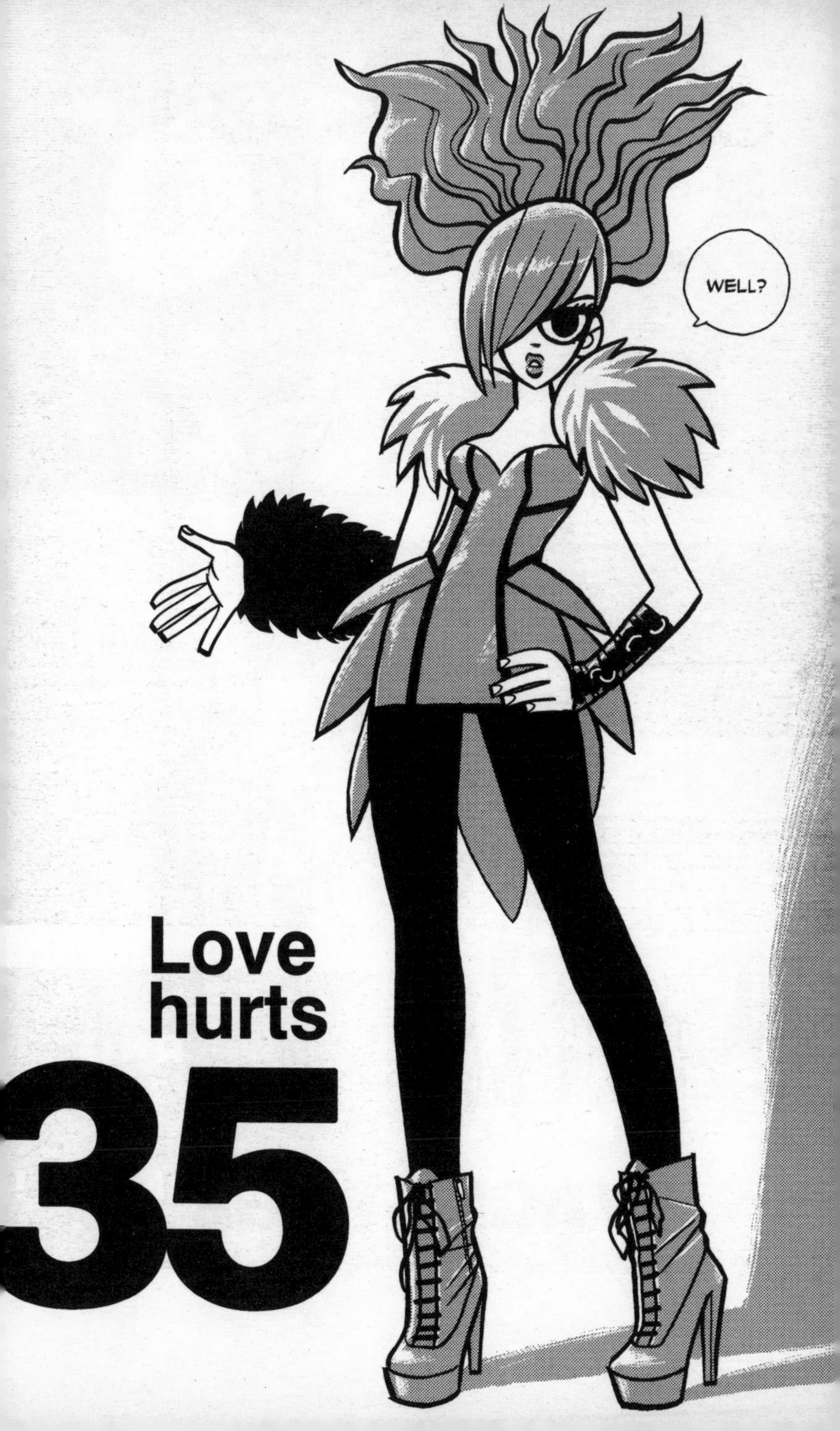
WELL?
Love hurts
35

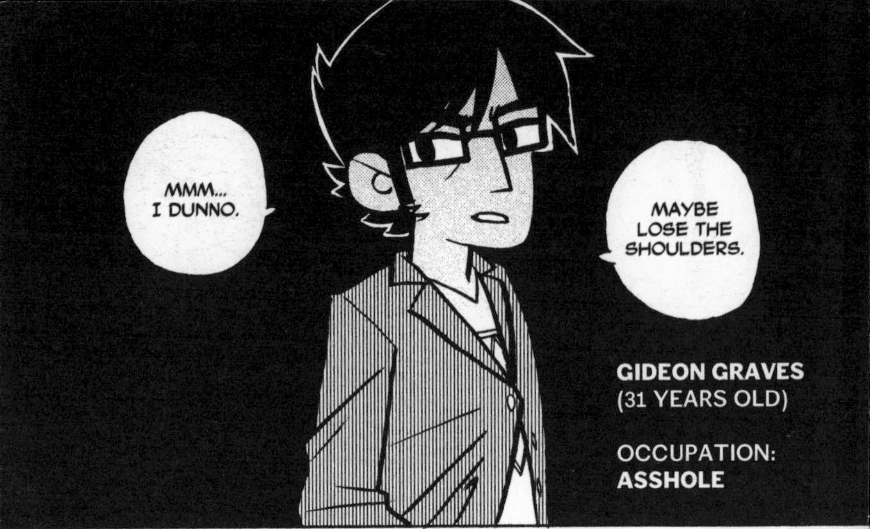
MMM... I DUNNO.
MAYBE LOSE THE SHOULDERS.
GIDEON GRAVES
(31 YEARS OLD)
OCCUPATION:
ASSHOLE

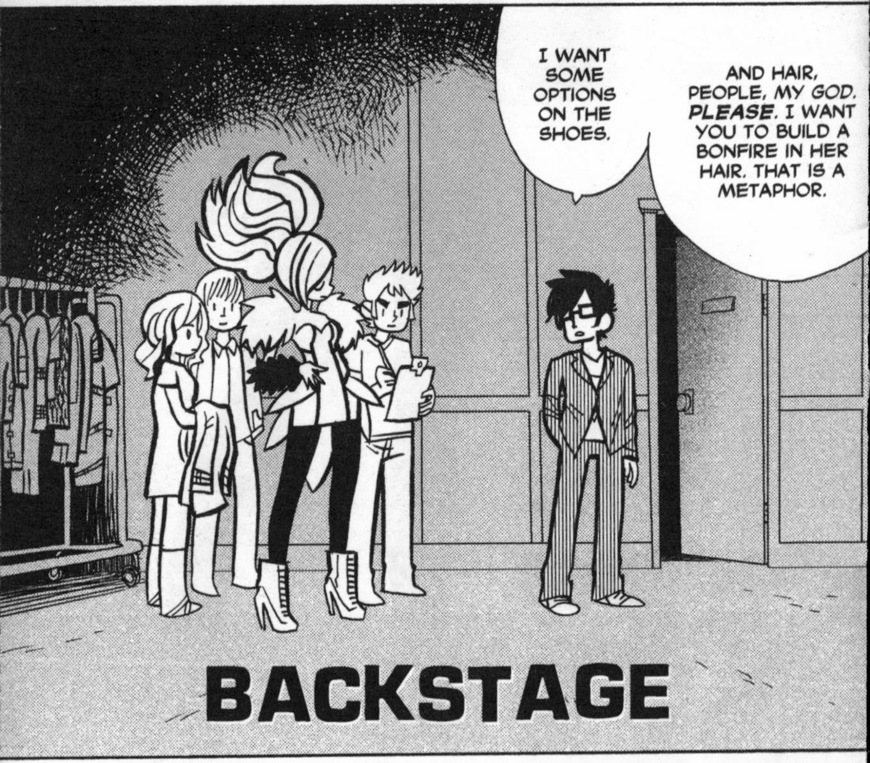
I WANT SOME OPTIONS ON THE SHOES.
AND HAIR, PEOPLE, MY GOD. PLEASE. I WANT YOU TO BUILD A BONFIRE IN HER HAIR. THAT IS A METAPHOR.
BACKSTAGE

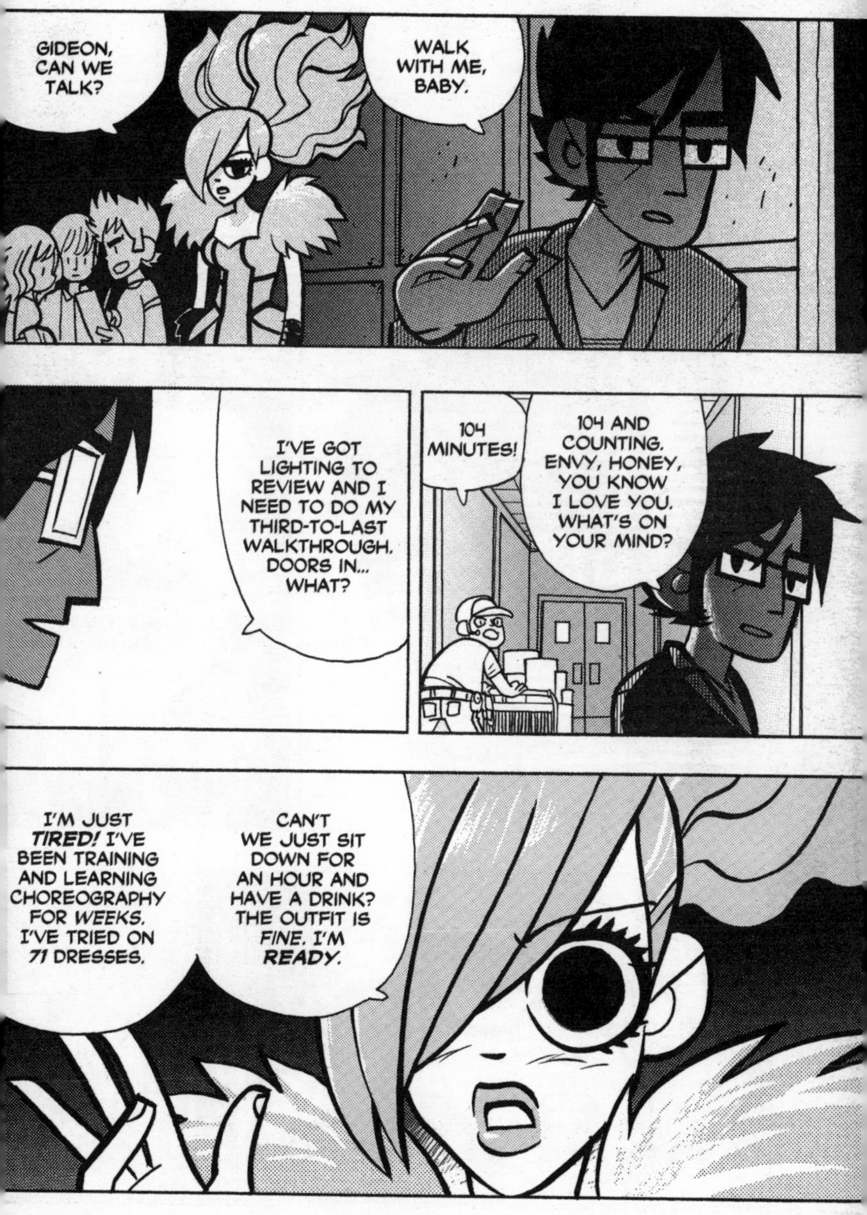
GIDEON, CAN WE TALK?
WALK WITH ME, BABY.
I'VE GOT LIGHTING TO REVIEW AND I NEED TO DO MY THIRD-TO-LAST WALKTHROUGH. DOORS IN... WHAT?
104 MINUTES!
104 AND COUNTING. ENVY, HONEY, YOU KNOW I LOVE YOU. WHAT'S ON YOUR MIND?
I'M JUST *TIRED!* I'VE BEEN TRAINING AND LEARNING CHOREOGRAPHY FOR *WEEKS.* I'VE TRIED ON *71* DRESSES.
CAN'T WE JUST SIT DOWN FOR AN HOUR AND HAVE A DRINK? THE OUTFIT IS *FINE.* I'M ***READY.***

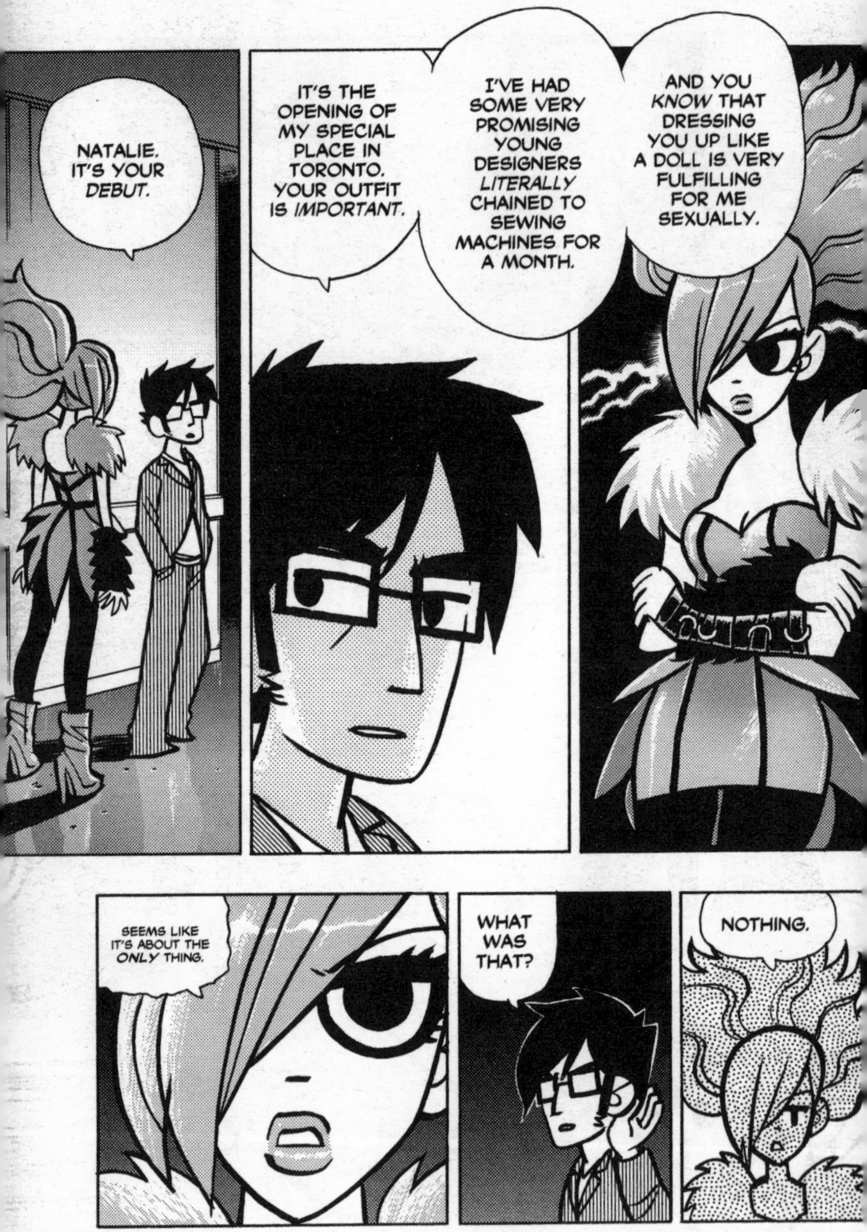
NATALIE. IT'S YOUR *DEBUT.*
IT'S THE OPENING OF MY SPECIAL PLACE IN TORONTO. YOUR OUTFIT IS *IMPORTANT.*
I'VE HAD SOME VERY PROMISING YOUNG DESIGNERS *LITERALLY* CHAINED TO SEWING MACHINES FOR A MONTH.
AND YOU *KNOW* THAT DRESSING YOU UP LIKE A DOLL IS VERY FULFILLING FOR ME SEXUALLY.
SEEMS LIKE IT'S ABOUT THE *ONLY* THING.
WHAT WAS THAT?
NOTHING.

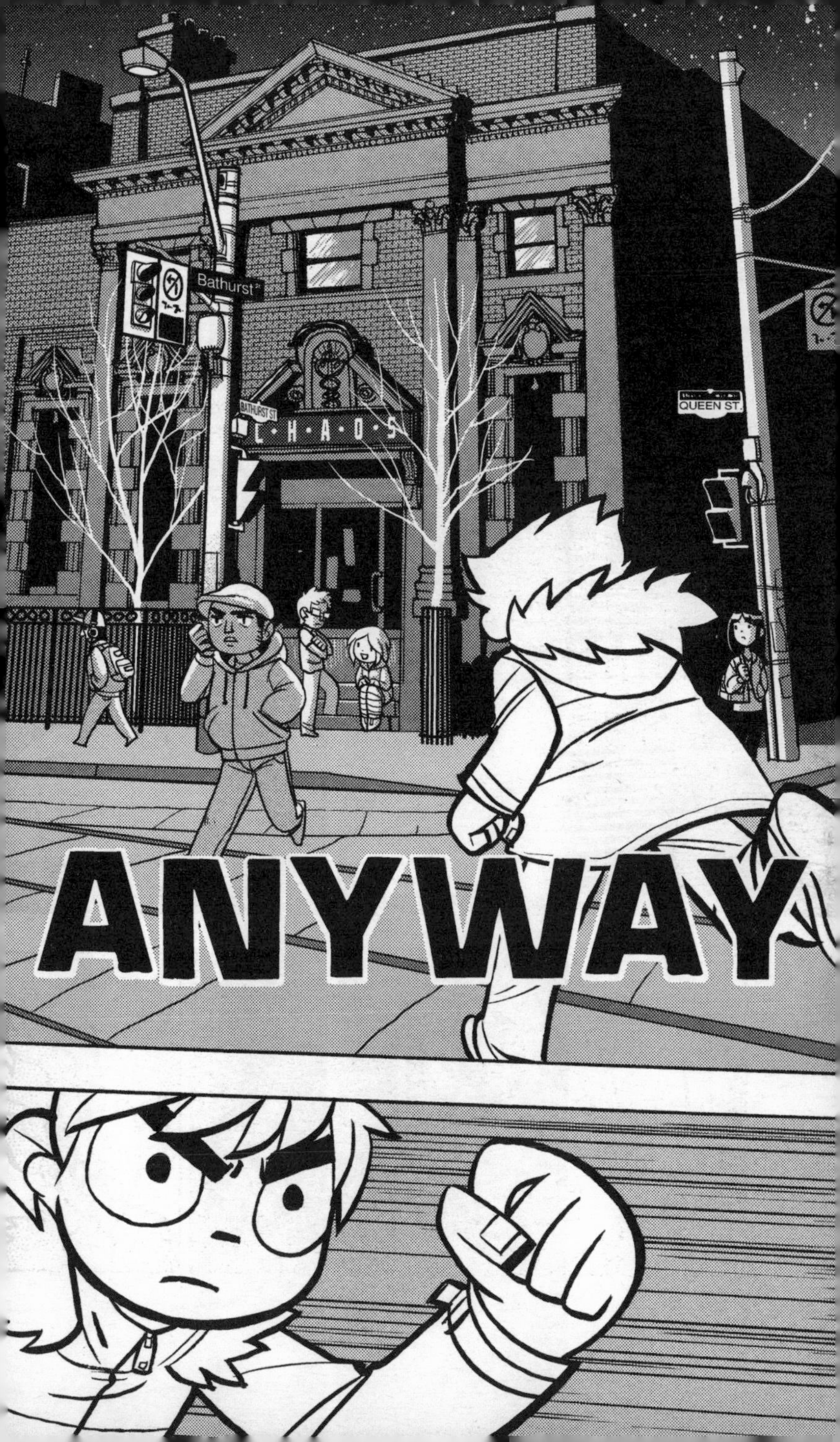

Bathurst St
BATHURST ST
C·H·A·O·S
QUEEN ST.
ANYWAY

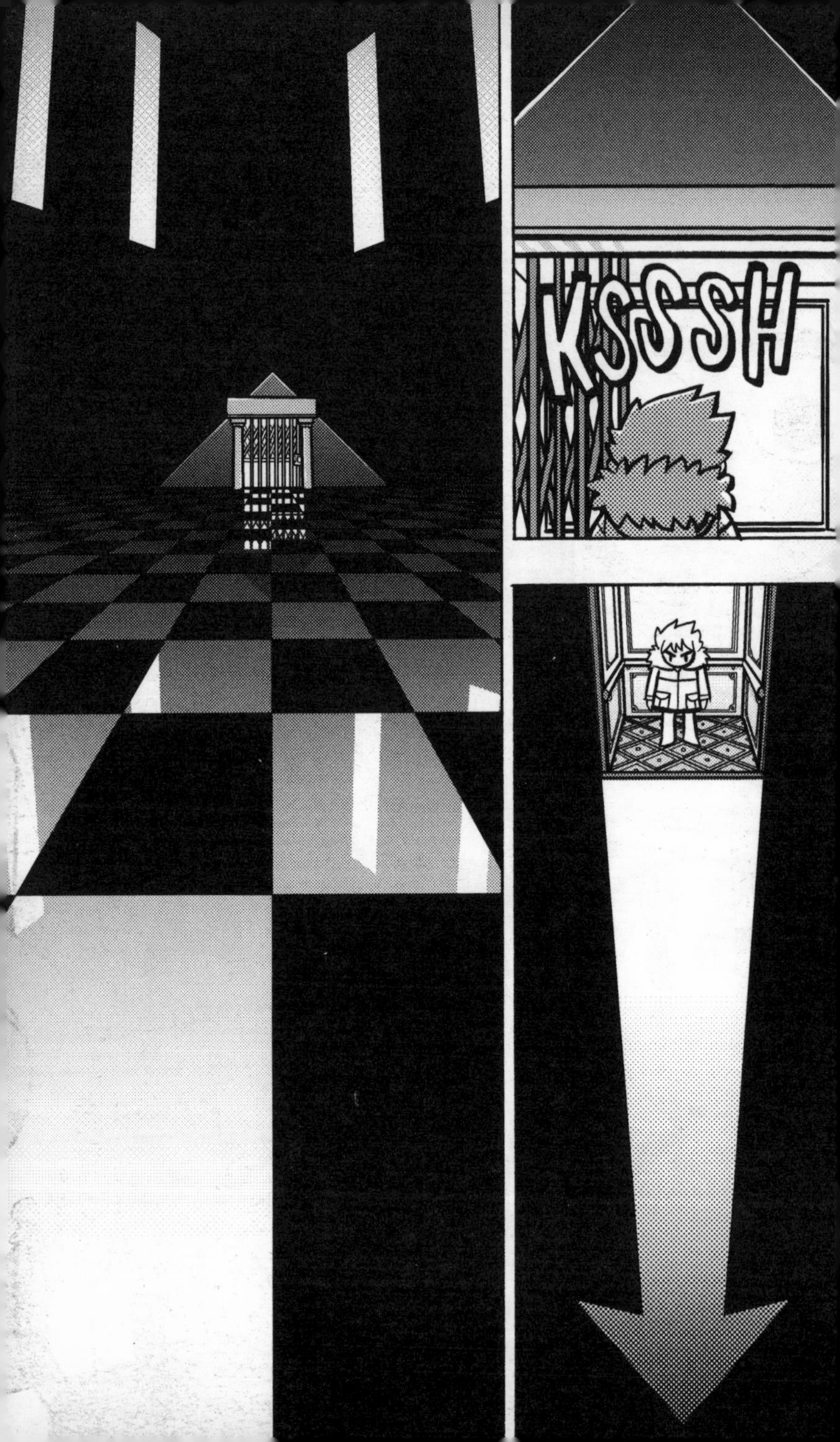
KSSSH

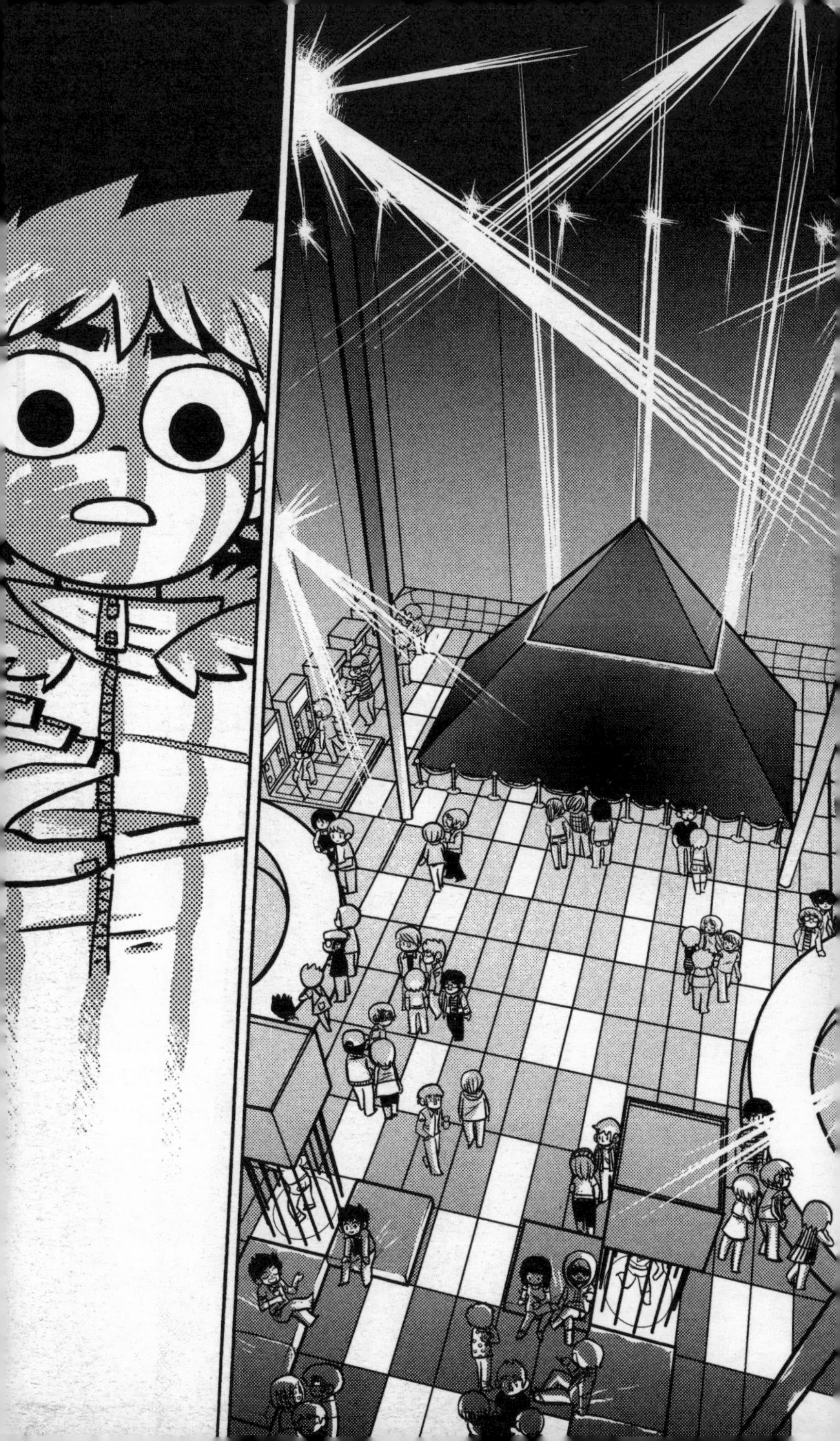

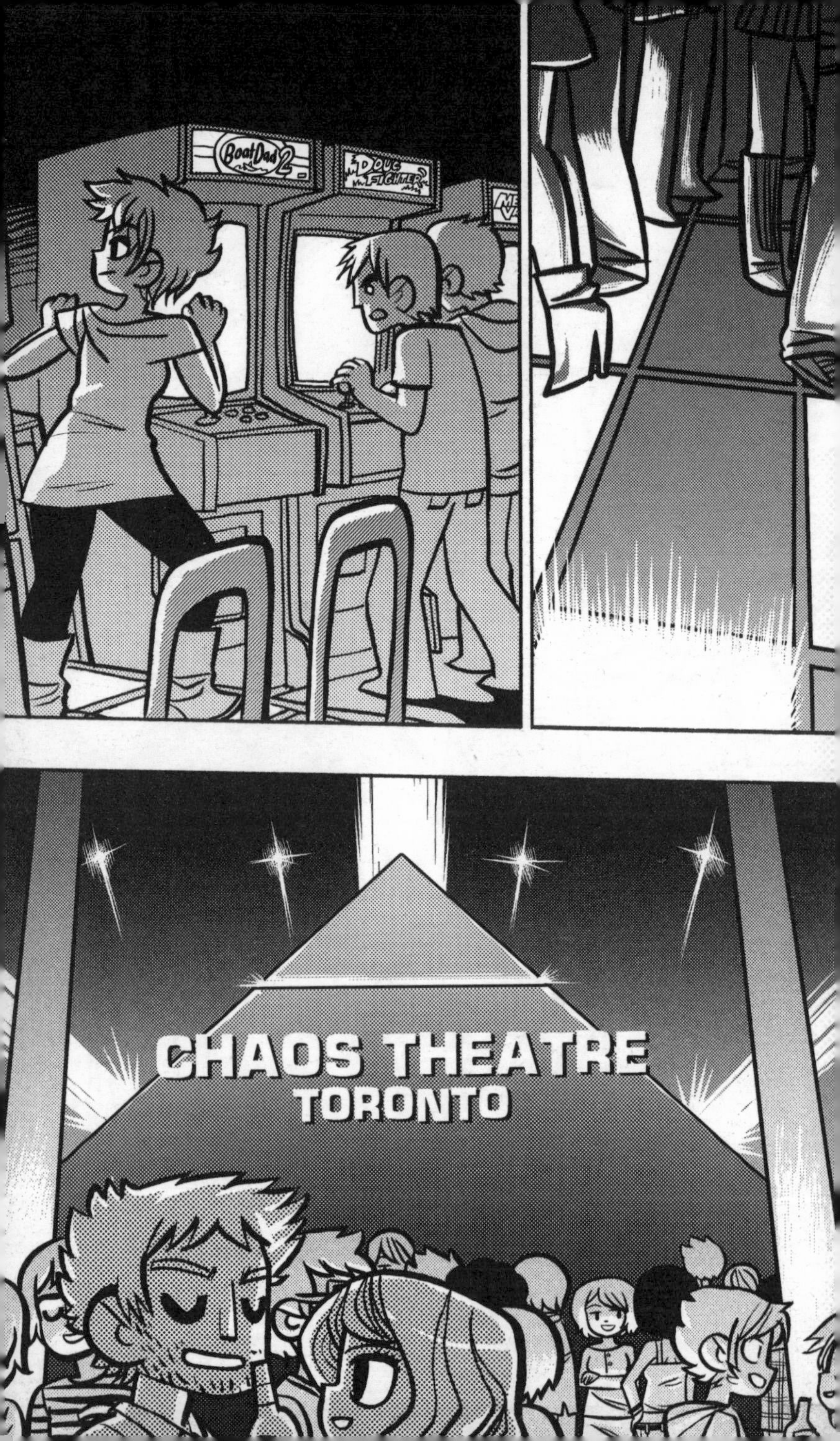

BoatDad 2
DOUG FIGHTER
CHAOS THEATRE
TORONTO

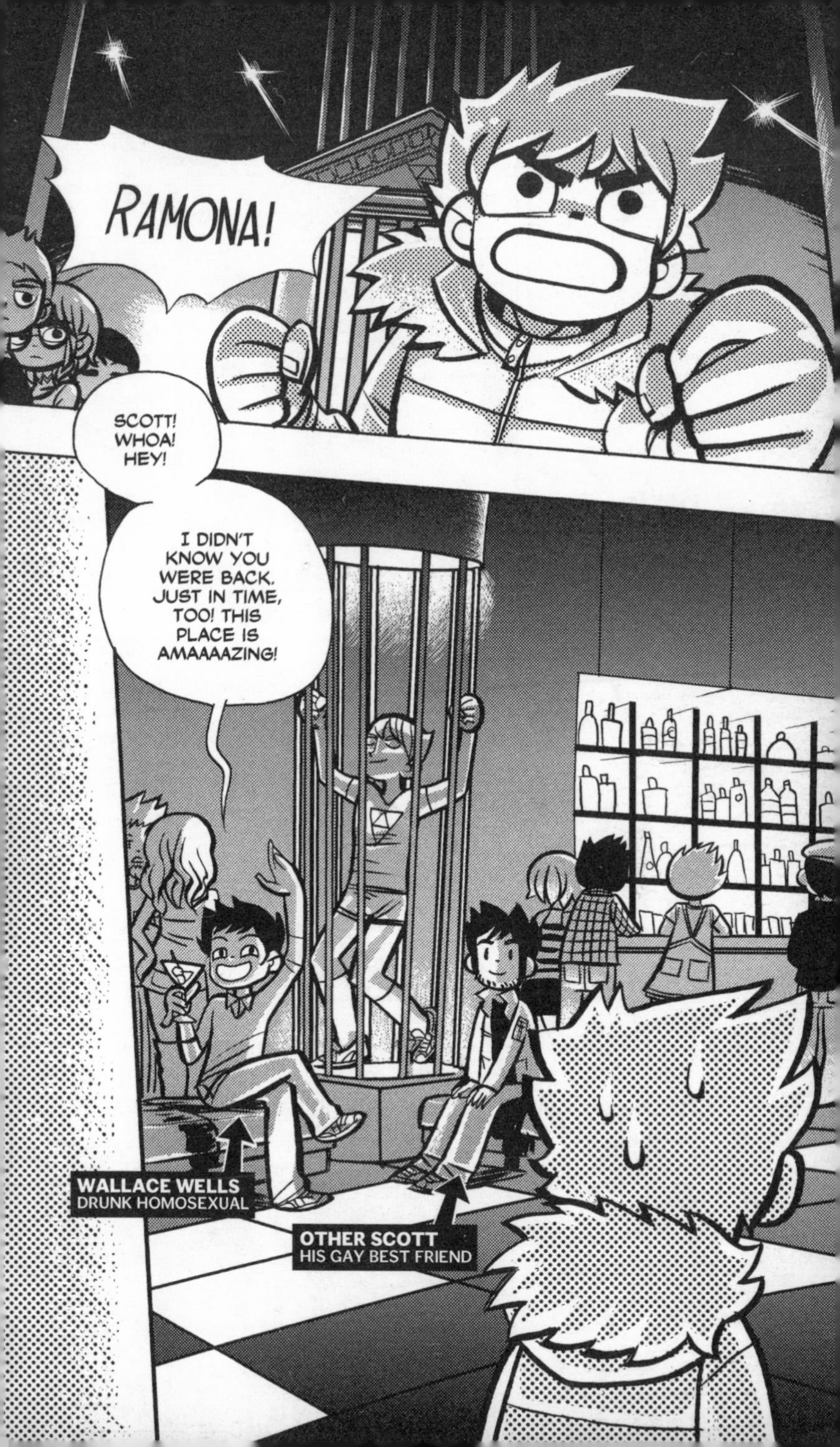
RAMONA!
SCOTT! WHOA! HEY!
I DIDN'T KNOW YOU WERE BACK. JUST IN TIME, TOO! THIS PLACE IS AMAAAAZING!
WALLACE WELLS
DRUNK HOMOSEXUAL
OTHER SCOTT
HIS GAY BEST FRIEND

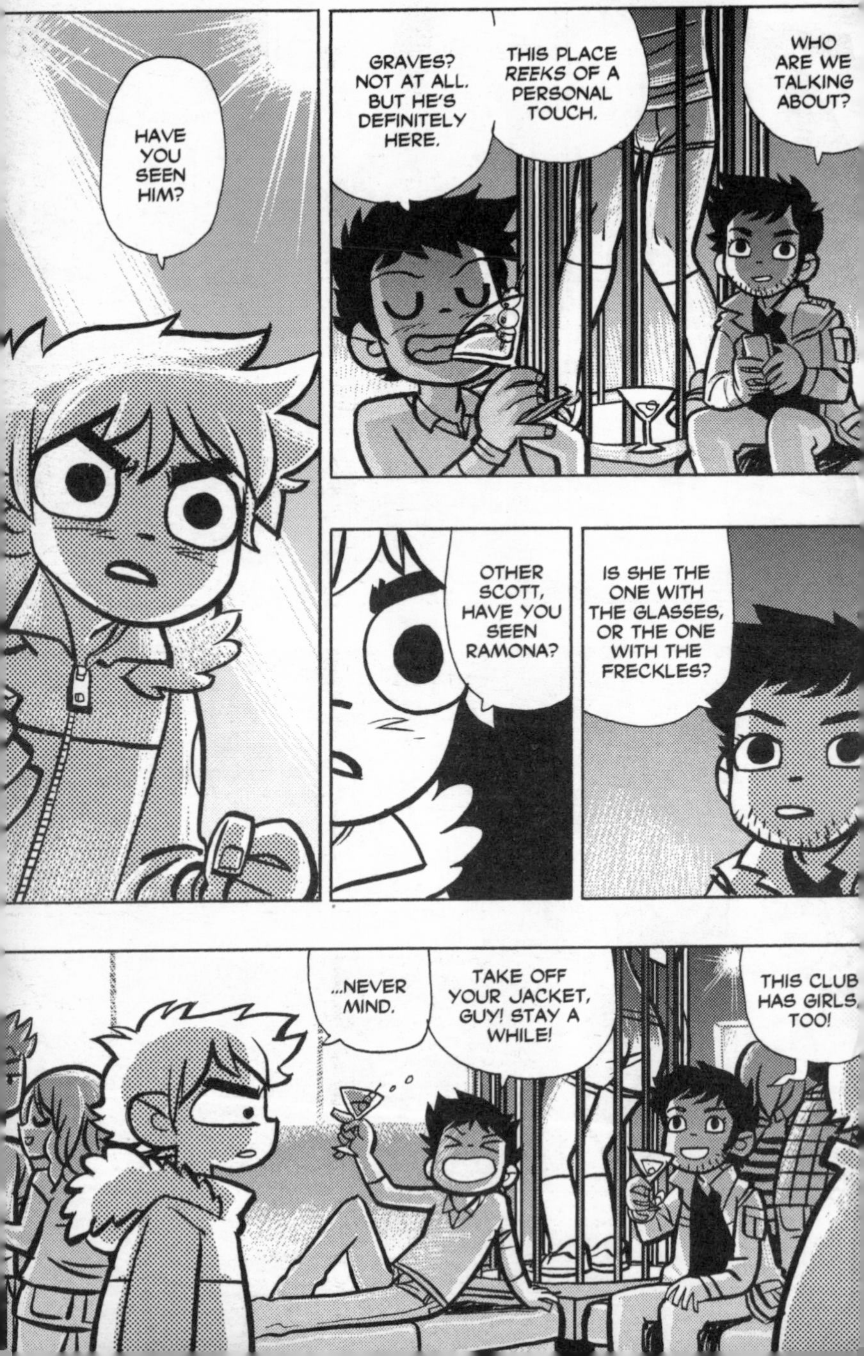
HAVE YOU SEEN HIM?
GRAVES? NOT AT ALL. BUT HE'S DEFINITELY HERE.
THIS PLACE REEKS OF A PERSONAL TOUCH.
WHO ARE WE TALKING ABOUT?
OTHER SCOTT, HAVE YOU SEEN RAMONA?
IS SHE THE ONE WITH THE GLASSES, OR THE ONE WITH THE FRECKLES?
...NEVER MIND.
TAKE OFF YOUR JACKET, GUY! STAY A WHILE!
THIS CLUB HAS GIRLS, TOO!

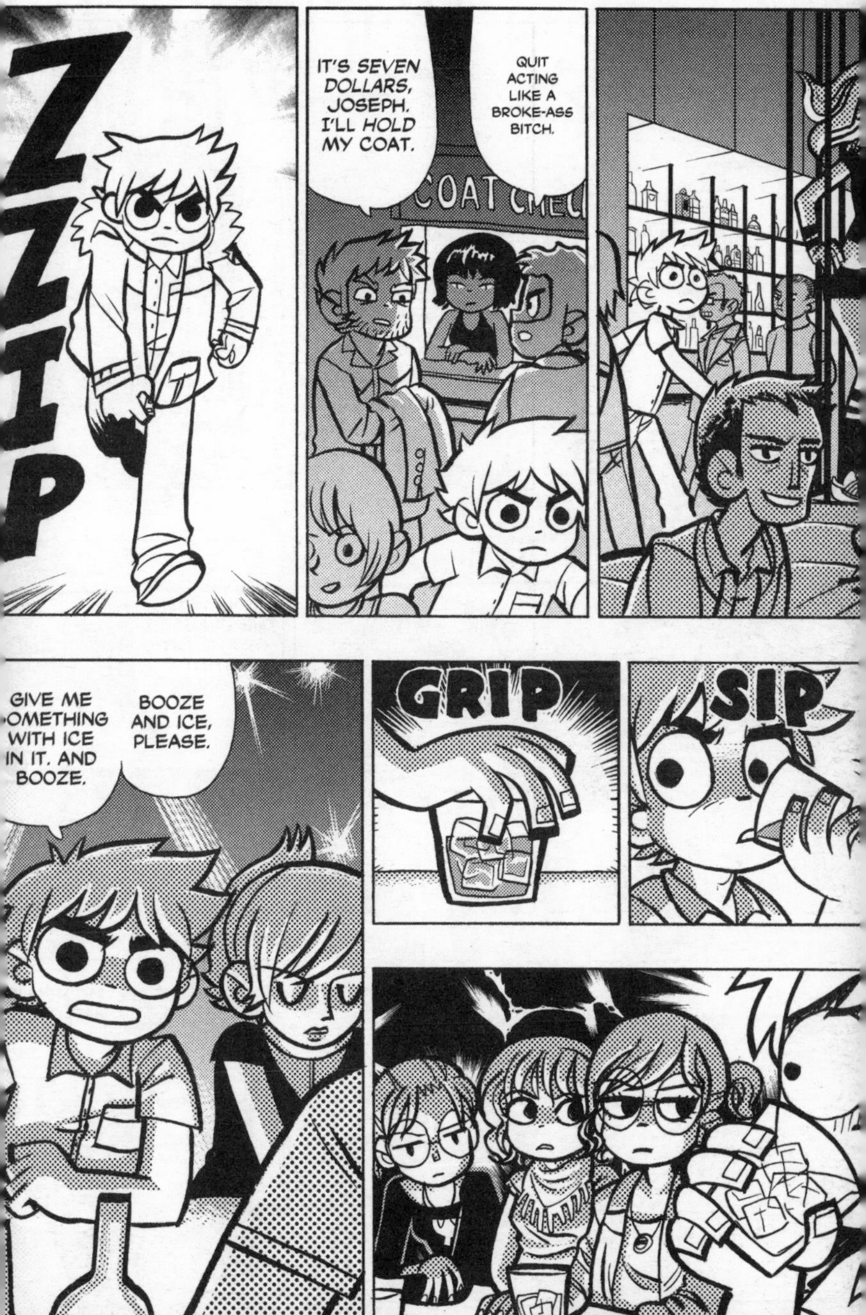
ZZIP
IT'S SEVEN DOLLARS, JOSEPH. I'LL HOLD MY COAT.
QUIT ACTING LIKE A BROKE-ASS BITCH.
COAT CHEC
GIVE ME SOMETHING WITH ICE IN IT. AND BOOZE.
BOOZE AND ICE, PLEASE.
GRIP
SIP

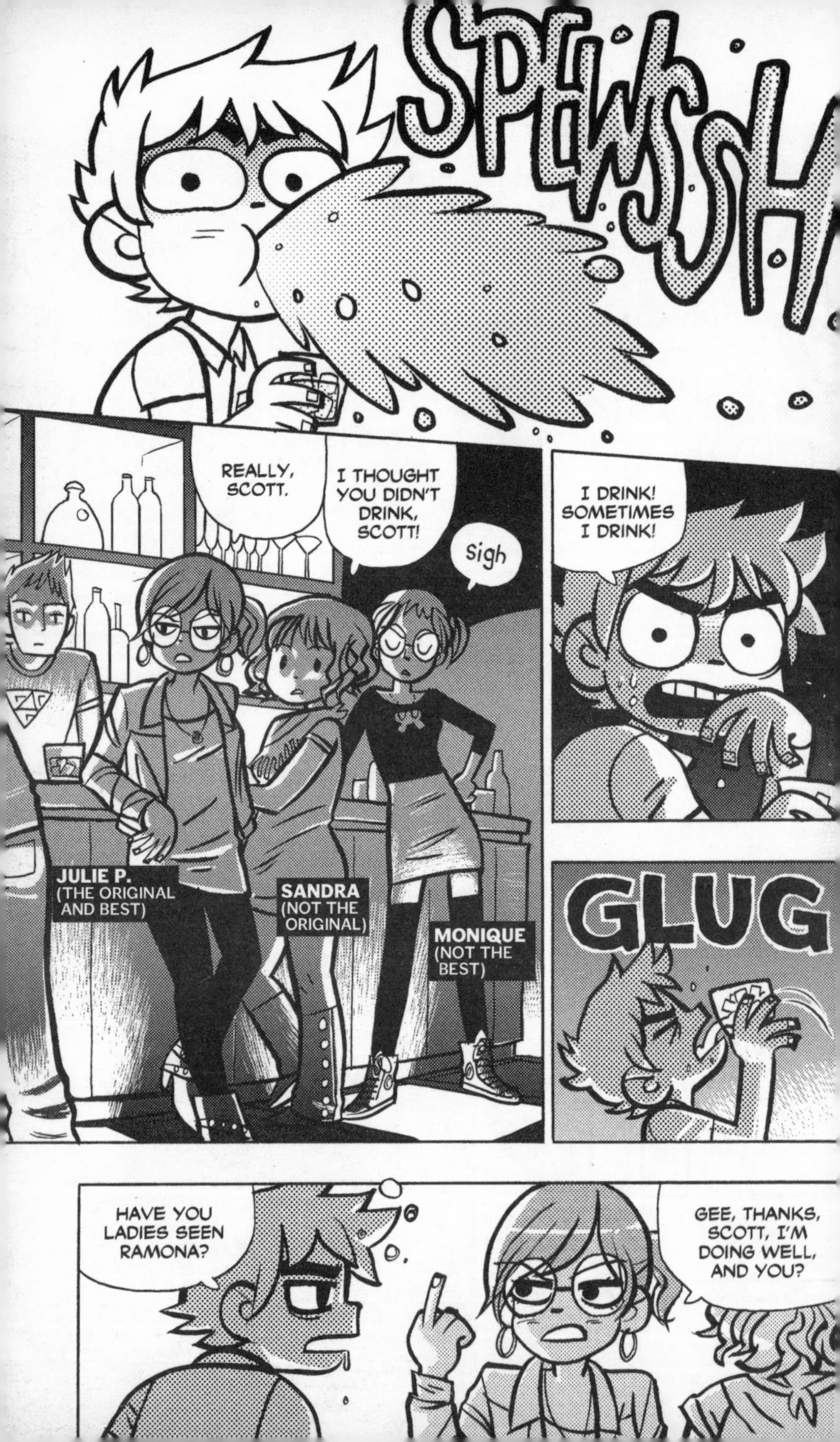
SPEWSSH
REALLY, SCOTT.
I THOUGHT YOU DIDN'T DRINK, SCOTT!
Sigh
JULIE P. (THE ORIGINAL AND BEST)
SANDRA (NOT THE ORIGINAL)
MONIQUE (NOT THE BEST)
I DRINK! SOMETIMES I DRINK!
GLUG
HAVE YOU LADIES SEEN RAMONA?
GEE, THANKS, SCOTT, I'M DOING WELL, AND YOU?

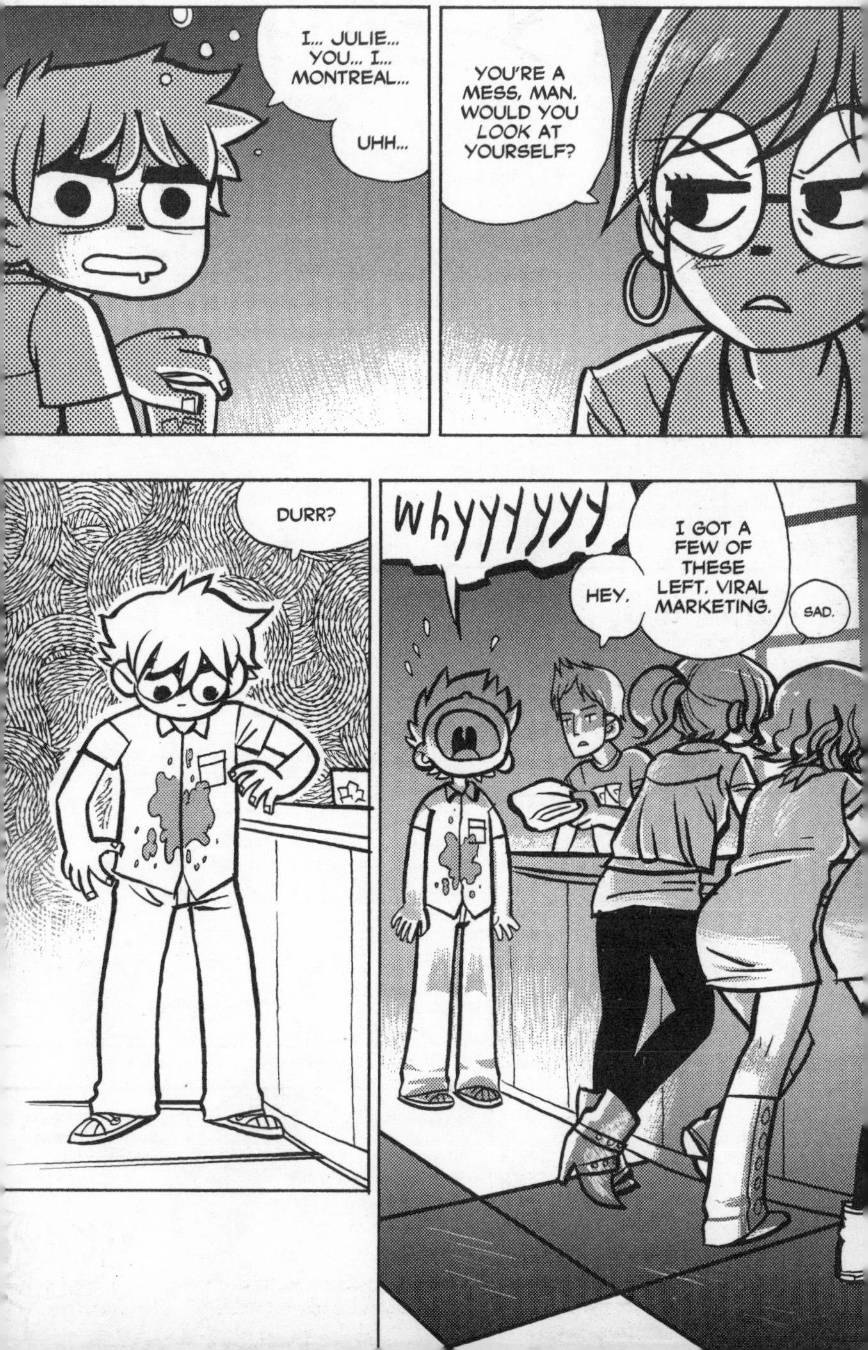
I... JULIE... YOU... I... MONTREAL...
UHH...
YOU'RE A MESS, MAN. WOULD YOU LOOK AT YOURSELF?
DURR?
WHYYYYYY
HEY.
I GOT A FEW OF THESE LEFT. VIRAL MARKETING.
SAD.

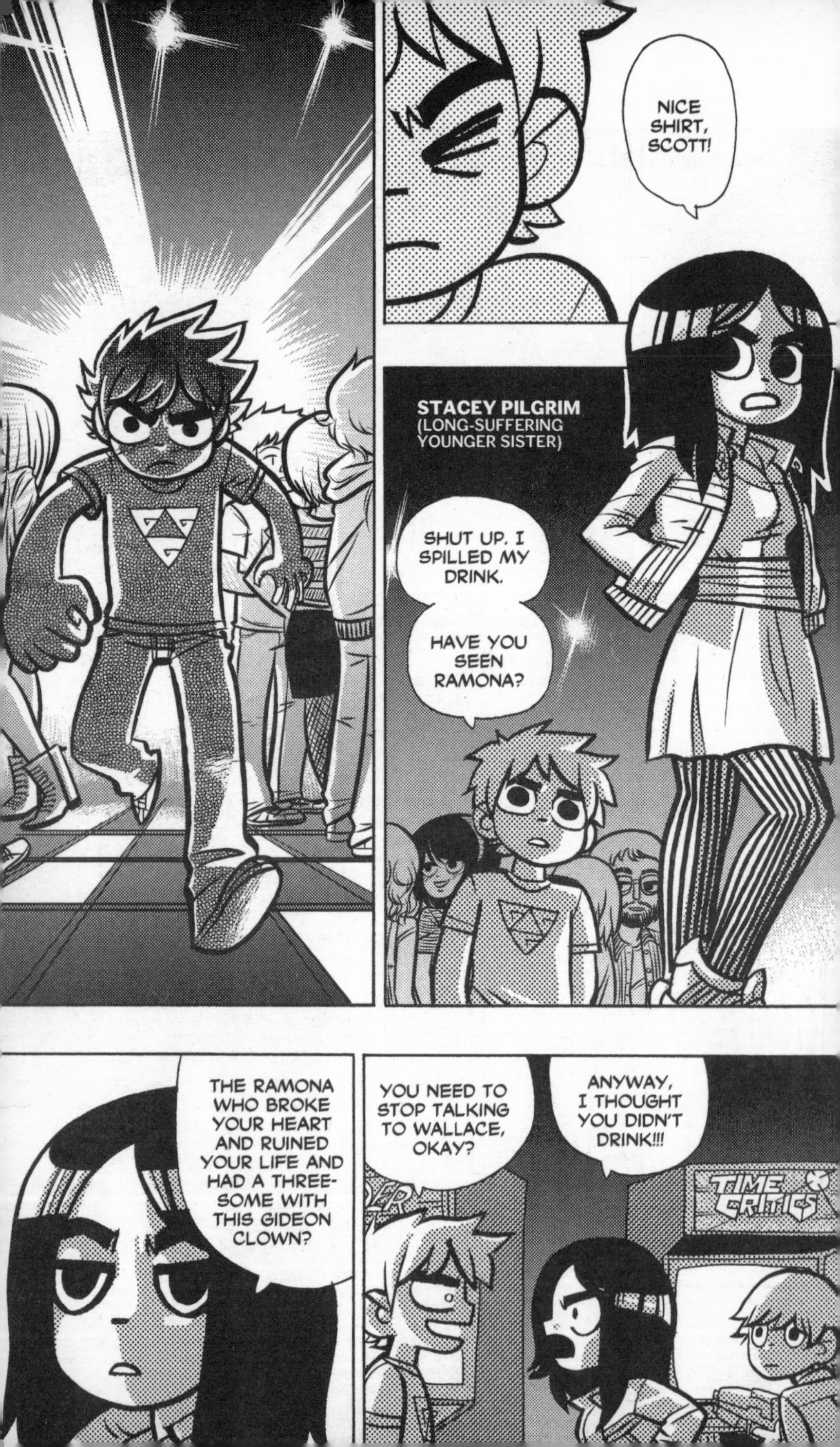
NICE SHIRT, SCOTT!
STACEY PILGRIM (LONG-SUFFERING YOUNGER SISTER)
SHUT UP. I SPILLED MY DRINK.
HAVE YOU SEEN RAMONA?
THE RAMONA WHO BROKE YOUR HEART AND RUINED YOUR LIFE AND HAD A THREE-SOME WITH THIS GIDEON CLOWN?
YOU NEED TO STOP TALKING TO WALLACE, OKAY?
ANYWAY, I THOUGHT YOU DIDN'T DRINK!!!
TIME CRITICS

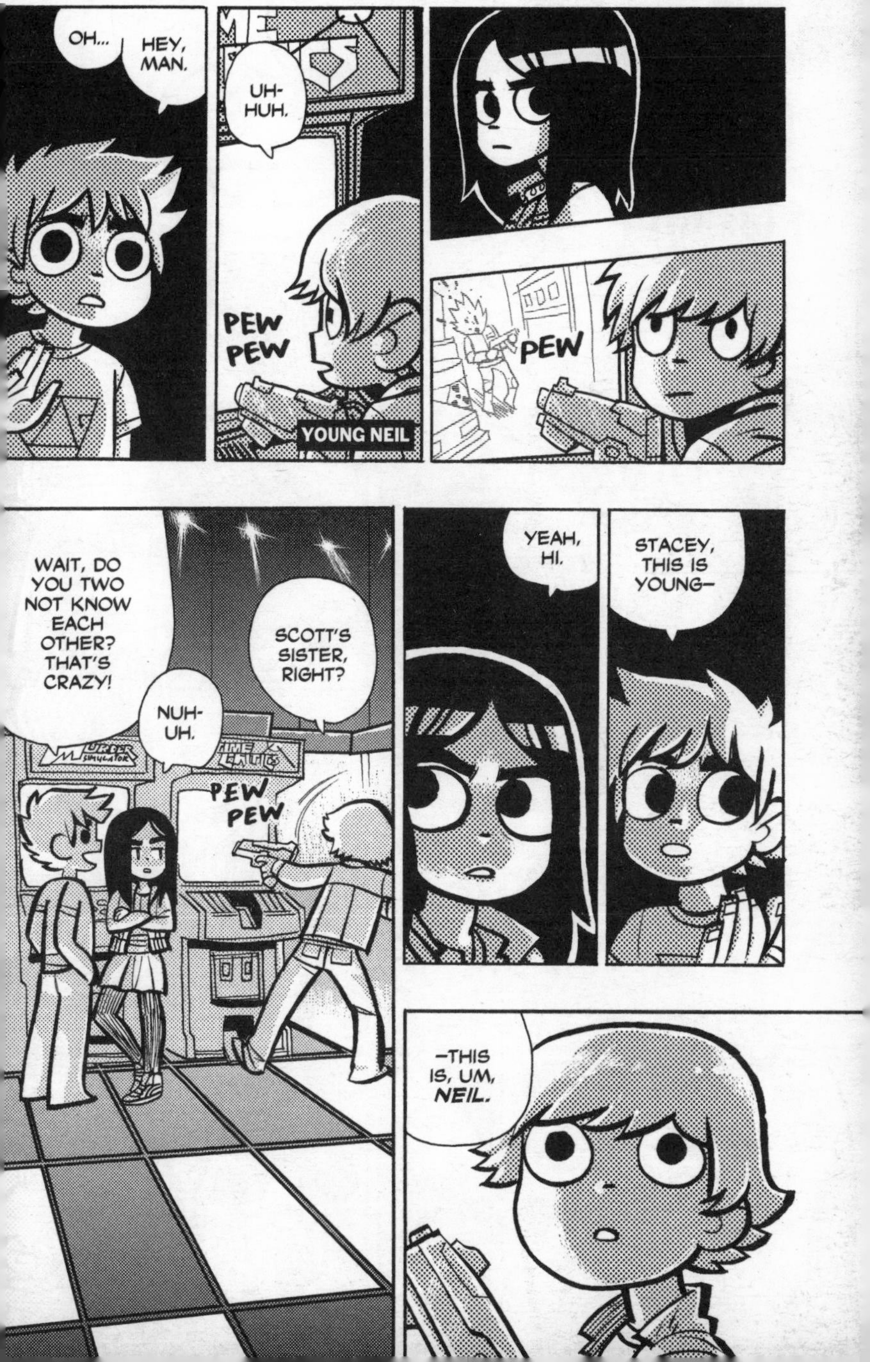
OH...
HEY, MAN.
UH-HUH.
PEW PEW
YOUNG NEIL
PEW
WAIT, DO YOU TWO NOT KNOW EACH OTHER? THAT'S CRAZY!
SCOTT'S SISTER, RIGHT?
NUH-UH.
PEW PEW
YEAH, HI.
STACEY, THIS IS YOUNG–
–THIS IS, UM, NEIL.

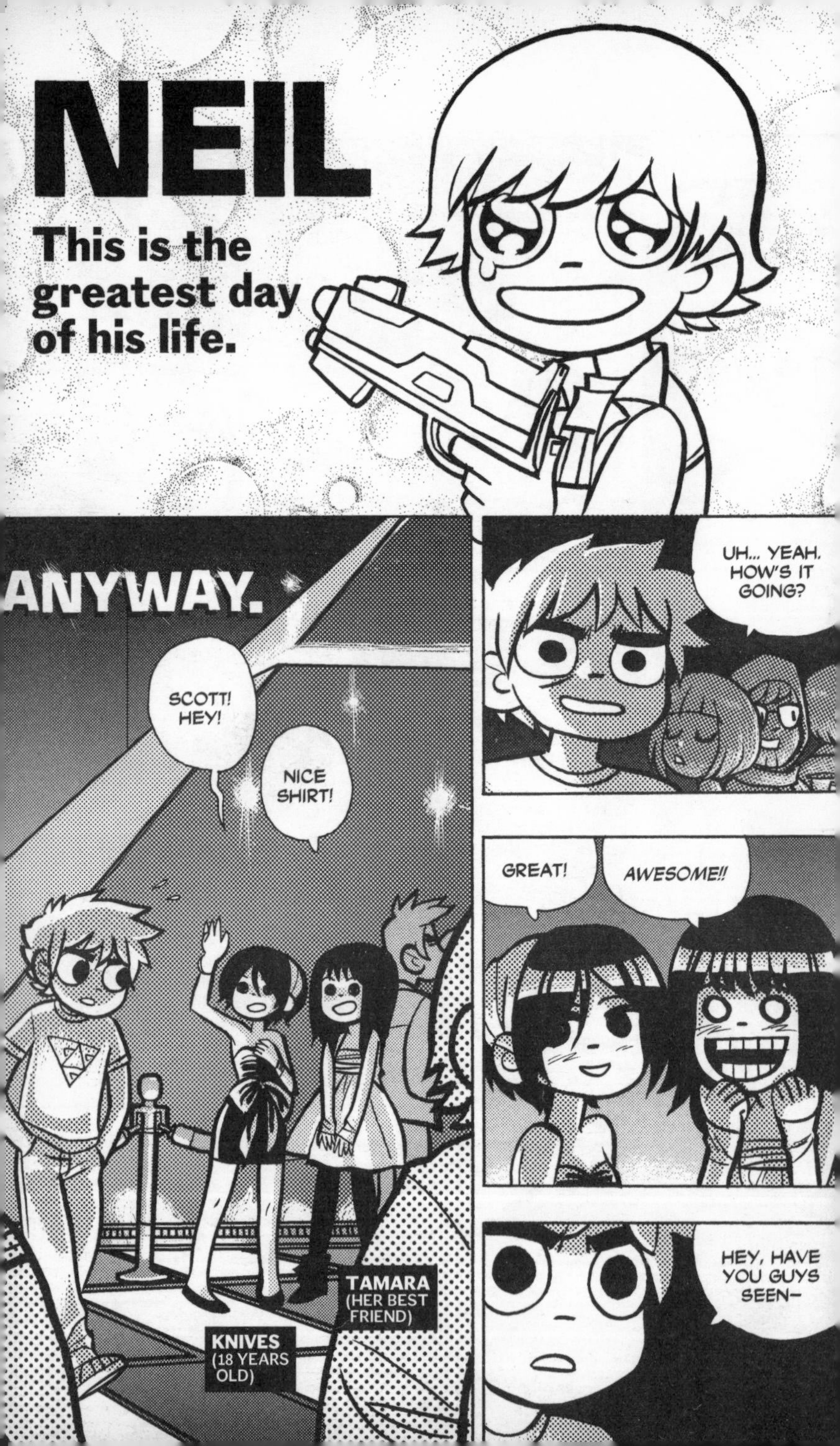
NEIL
This is the greatest day of his life.
ANYWAY.
SCOTT! HEY!
NICE SHIRT!
TAMARA (HER BEST FRIEND)
KNIVES (18 YEARS OLD)
UH... YEAH. HOW'S IT GOING?
GREAT!
AWESOME!!
HEY, HAVE YOU GUYS SEEN–

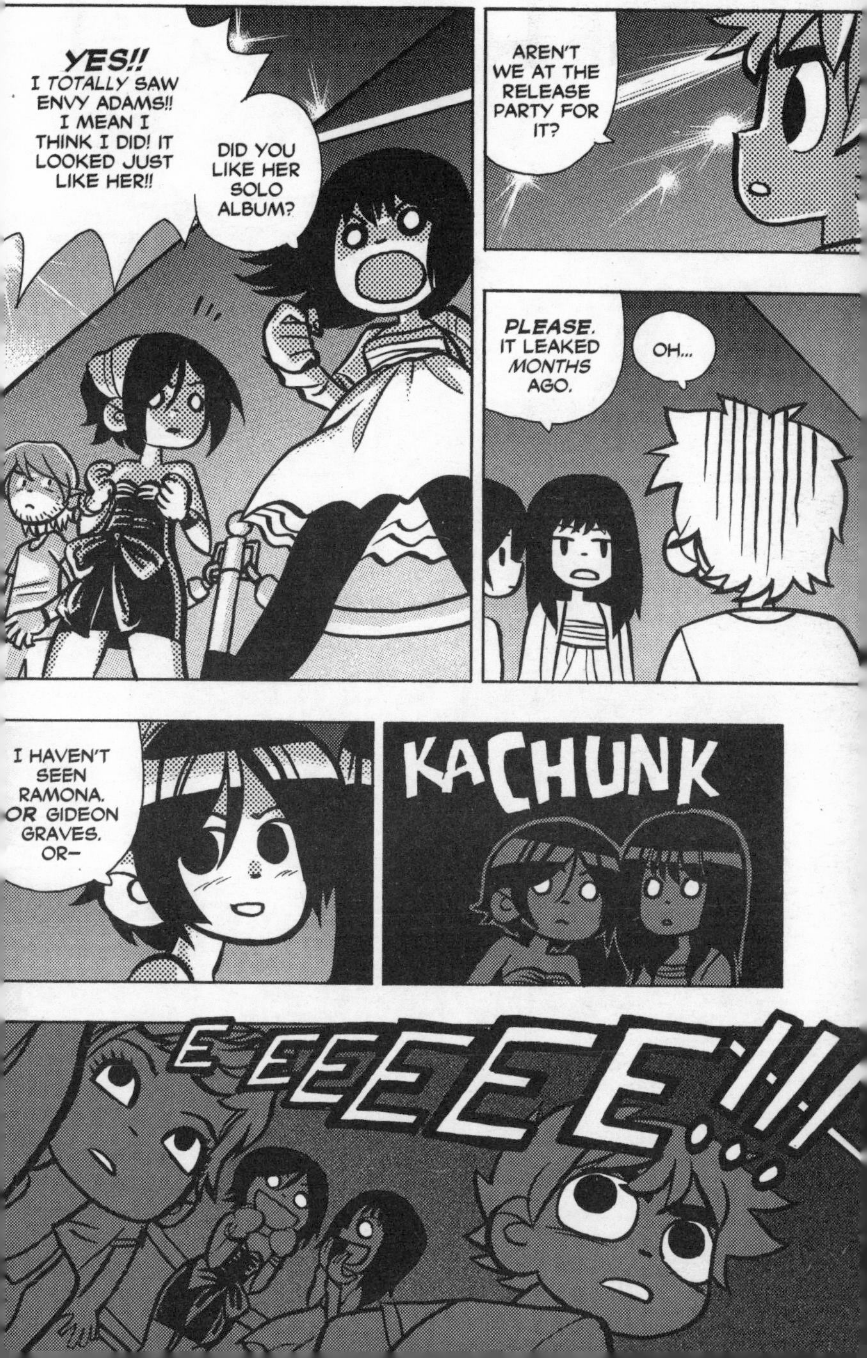
YES!! I TOTALLY SAW ENVY ADAMS!! I MEAN I THINK I DID! IT LOOKED JUST LIKE HER!!
DID YOU LIKE HER SOLO ALBUM?
AREN'T WE AT THE RELEASE PARTY FOR IT?
PLEASE. IT LEAKED MONTHS AGO.
OH...
I HAVEN'T SEEN RAMONA. OR GIDEON GRAVES. OR–
KACHUNK
E EEEEE!!!

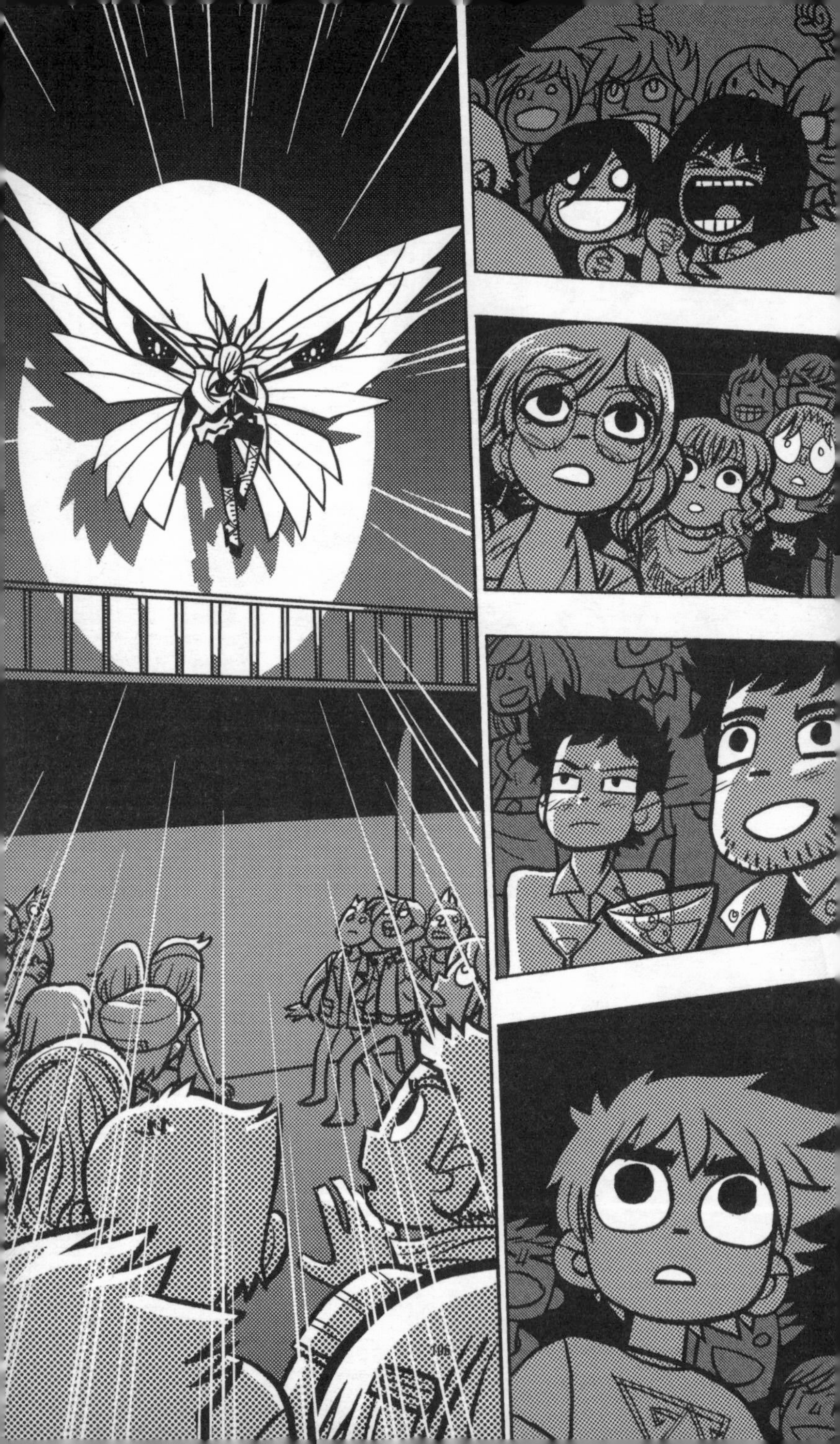

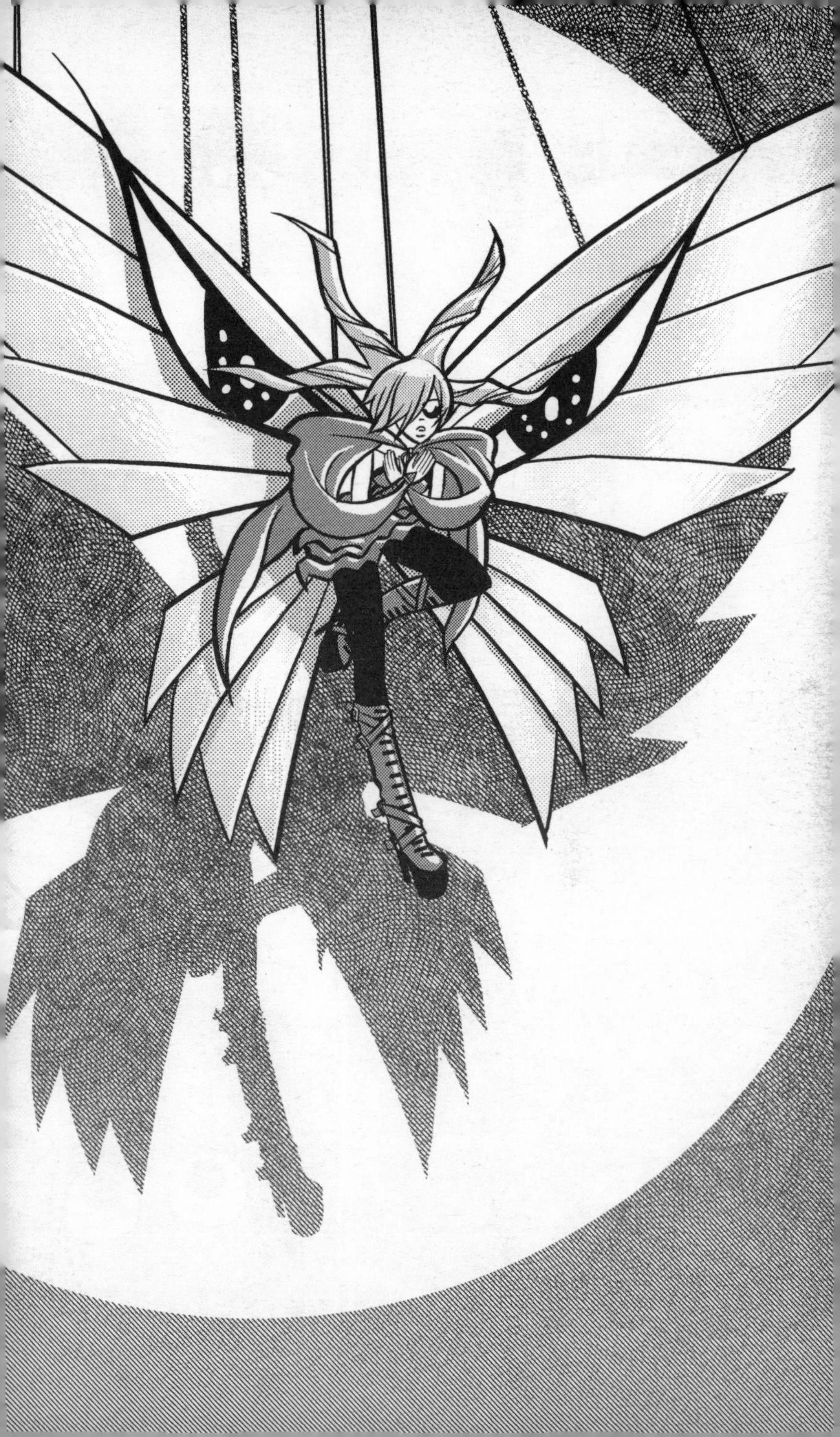

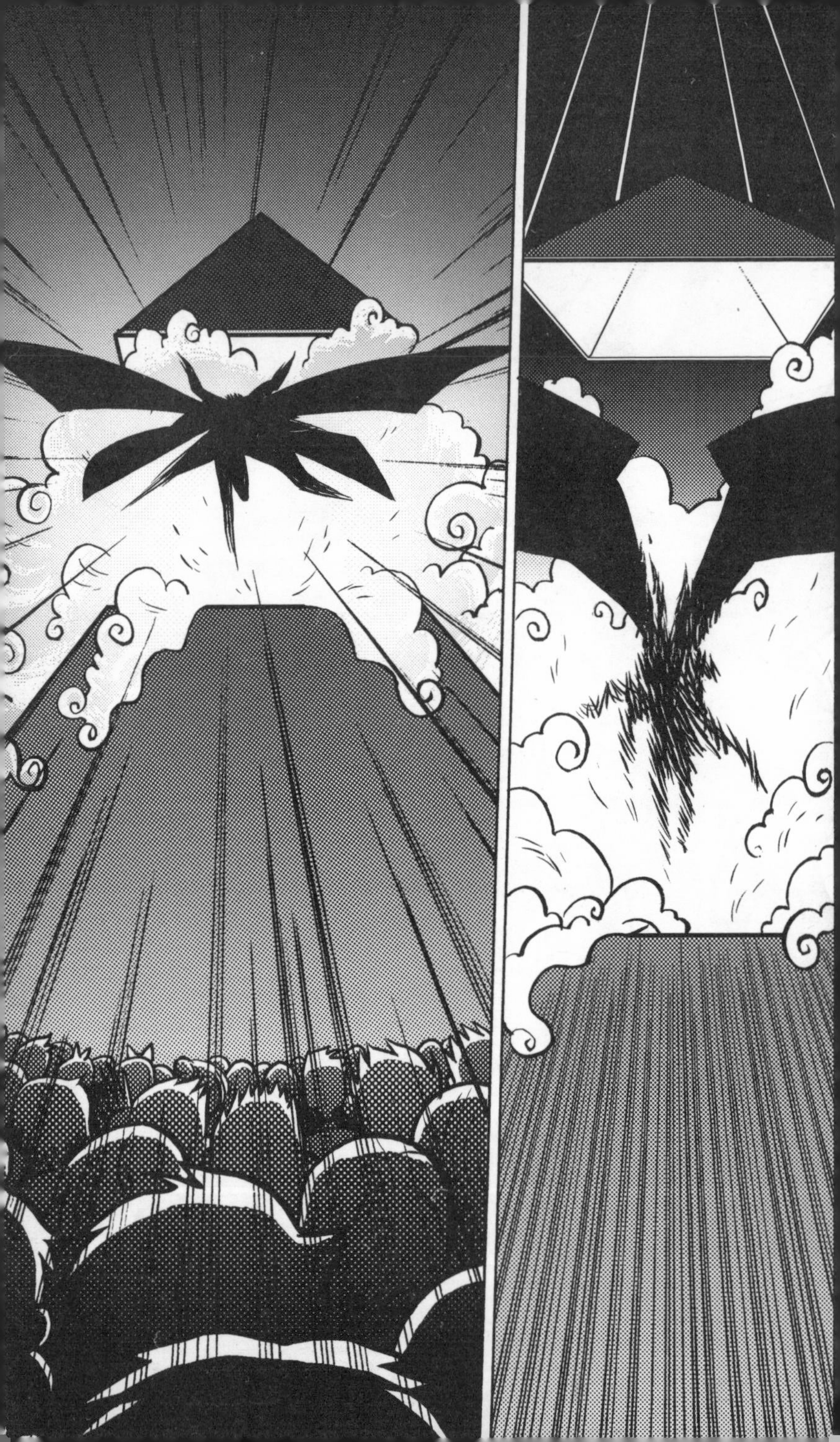

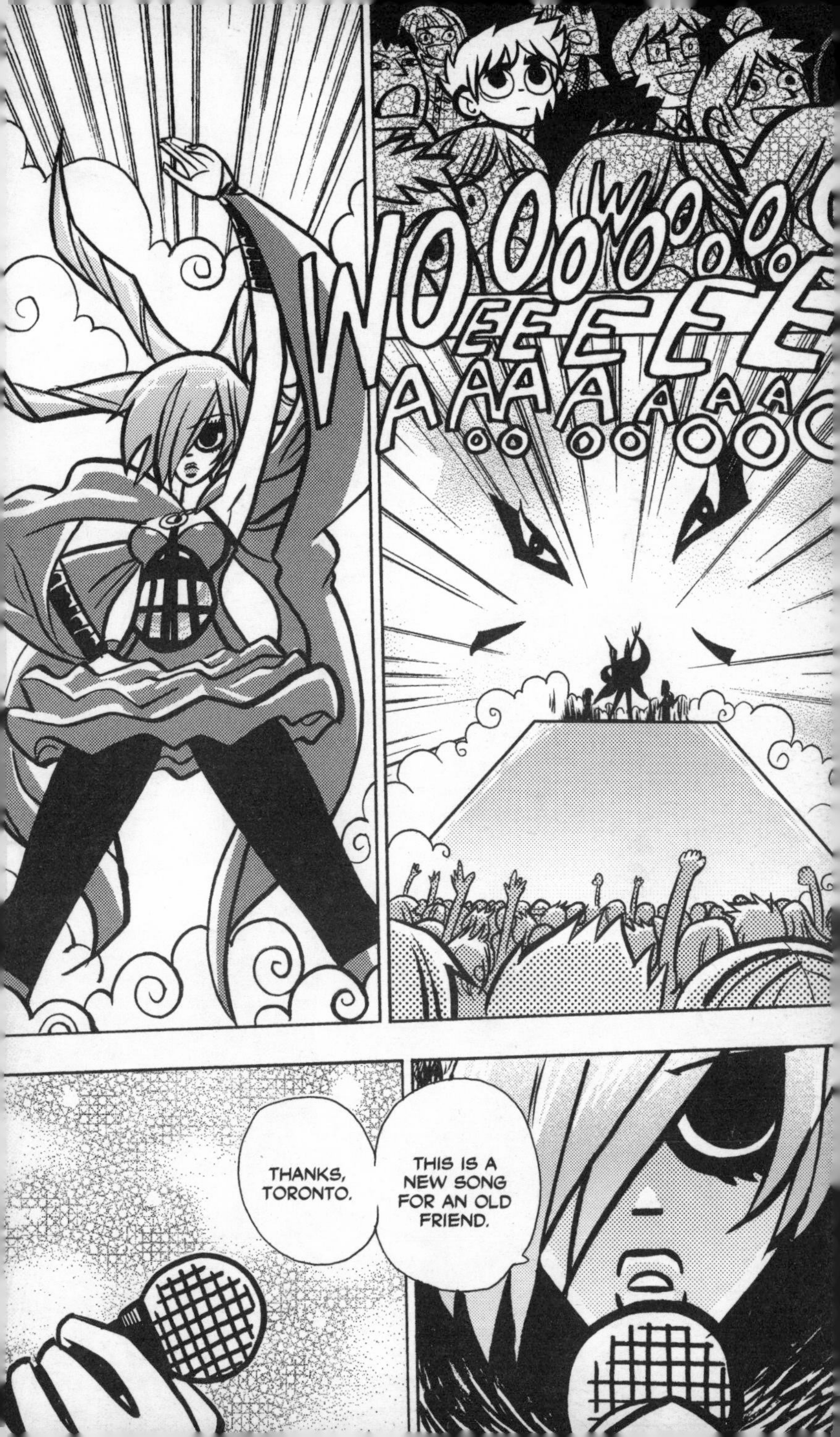

THANKS, TORONTO.
THIS IS A NEW SONG FOR AN OLD FRIEND.

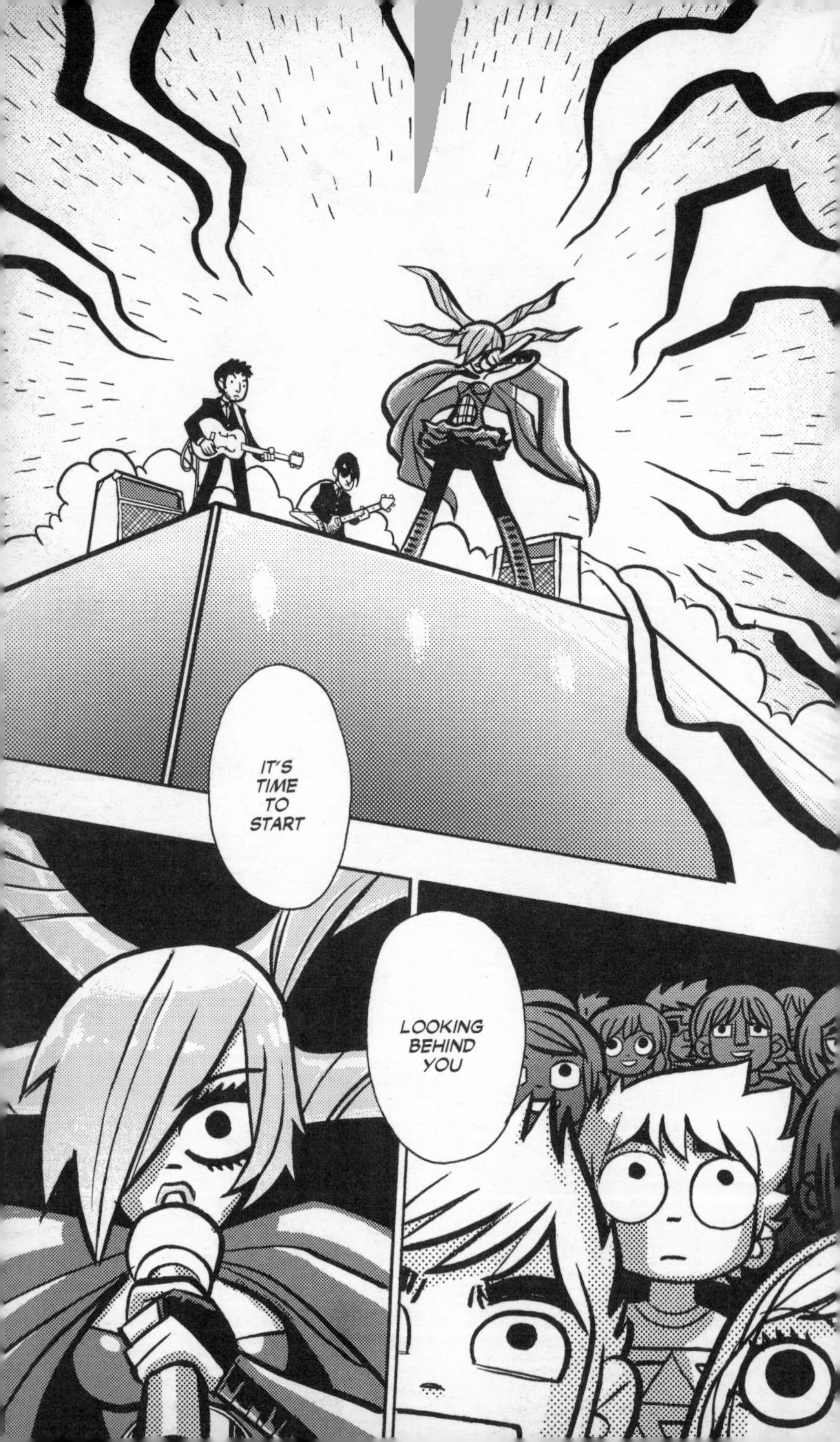
IT'S TIME TO START
LOOKING BEHIND YOU

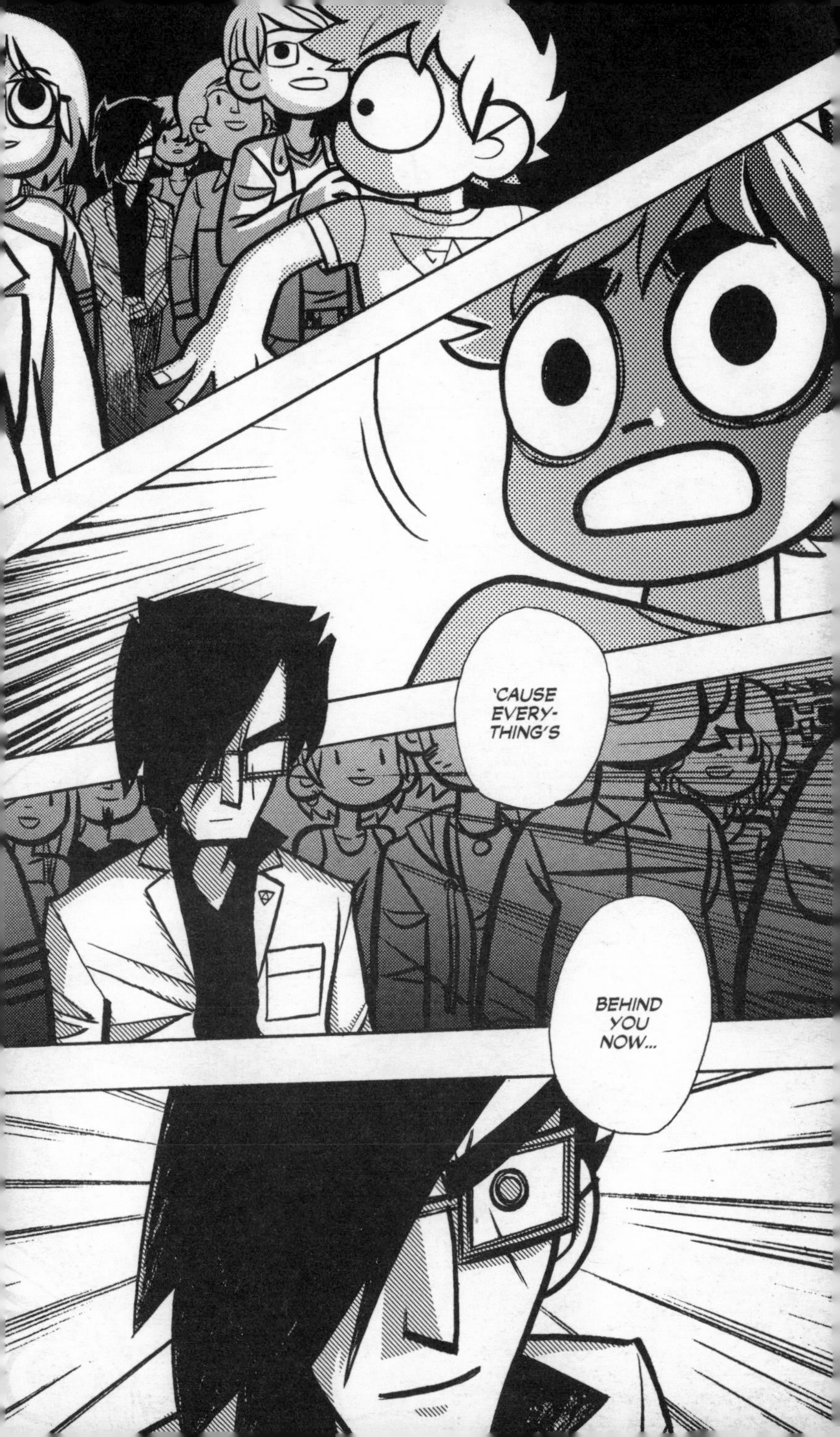
'CAUSE EVERY-THING'S
BEHIND YOU NOW...

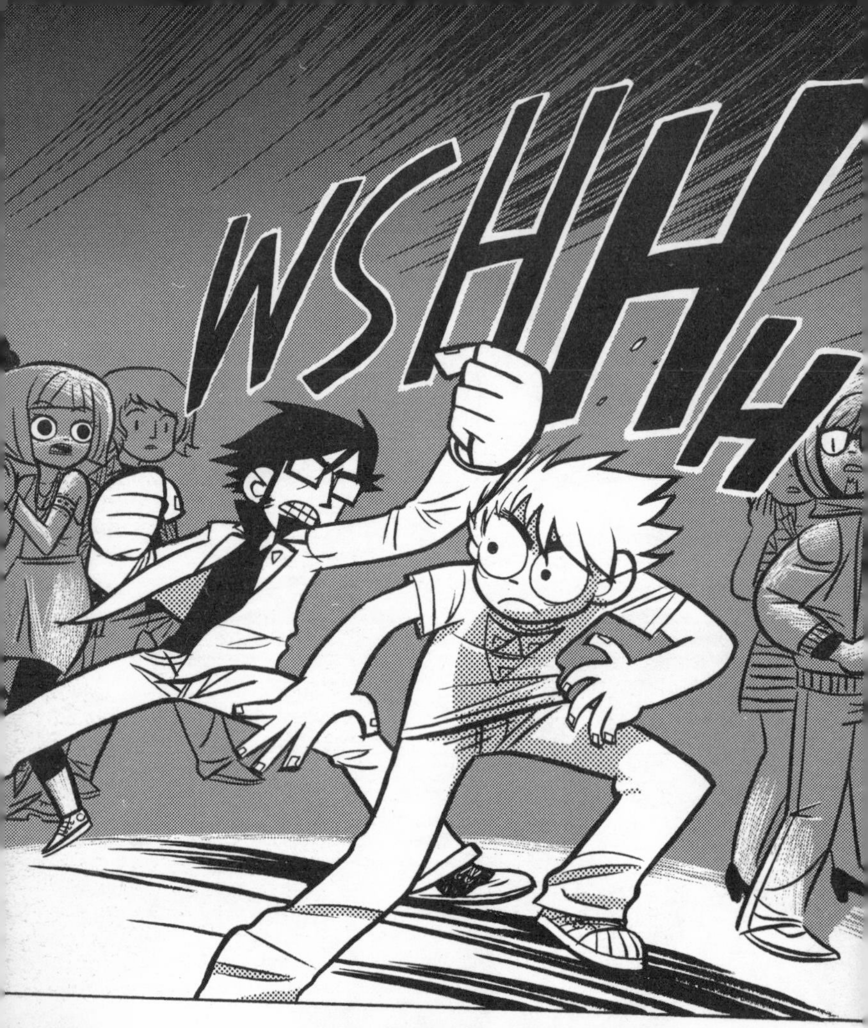
WSHHH

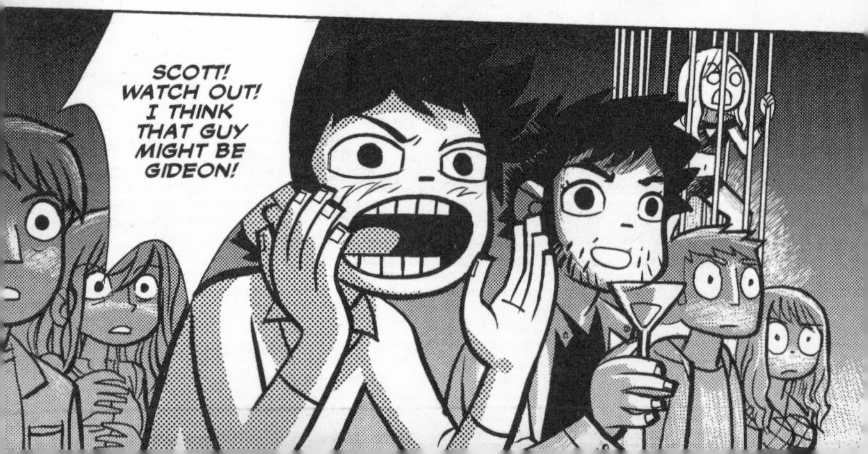
SCOTT! WATCH OUT! I THINK THAT GUY MIGHT BE GIDEON!

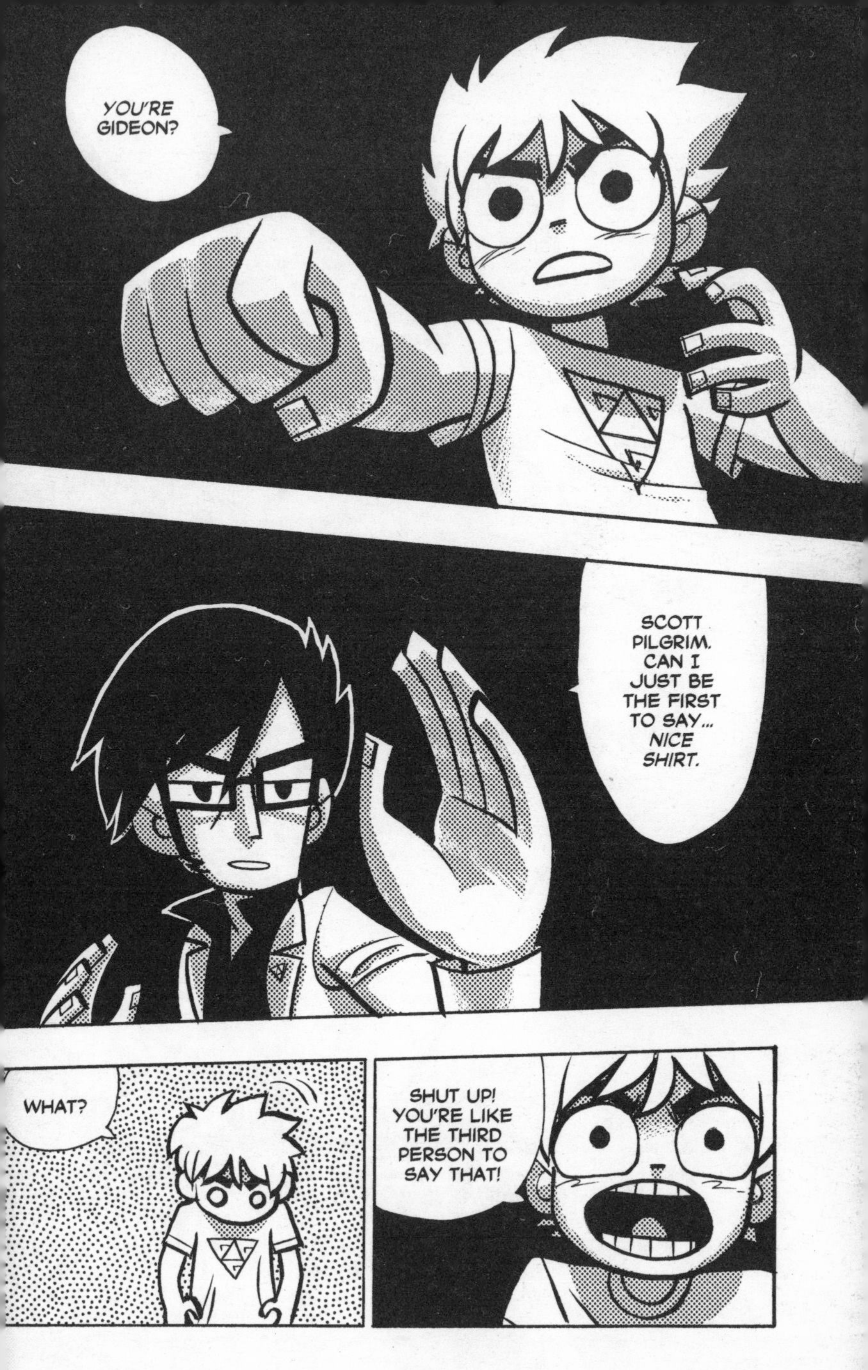
YOU'RE GIDEON?
SCOTT PILGRIM. CAN I JUST BE THE FIRST TO SAY... NICE SHIRT.
WHAT?
SHUT UP! YOU'RE LIKE THE THIRD PERSON TO SAY THAT!

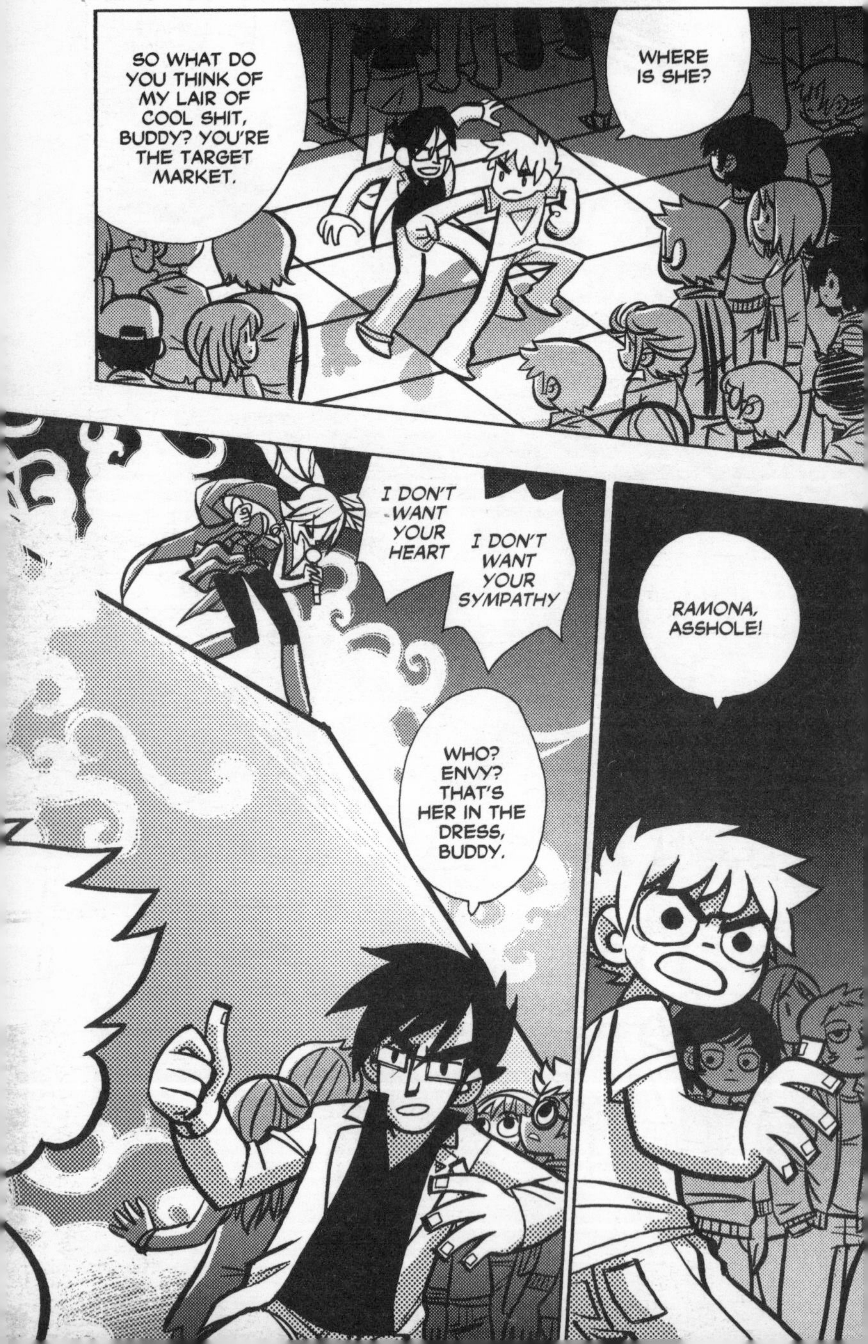

SO WHAT DO YOU THINK OF MY LAIR OF COOL SHIT, BUDDY? YOU'RE THE TARGET MARKET.
WHERE IS SHE?
I DON'T WANT YOUR HEART
I DON'T WANT YOUR SYMPATHY
WHO? ENVY? THAT'S HER IN THE DRESS, BUDDY.
RAMONA, ASSHOLE!

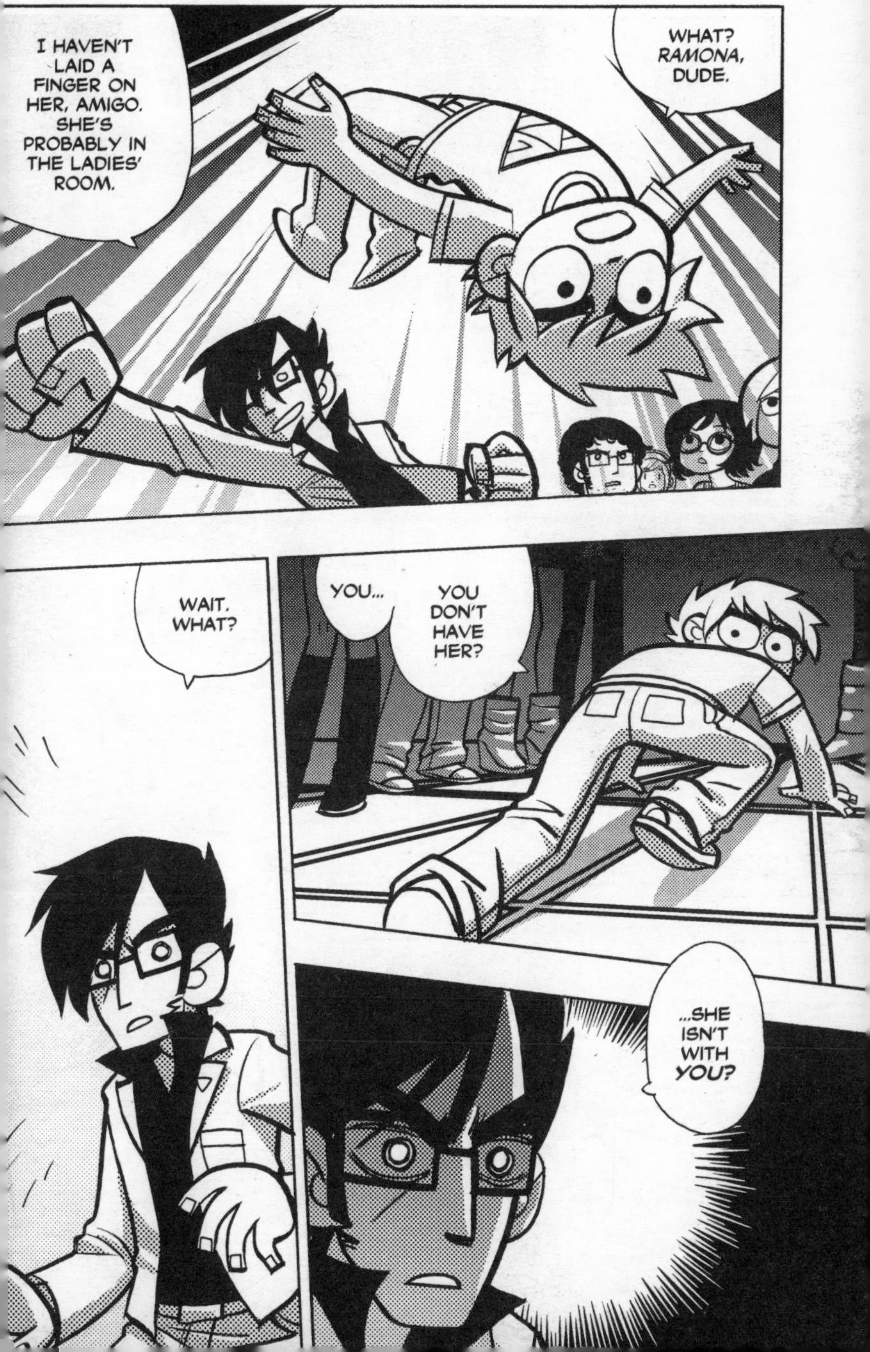
I HAVEN'T LAID A FINGER ON HER, AMIGO. SHE'S PROBABLY IN THE LADIES' ROOM.
WHAT? *RAMONA*, DUDE.
WAIT. WHAT?
YOU...
YOU DON'T HAVE HER?
...SHE ISN'T WITH *YOU*?

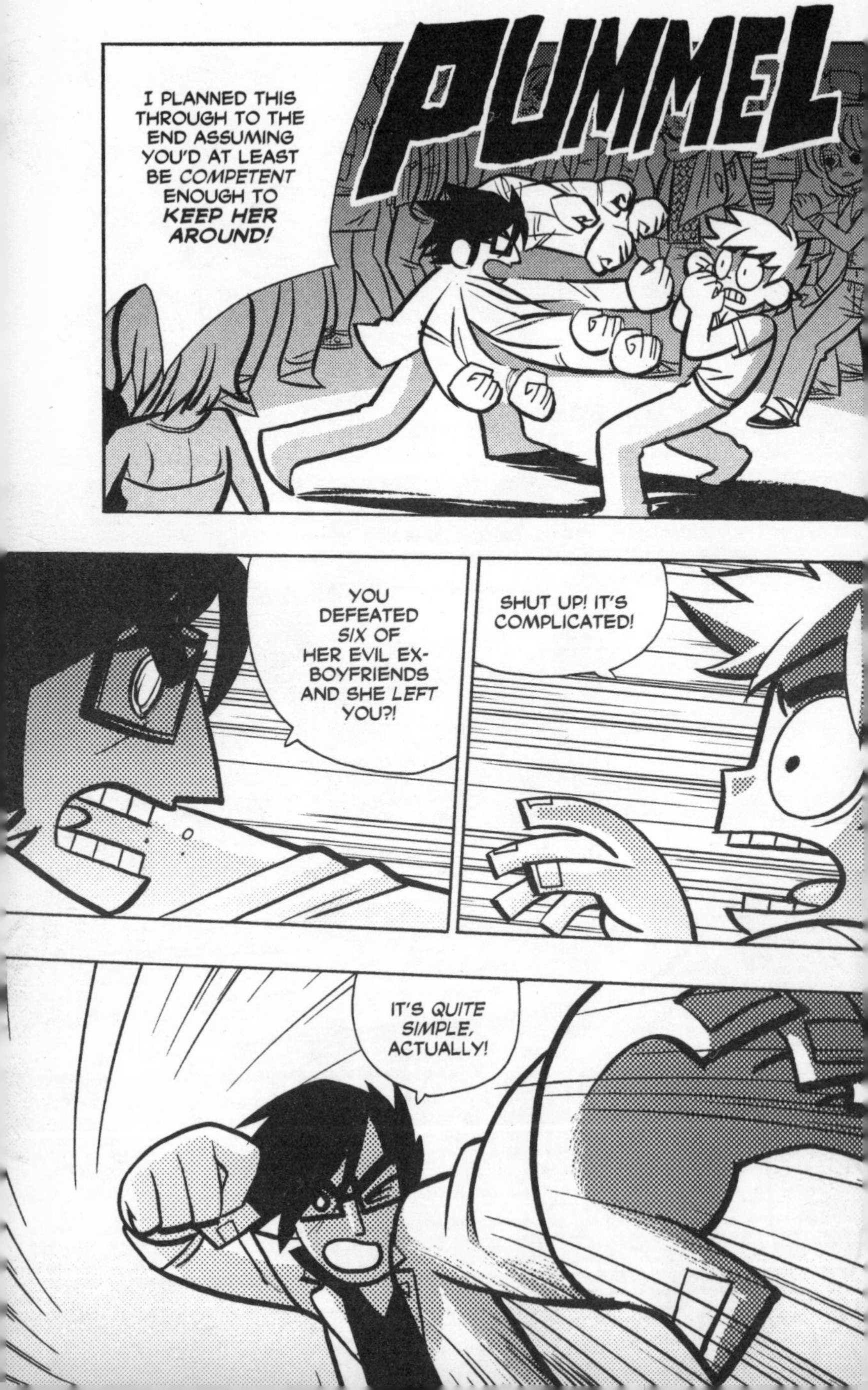

PUMMEL
I PLANNED THIS THROUGH TO THE END ASSUMING YOU'D AT LEAST BE *COMPETENT* ENOUGH TO ***KEEP HER AROUND!***
YOU DEFEATED *SIX* OF HER EVIL EX-BOYFRIENDS AND SHE *LEFT* YOU?!
SHUT UP! IT'S COMPLICATED!
IT'S *QUITE SIMPLE,* ACTUALLY!

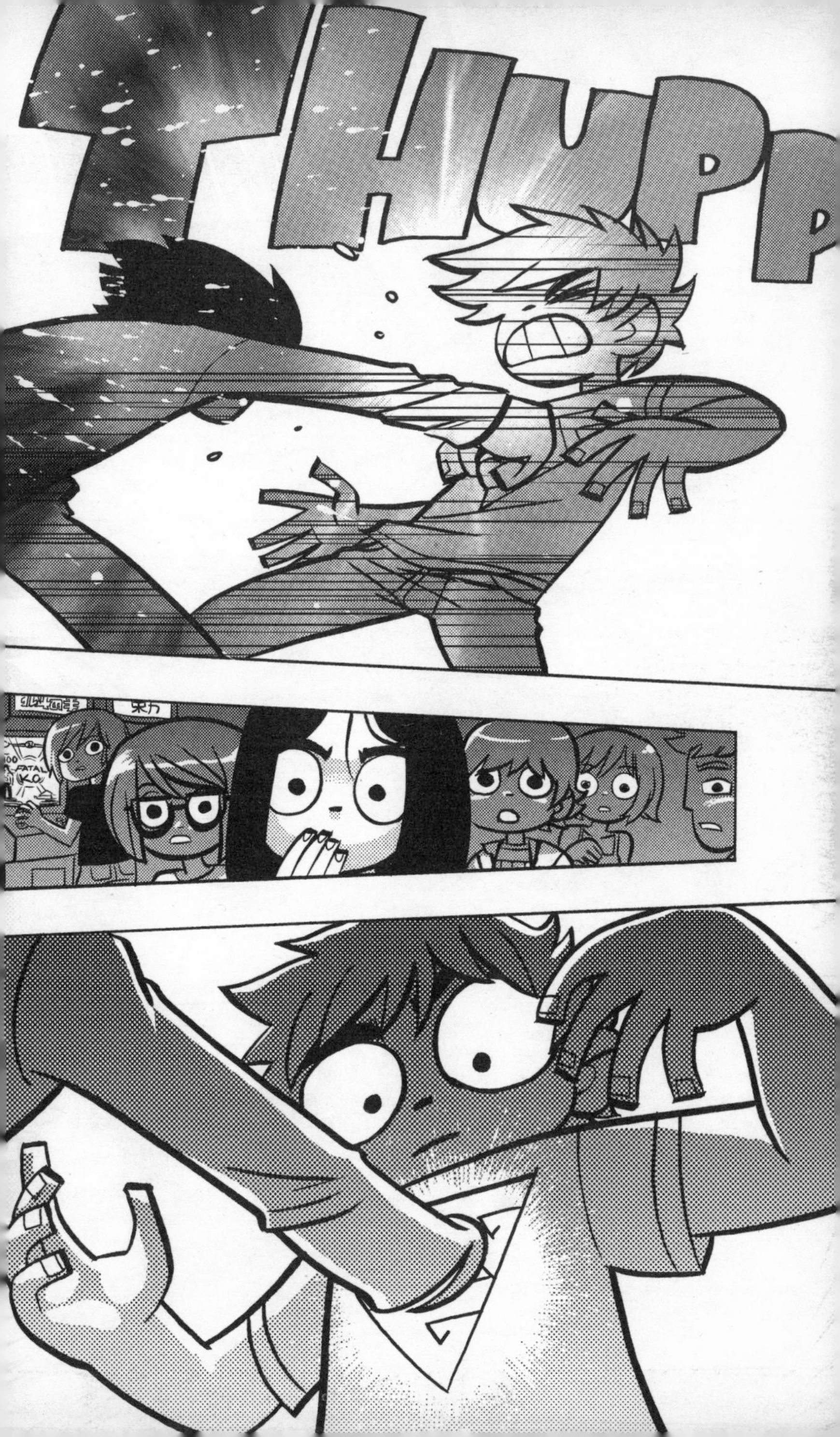
THUPP

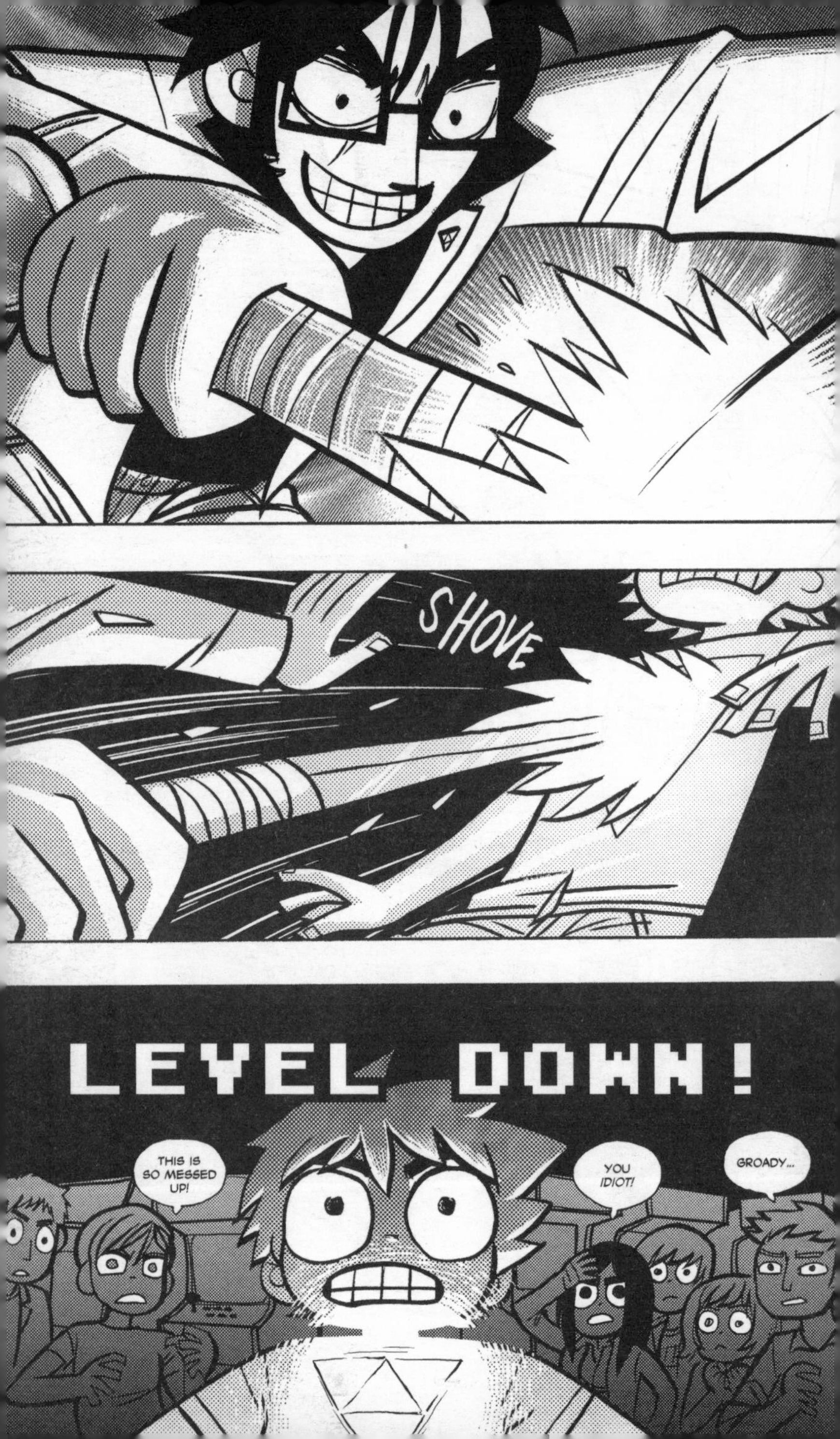
SHOVE
LEVEL DOWN!
THIS IS SO MESSED UP!
YOU IDIOT!
GROADY...

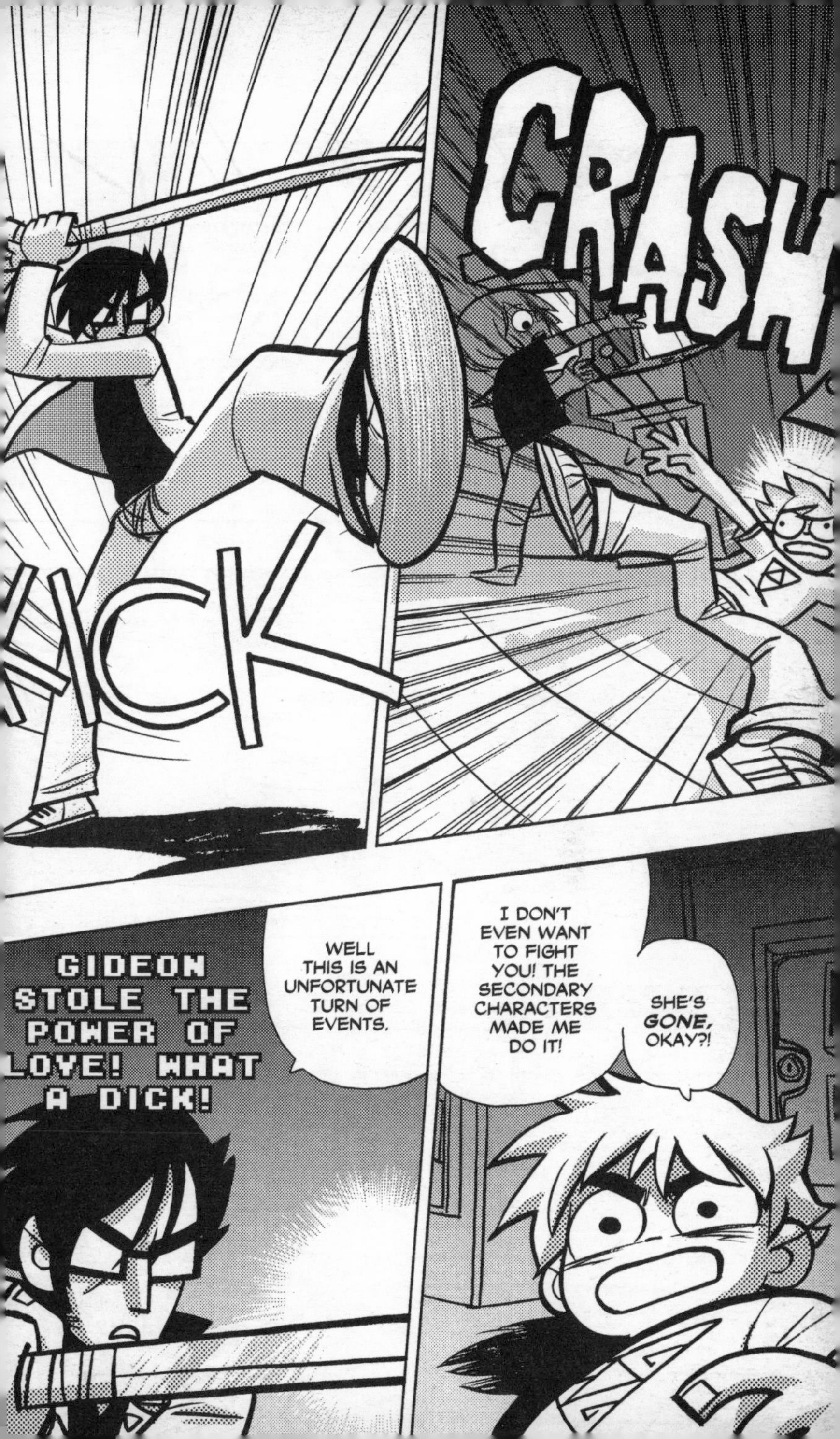
CRASH
KICK
GIDEON STOLE THE POWER OF LOVE! WHAT A DICK!
WELL THIS IS AN UNFORTUNATE TURN OF EVENTS.
I DON'T EVEN WANT TO FIGHT YOU! THE SECONDARY CHARACTERS MADE ME DO IT!
SHE'S *GONE,* OKAY?!

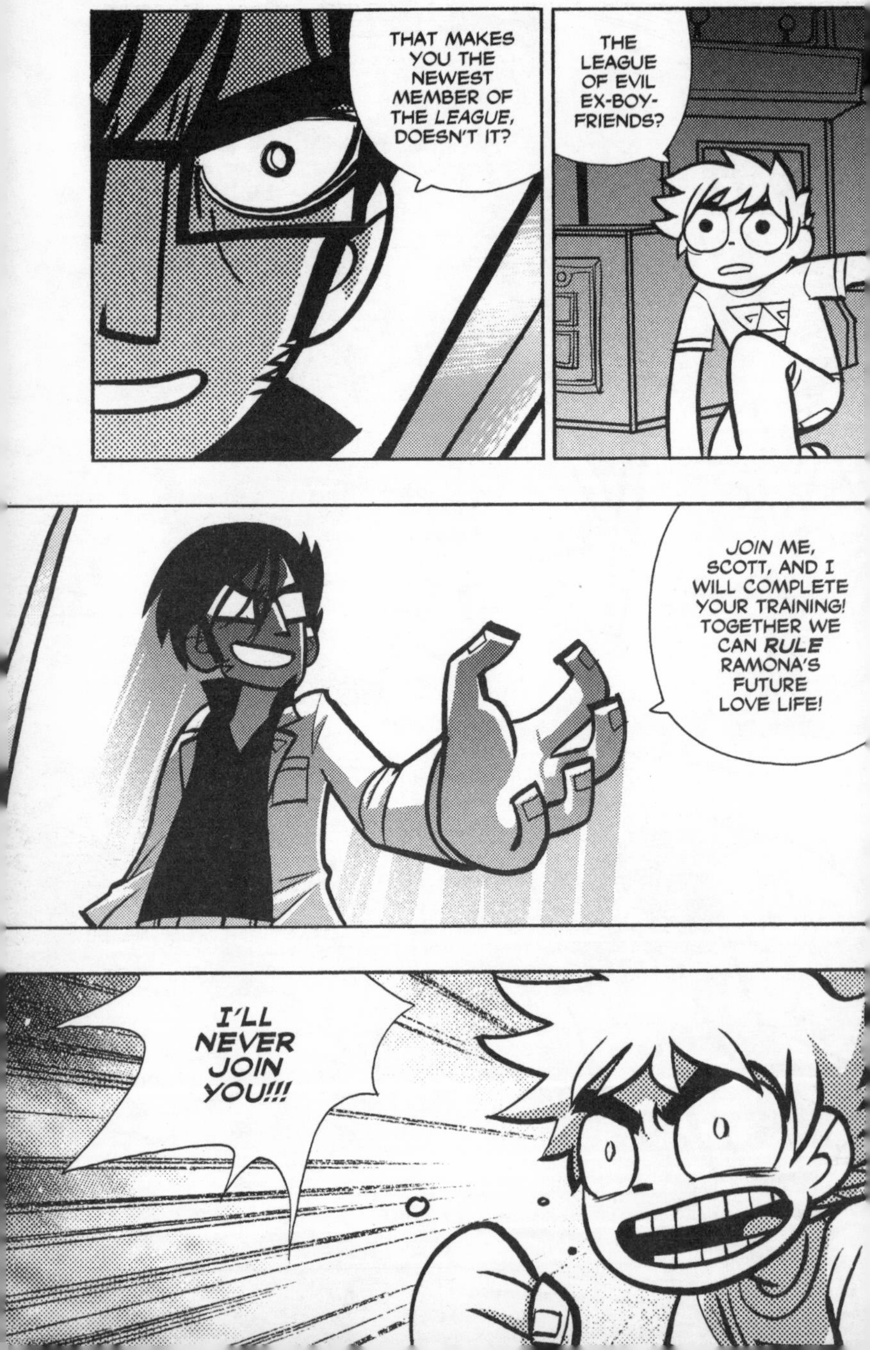
THAT MAKES YOU THE NEWEST MEMBER OF THE *LEAGUE,* DOESN'T IT?
THE LEAGUE OF EVIL EX-BOY-FRIENDS?
JOIN ME, SCOTT, AND I WILL COMPLETE YOUR TRAINING! TOGETHER WE CAN ***RULE*** RAMONA'S FUTURE LOVE LIFE!
I'LL NEVER JOIN YOU!!!

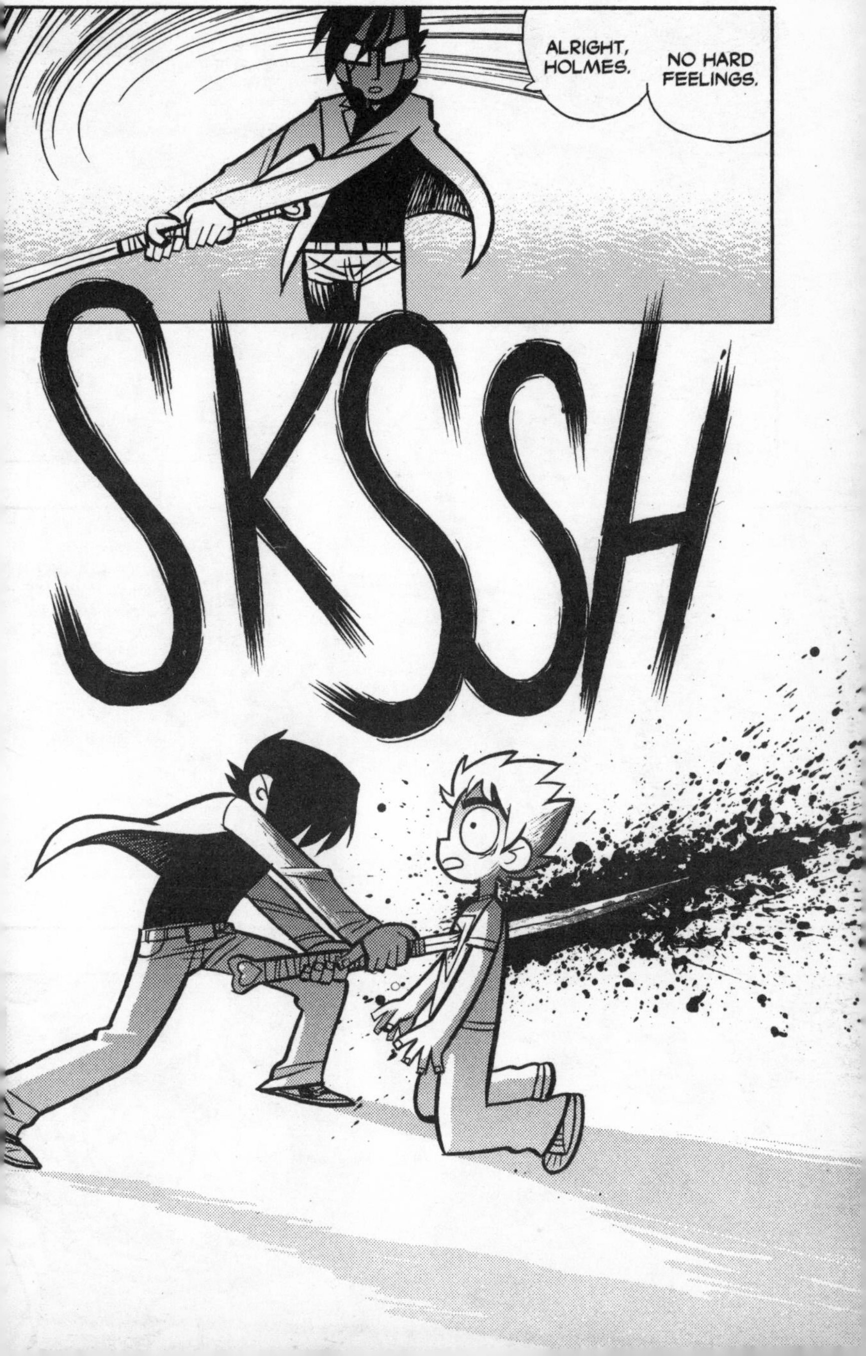
ALRIGHT, HOLMES.
NO HARD FEELINGS.
SKSSH

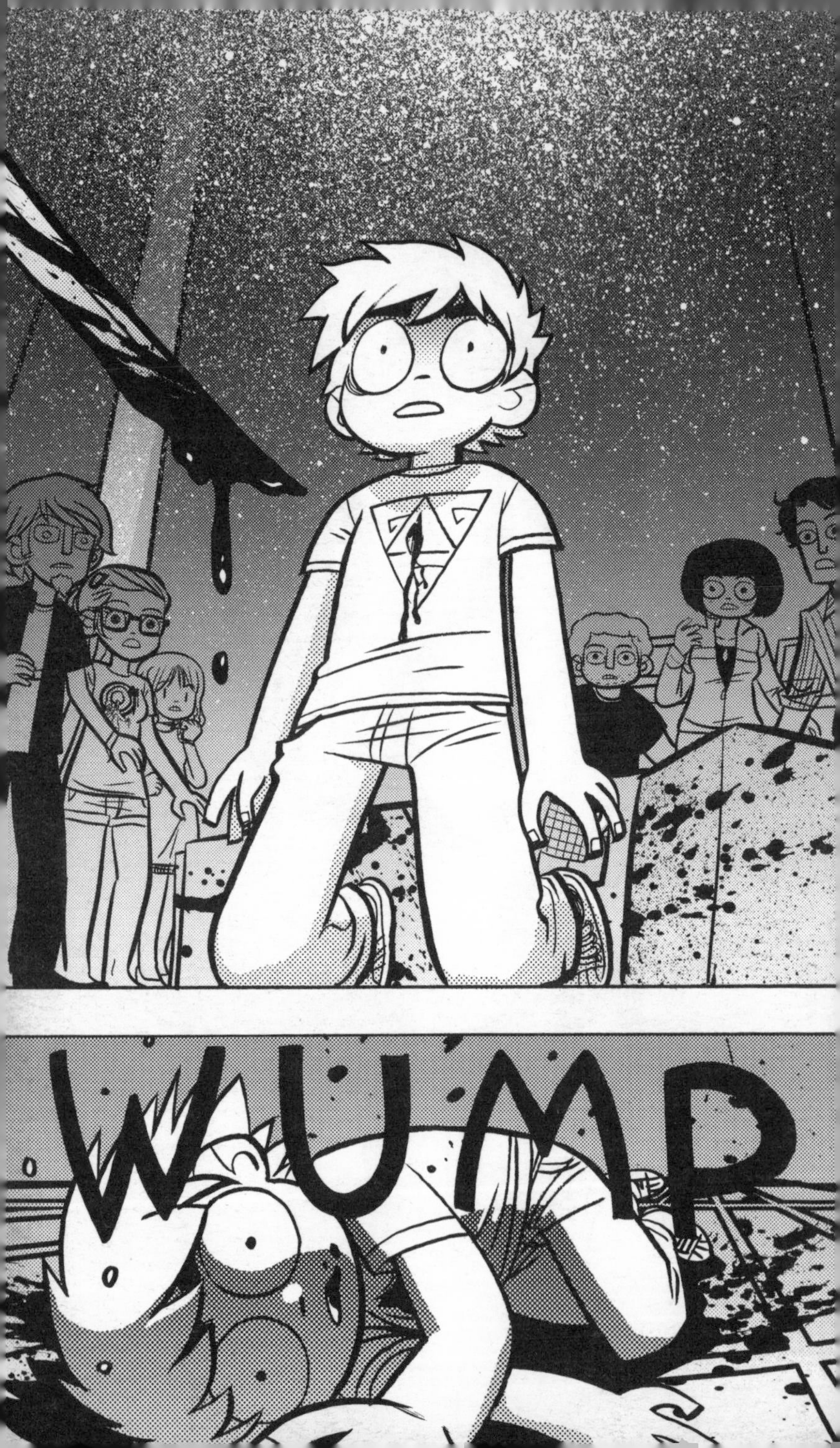
WUMP

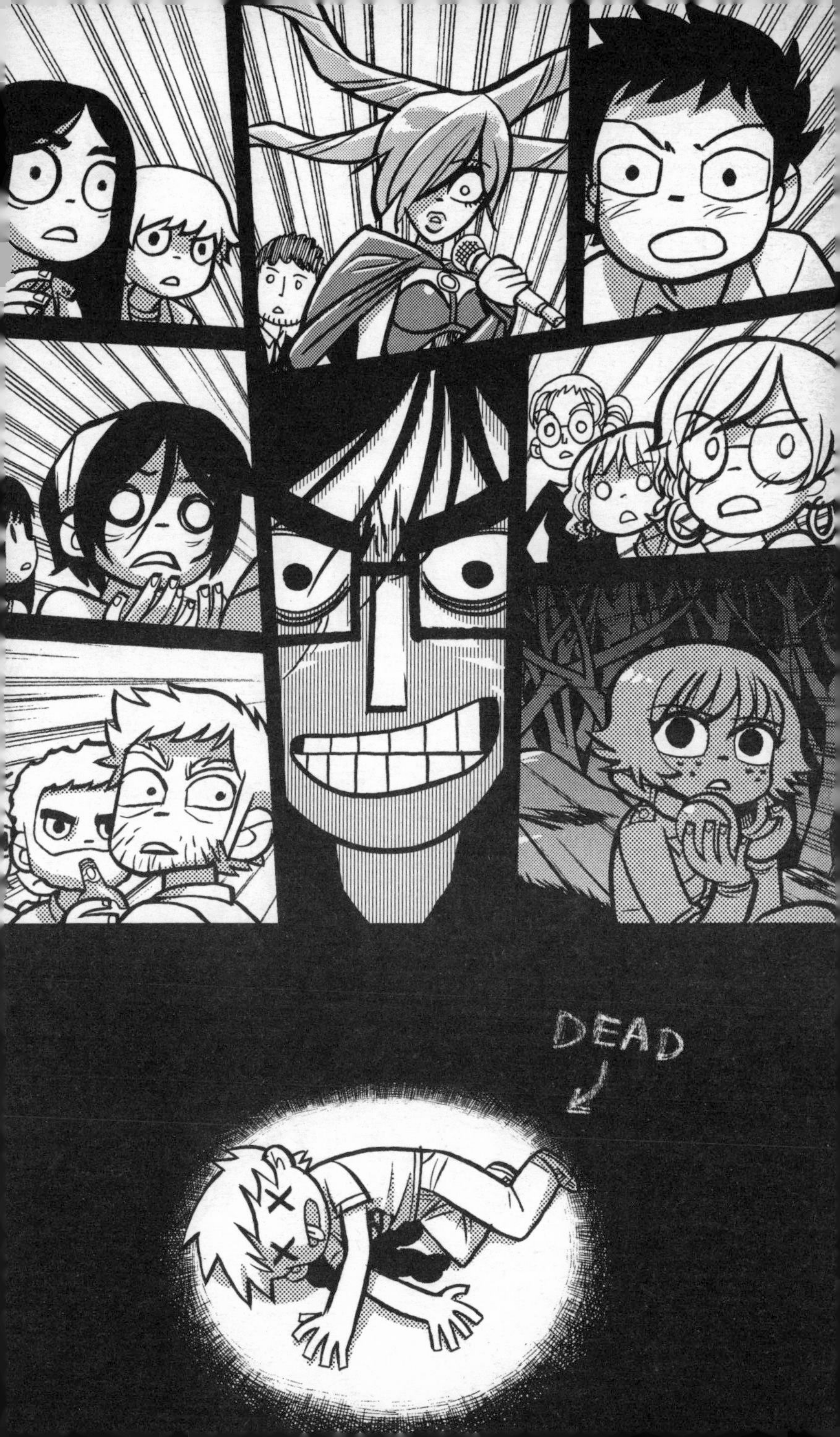
DEAD

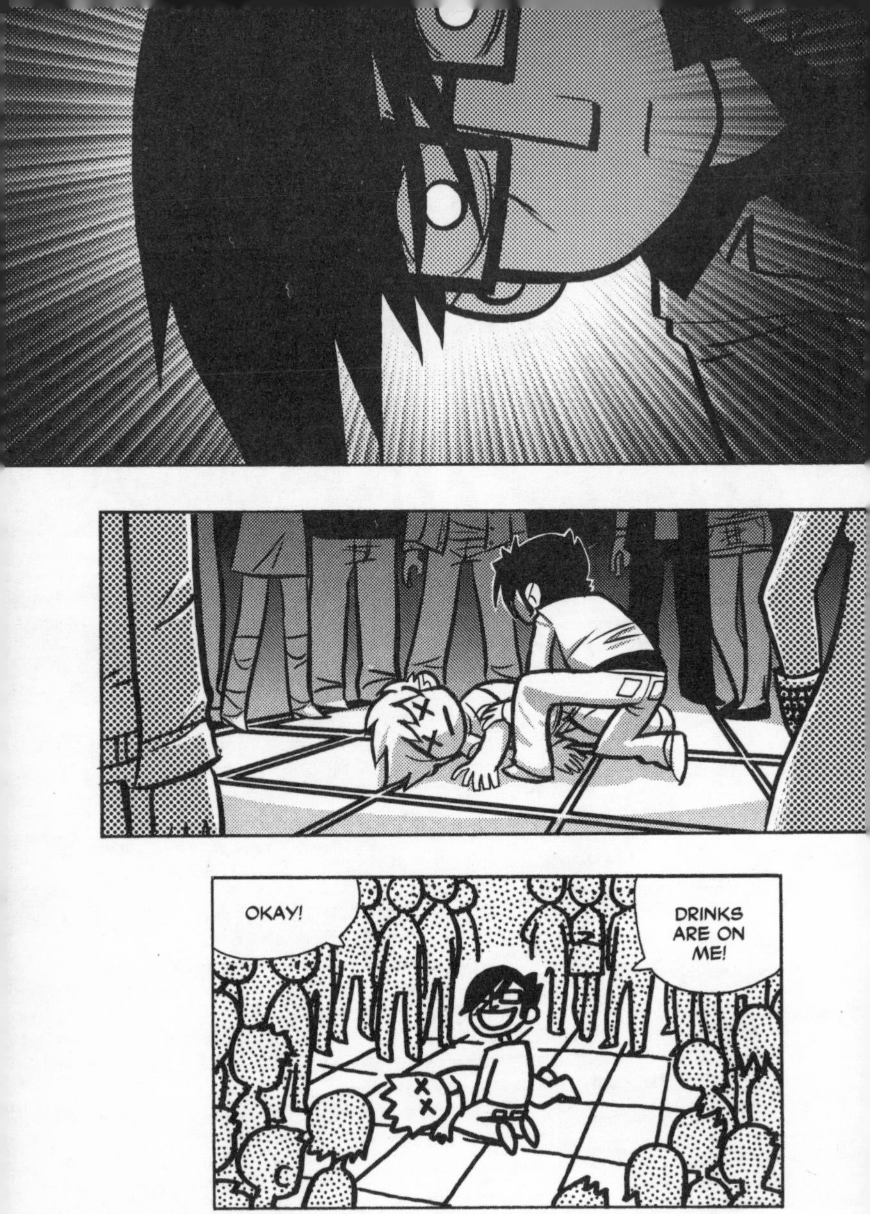
OKAY!
DRINKS ARE ON ME!

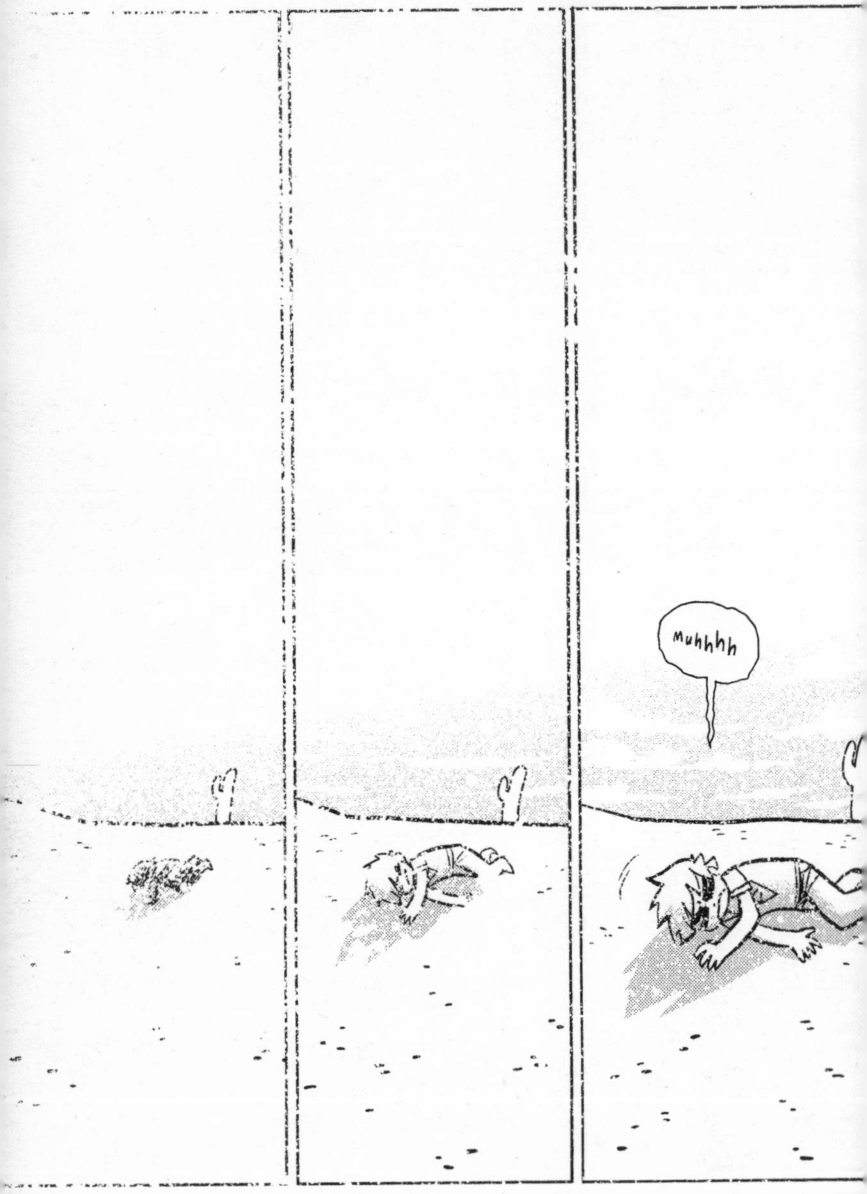
Muhhhh

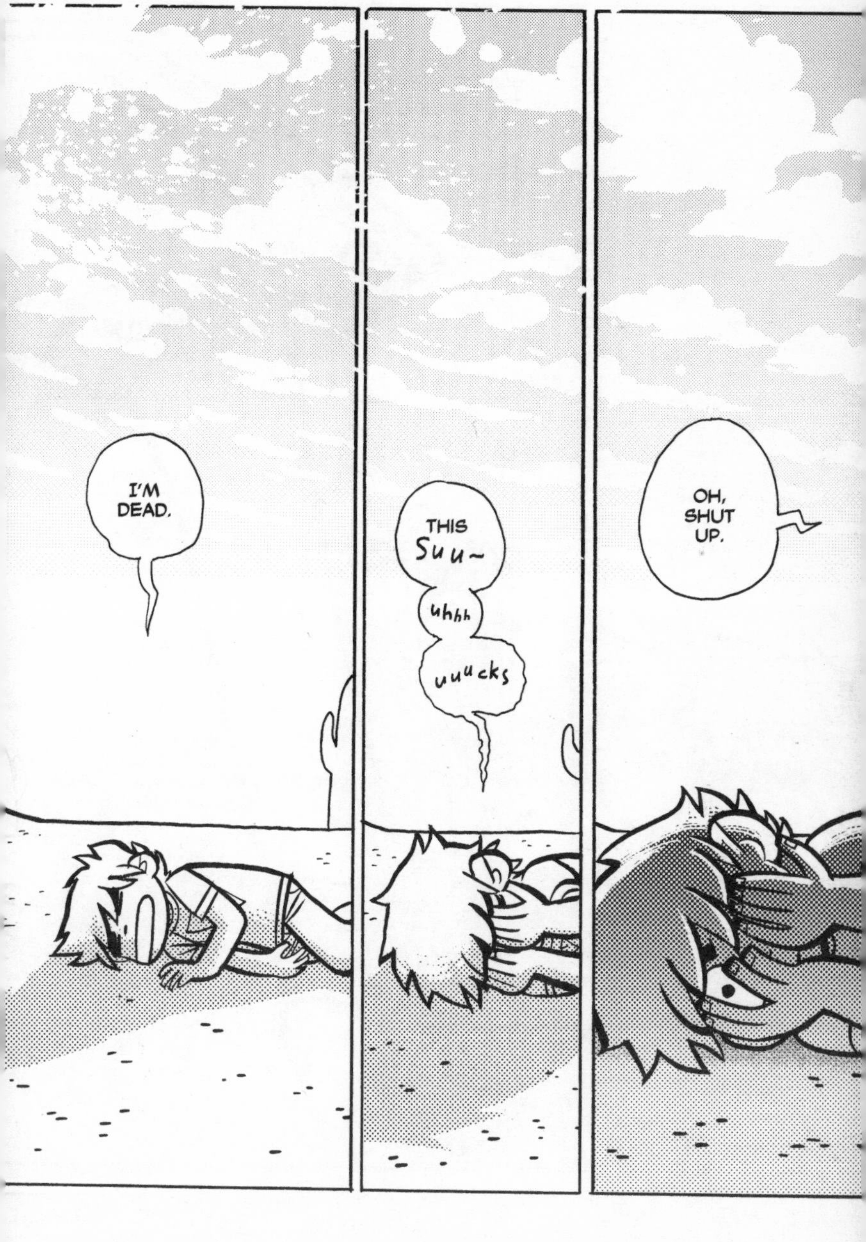
I'M DEAD.
THIS Suu~
uhhh
uuucks
OH, SHUT UP.

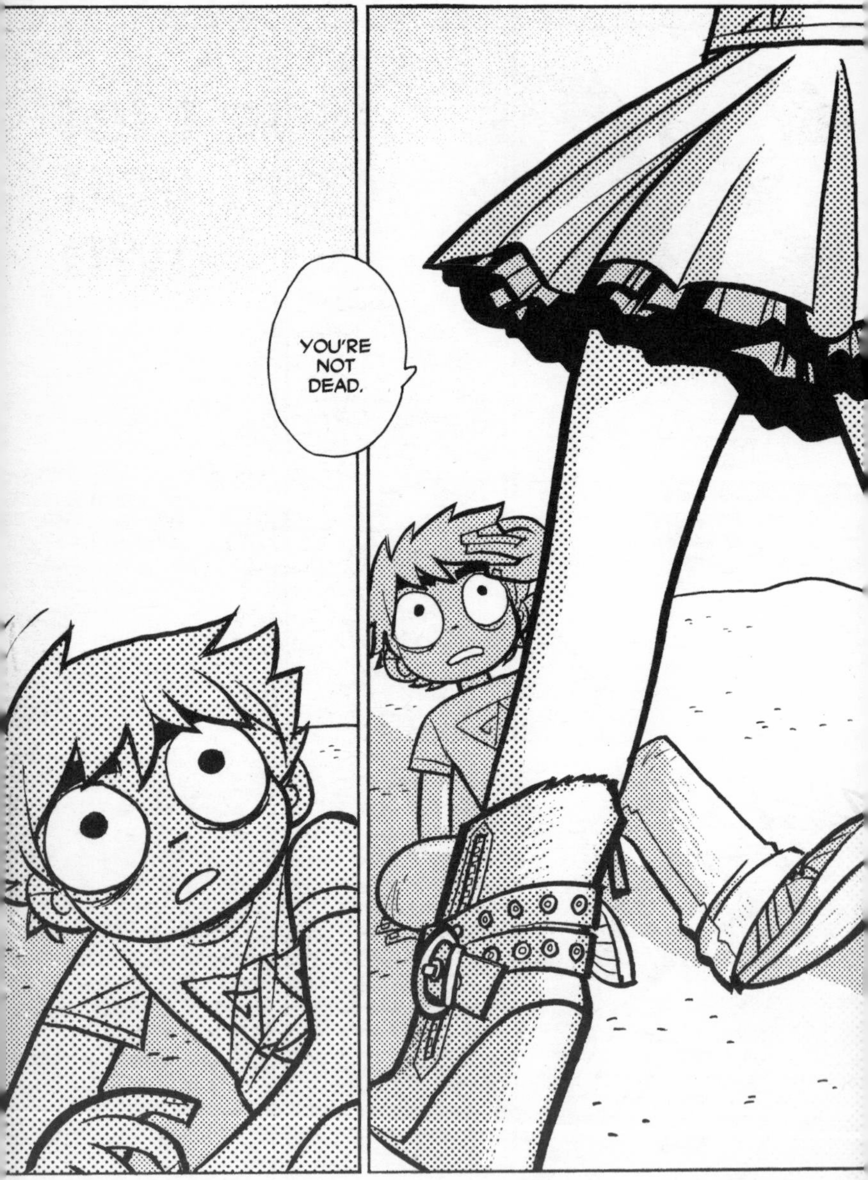
YOU'RE NOT DEAD.

36 Don't let it get you down

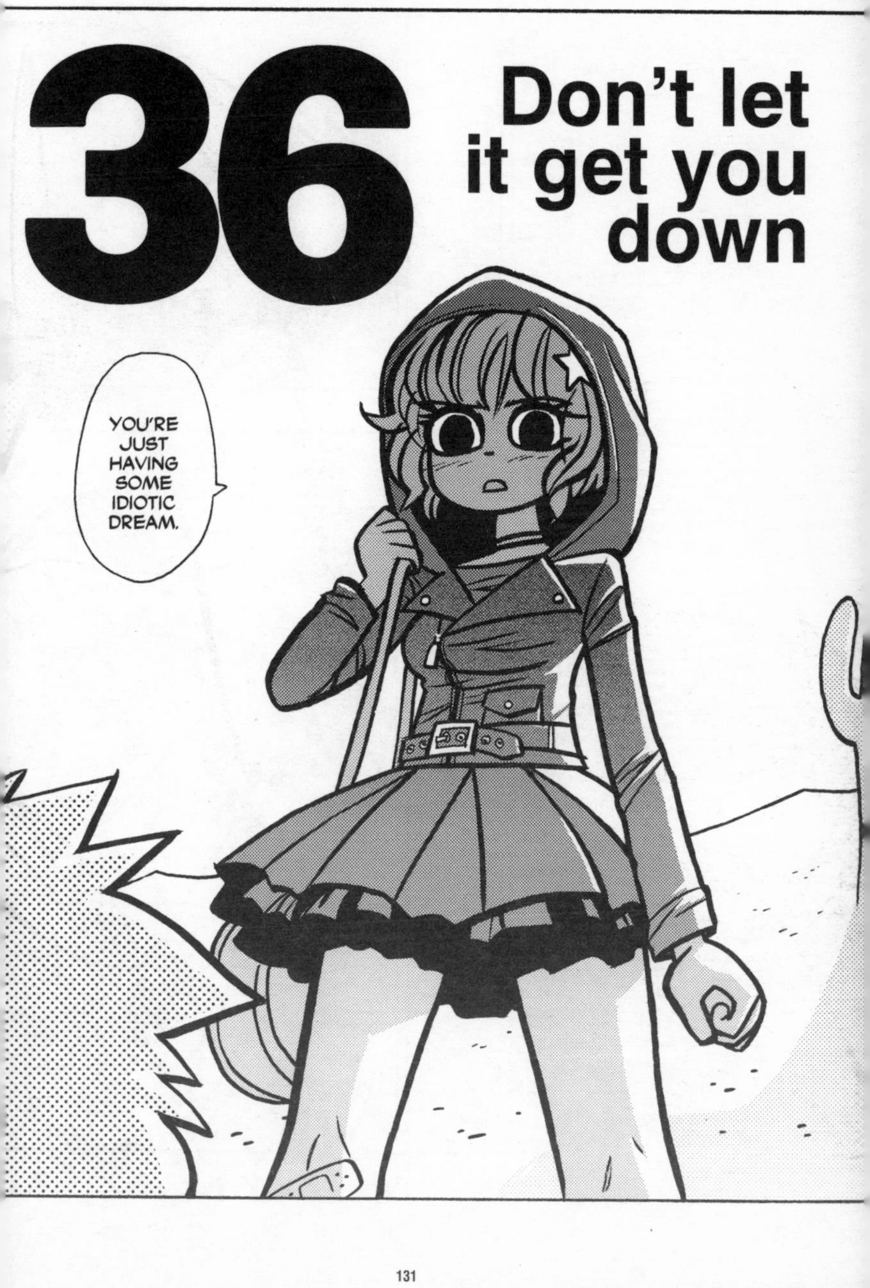

YOU'RE JUST HAVING SOME IDIOTIC DREAM.

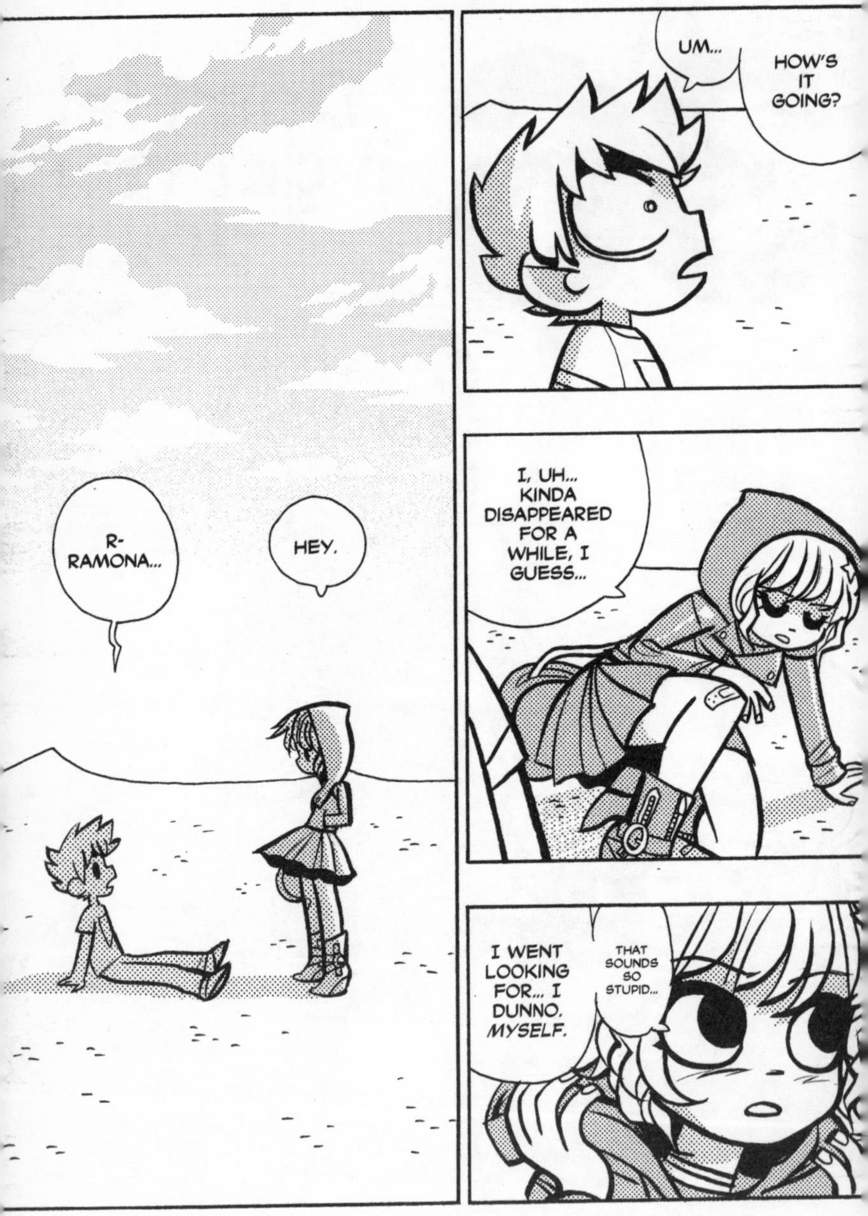
R-RAMONA...
HEY.
UM...
HOW'S IT GOING?
I, UH... KINDA DISAPPEARED FOR A WHILE, I GUESS...
I WENT LOOKING FOR... I DUNNO. *MYSELF.*
THAT SOUNDS SO STUPID...

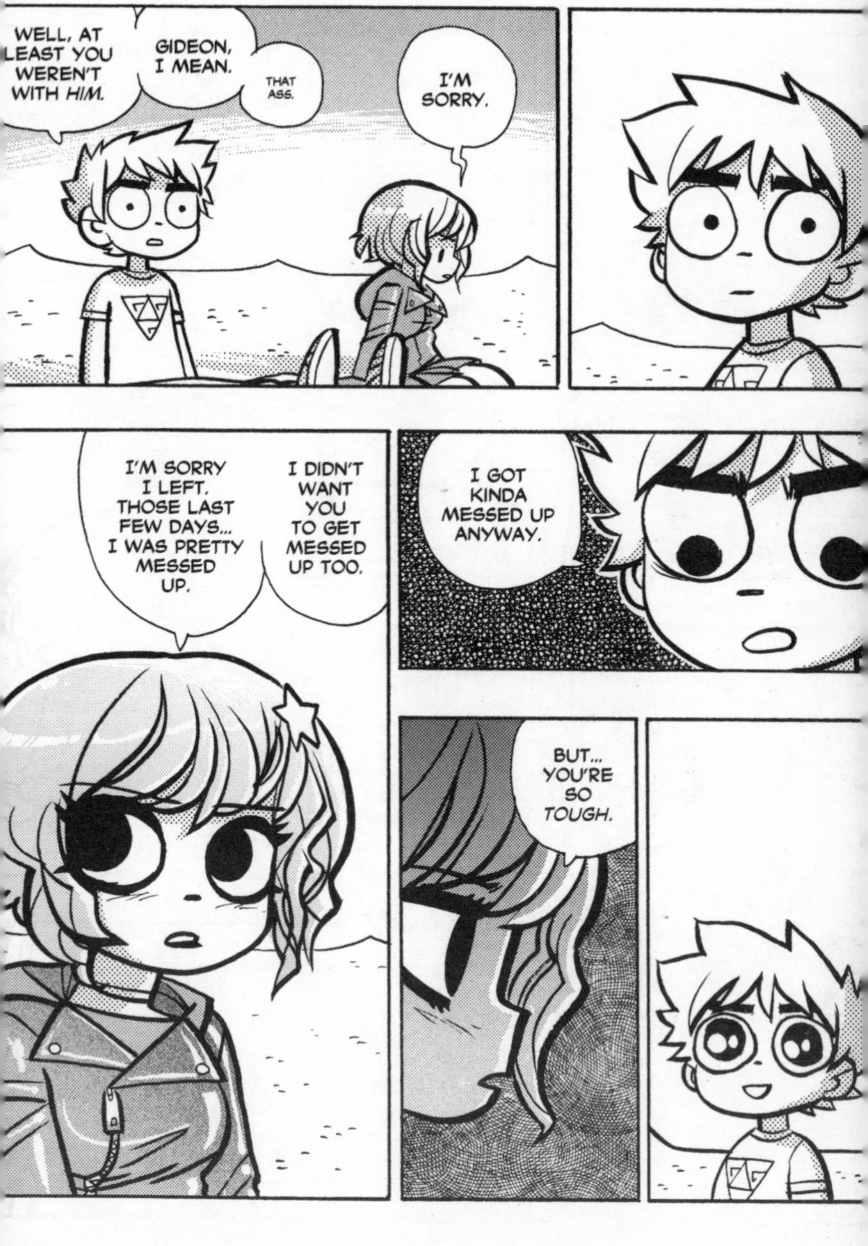
WELL, AT LEAST YOU WEREN'T WITH *HIM*.
GIDEON, I MEAN.
THAT ASS.
I'M SORRY.
I'M SORRY I LEFT. THOSE LAST FEW DAYS... I WAS PRETTY MESSED UP.
I DIDN'T WANT YOU TO GET MESSED UP TOO.
I GOT KINDA MESSED UP ANYWAY.
BUT... YOU'RE SO *TOUGH*.

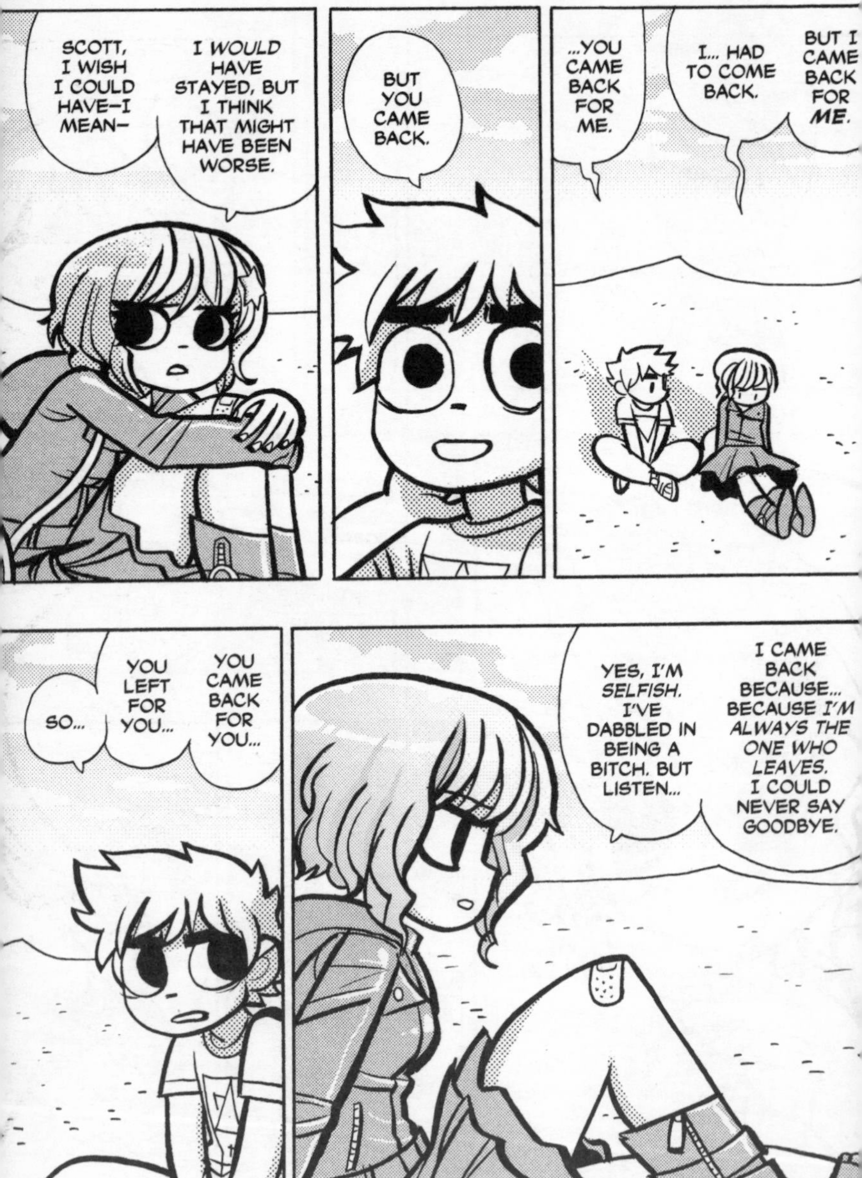
SCOTT, I WISH I COULD HAVE—I MEAN—
I *WOULD* HAVE STAYED, BUT I THINK THAT MIGHT HAVE BEEN WORSE.
BUT YOU CAME BACK.
...YOU CAME BACK FOR ME.
I... HAD TO COME BACK.
BUT I CAME BACK FOR ***ME***.
SO...
YOU LEFT FOR YOU...
YOU CAME BACK FOR YOU...
YES, I'M *SELFISH.* I'VE DABBLED IN BEING A BITCH. BUT LISTEN...
I CAME BACK BECAUSE... BECAUSE *I'M ALWAYS THE ONE WHO LEAVES.* I COULD NEVER SAY GOODBYE.

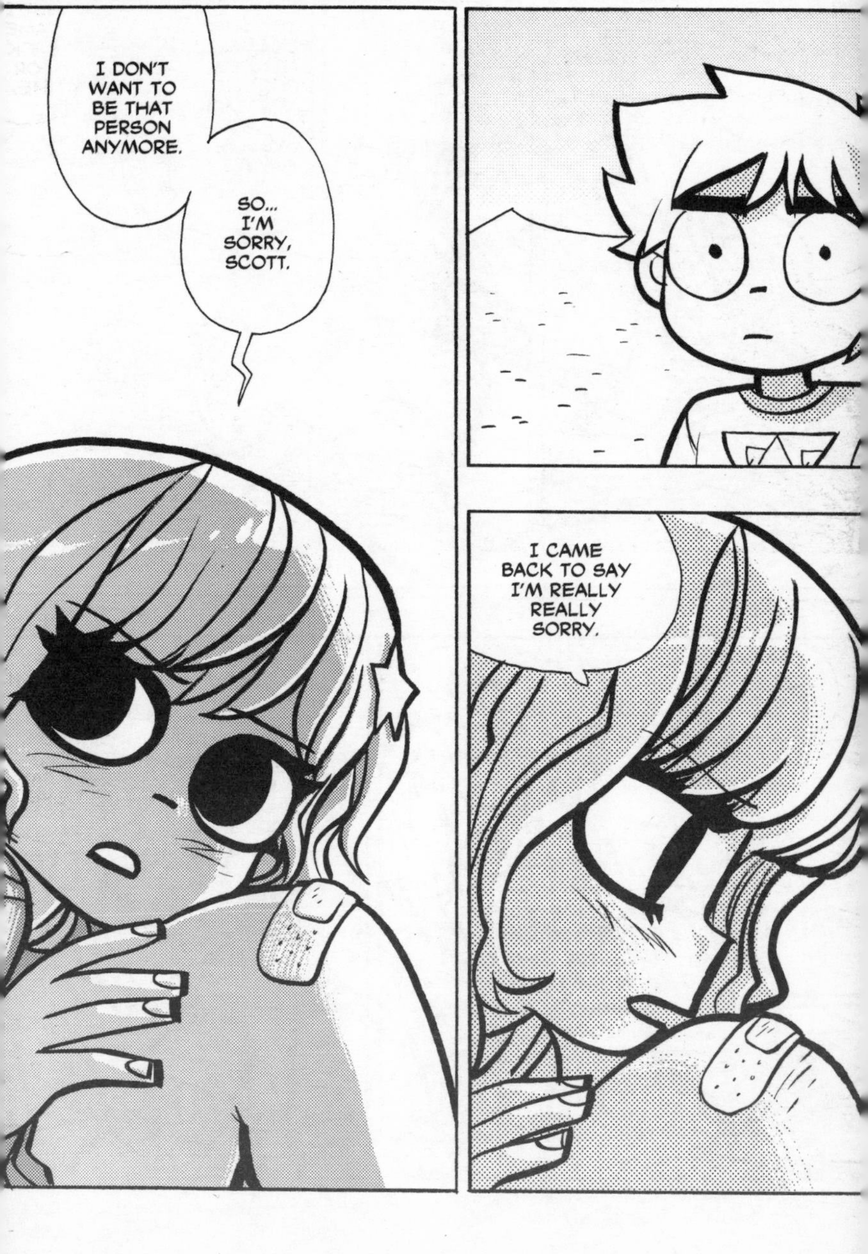
I DON'T WANT TO BE THAT PERSON ANYMORE.
SO... I'M SORRY, SCOTT.
I CAME BACK TO SAY I'M REALLY REALLY SORRY.

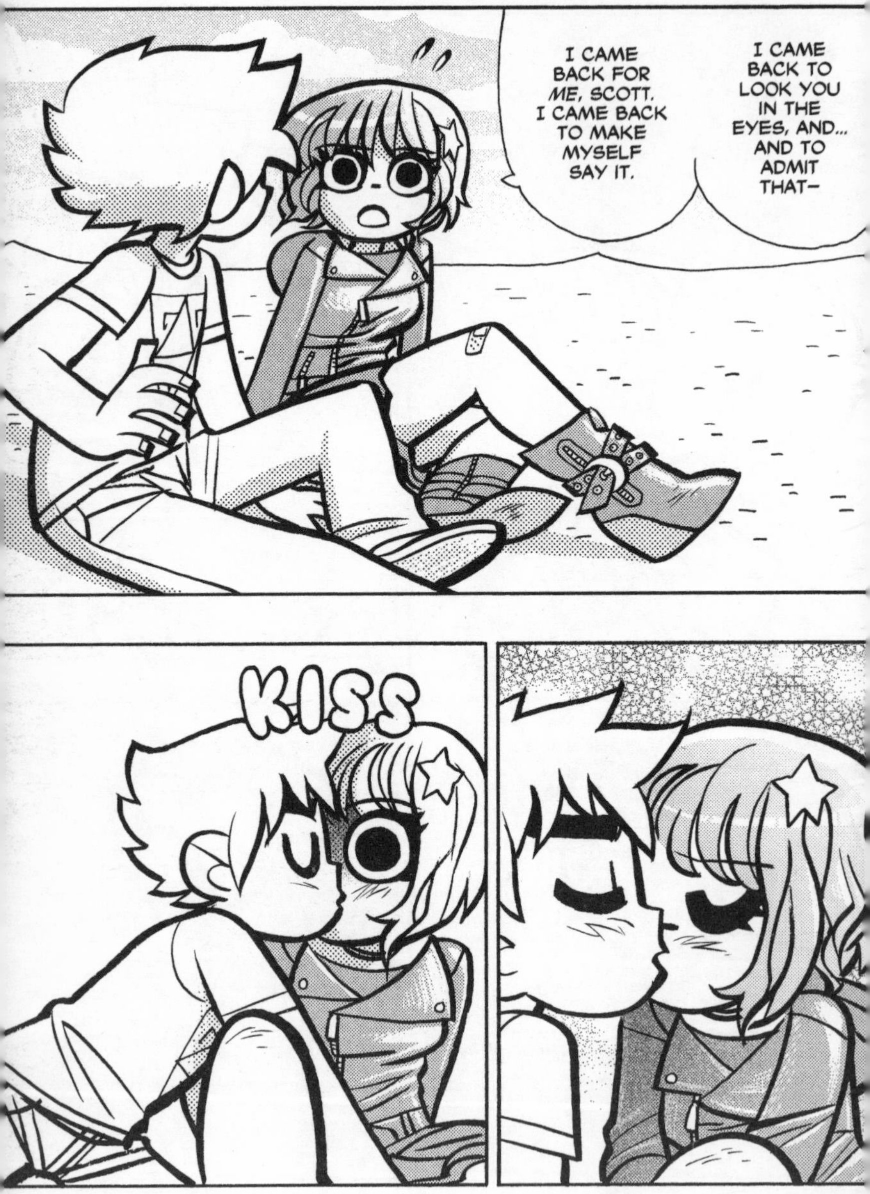
I CAME BACK FOR *ME*, SCOTT. I CAME BACK TO MAKE MYSELF SAY IT.
I CAME BACK TO LOOK YOU IN THE EYES, AND... AND TO ADMIT THAT–
KISS

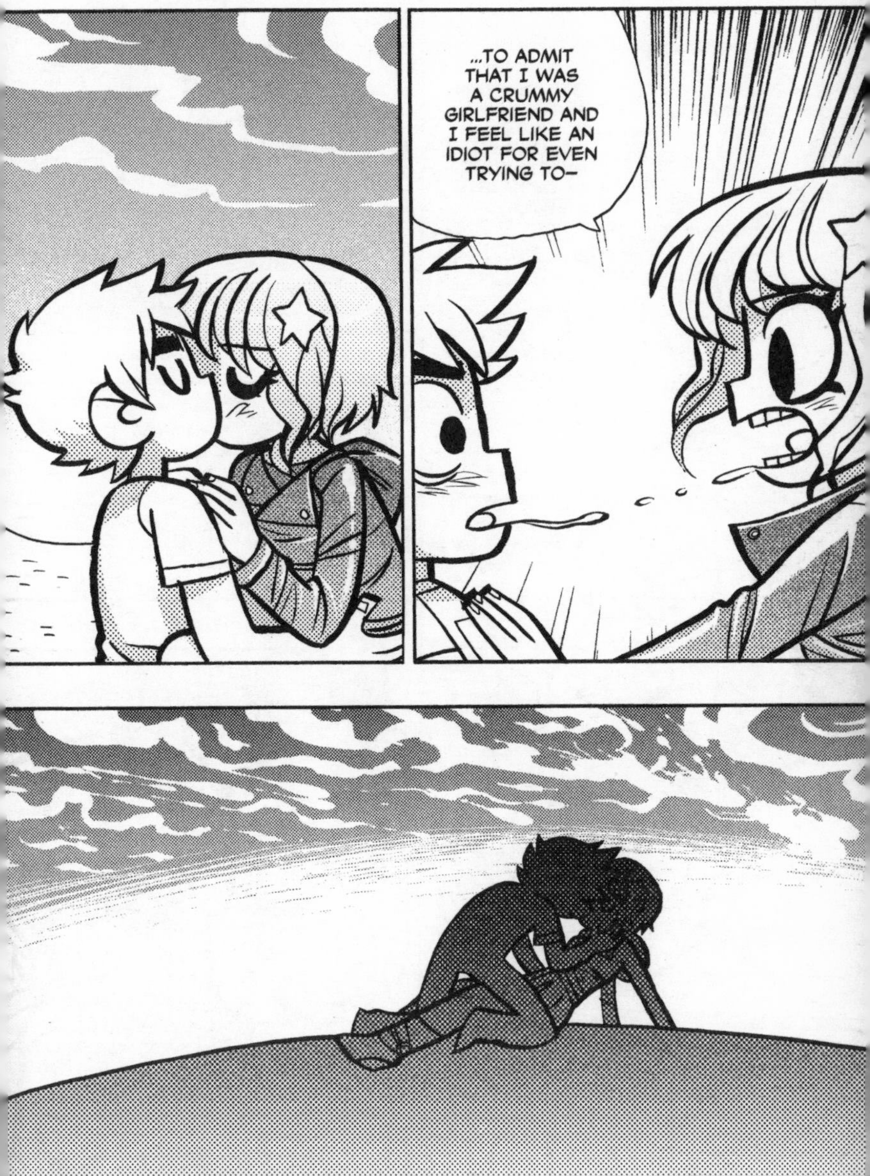
...TO ADMIT THAT I WAS A CRUMMY GIRLFRIEND AND I FEEL LIKE AN IDIOT FOR EVEN TRYING TO—

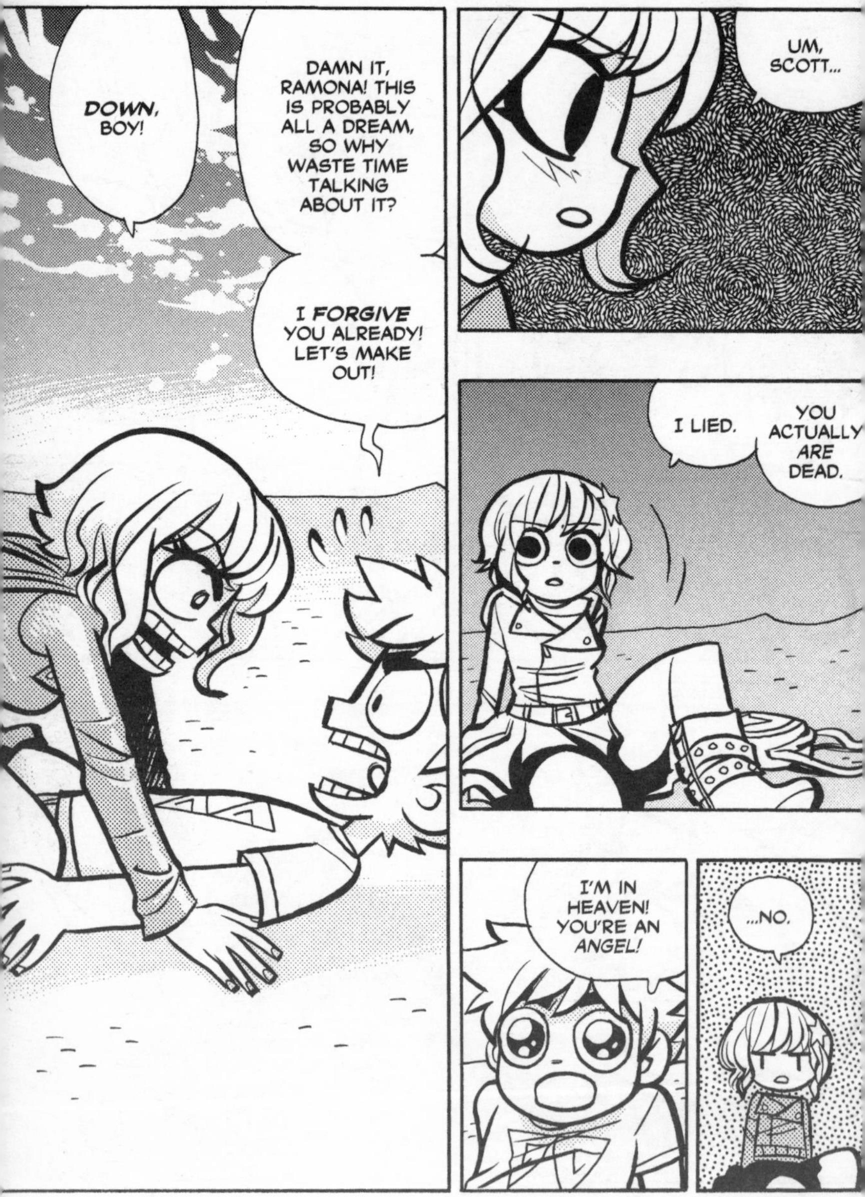
DOWN, BOY!
DAMN IT, RAMONA! THIS IS PROBABLY ALL A DREAM, SO WHY WASTE TIME TALKING ABOUT IT?
I FORGIVE YOU ALREADY! LET'S MAKE OUT!
UM, SCOTT...
I LIED.
YOU ACTUALLY ARE DEAD.
I'M IN HEAVEN! YOU'RE AN ANGEL!
...NO.

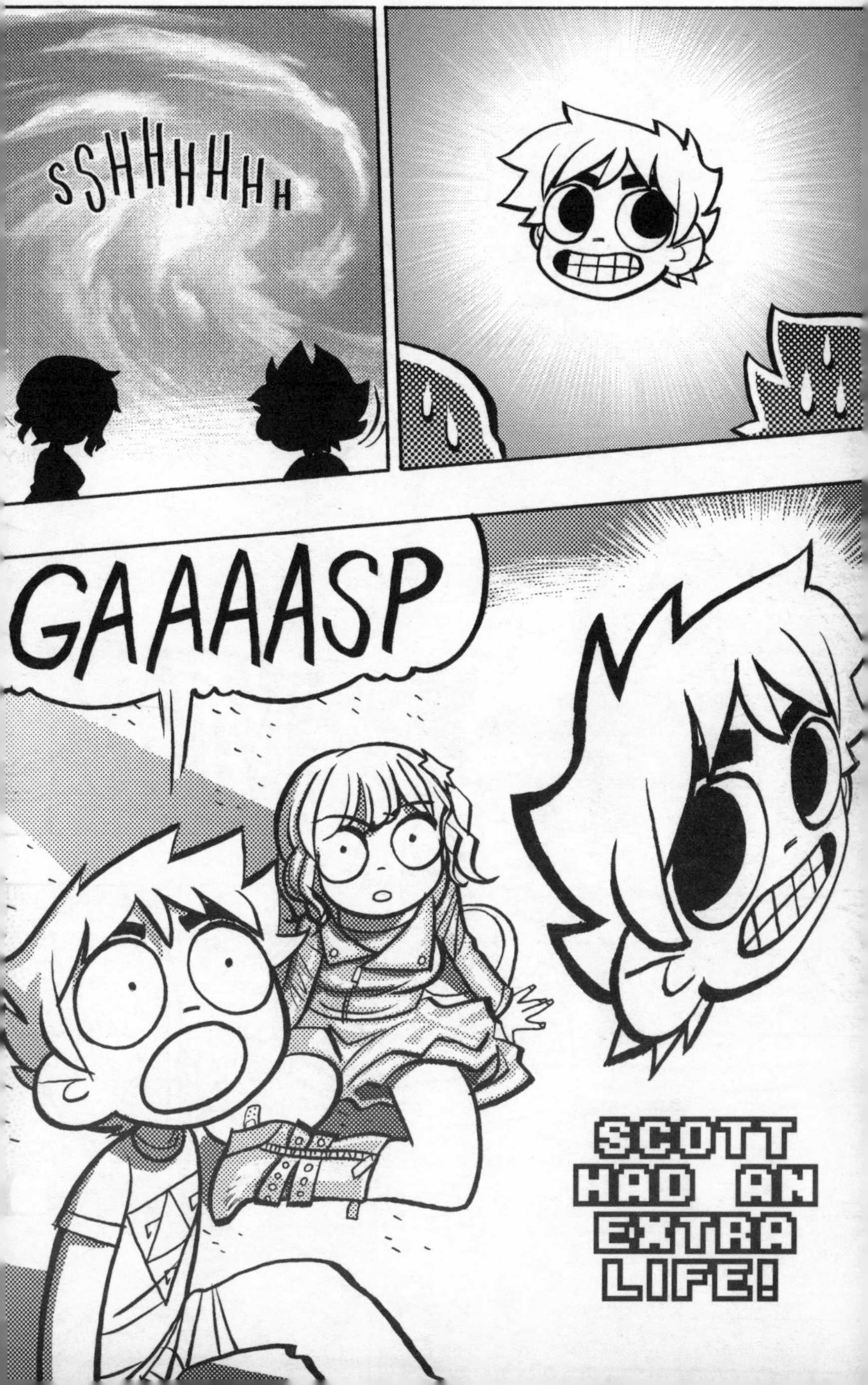
SSHHHHHHH
GAAAASP
SCOTT HAD AN EXTRA LIFE!

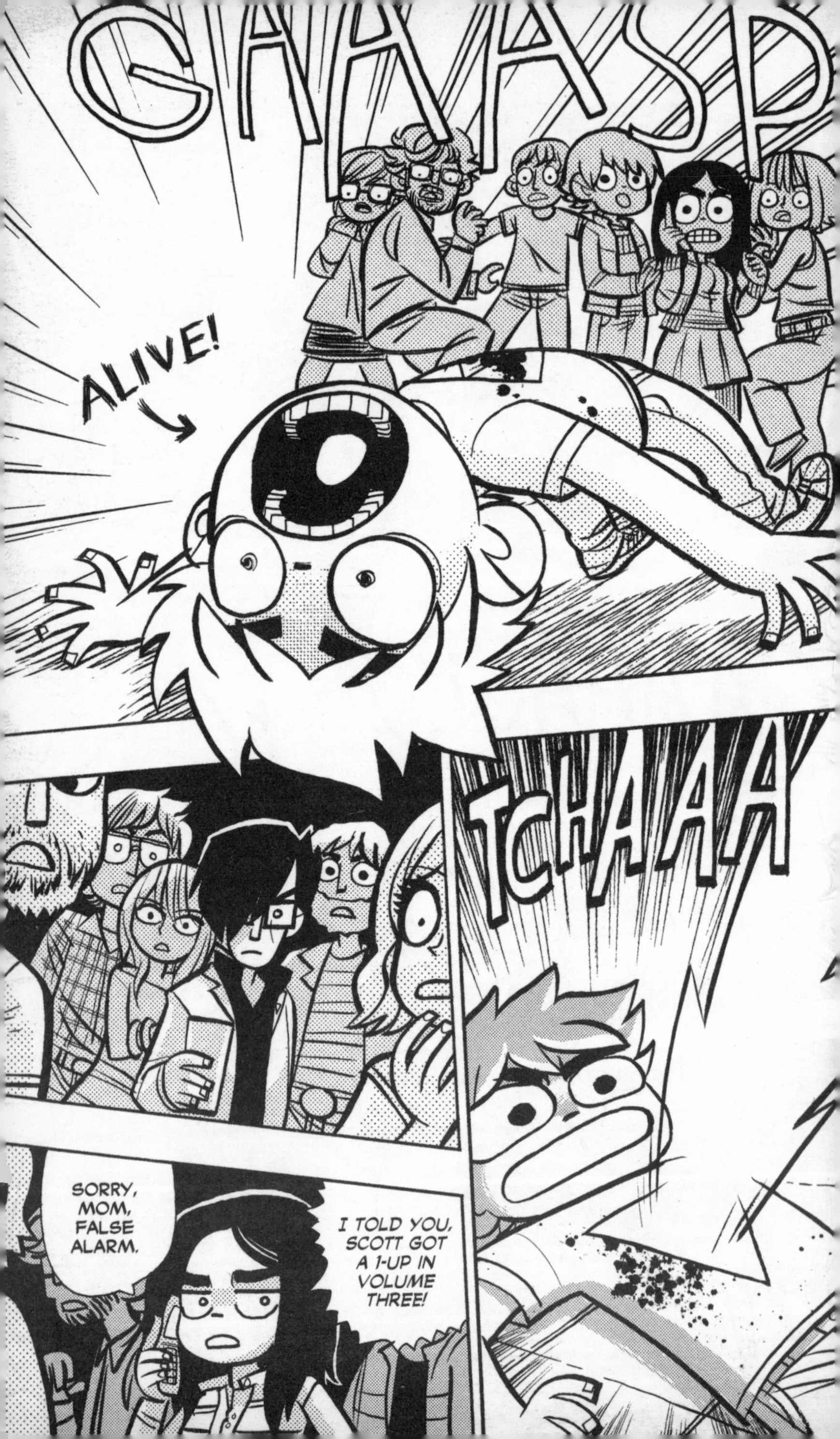
GAASP
ALIVE!
TCHAAA
SORRY, MOM, FALSE ALARM.
I TOLD YOU, SCOTT GOT A 1-UP IN VOLUME THREE!

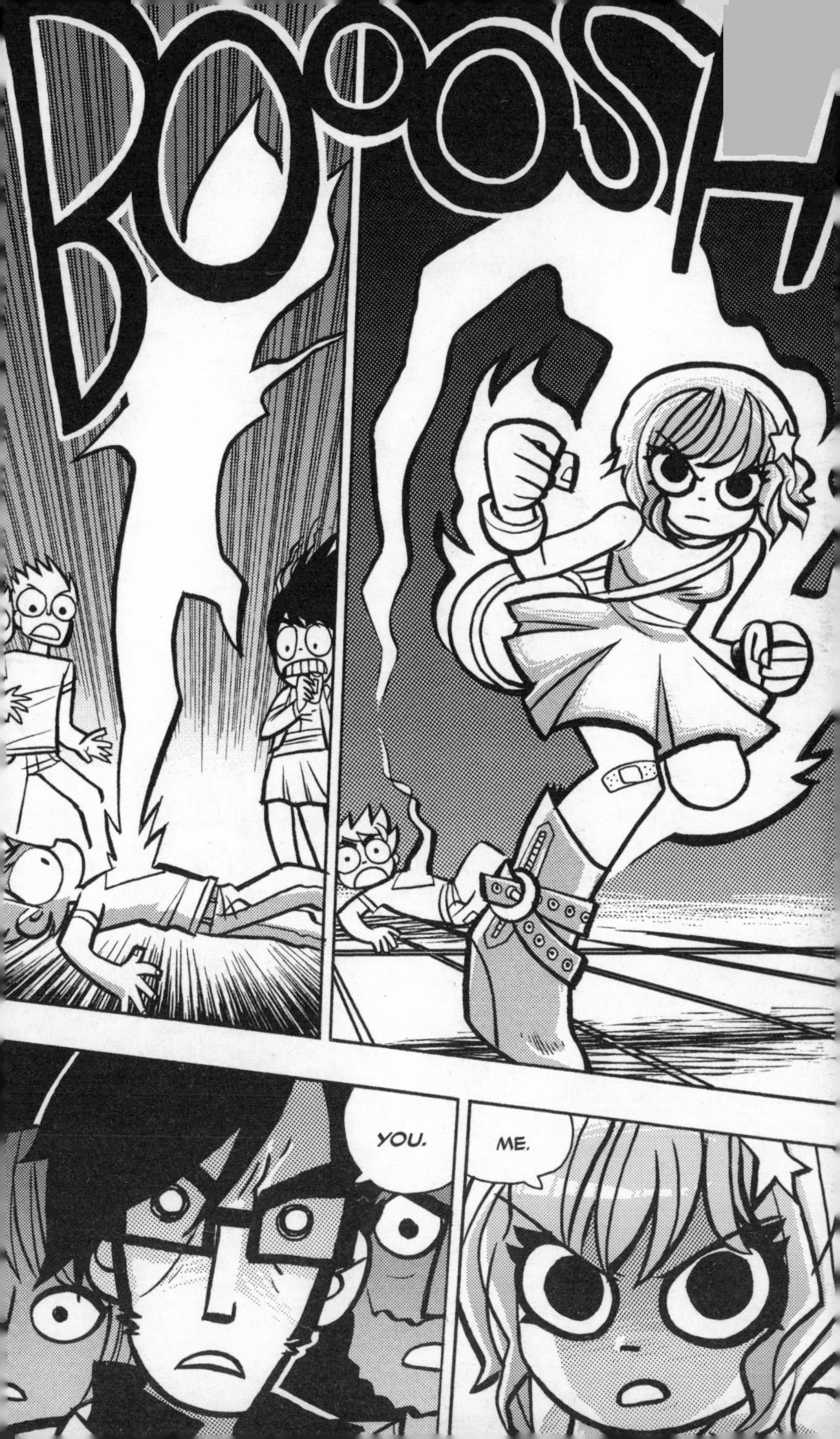
BOOOSH!
YOU.
ME.

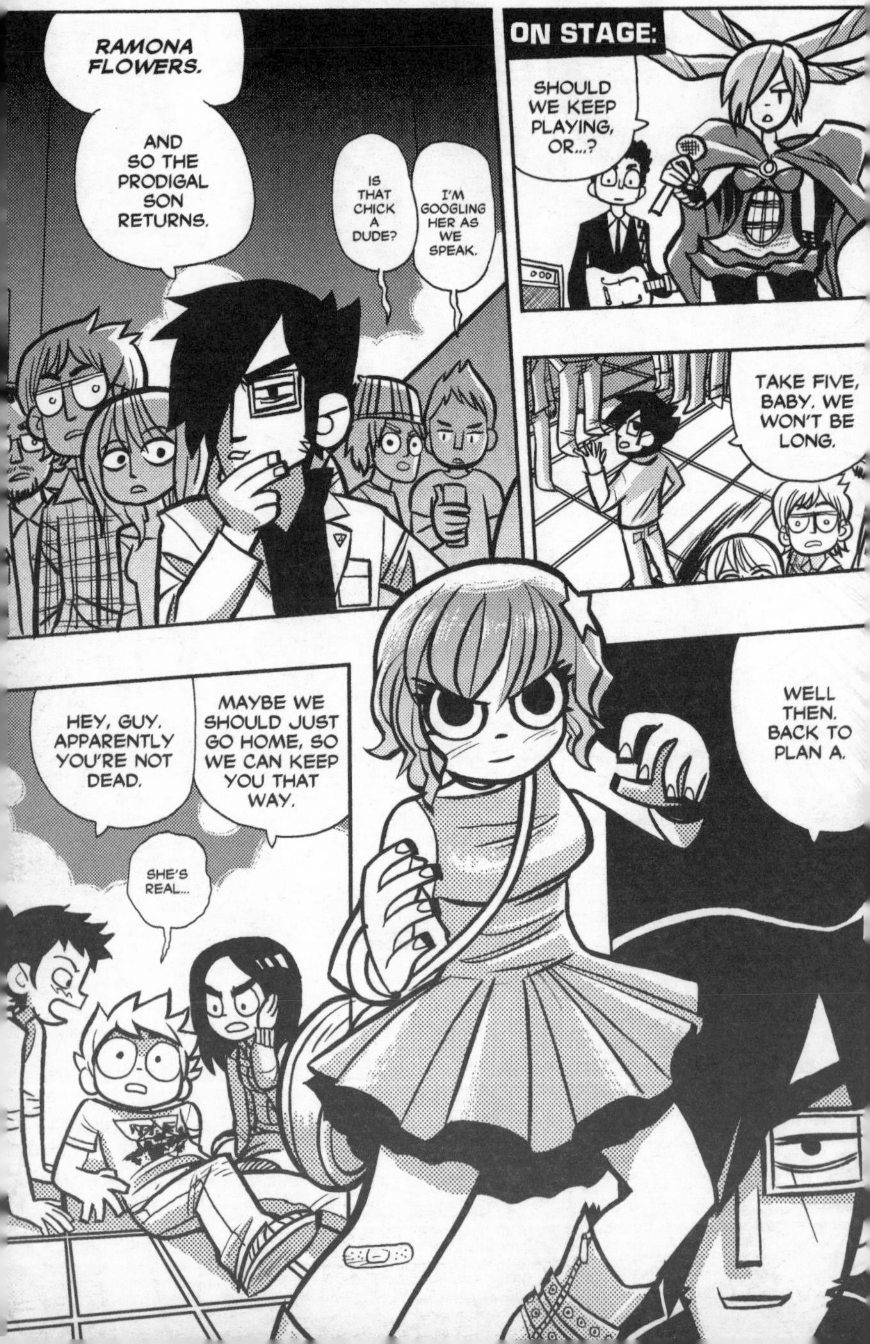
RAMONA FLOWERS.
AND SO THE PRODIGAL SON RETURNS.
IS THAT CHICK A DUDE?
I'M GOOGLING HER AS WE SPEAK.
ON STAGE:
SHOULD WE KEEP PLAYING, OR...?
TAKE FIVE, BABY. WE WON'T BE LONG.
HEY, GUY. APPARENTLY YOU'RE NOT DEAD.
MAYBE WE SHOULD JUST GO HOME, SO WE CAN KEEP YOU THAT WAY.
SHE'S REAL...
WELL THEN. BACK TO PLAN A.

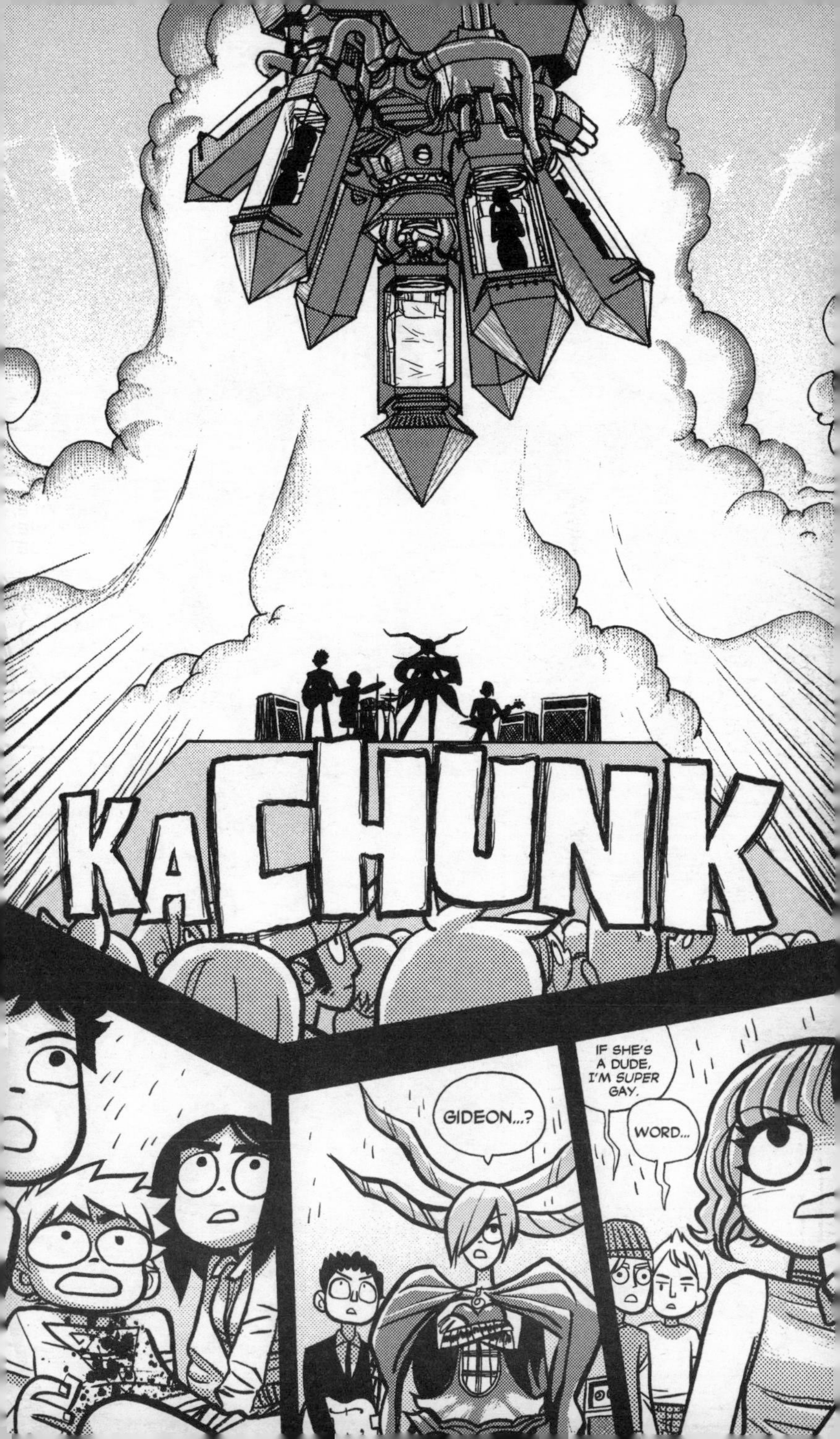
KACHUNK
GIDEON...?
IF SHE'S A DUDE, I'M SUPER GAY.
WORD...

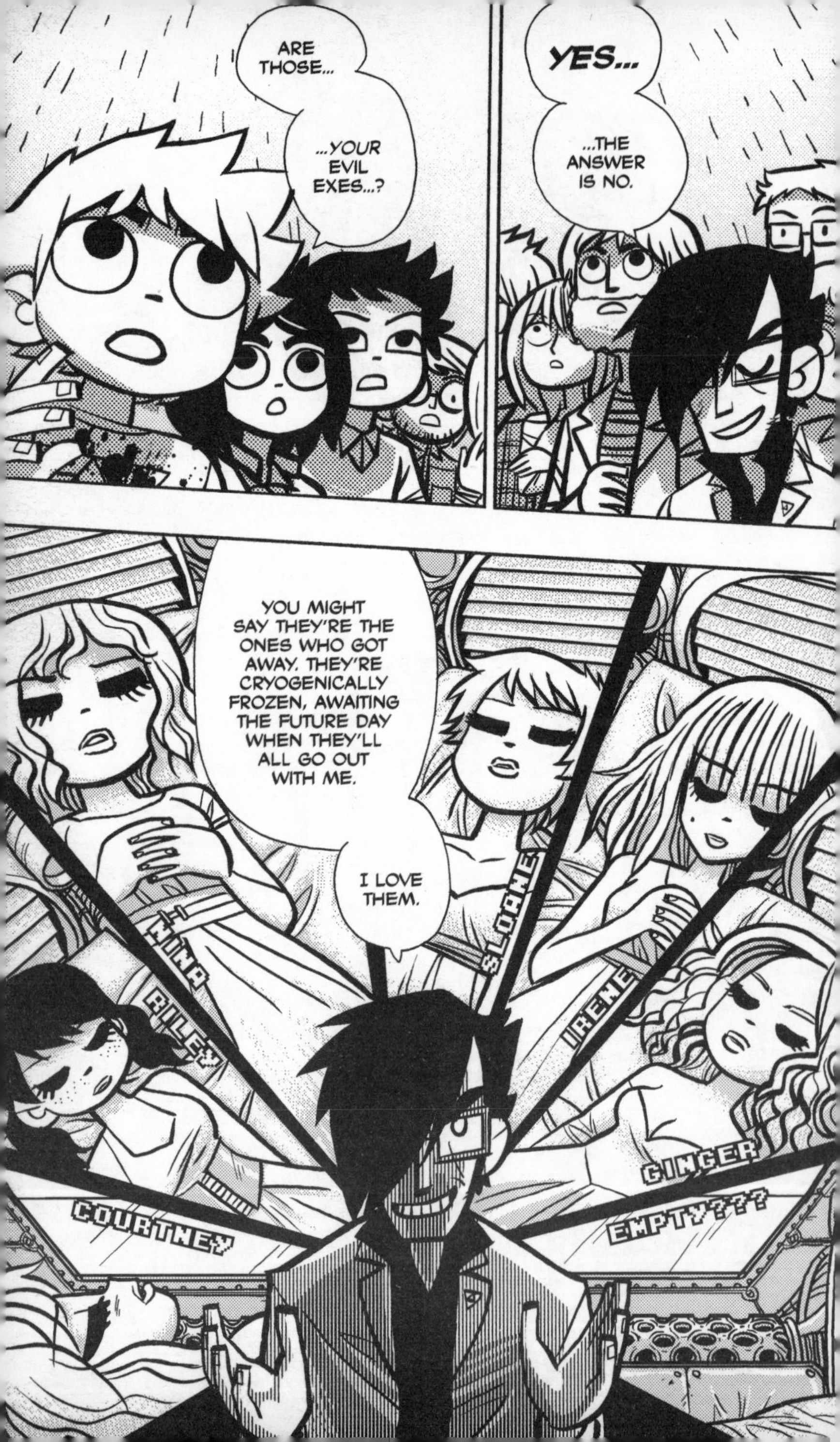
ARE THOSE...
...YOUR EVIL EXES...?
YES...
...THE ANSWER IS NO.
YOU MIGHT SAY THEY'RE THE ONES WHO GOT AWAY. THEY'RE CRYOGENICALLY FROZEN, AWAITING THE FUTURE DAY WHEN THEY'LL ALL GO OUT WITH ME.
I LOVE THEM.
NINA
RILEY
SLOANE
IRENE
GINGER
COURTNEY
EMPTY???

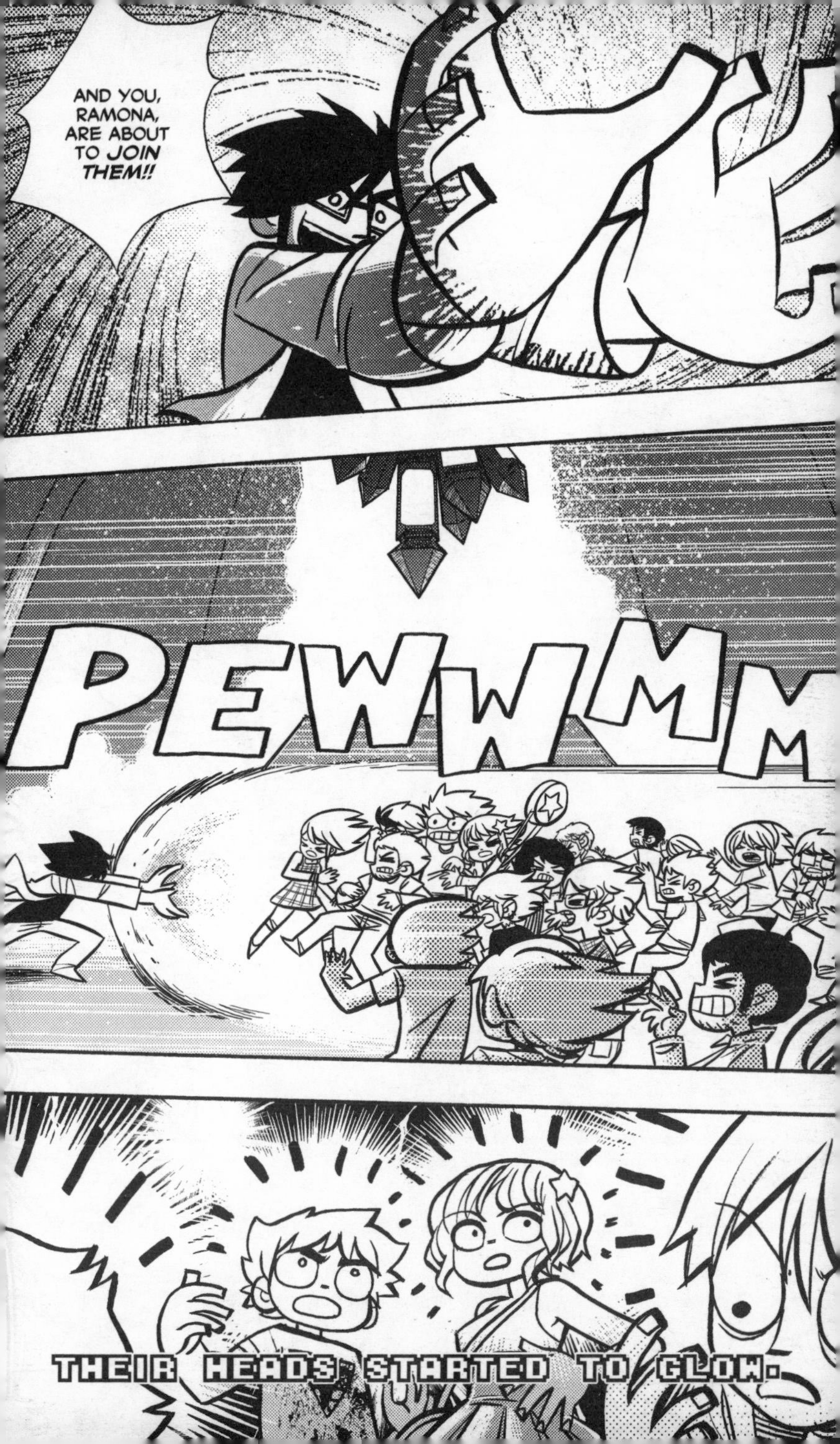
AND YOU, RAMONA, ARE ABOUT TO JOIN THEM!!
PEWWMM
THEIR HEADS STARTED TO GLOW.

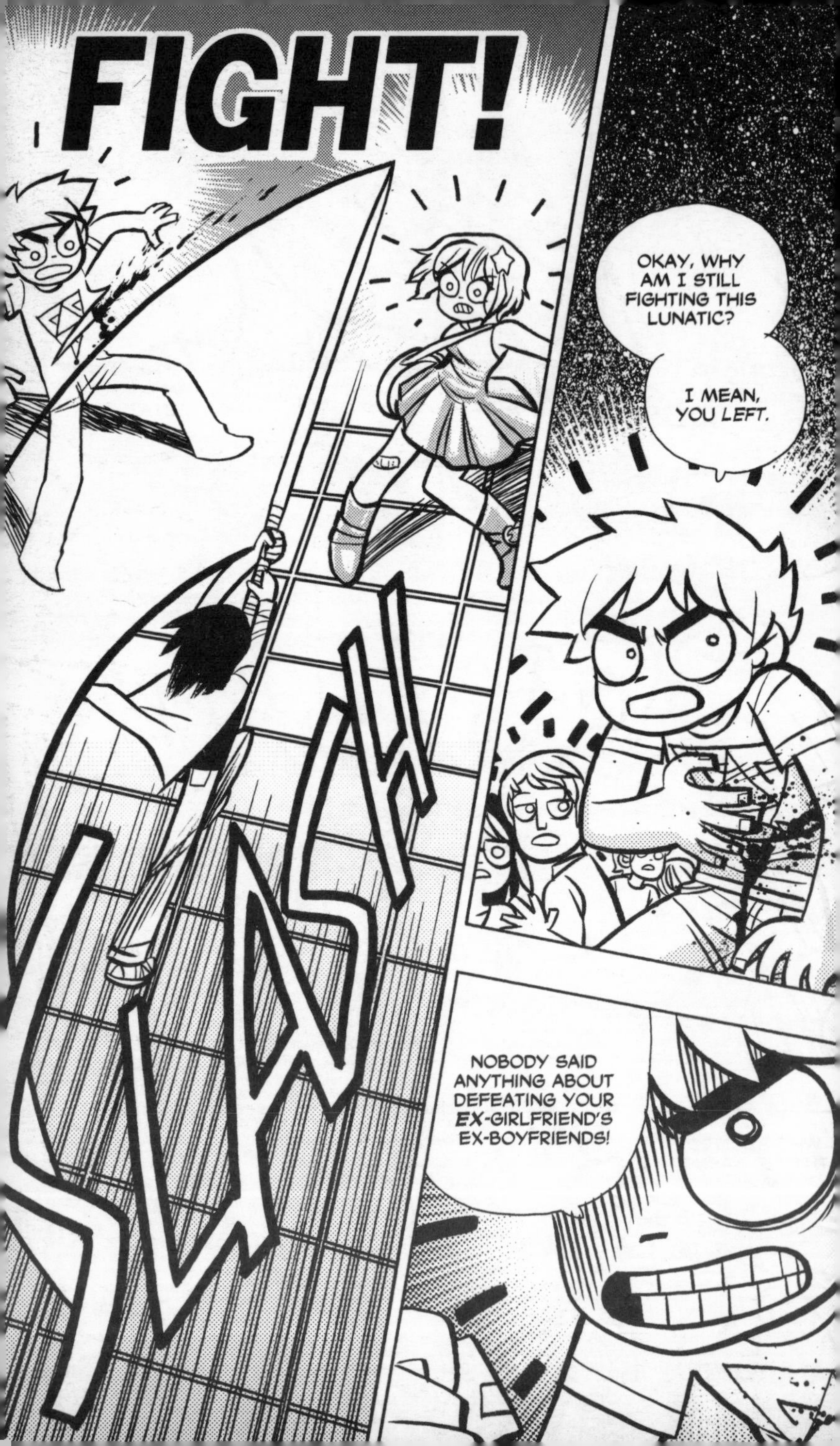
FIGHT!
OKAY, WHY AM I STILL FIGHTING THIS LUNATIC?
I MEAN, YOU *LEFT*.
NOBODY SAID ANYTHING ABOUT DEFEATING YOUR ***EX***-GIRLFRIEND'S EX-BOYFRIENDS!

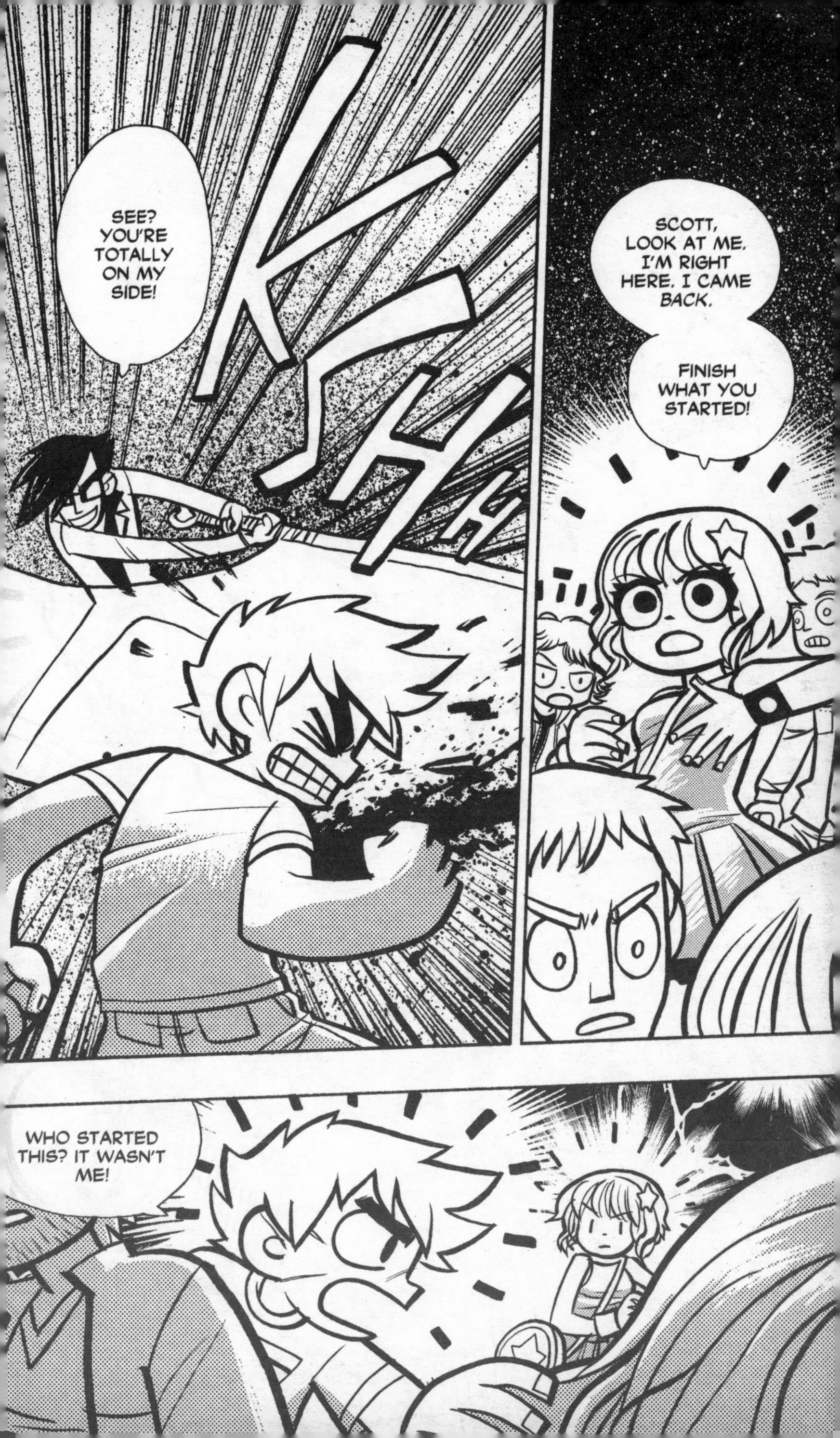
SEE? YOU'RE TOTALLY ON MY SIDE!
KKHHK
SCOTT, LOOK AT ME. I'M RIGHT HERE. I CAME BACK.
FINISH WHAT YOU STARTED!
WHO STARTED THIS? IT WASN'T ME!

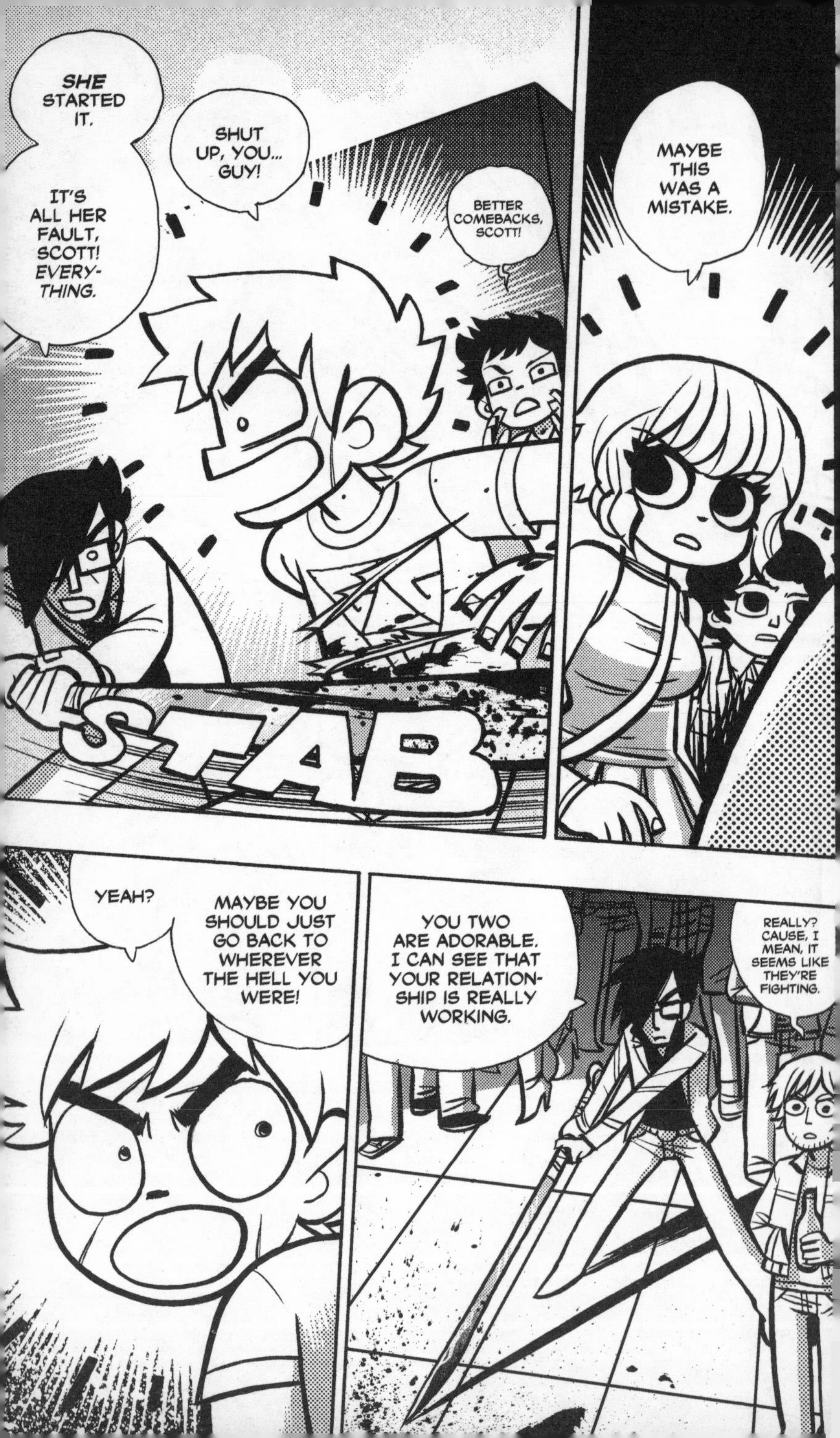
SHE STARTED IT.
IT'S ALL HER FAULT, SCOTT! EVERY-THING.
SHUT UP, YOU... GUY!
BETTER COMEBACKS, SCOTT!
STAB
MAYBE THIS WAS A MISTAKE.
YEAH?
MAYBE YOU SHOULD JUST GO BACK TO WHEREVER THE HELL YOU WERE!
YOU TWO ARE ADORABLE. I CAN SEE THAT YOUR RELATION-SHIP IS REALLY WORKING.
REALLY? CAUSE, I MEAN, IT SEEMS LIKE THEY'RE FIGHTING.

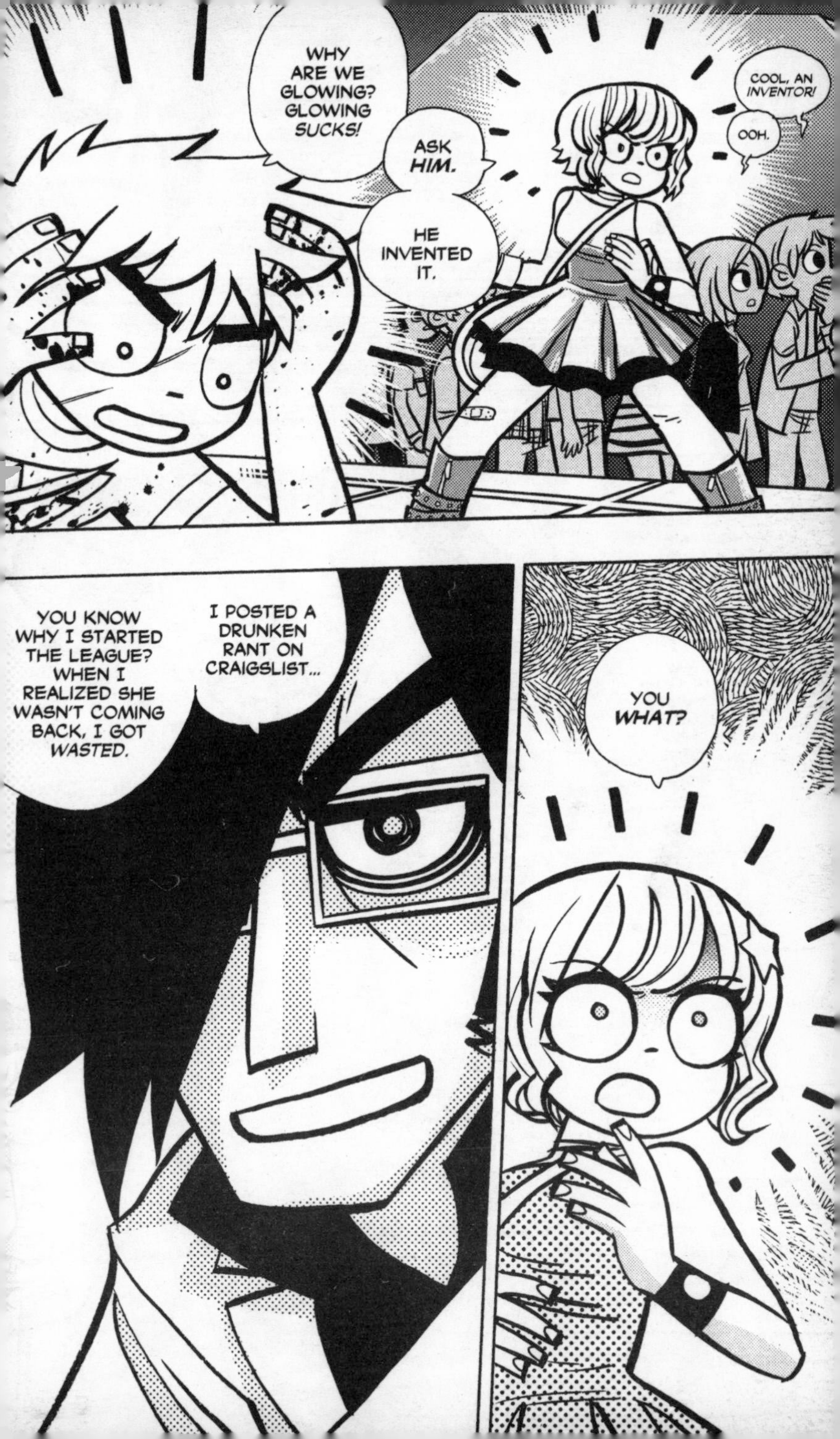
WHY ARE WE GLOWING? GLOWING SUCKS!
ASK HIM.
HE INVENTED IT.
COOL, AN INVENTOR!
OOH.
YOU KNOW WHY I STARTED THE LEAGUE? WHEN I REALIZED SHE WASN'T COMING BACK, I GOT WASTED.
I POSTED A DRUNKEN RANT ON CRAIGSLIST...
YOU WHAT?

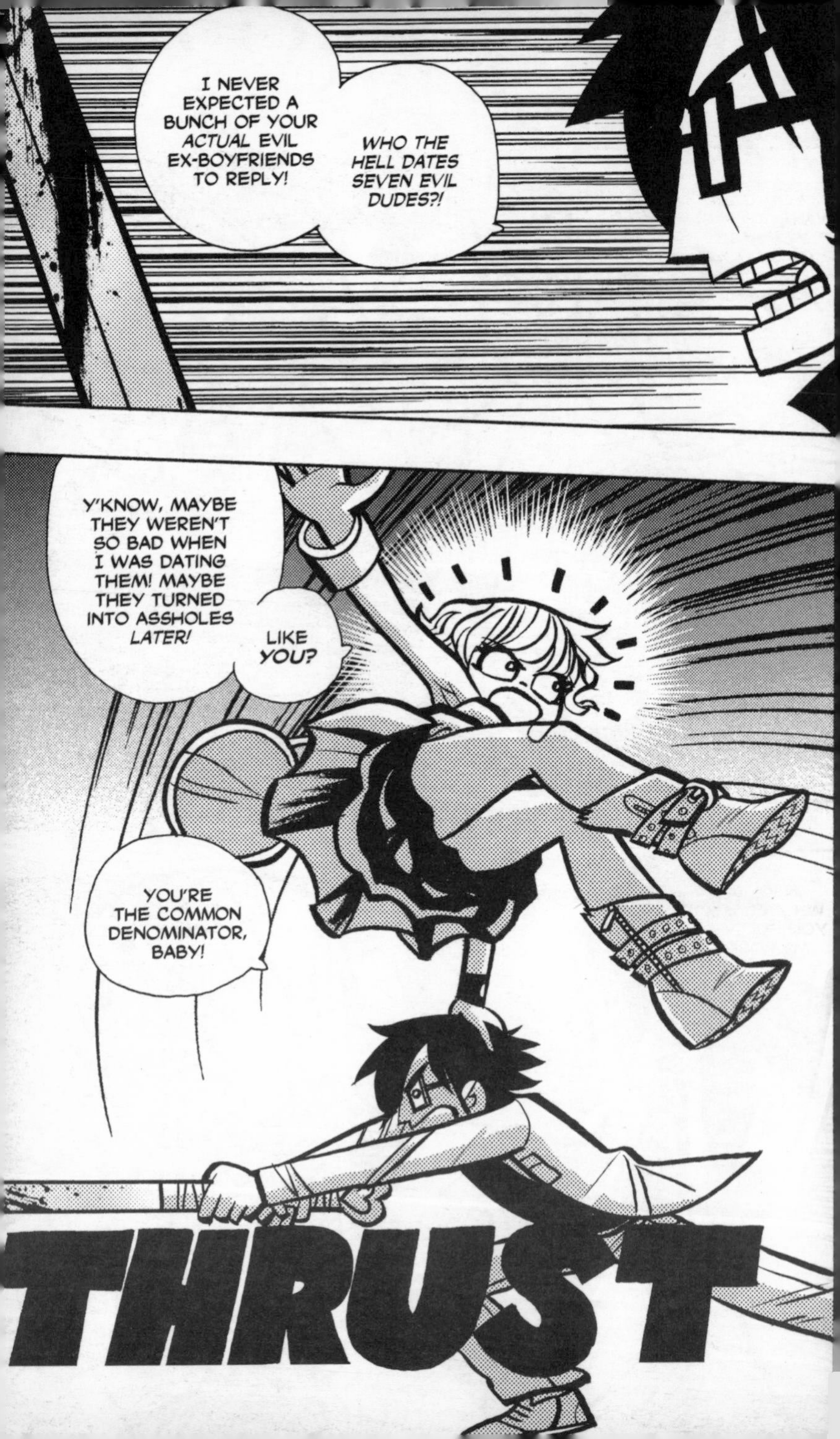
I NEVER EXPECTED A BUNCH OF YOUR *ACTUAL* EVIL EX-BOYFRIENDS TO REPLY!
WHO THE HELL DATES SEVEN EVIL DUDES?!
Y'KNOW, MAYBE THEY WEREN'T SO BAD WHEN I WAS DATING THEM! MAYBE THEY TURNED INTO ASSHOLES *LATER!*
LIKE *YOU?*
YOU'RE THE COMMON DENOMINATOR, BABY!
THRUST

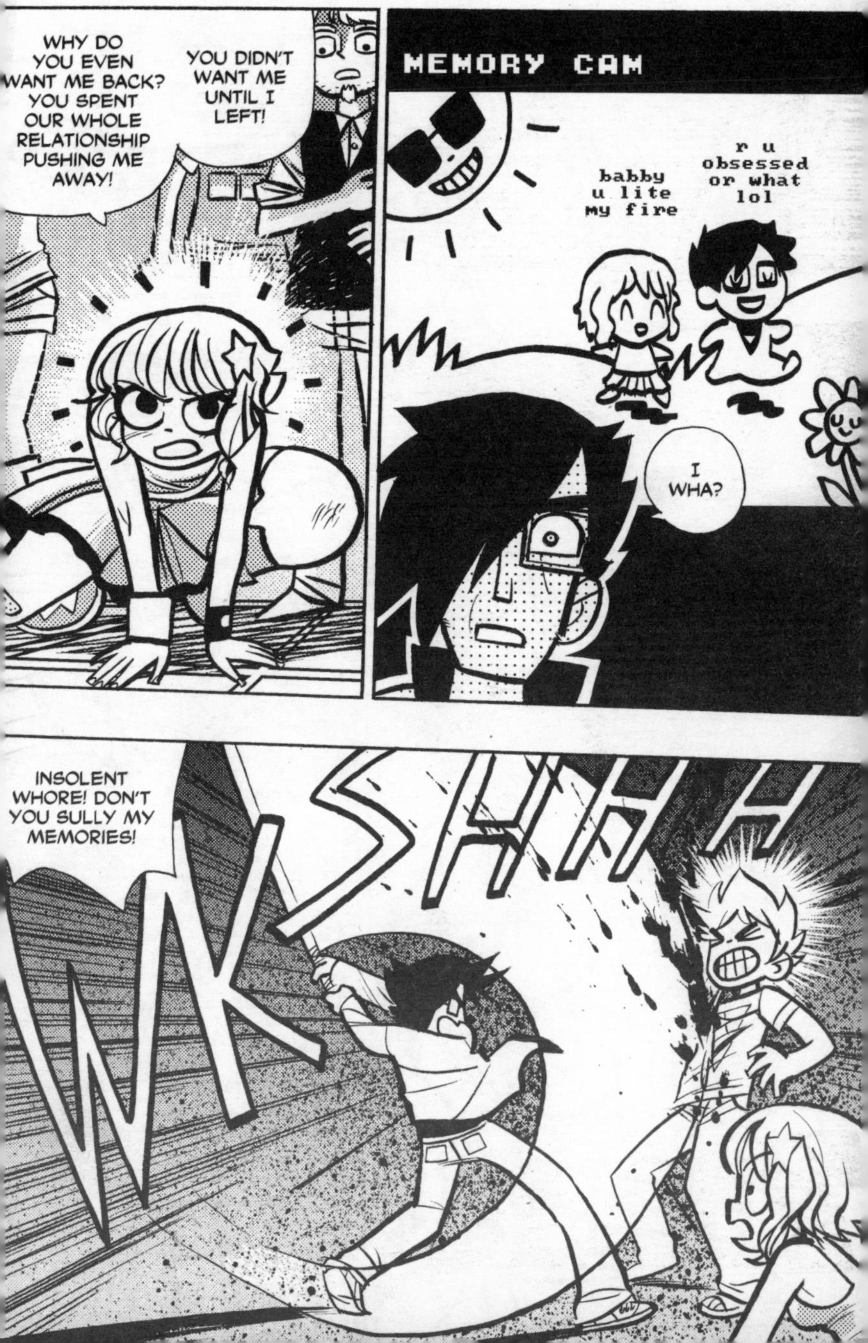
WHY DO YOU EVEN WANT ME BACK? YOU SPENT OUR WHOLE RELATIONSHIP PUSHING ME AWAY!
YOU DIDN'T WANT ME UNTIL I LEFT!
MEMORY CAM
babby u lite my fire
r u obsessed or what lol
I WHA?
INSOLENT WHORE! DON'T YOU SULLY MY MEMORIES!
SHHH
WK

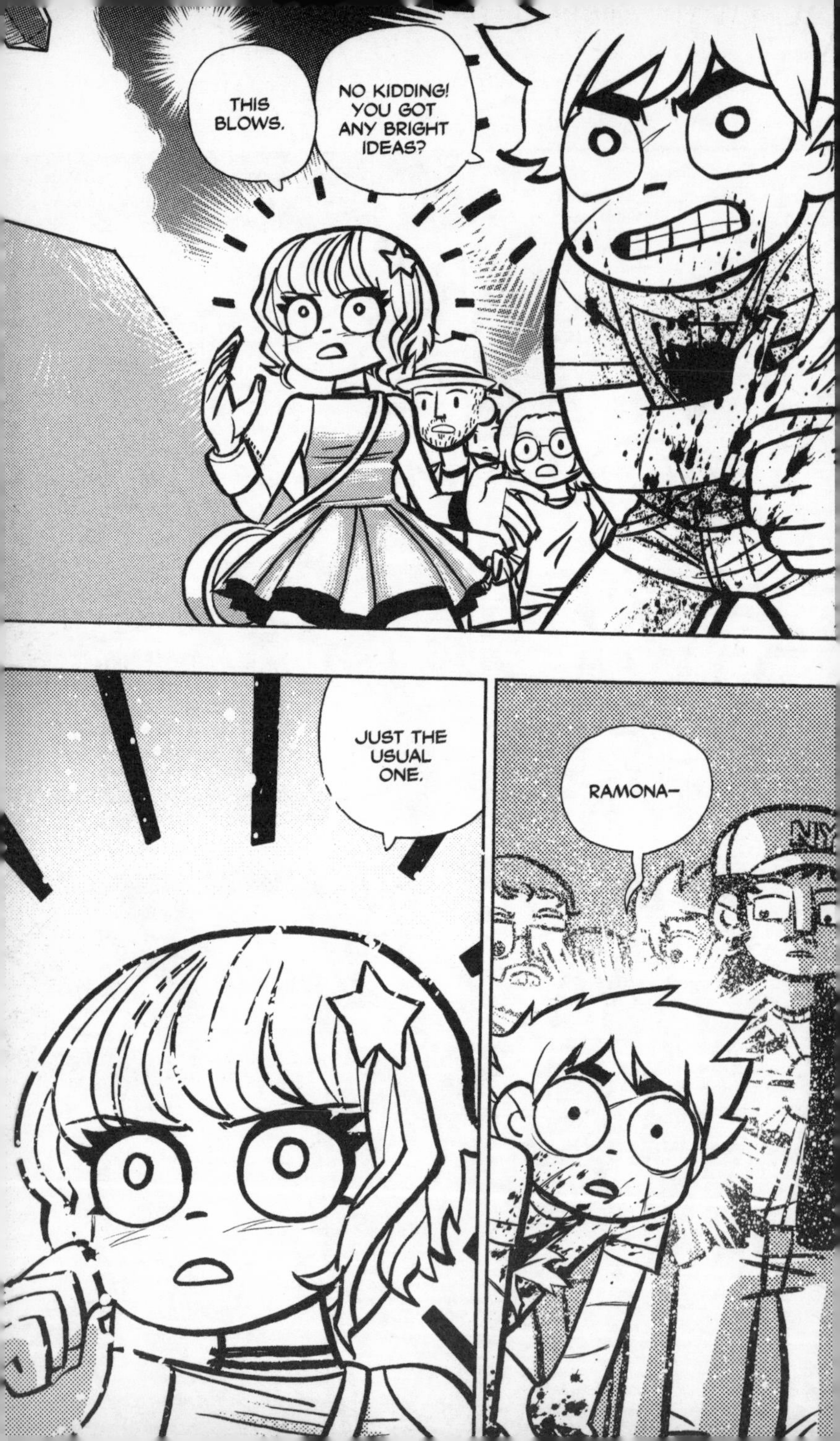
THIS BLOWS.
NO KIDDING! YOU GOT ANY BRIGHT IDEAS?
JUST THE USUAL ONE.
RAMONA–

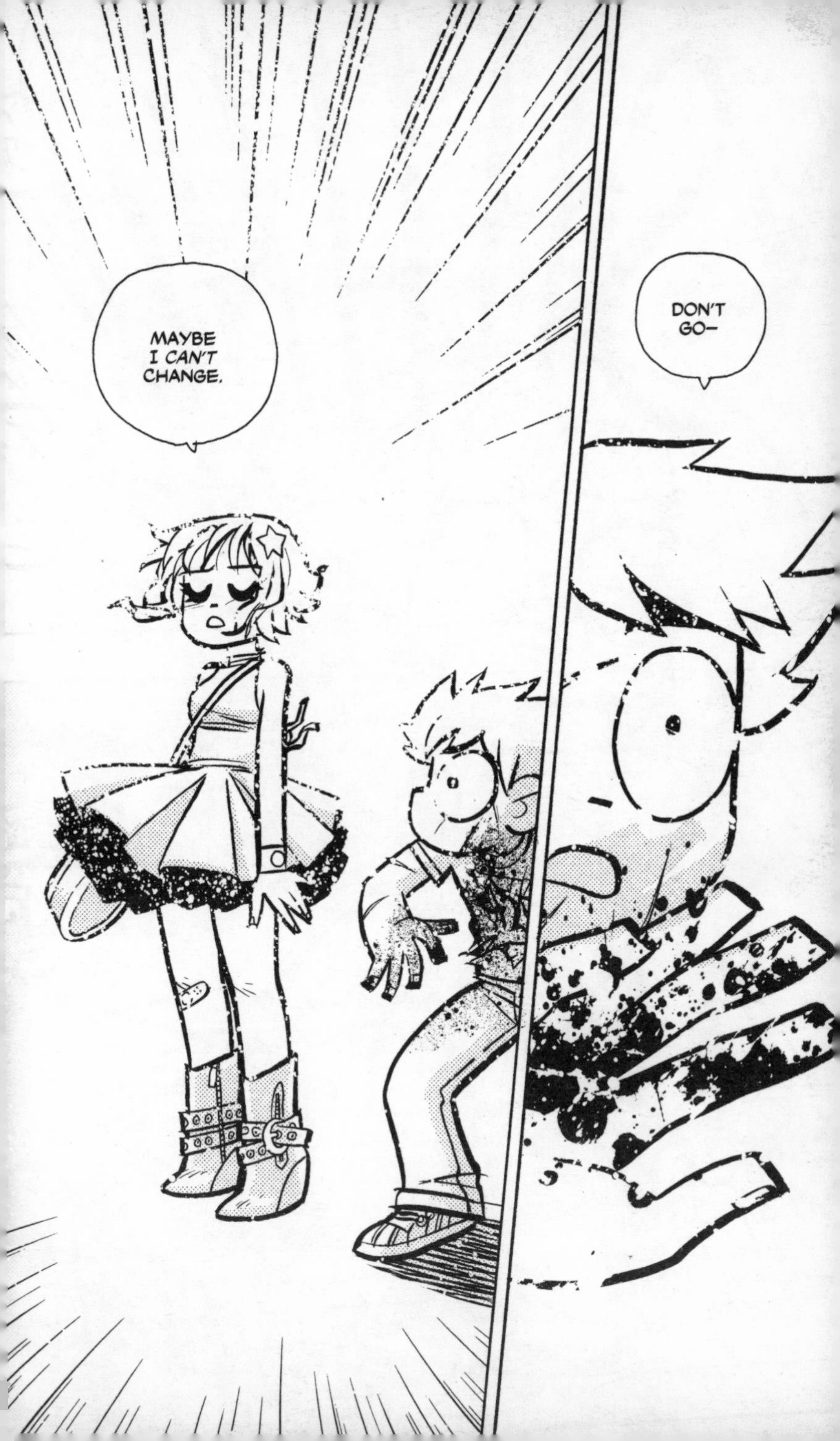
MAYBE I CAN'T CHANGE.
DON'T GO—

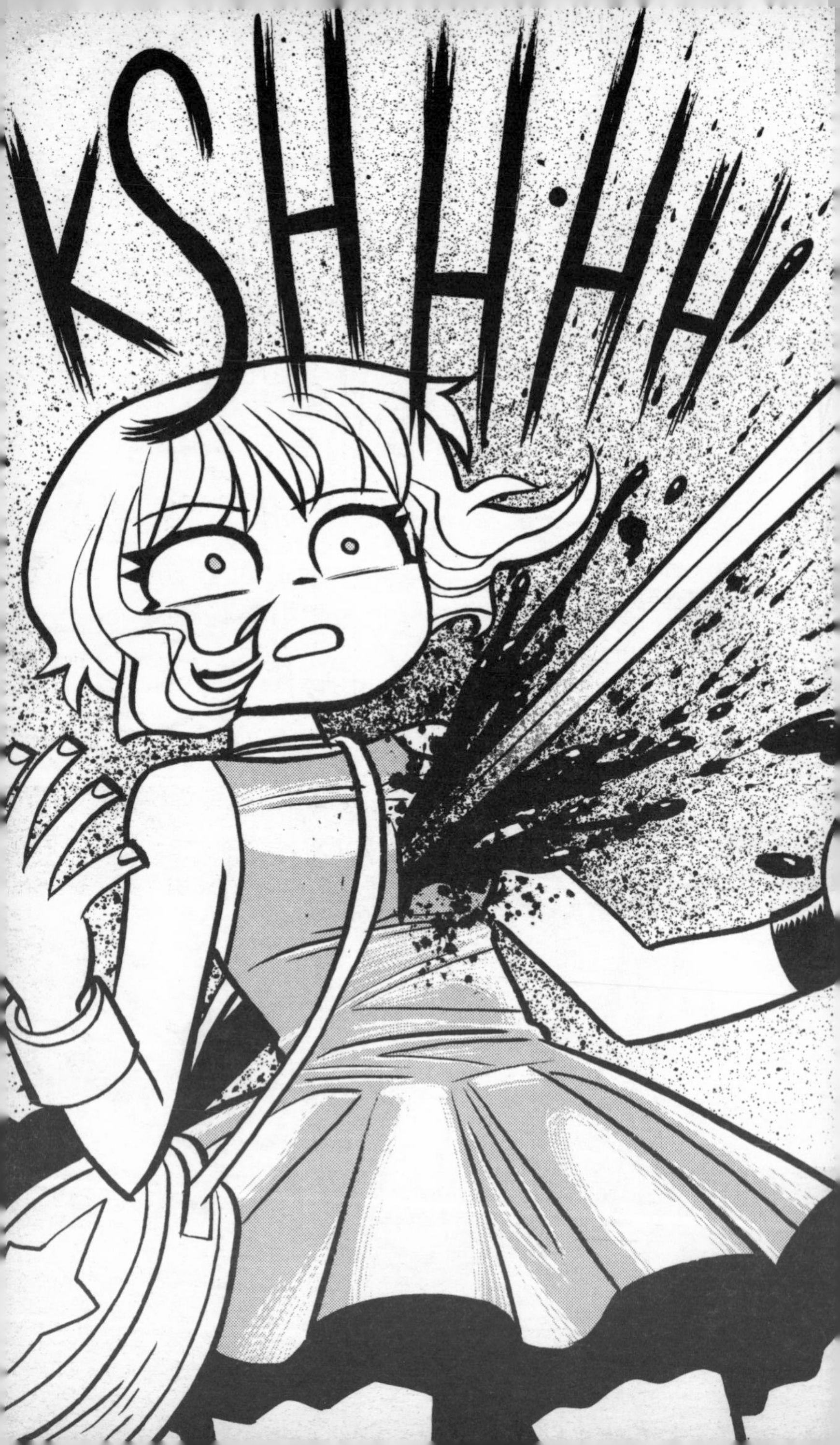
KSHHHH

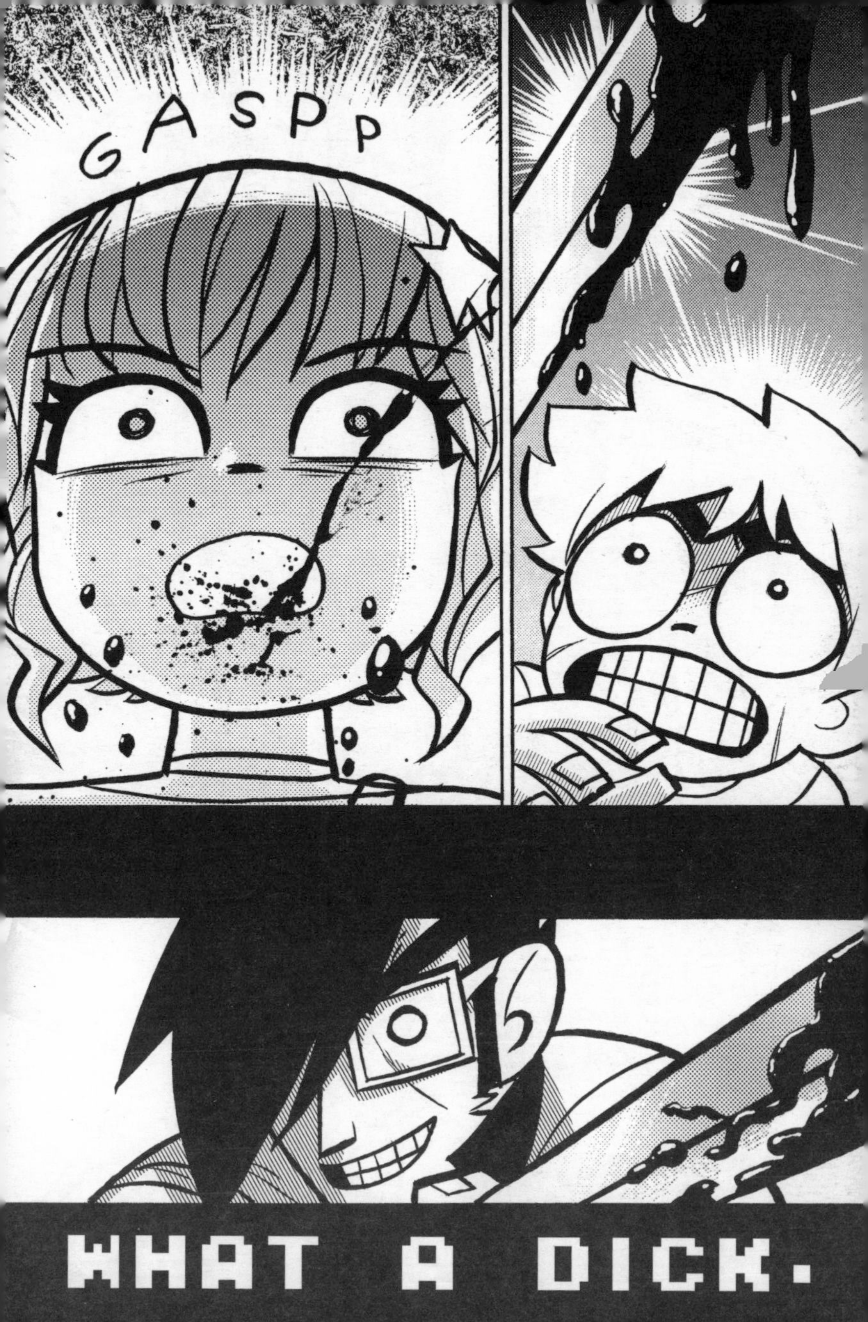
GASPP
WHAT A DICK.

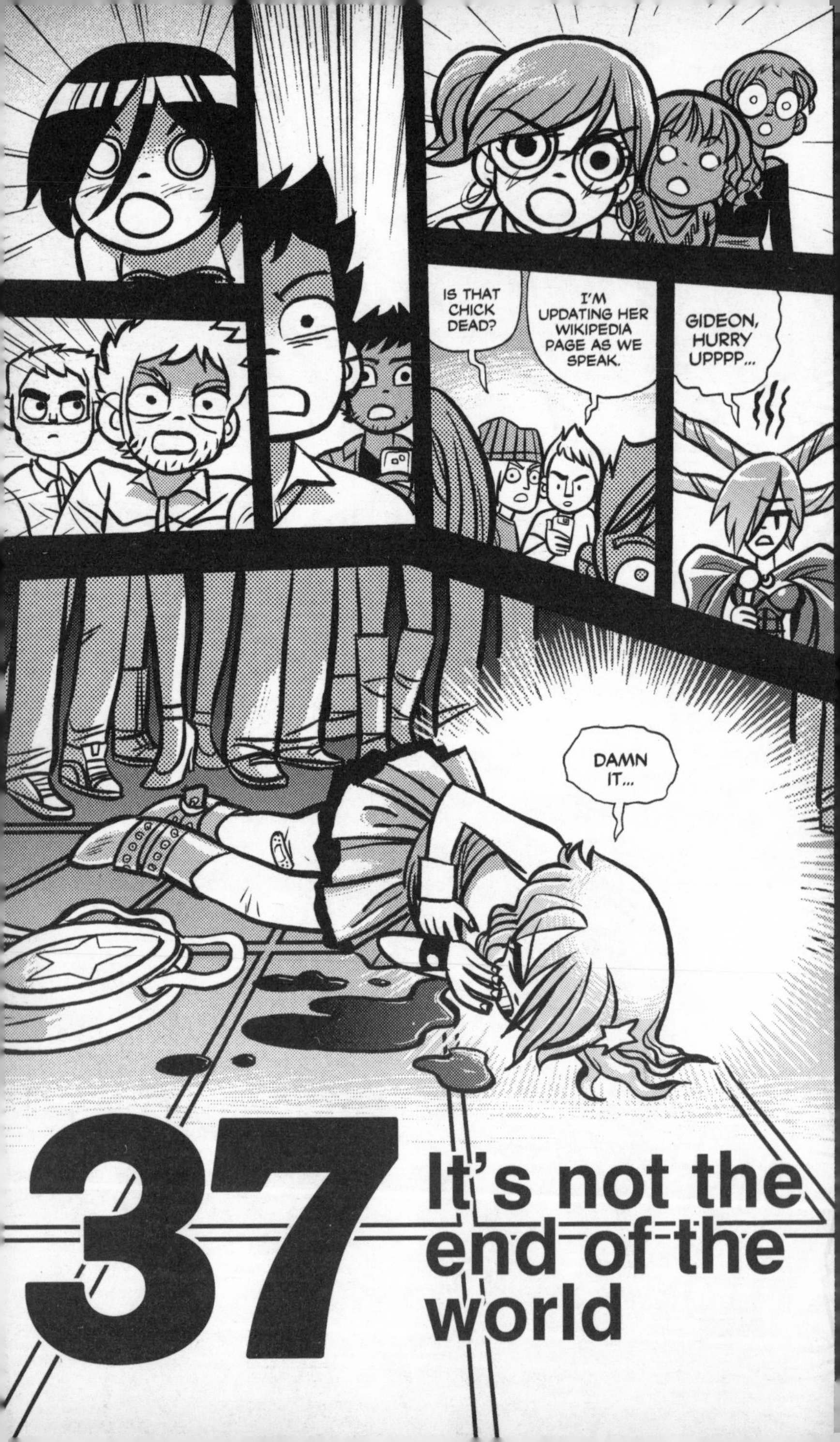
IS THAT CHICK DEAD?
I'M UPDATING HER WIKIPEDIA PAGE AS WE SPEAK.
GIDEON, HURRY UPPPP...
DAMN IT...

37 It's not the end of the world

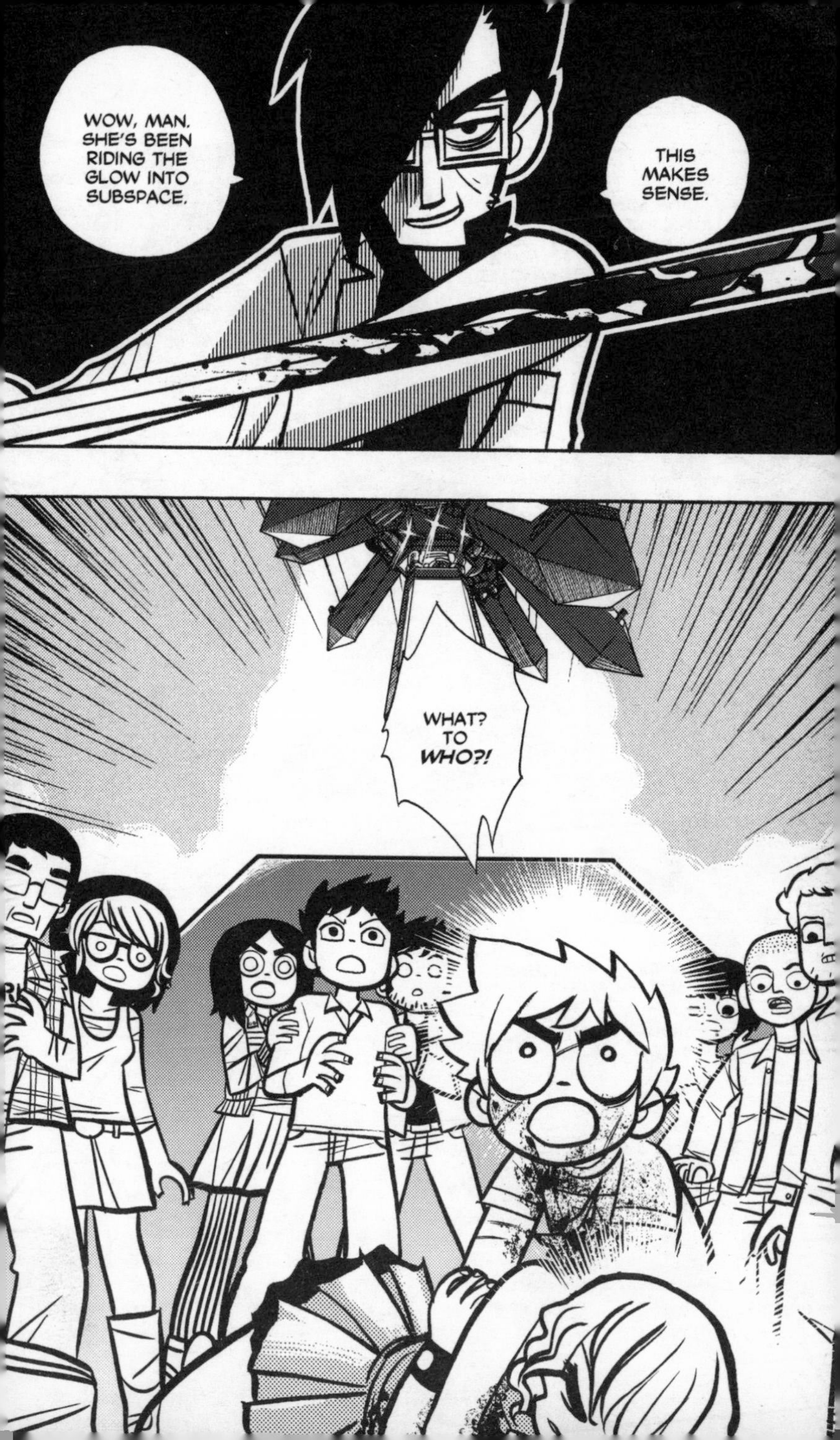
WOW, MAN. SHE'S BEEN RIDING THE GLOW INTO SUBSPACE.
THIS MAKES SENSE.
WHAT? TO *WHO?!*

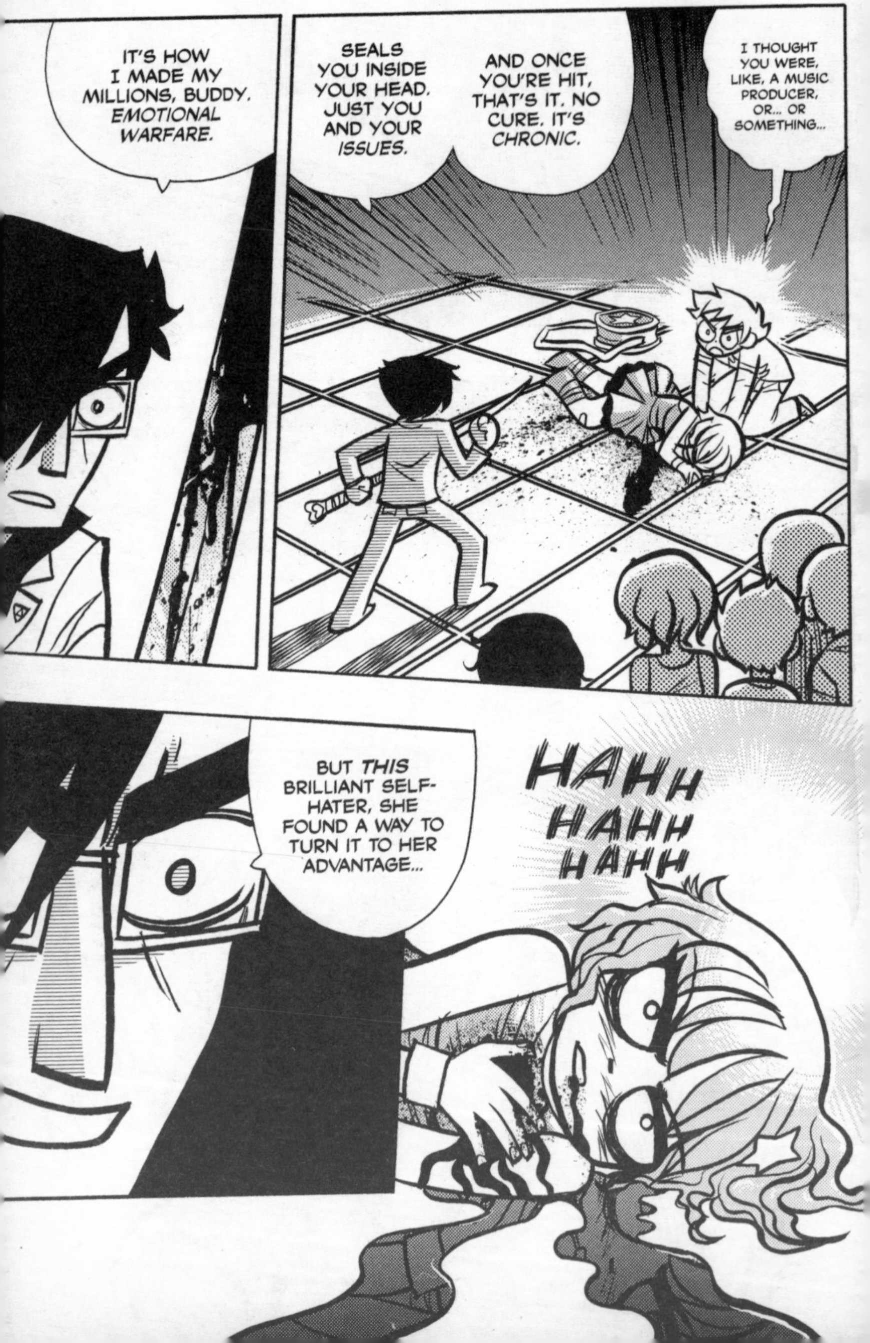
IT'S HOW I MADE MY MILLIONS, BUDDY. EMOTIONAL WARFARE.
SEALS YOU INSIDE YOUR HEAD. JUST YOU AND YOUR ISSUES.
AND ONCE YOU'RE HIT, THAT'S IT. NO CURE. IT'S CHRONIC.
I THOUGHT YOU WERE, LIKE, A MUSIC PRODUCER, OR... OR SOMETHING...
BUT THIS BRILLIANT SELF-HATER, SHE FOUND A WAY TO TURN IT TO HER ADVANTAGE...
HAHH HAHH HAHH

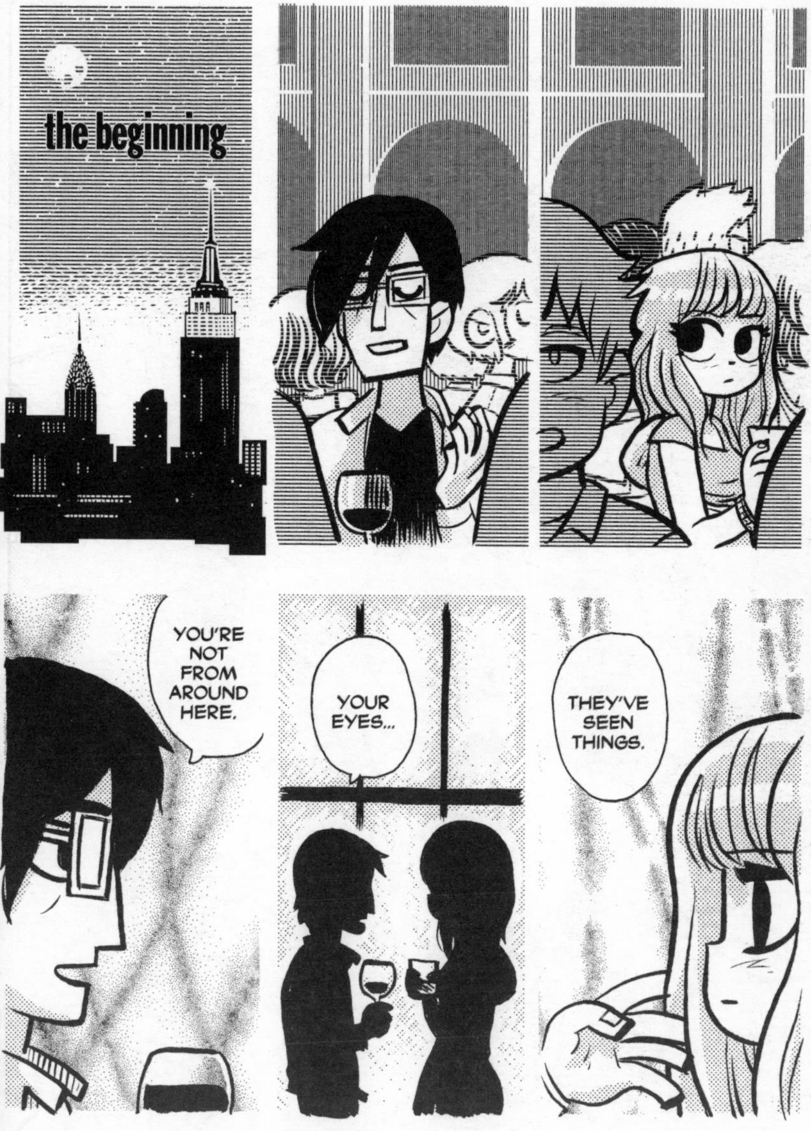
the beginning
YOU'RE NOT FROM AROUND HERE.
YOUR EYES...
THEY'VE SEEN THINGS.

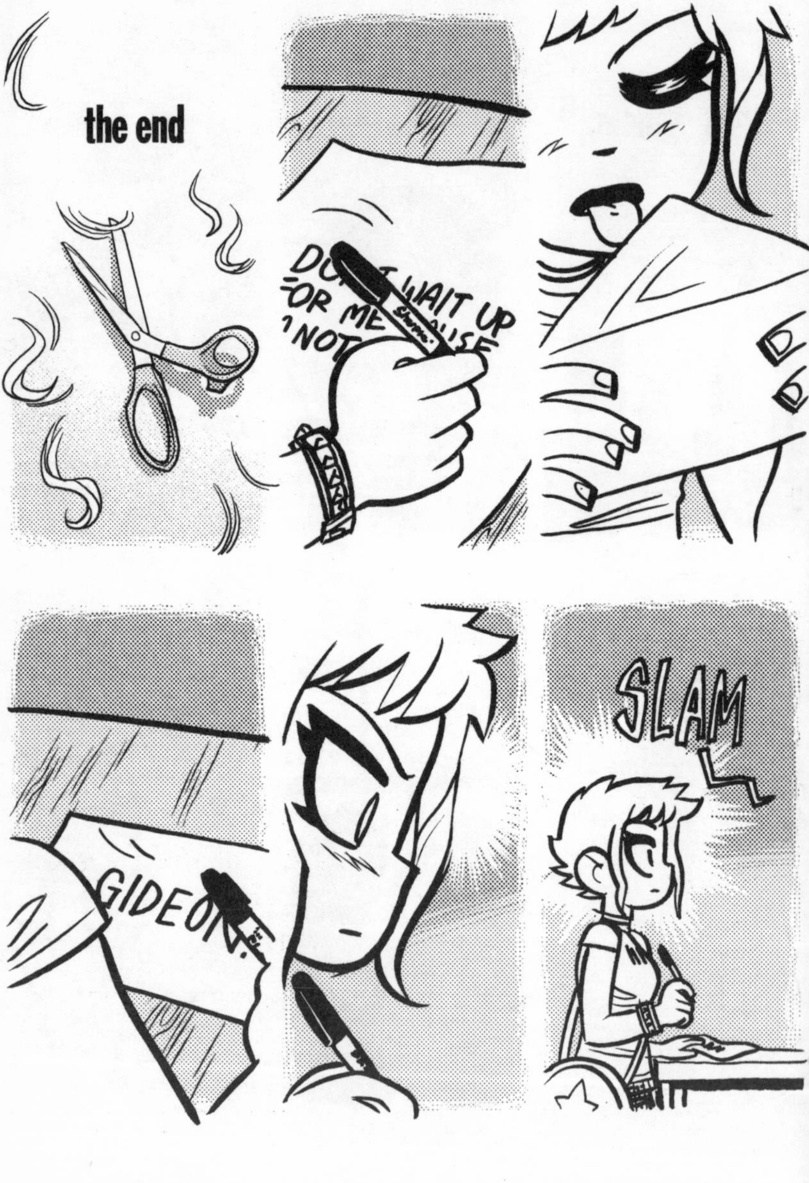
the end
WAIT UP
FOR ME
NOT
Sharpie
GIDEON.
SLAM

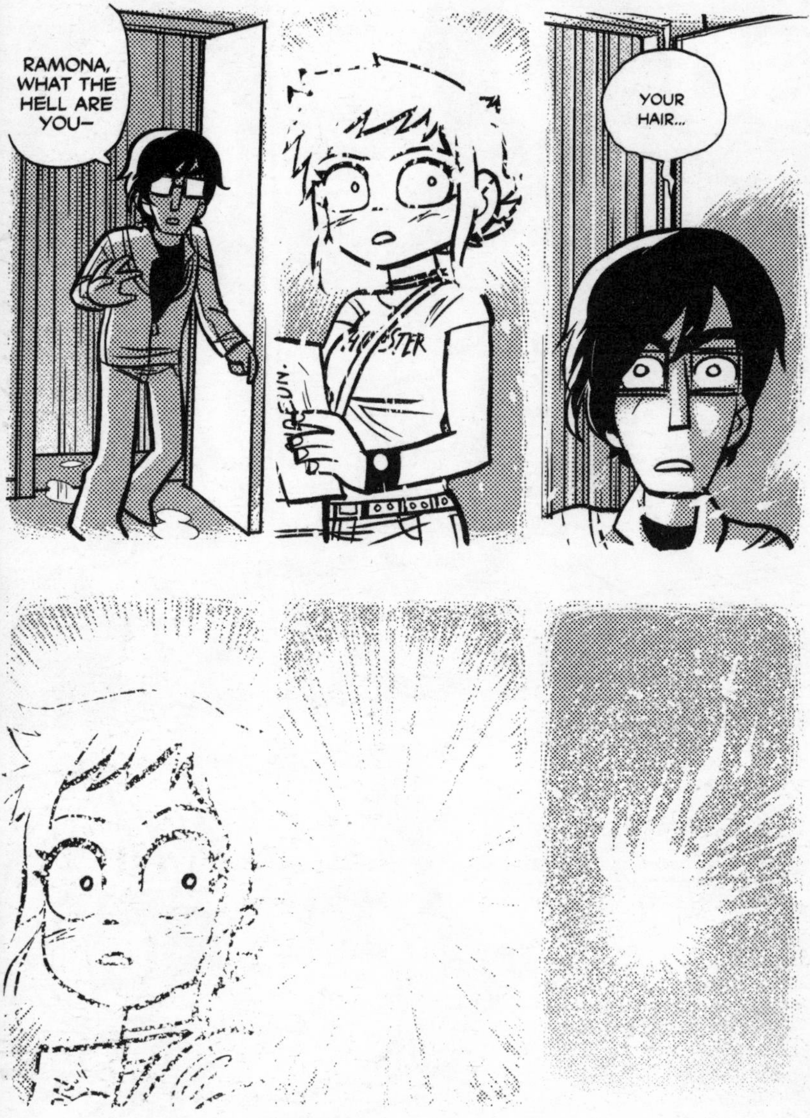
RAMONA, WHAT THE HELL ARE YOU—
YOUR HAIR...

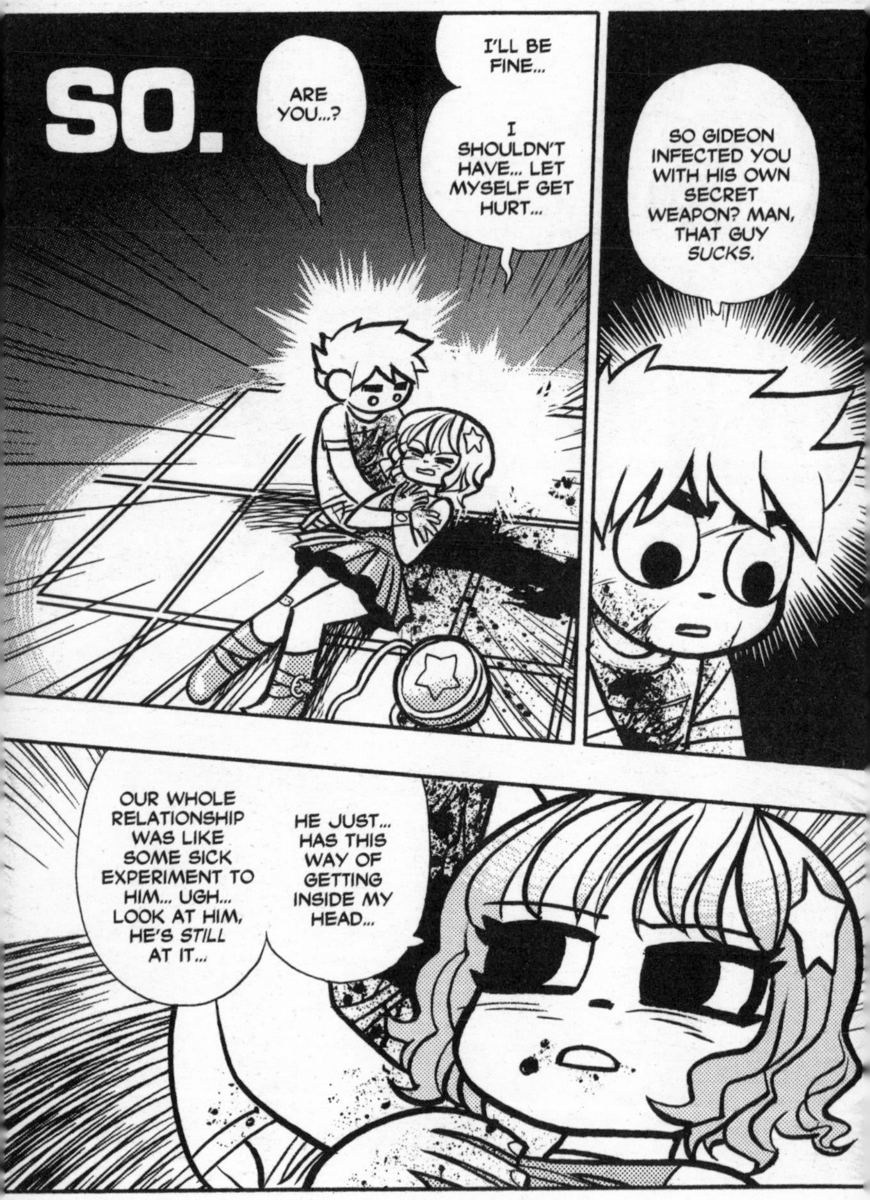
SO.
ARE YOU...?
I'LL BE FINE...
I SHOULDN'T HAVE... LET MYSELF GET HURT...
SO GIDEON INFECTED YOU WITH HIS OWN SECRET WEAPON? MAN, THAT GUY *SUCKS.*
OUR WHOLE RELATIONSHIP WAS LIKE SOME SICK EXPERIMENT TO HIM... UGH... LOOK AT HIM, HE'S *STILL* AT IT...
HE JUST... HAS THIS WAY OF GETTING INSIDE MY HEAD...

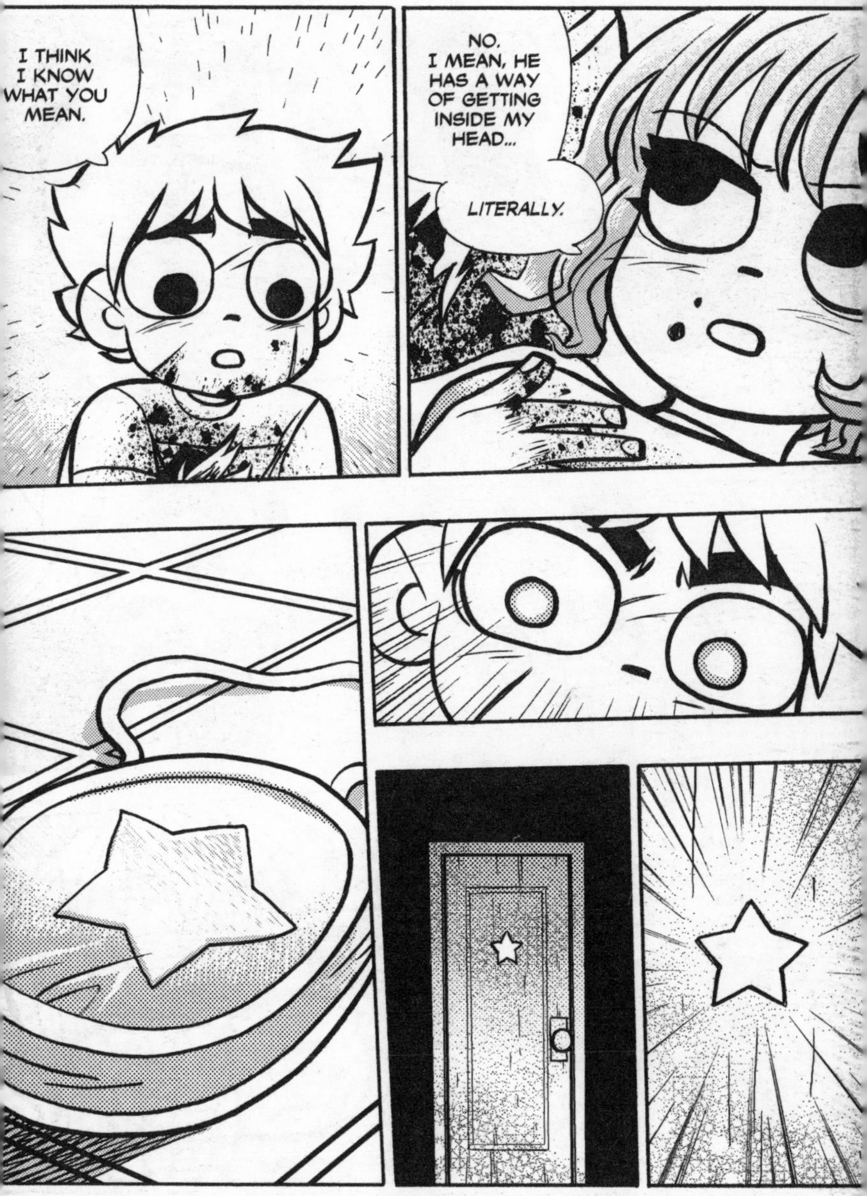
I THINK I KNOW WHAT YOU MEAN.
NO. I MEAN, HE HAS A WAY OF GETTING INSIDE MY HEAD...
LITERALLY.

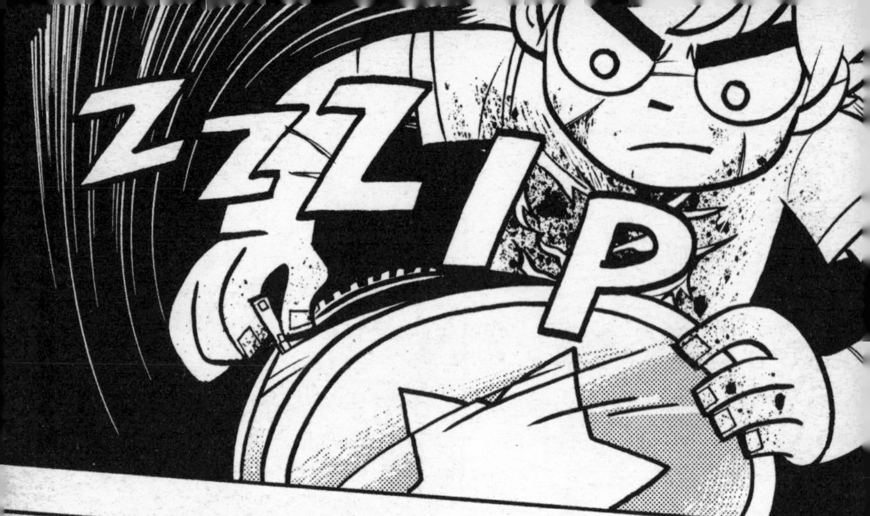
ZZZIP

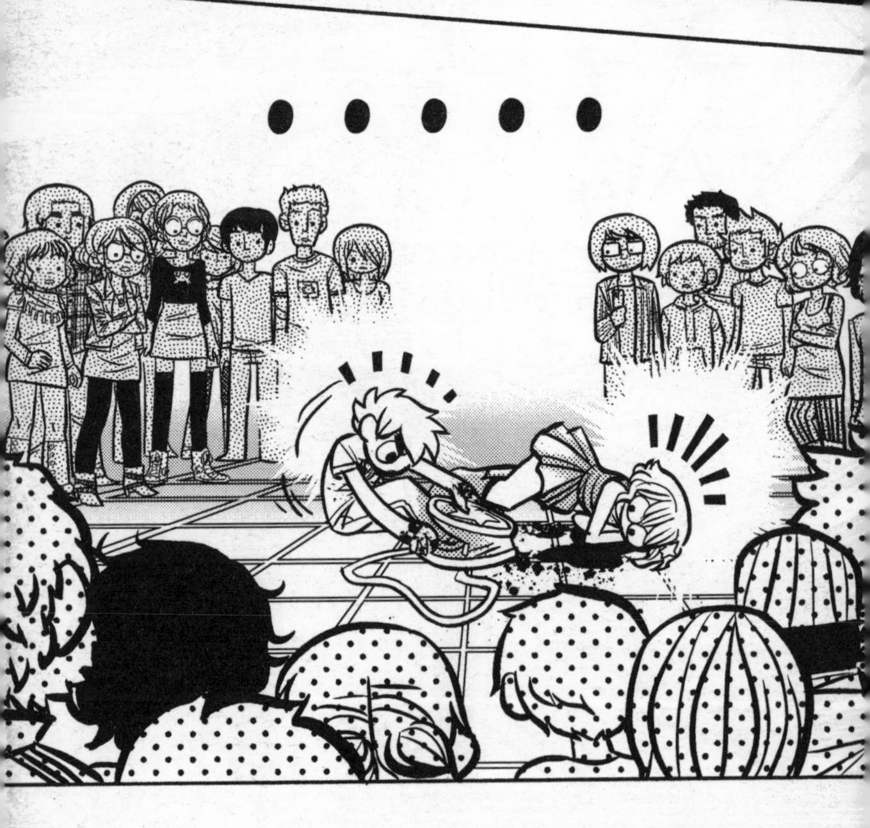
.....

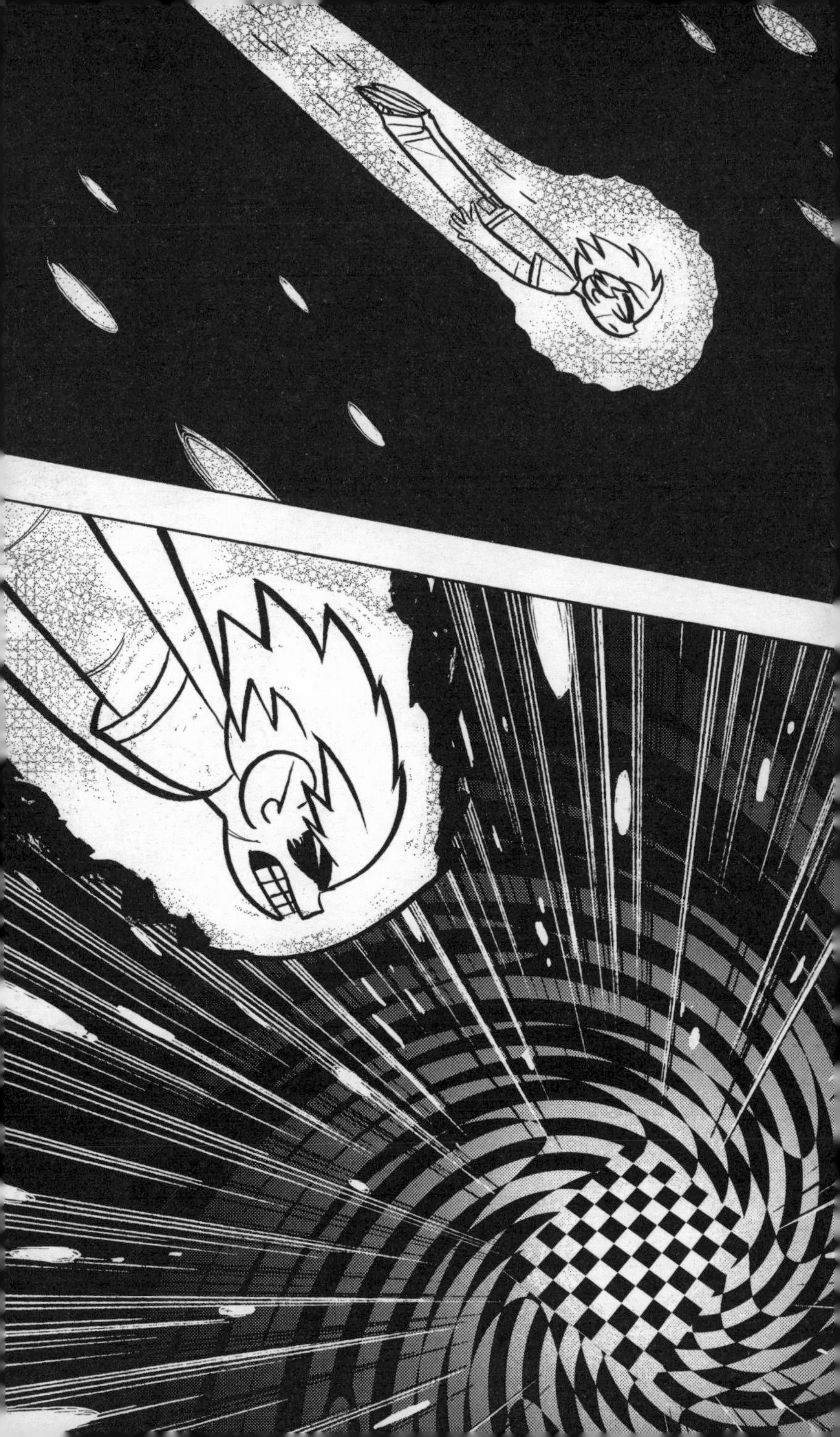

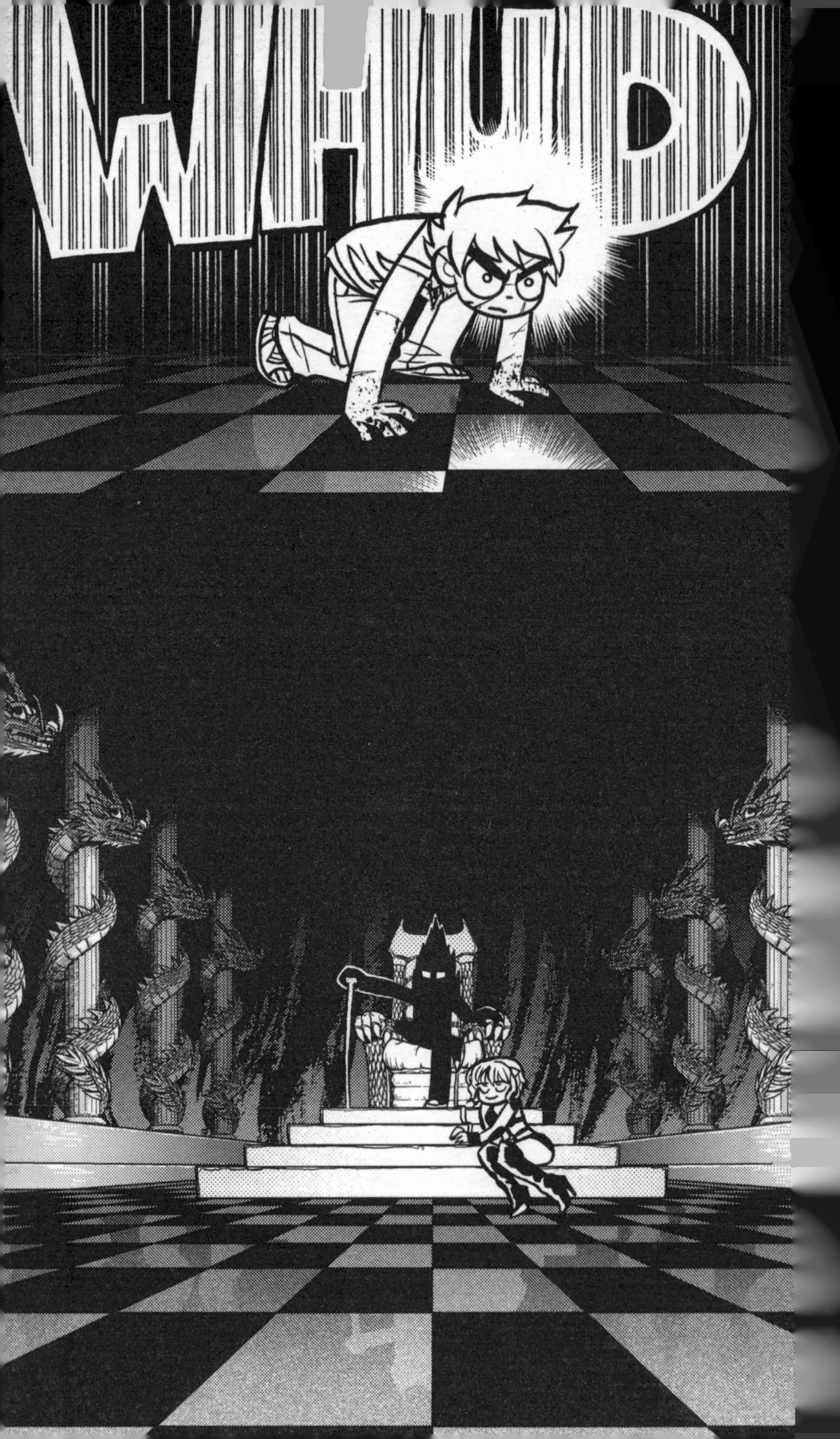
WHUD

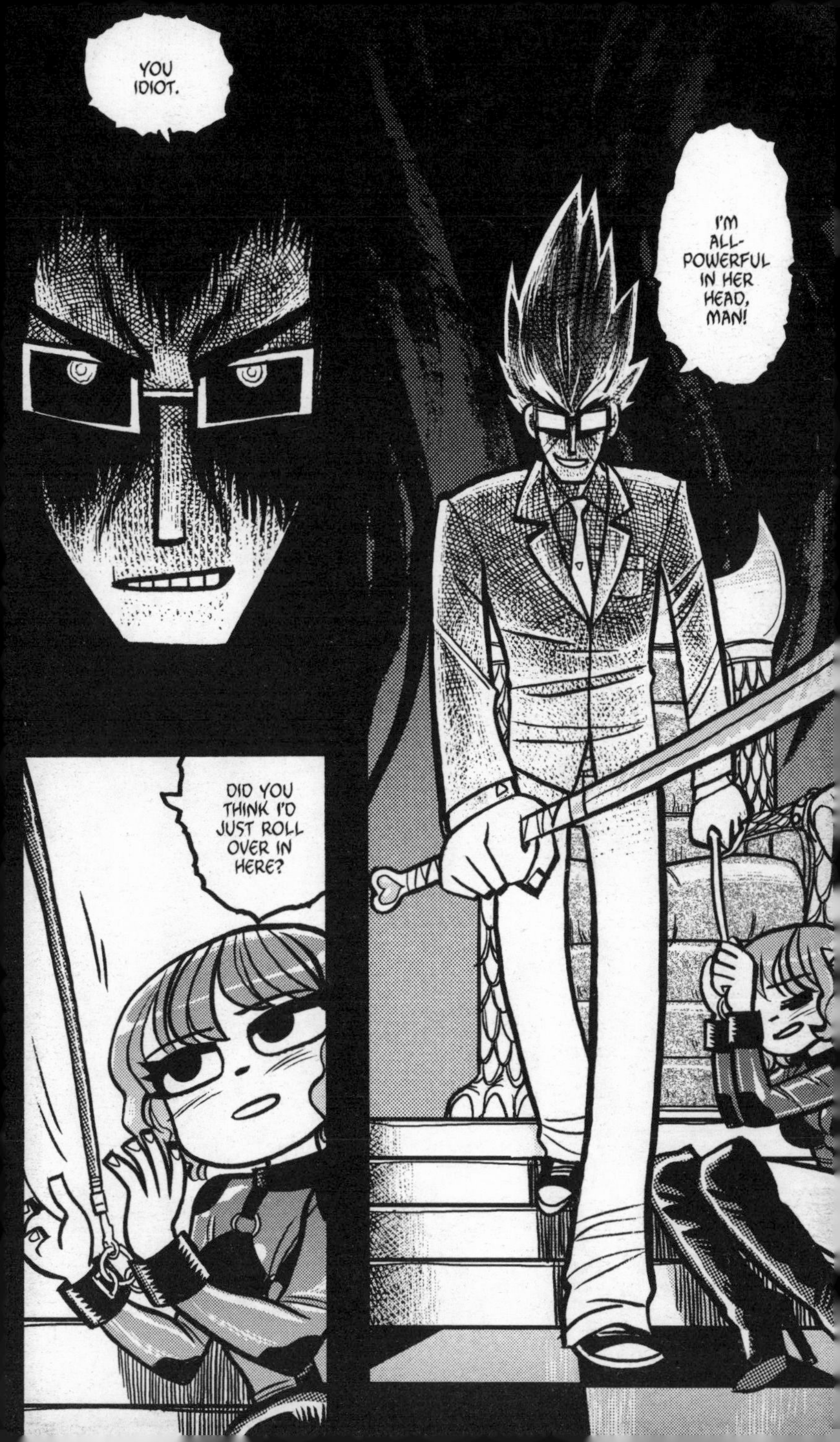
YOU IDIOT.
I'M ALL-POWERFUL IN HER HEAD, MAN!
DID YOU THINK I'D JUST ROLL OVER IN HERE?

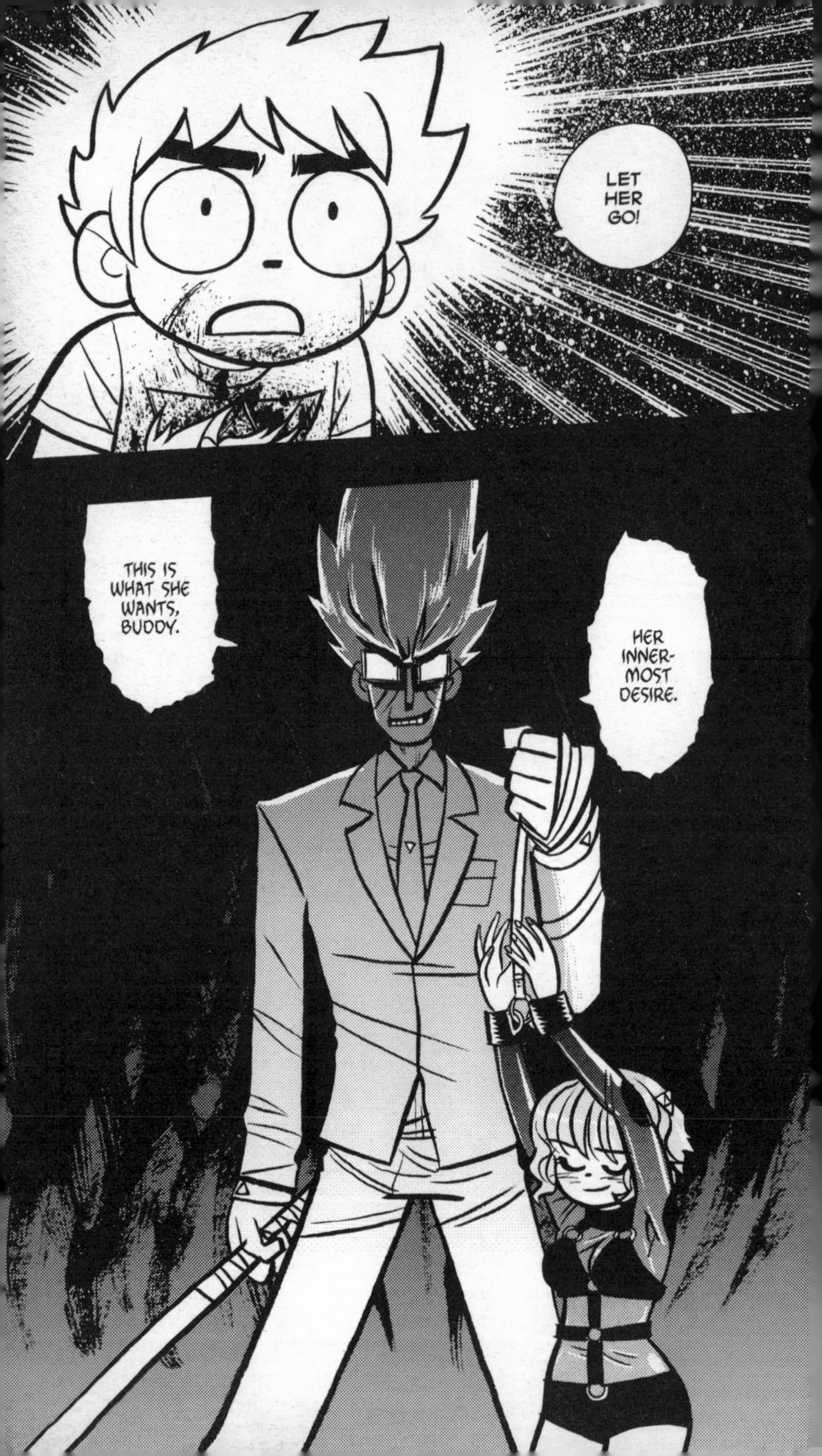
LET HER GO!
THIS IS WHAT SHE WANTS, BUDDY.
HER INNER-MOST DESIRE.

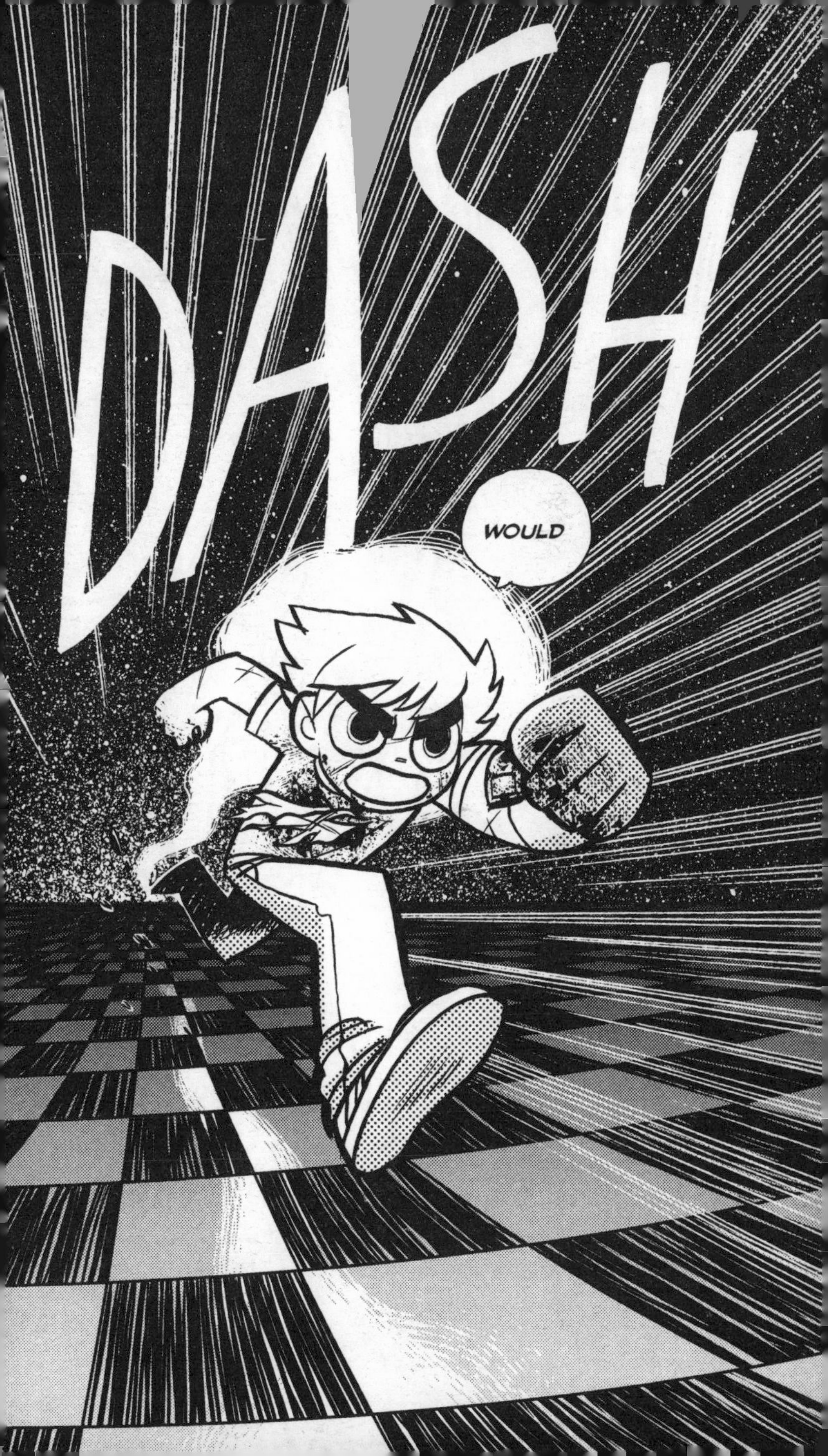
DASH
WOULD

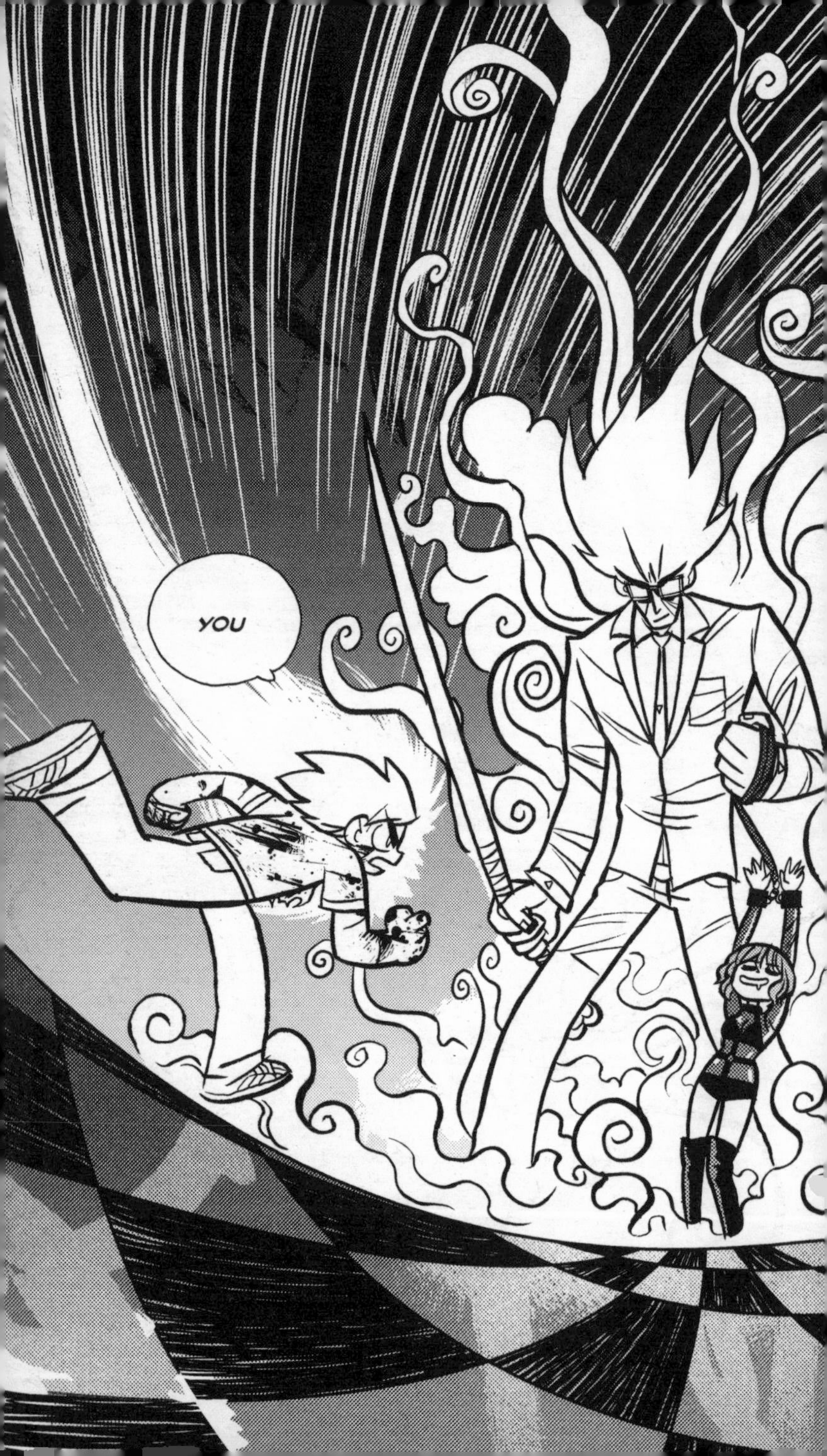
YOU

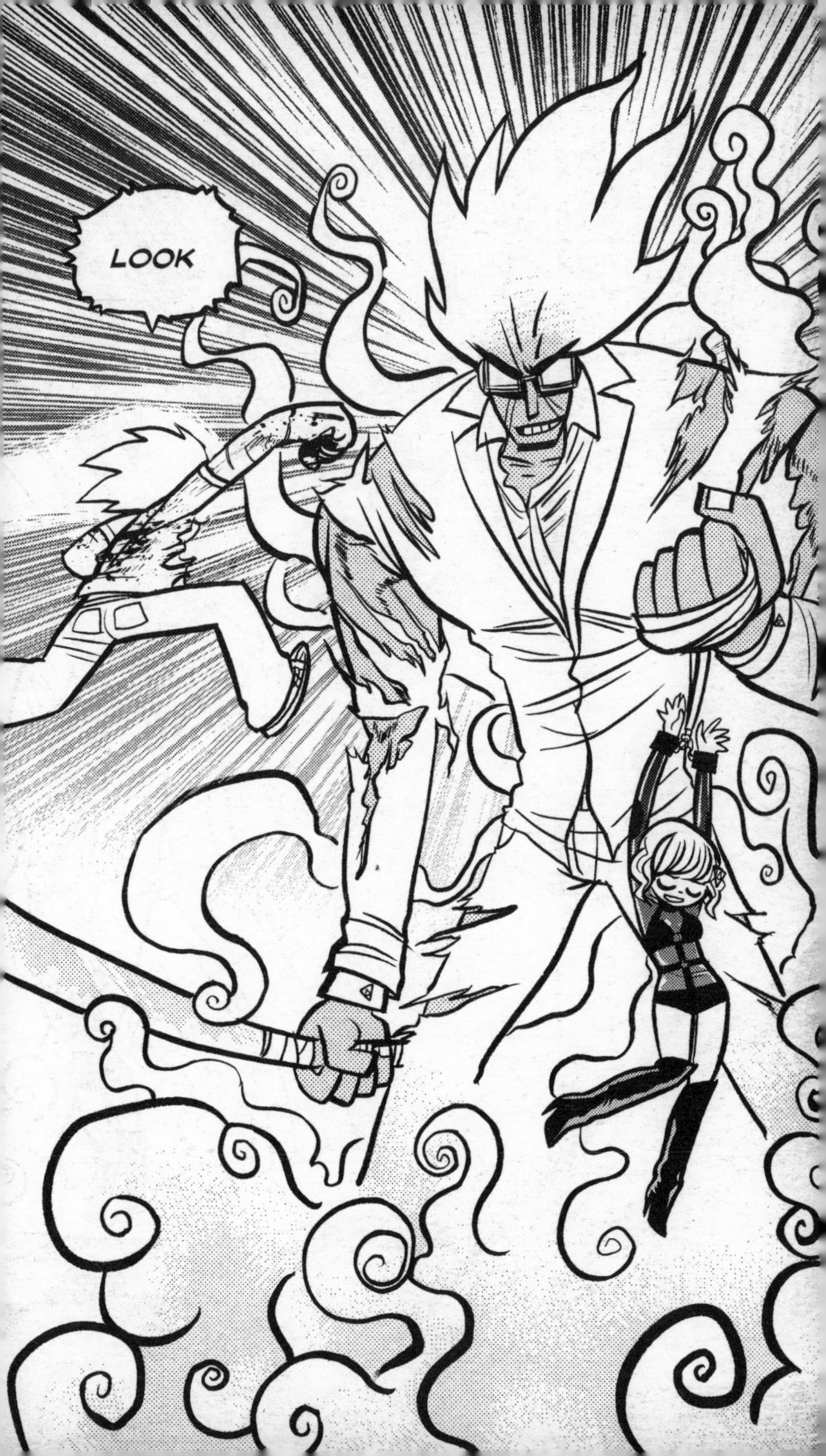
LOOK

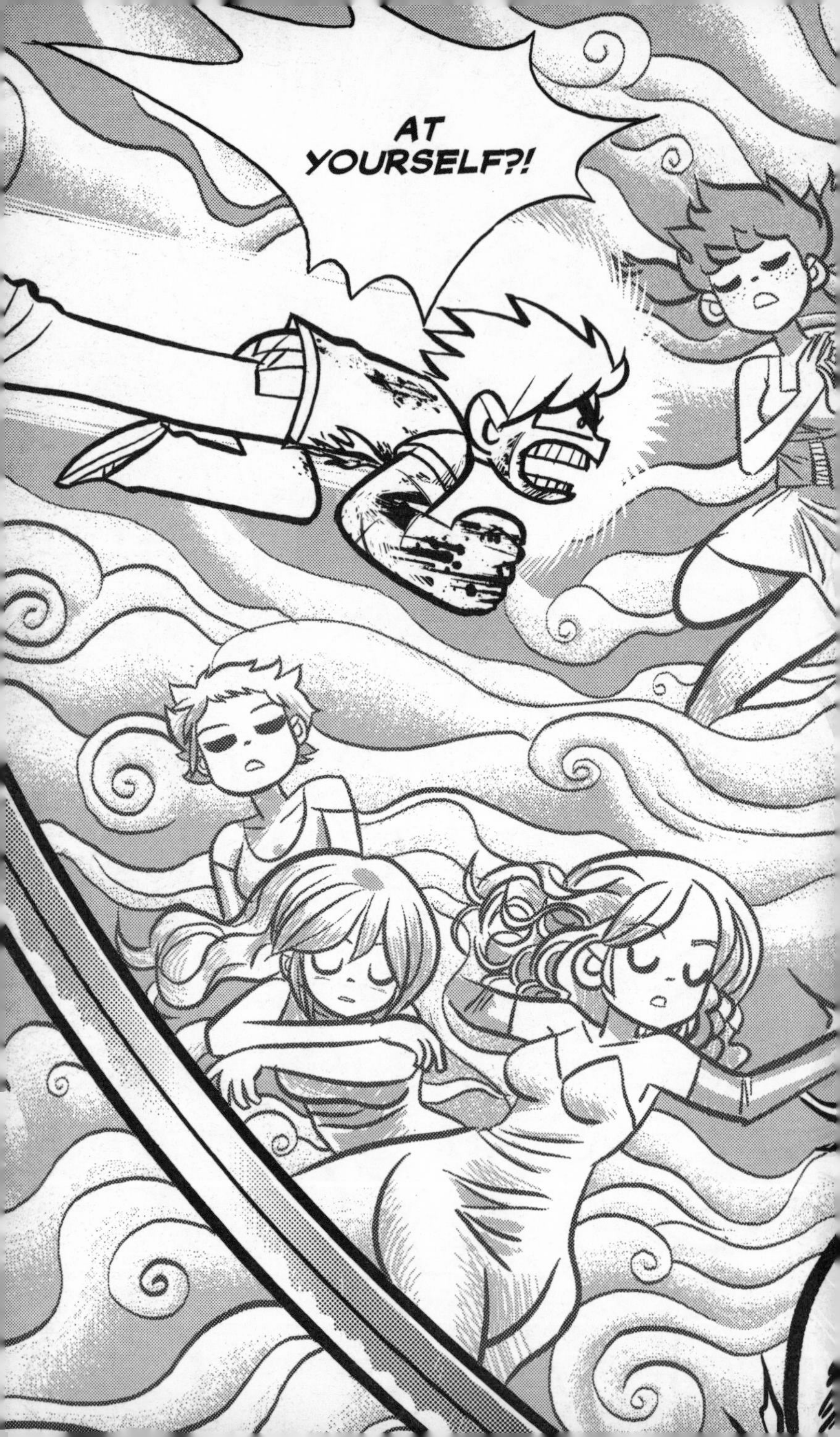
AT YOURSELF?!

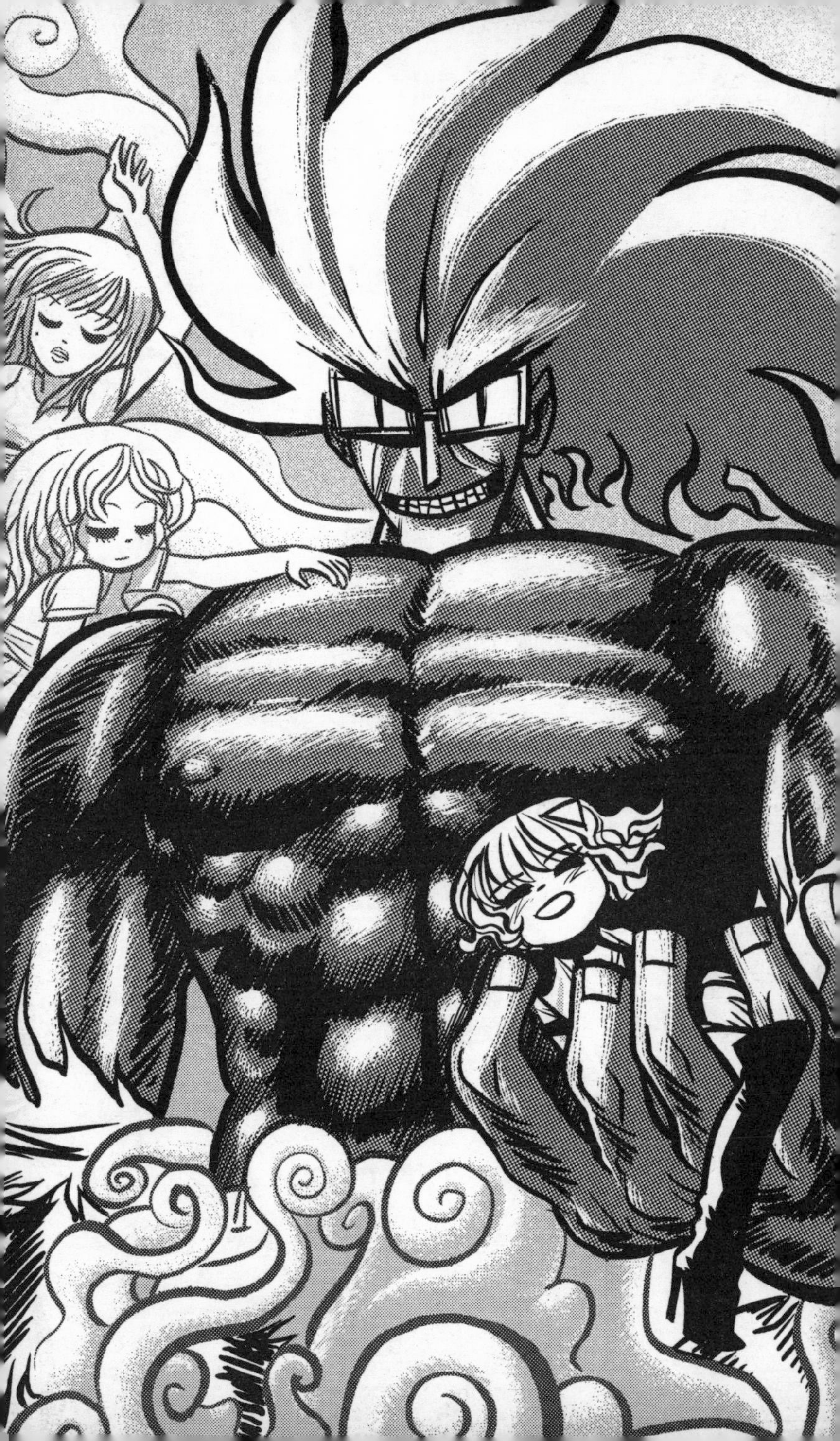

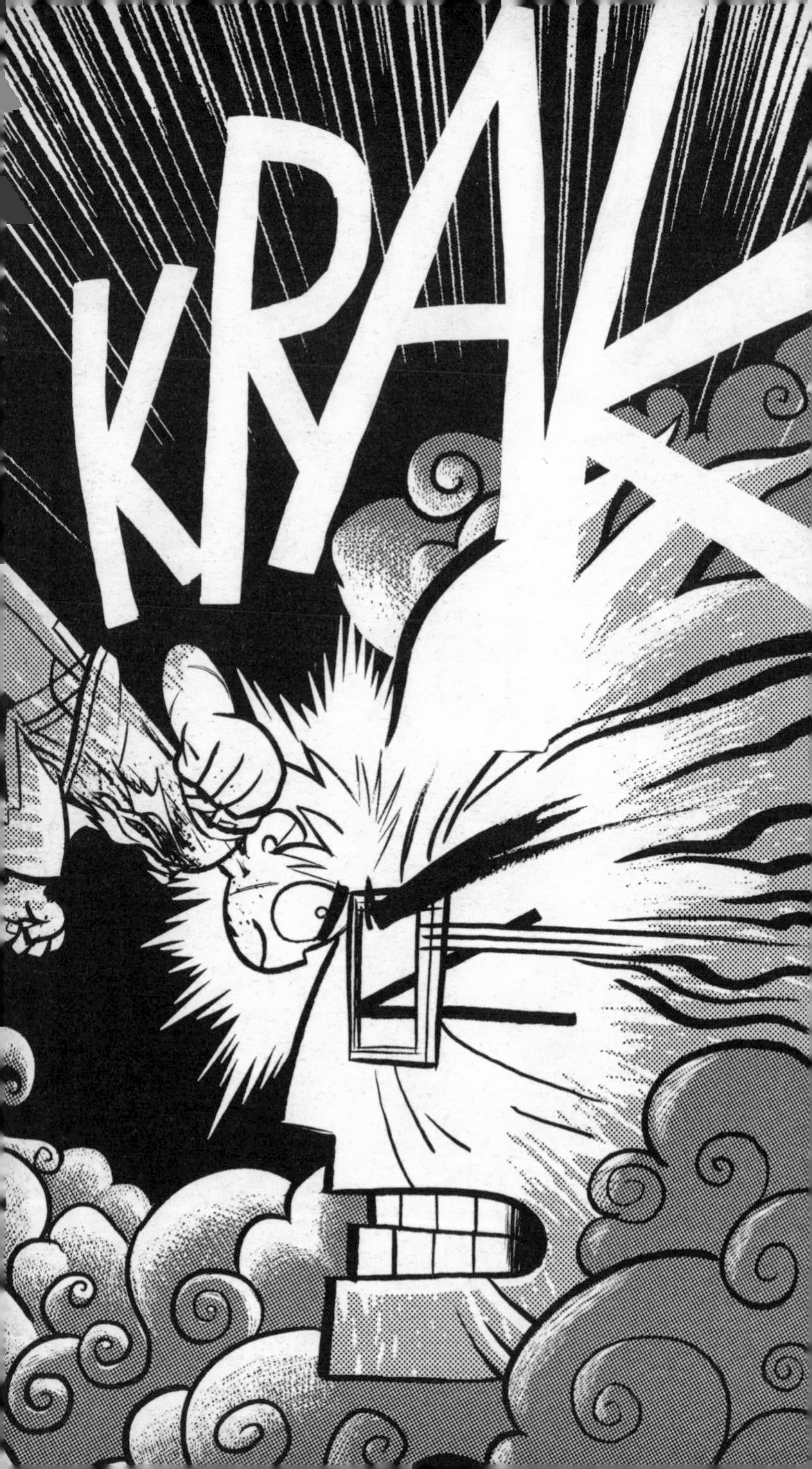
KRAK

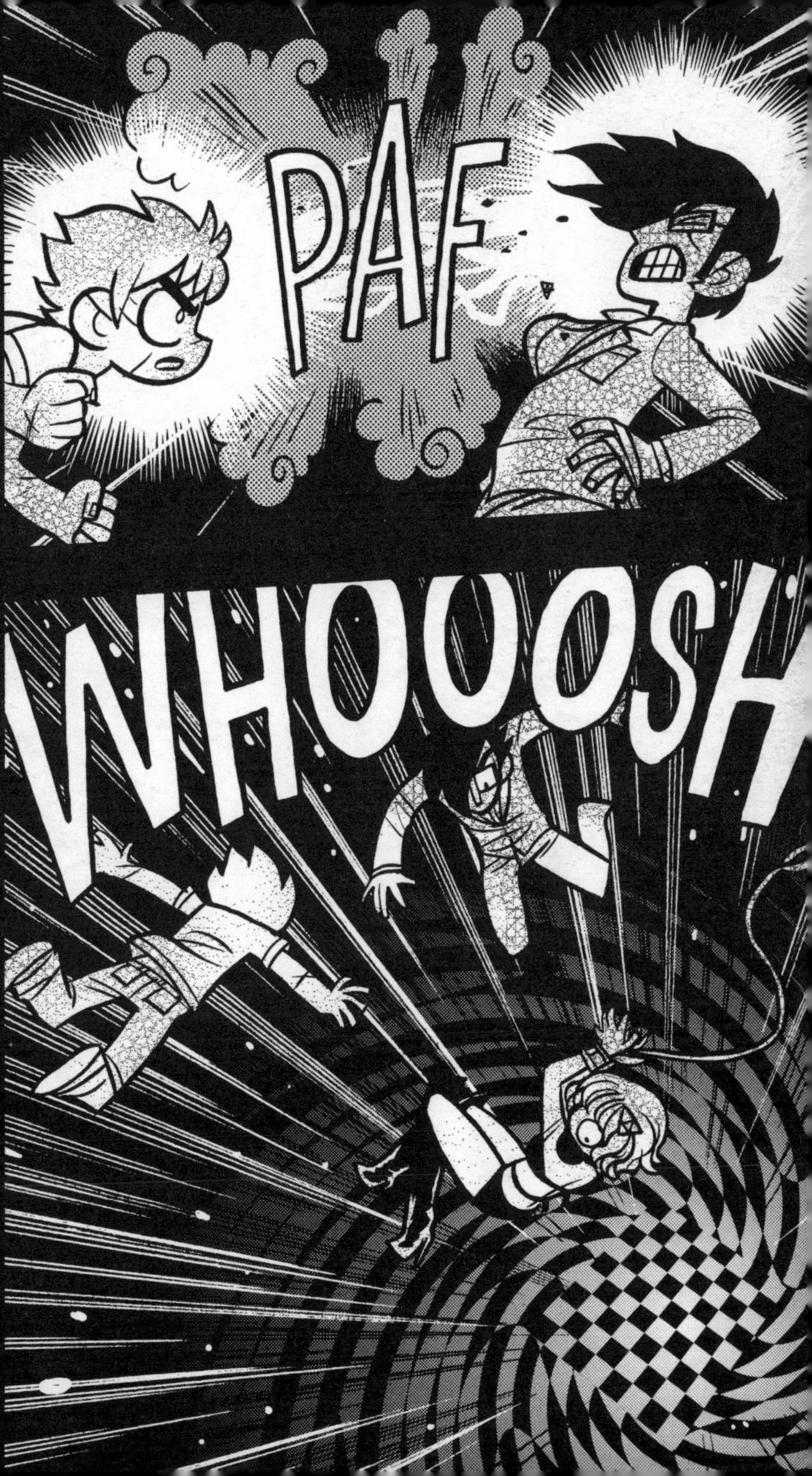
PAF
WHOOOSH

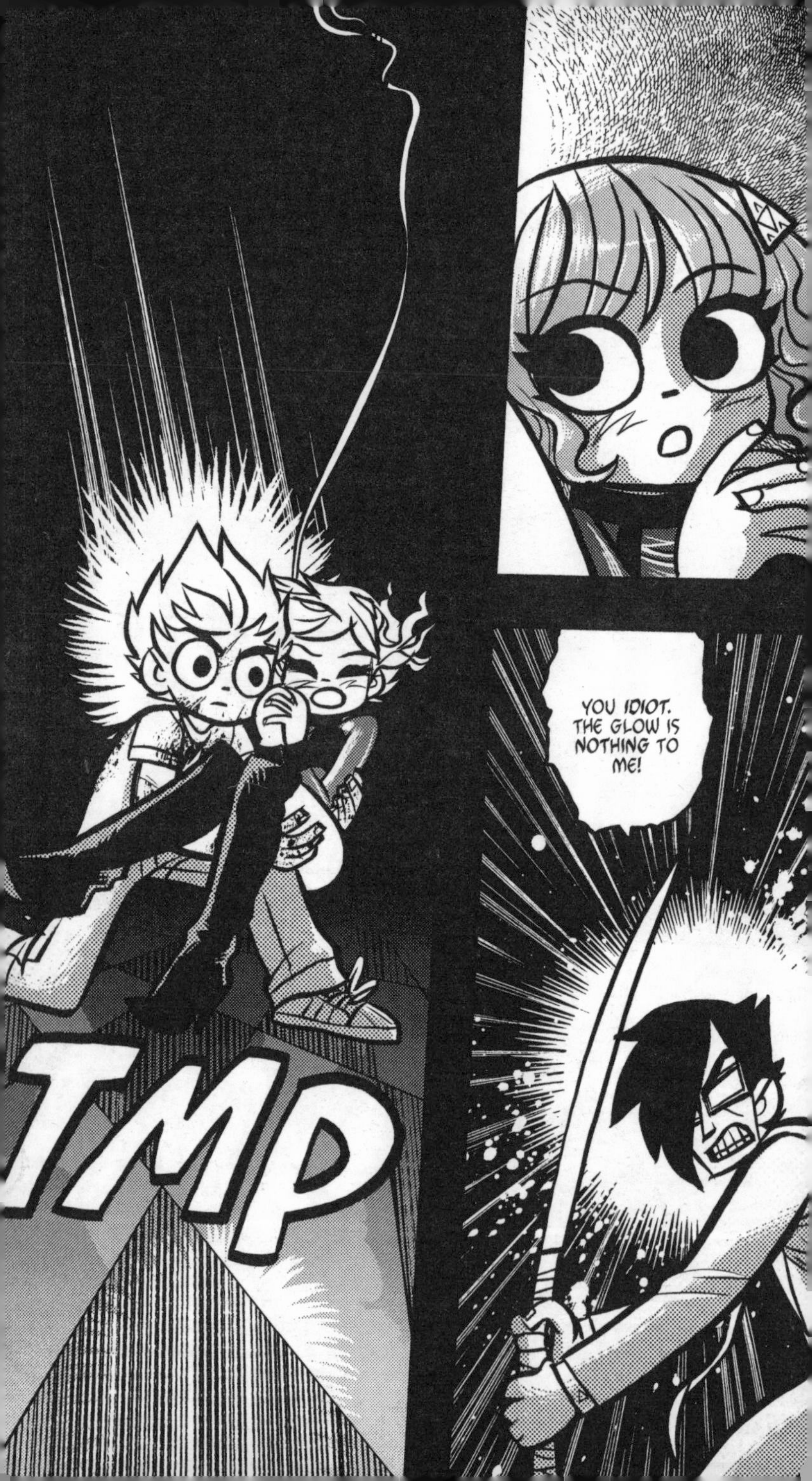
TMP
YOU IDIOT. THE GLOW IS NOTHING TO ME!

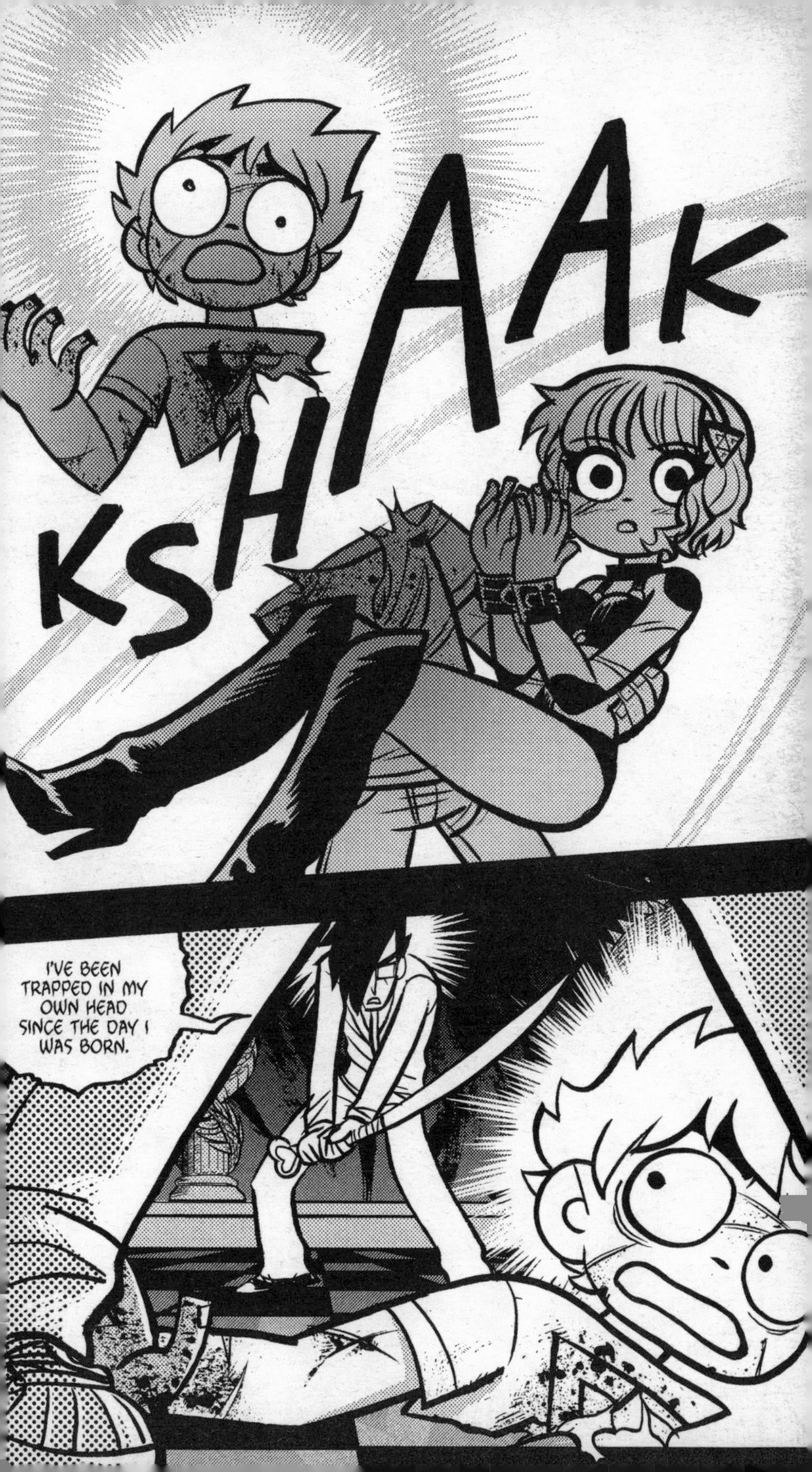
KSHAAAK
I'VE BEEN TRAPPED IN MY OWN HEAD SINCE THE DAY I WAS BORN.

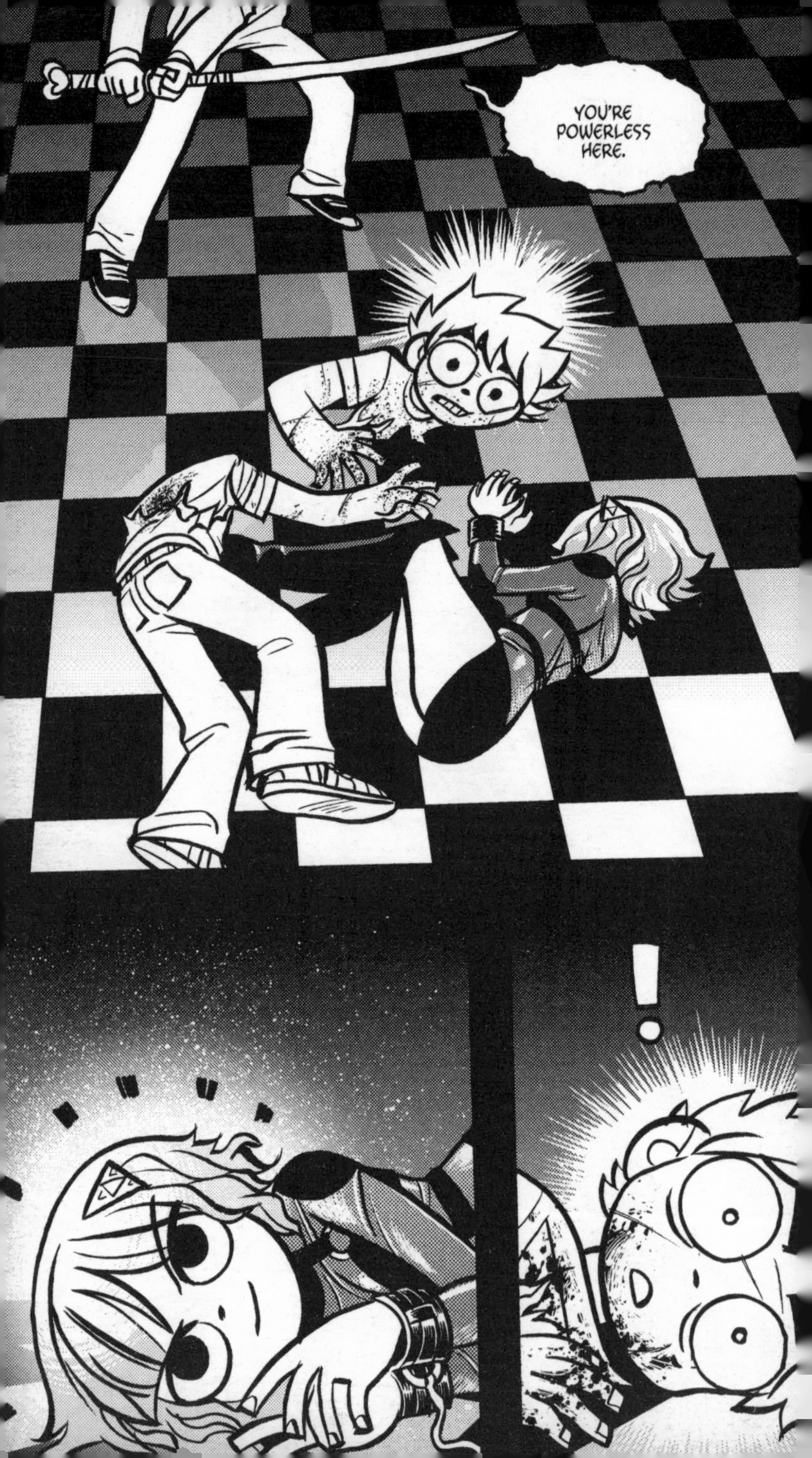

YOU'RE POWERLESS HERE.
!

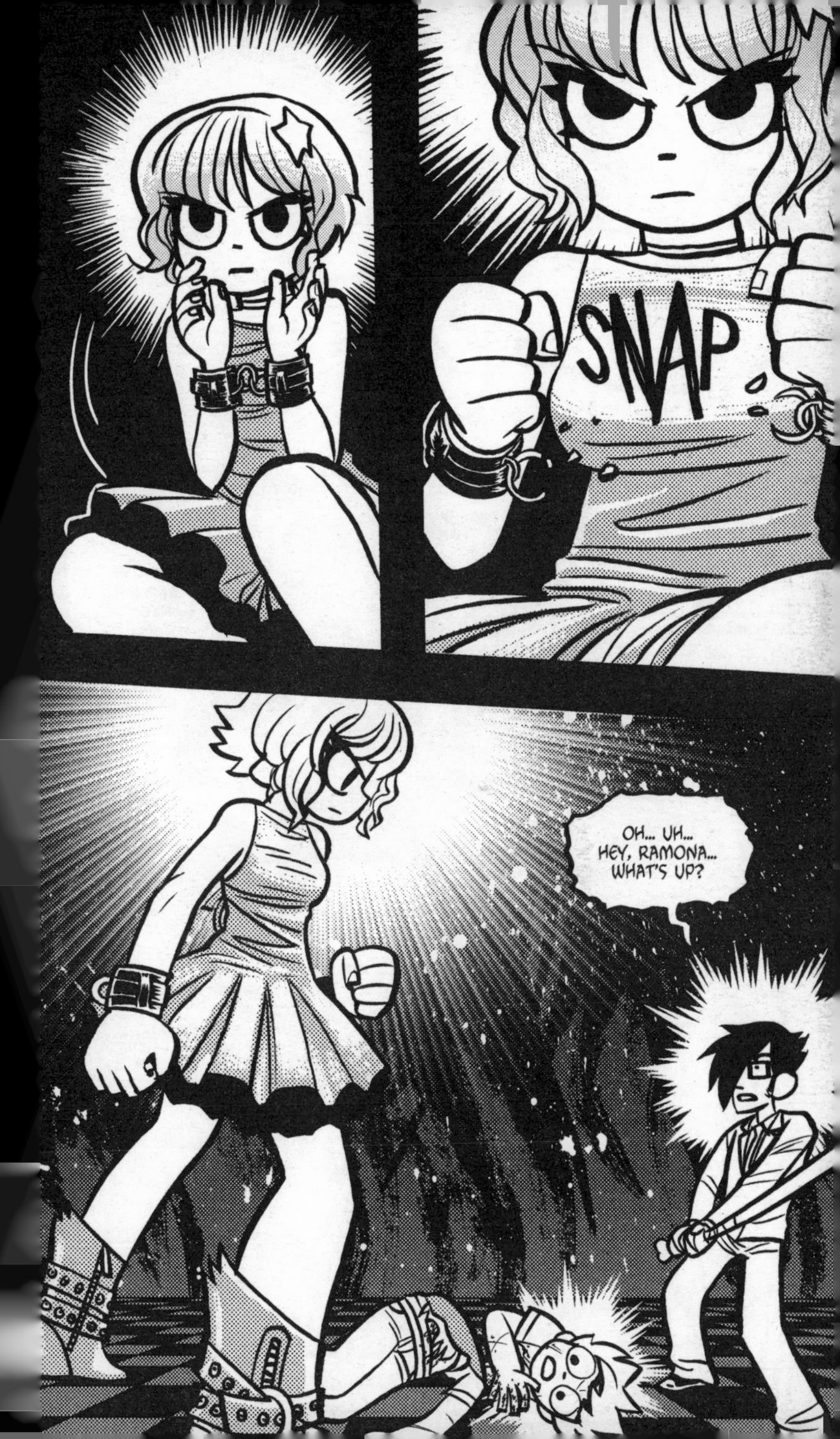
SNAP
OH... UH...
HEY, RAMONA...
WHAT'S UP?

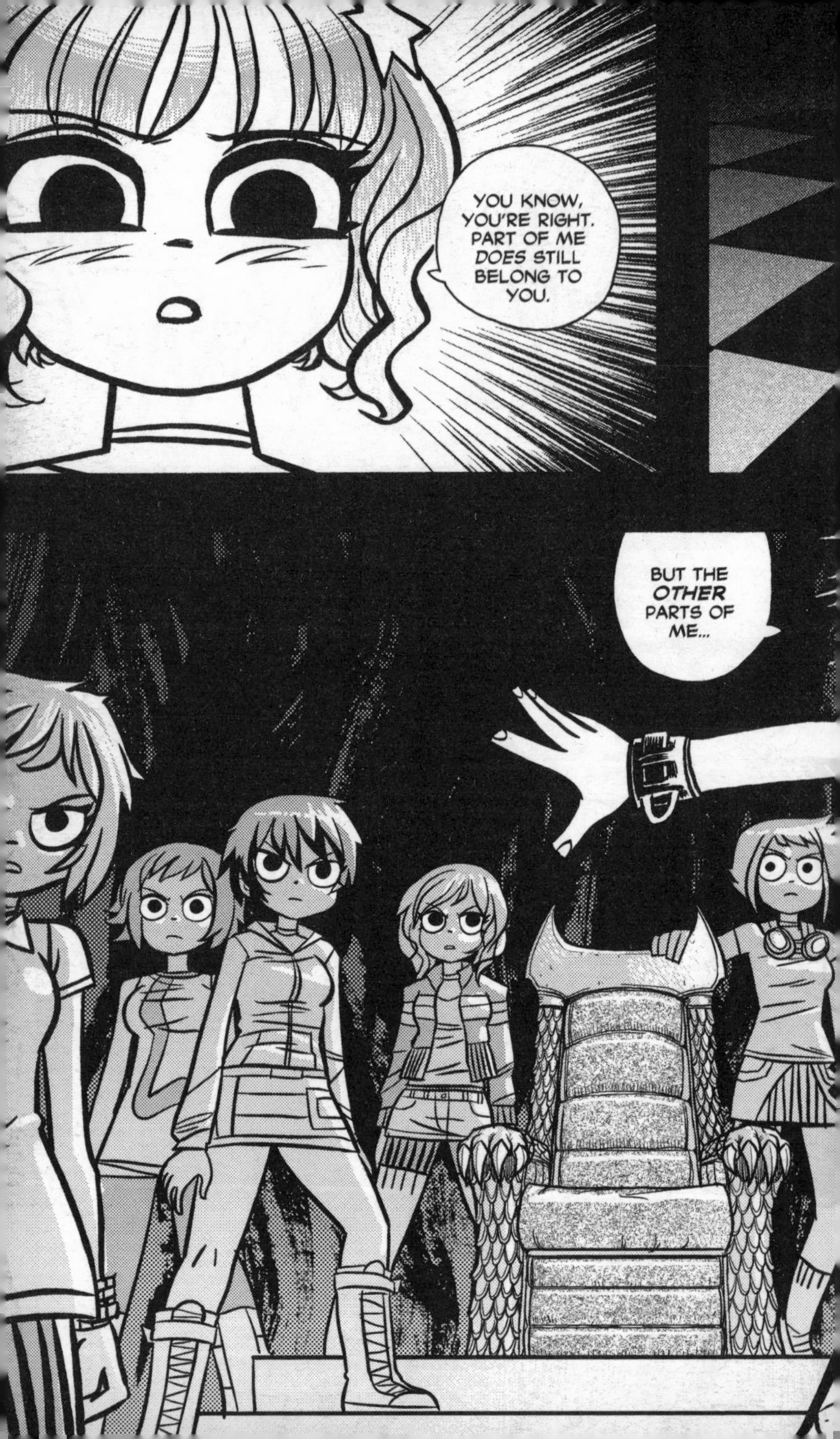
YOU KNOW, YOU'RE RIGHT. PART OF ME *DOES* STILL BELONG TO YOU.
BUT THE *OTHER* PARTS OF ME...

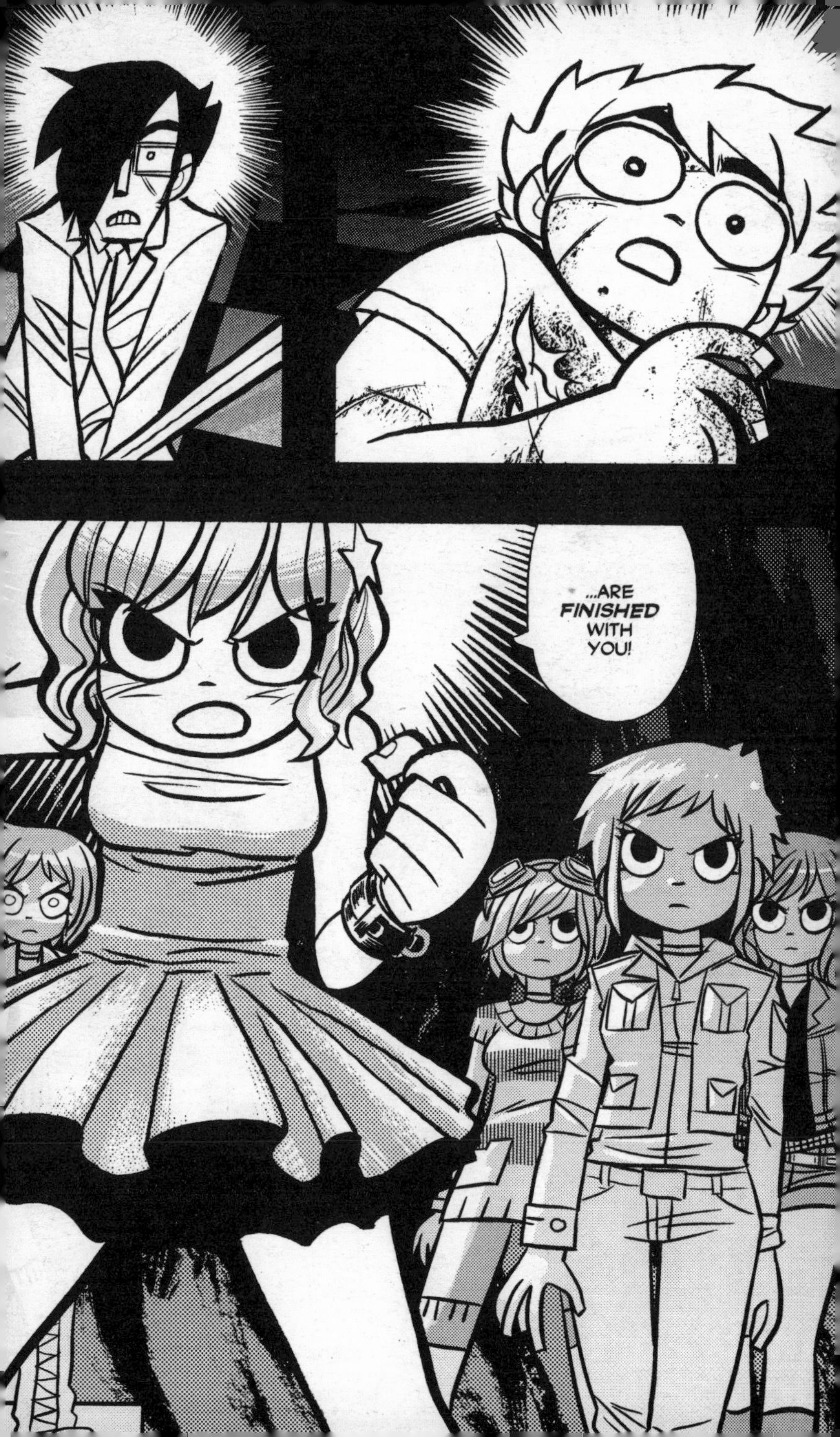
...ARE FINISHED WITH YOU!

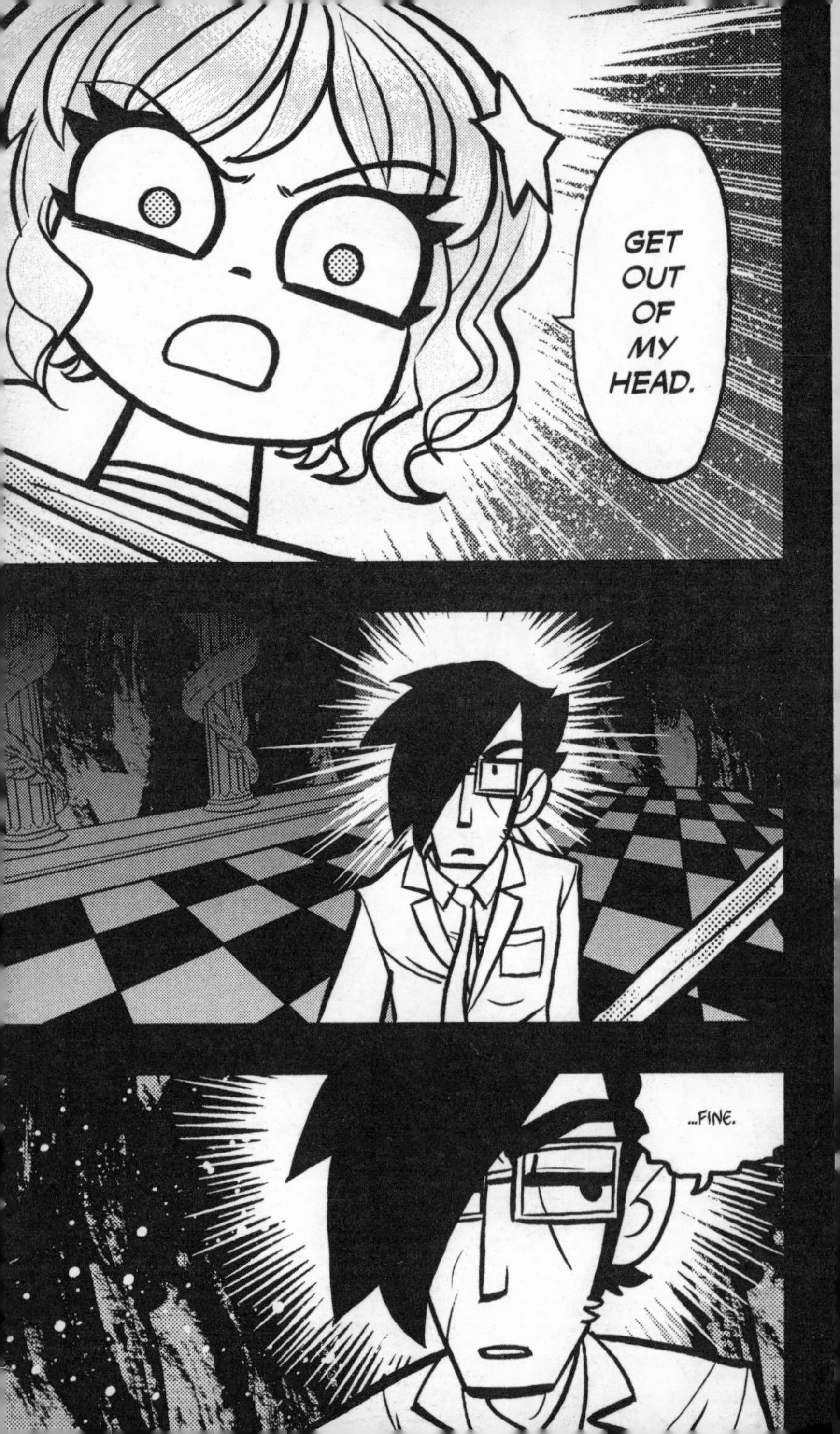
GET OUT OF MY HEAD.
...FINE.

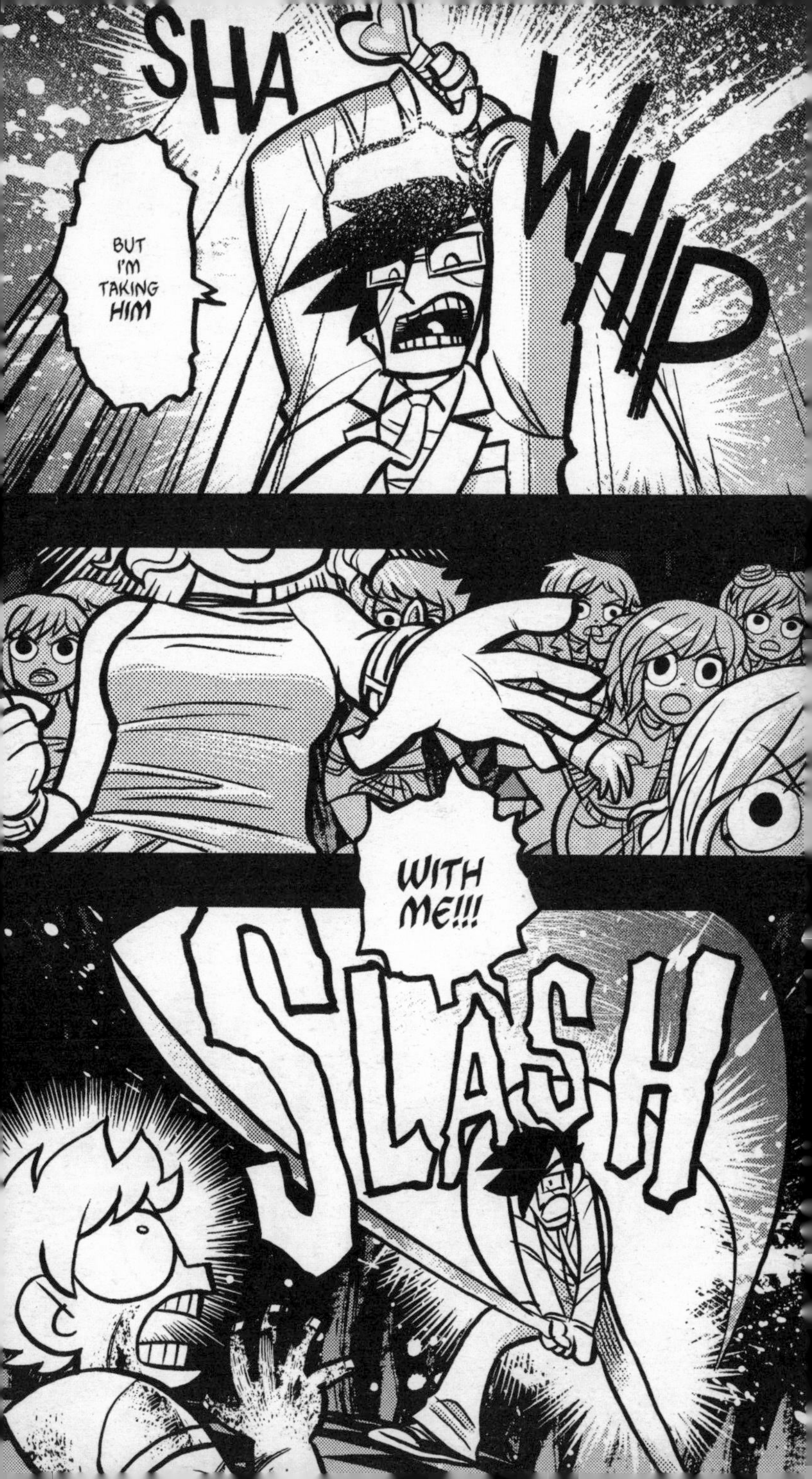
SHA
WHIP
BUT I'M TAKING HIM
WITH ME!!!
SLASH

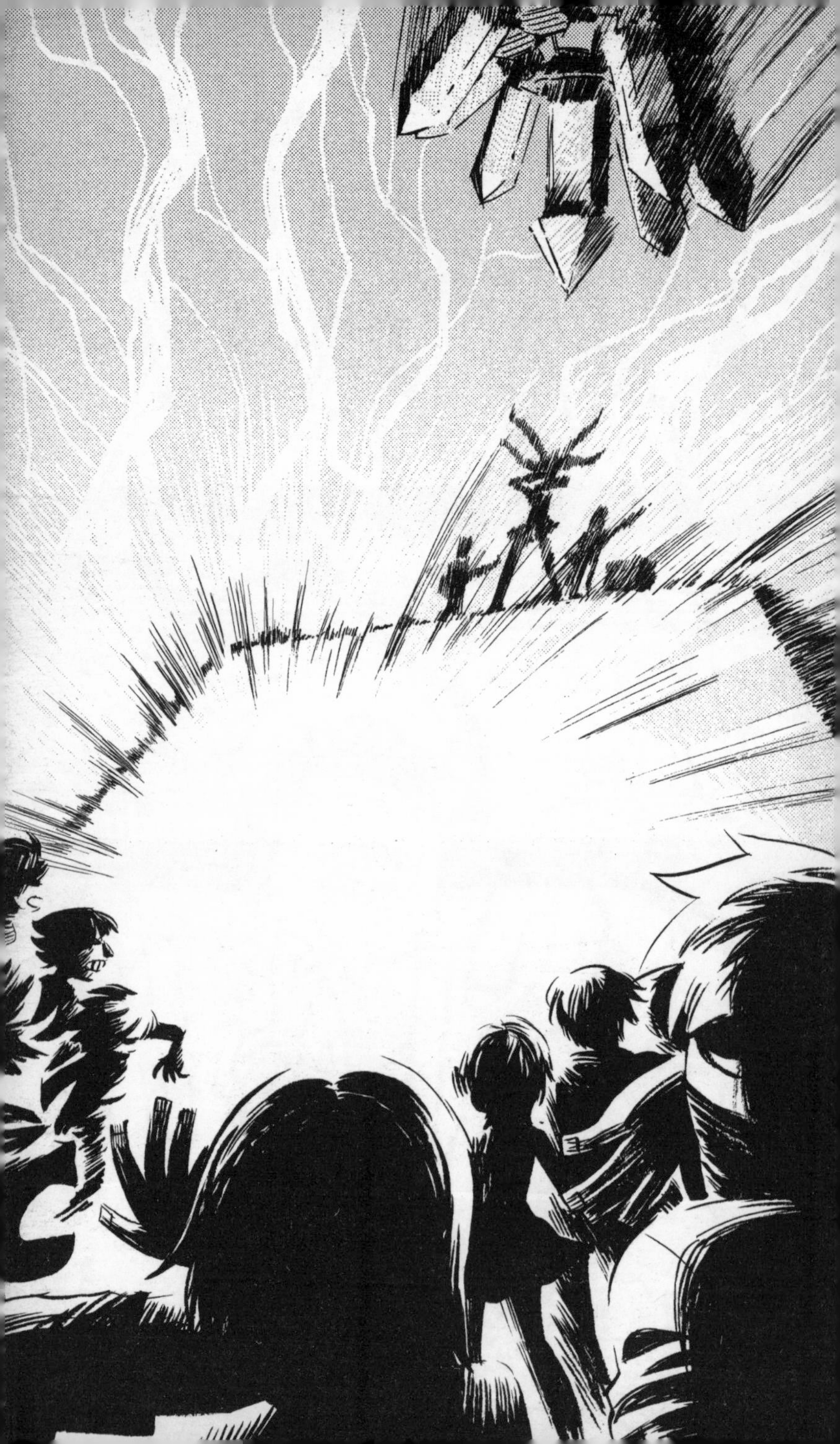

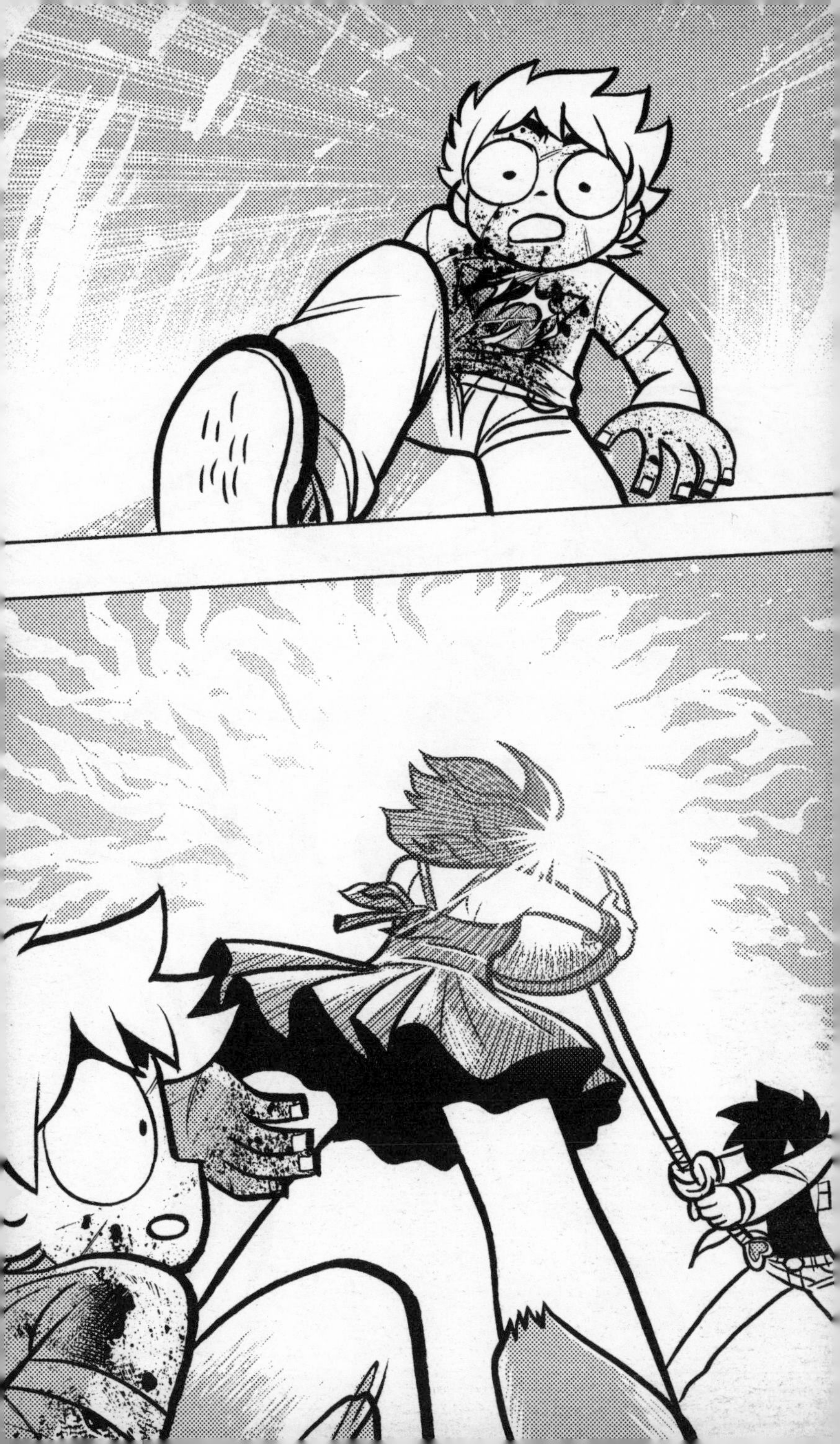

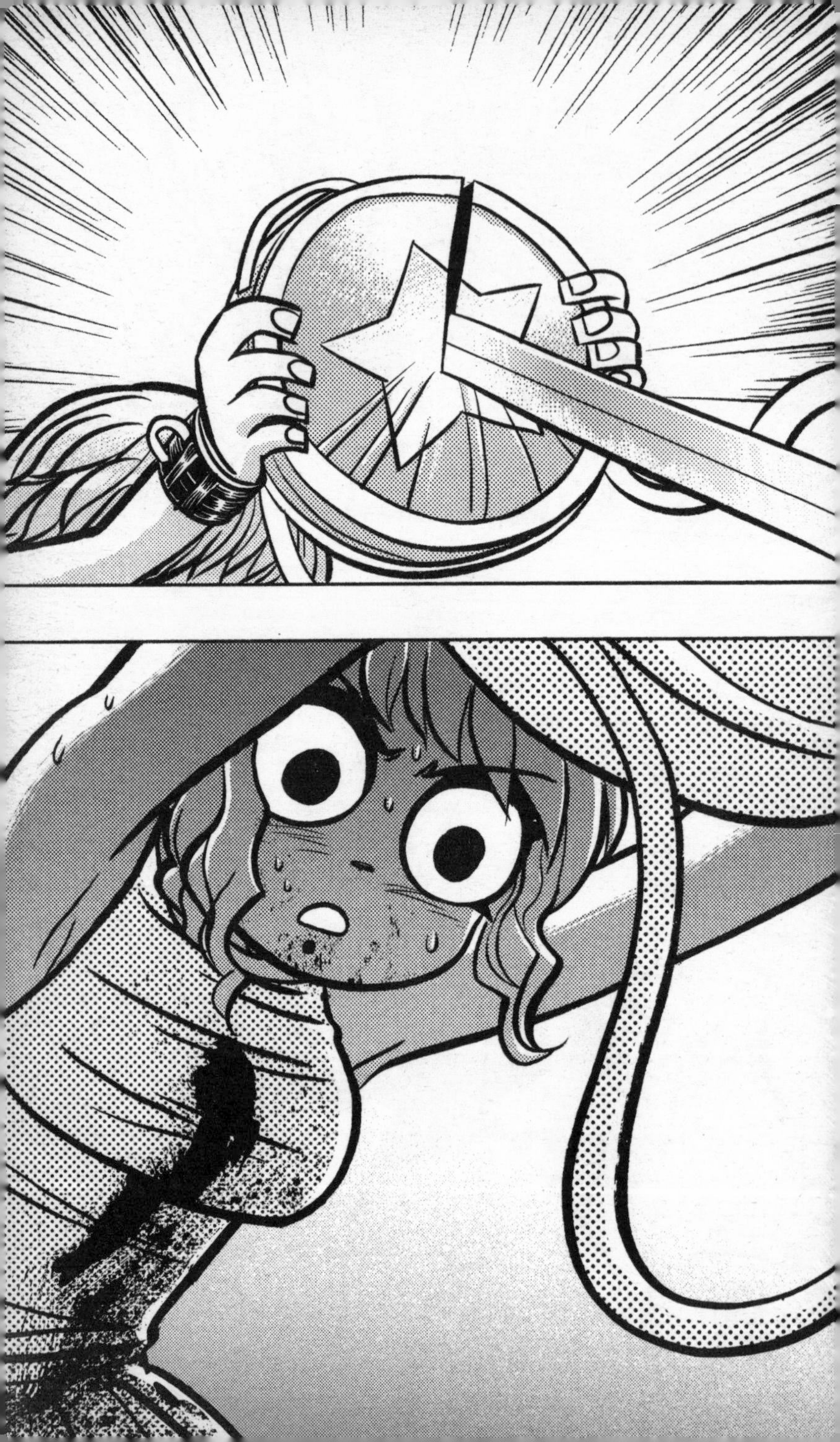

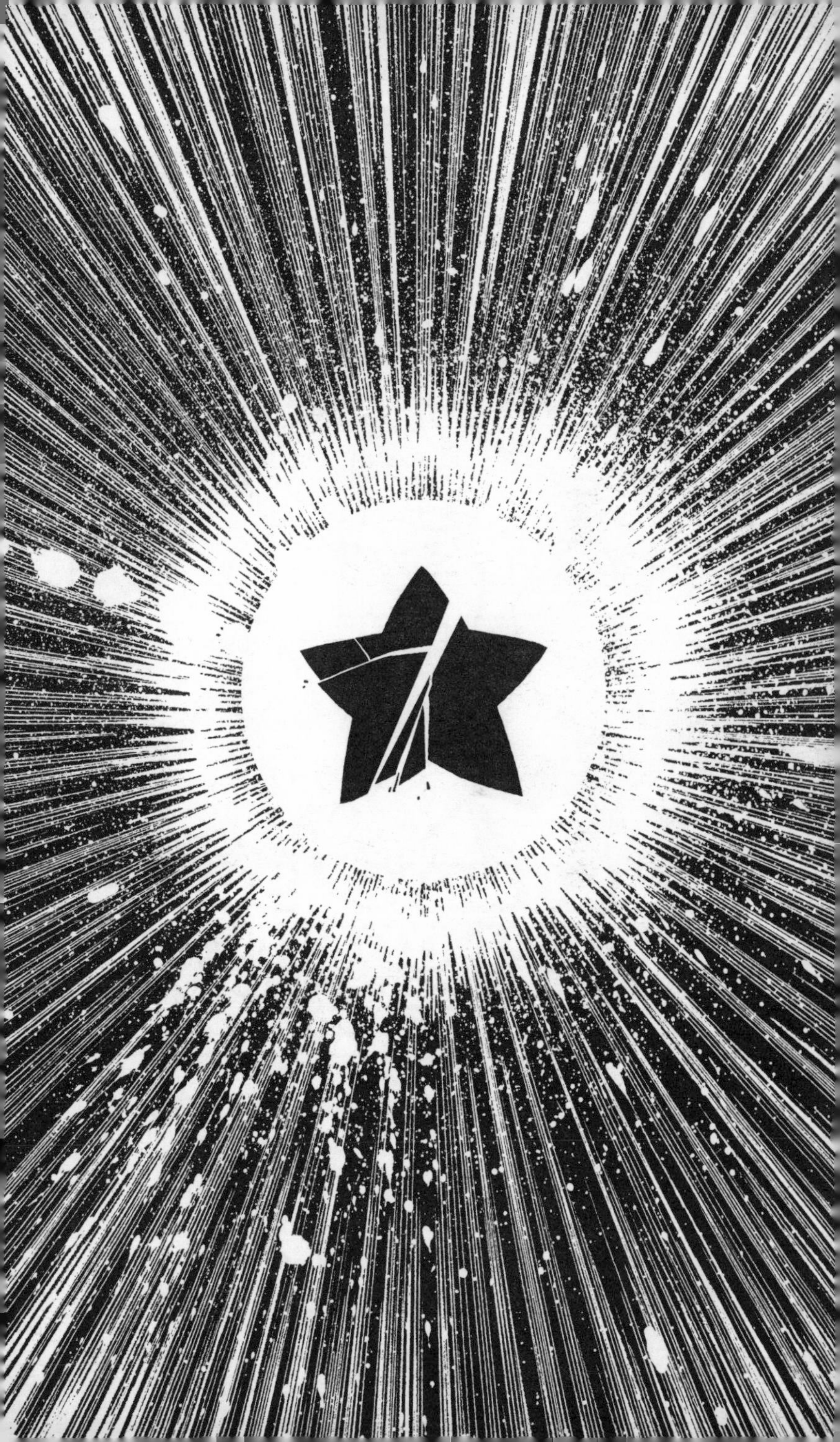

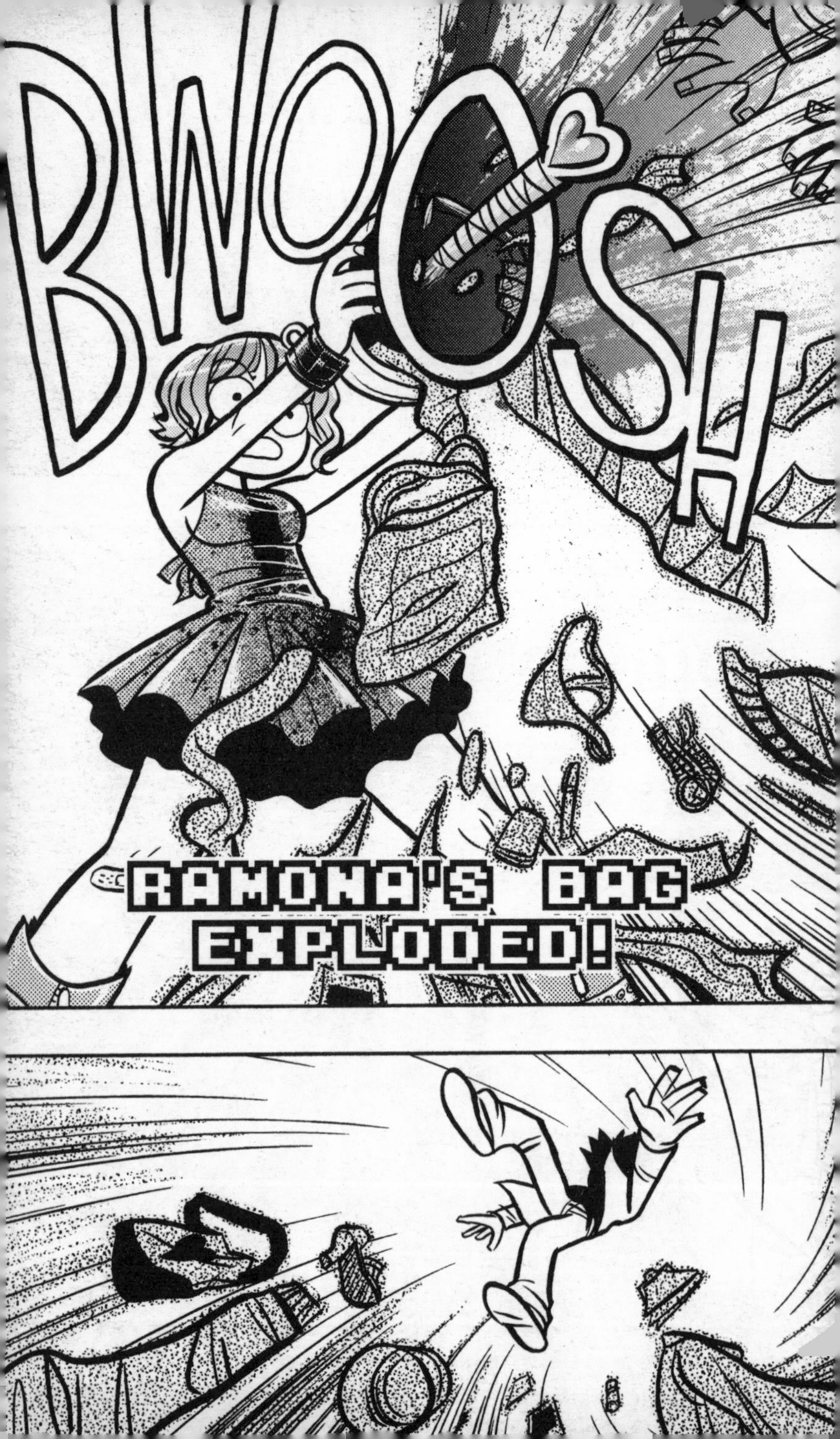
BWOOSH
RAMONA'S BAG EXPLODED!

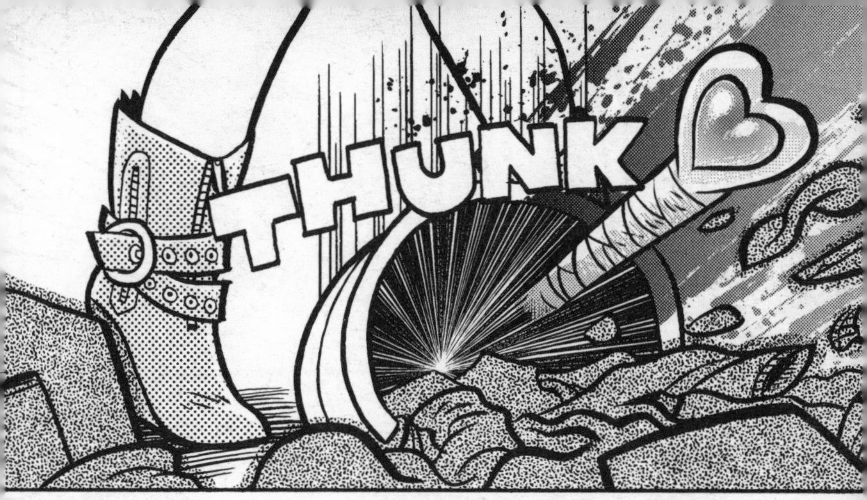
THUNK

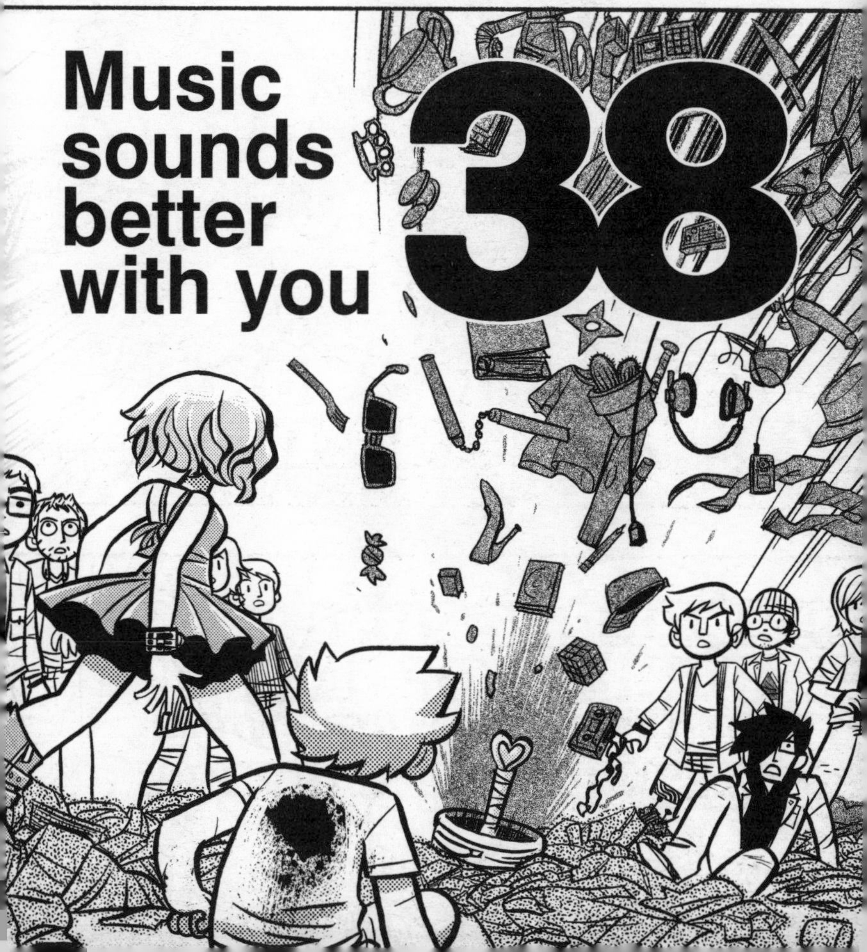
Music sounds better with you
38

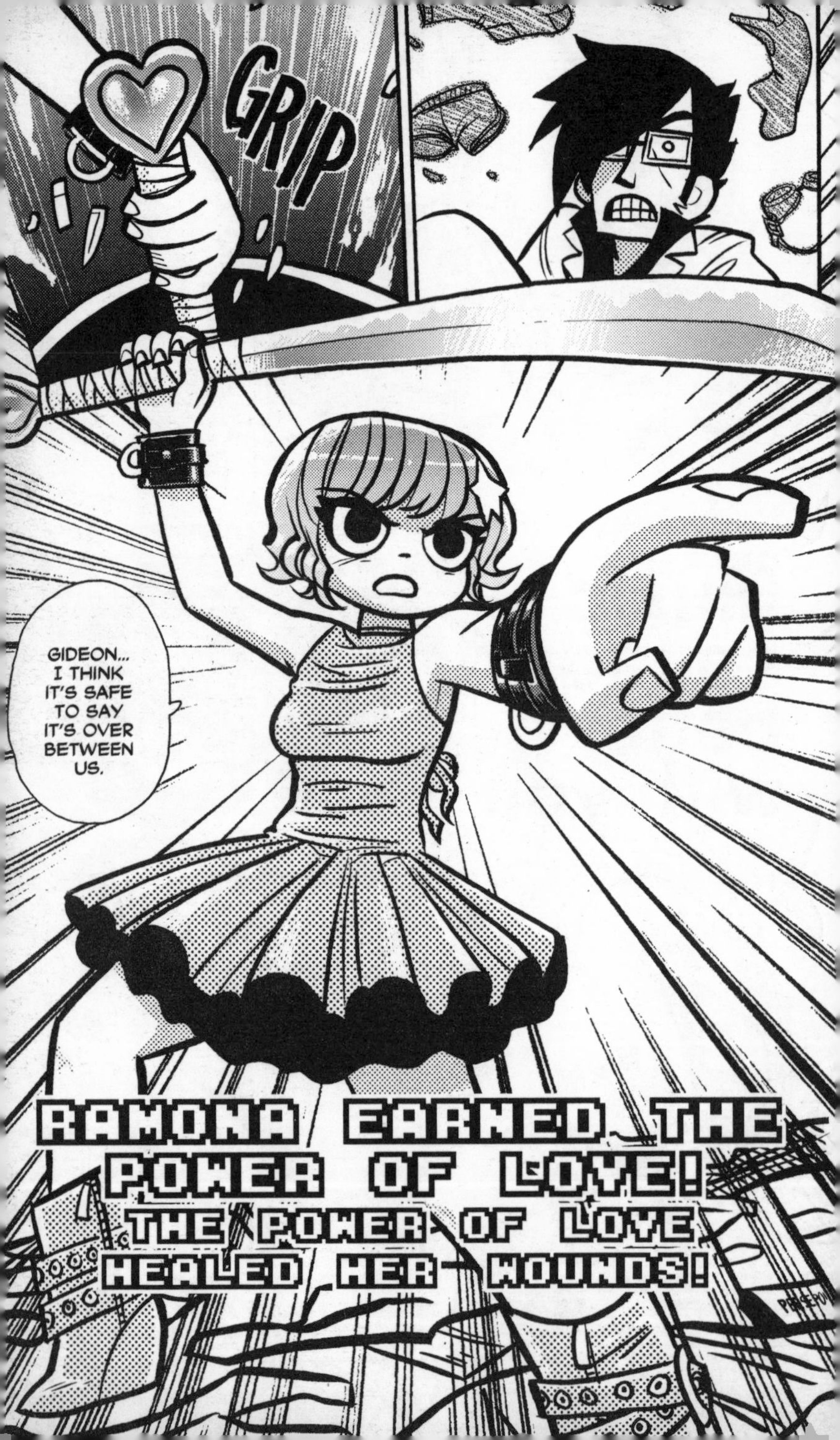
GRIP
GIDEON... I THINK IT'S SAFE TO SAY IT'S OVER BETWEEN US.
RAMONA EARNED THE POWER OF LOVE!
THE POWER OF LOVE HEALED HER WOUNDS!

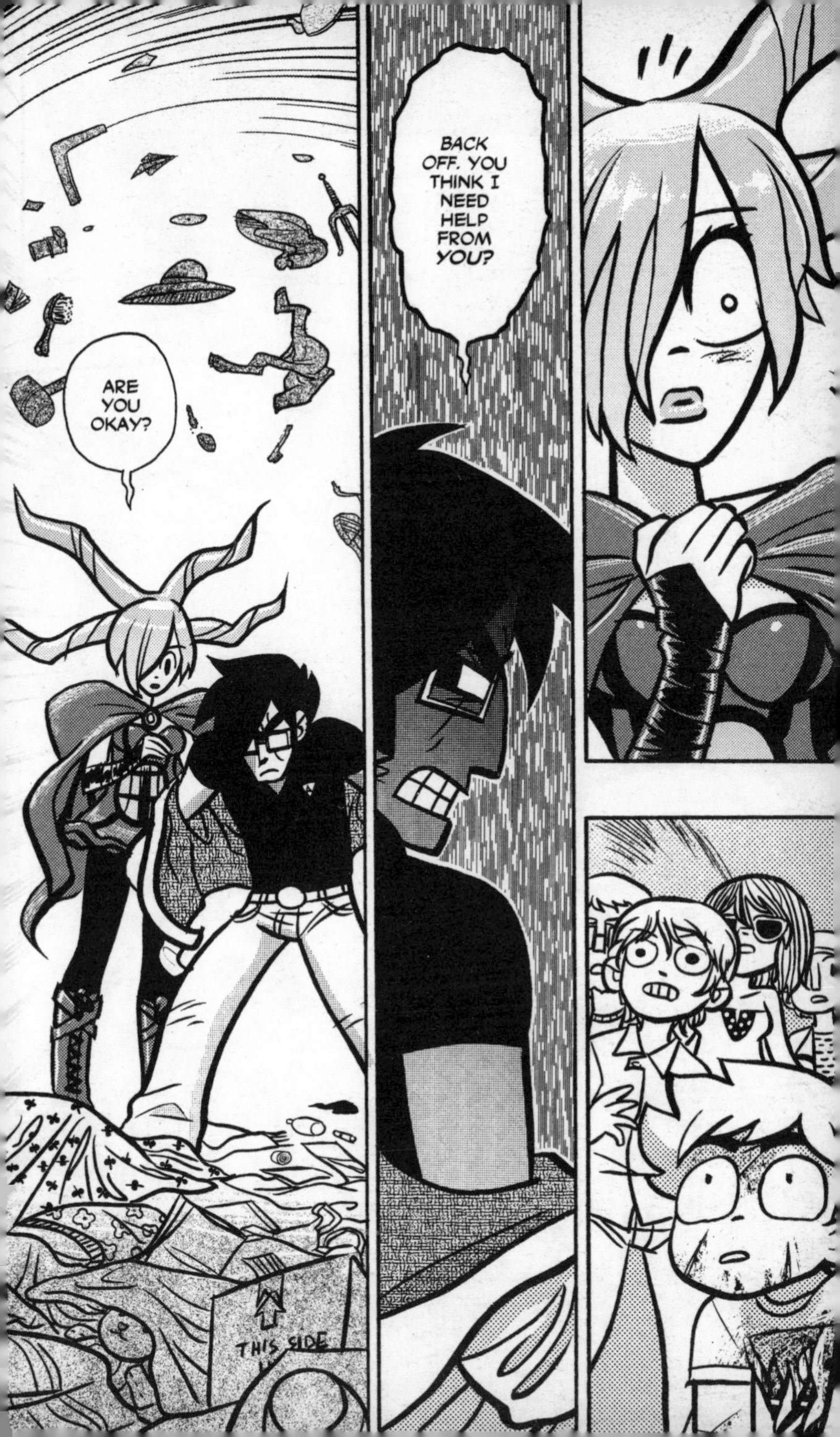
ARE YOU OKAY?
THIS SIDE
BACK OFF. YOU THINK I NEED HELP FROM YOU?

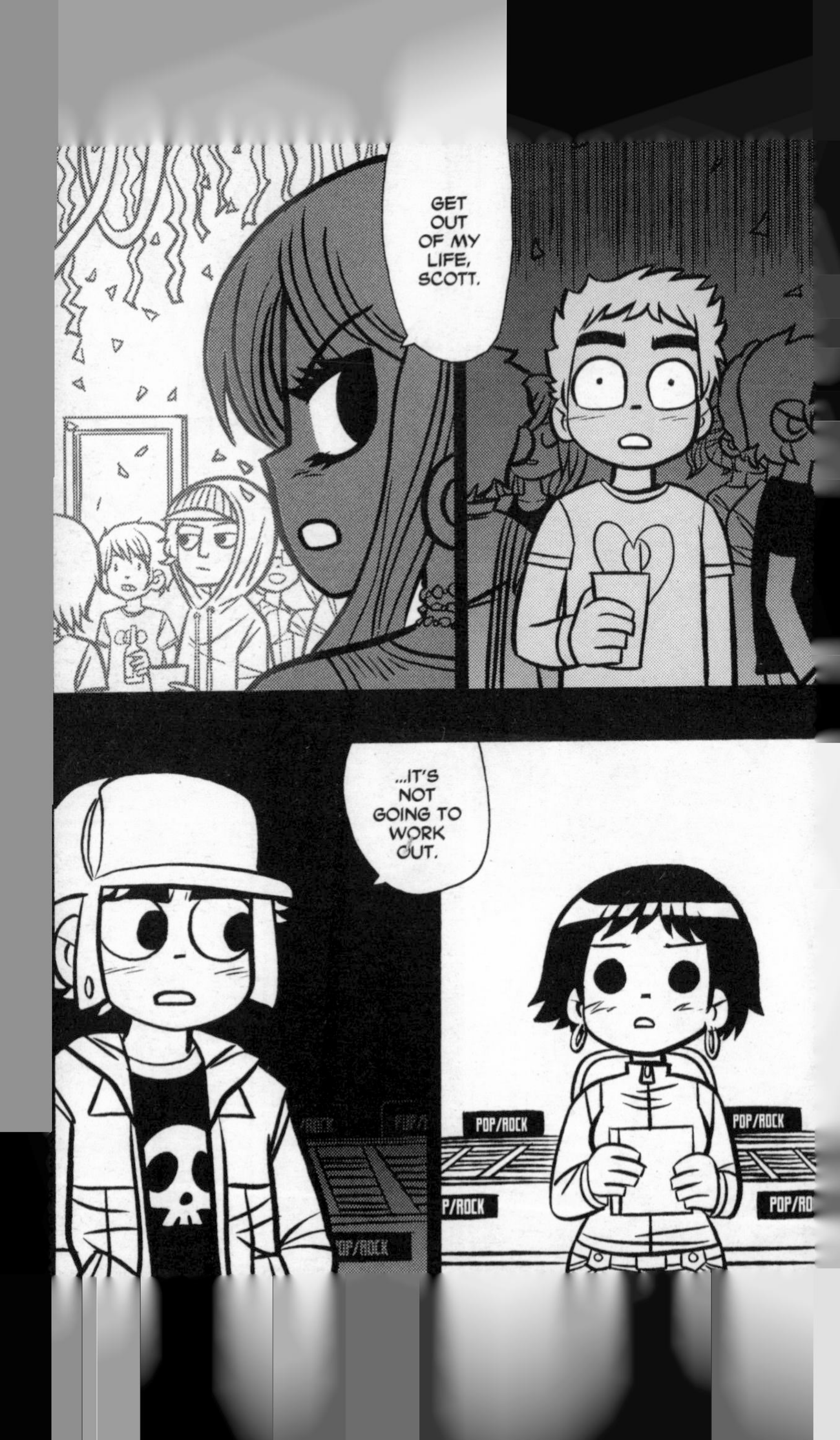
GET OUT OF MY LIFE, SCOTT.
...IT'S NOT GOING TO WORK OUT.
POP/ROCK
POP/ROCK

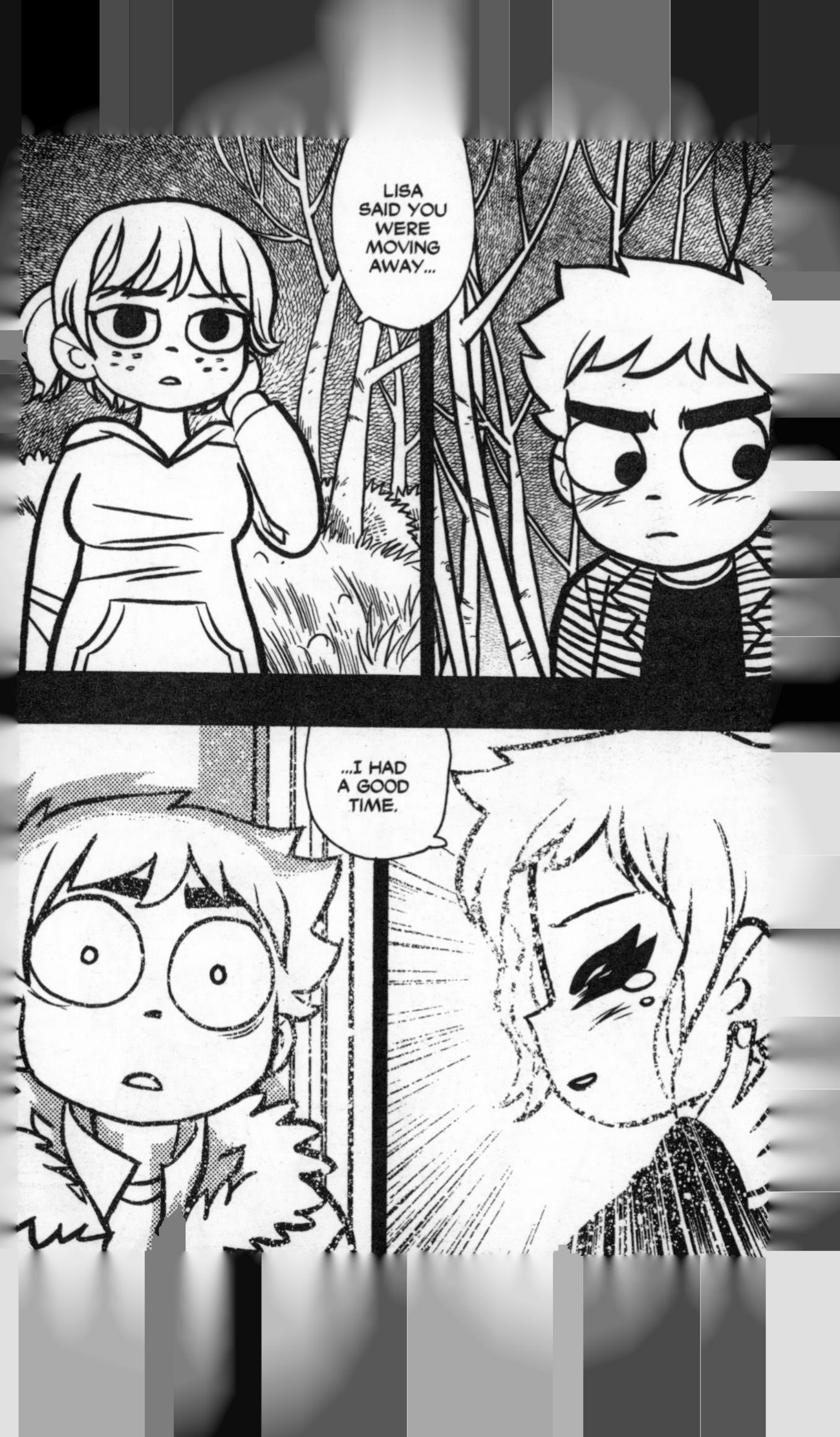
LISA SAID YOU WERE MOVING AWAY...
...I HAD A GOOD TIME.

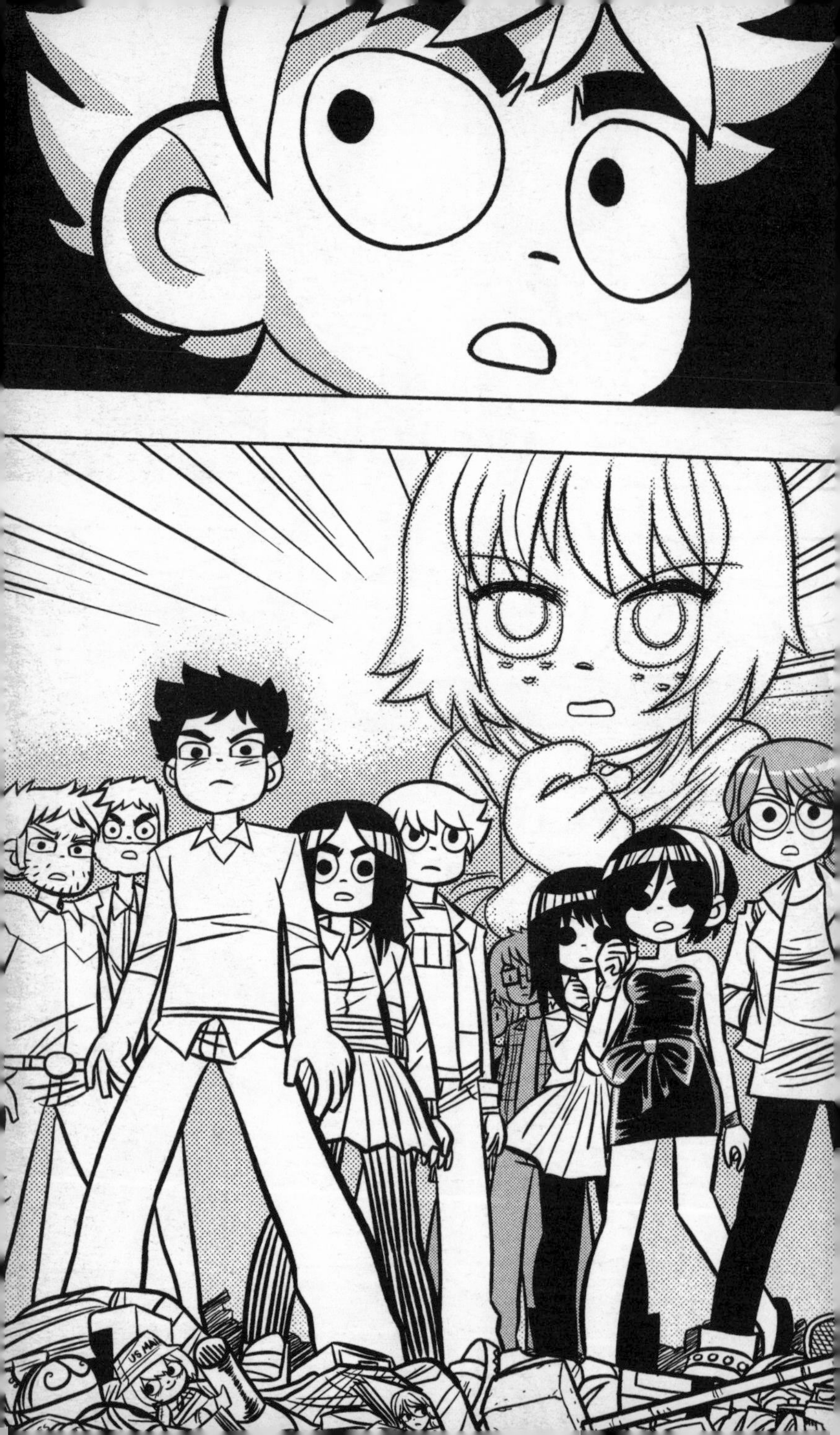

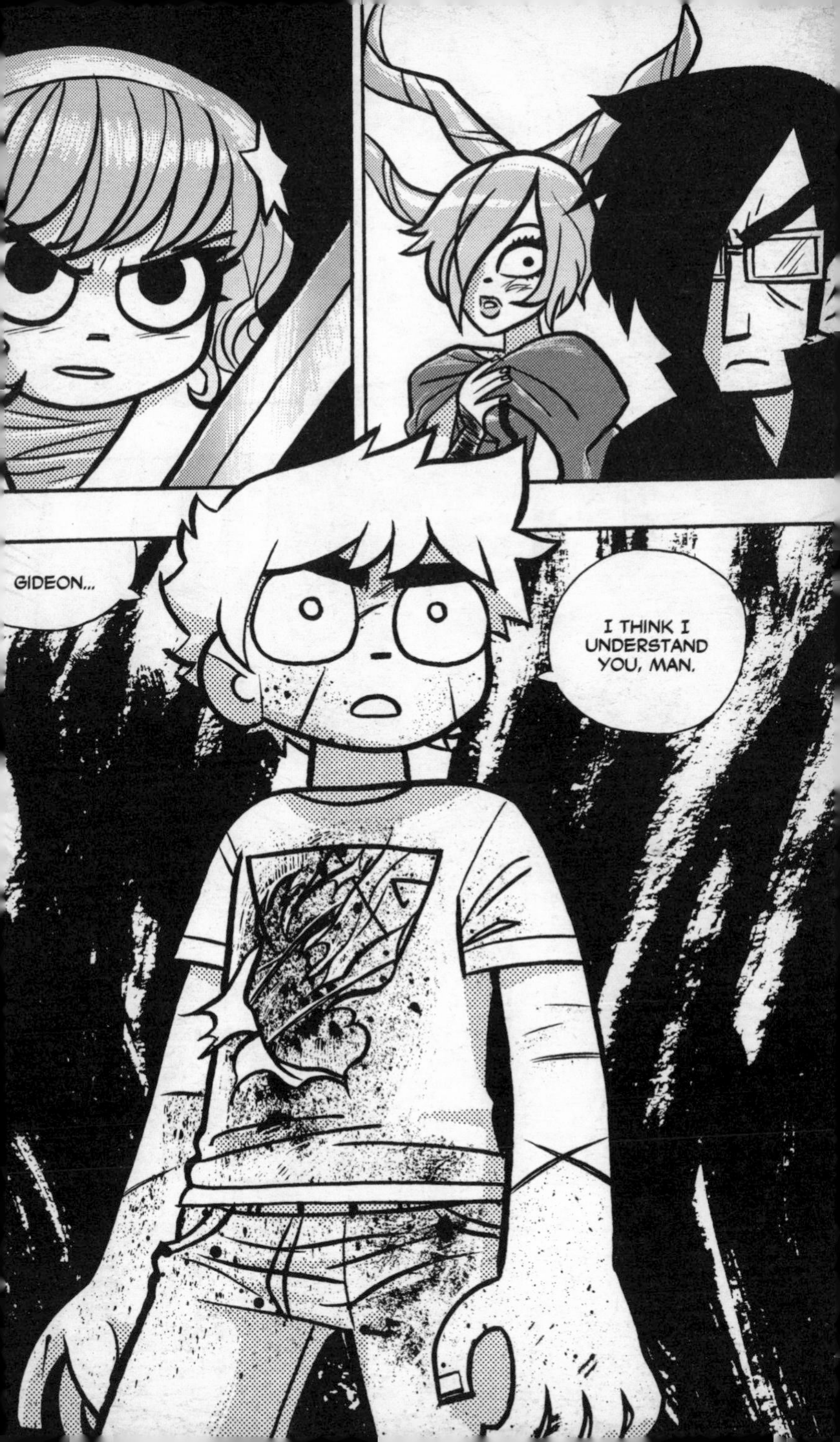
GIDEON...
I THINK I UNDERSTAND YOU, MAN.

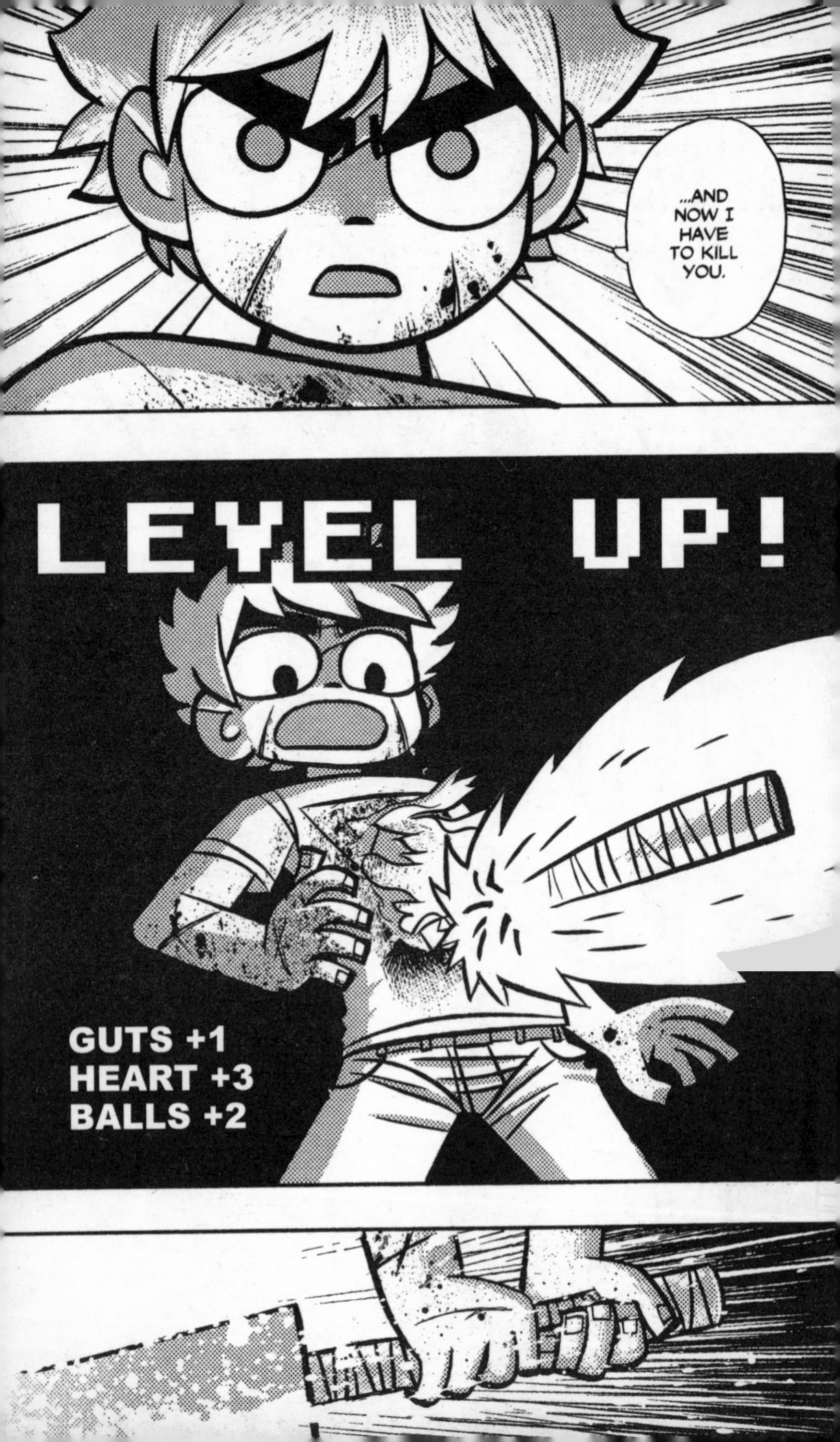

...AND NOW I HAVE TO KILL YOU.
LEVEL UP!
GUTS +1
HEART +3
BALLS +2

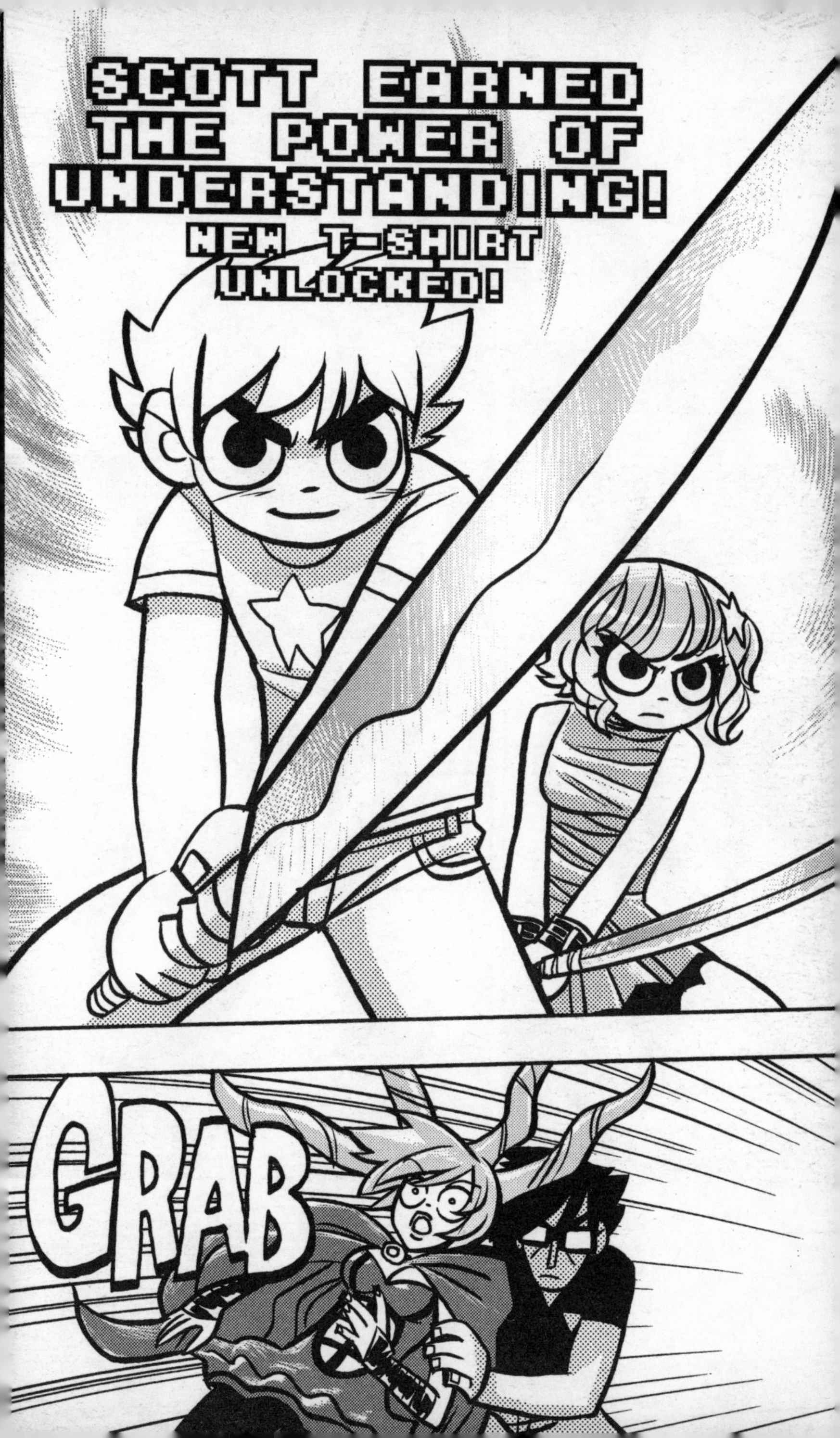
SCOTT EARNED THE POWER OF UNDERSTANDING!
NEW T-SHIRT UNLOCKED!
GRAB

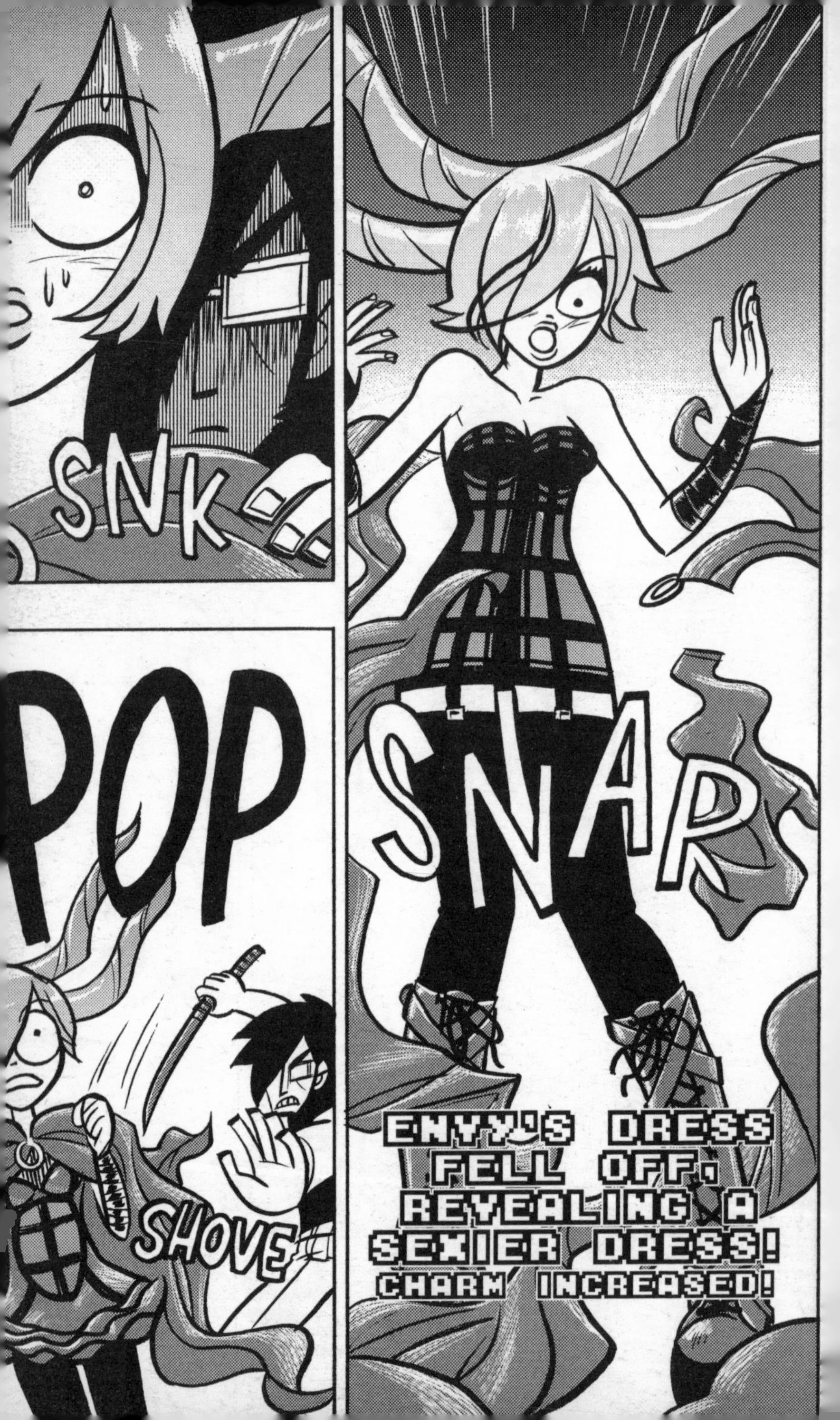
SNK
POP
SHOVE
SNAP
ENVY'S DRESS FELL OFF, REVEALING A SEXIER DRESS!
CHARM INCREASED!

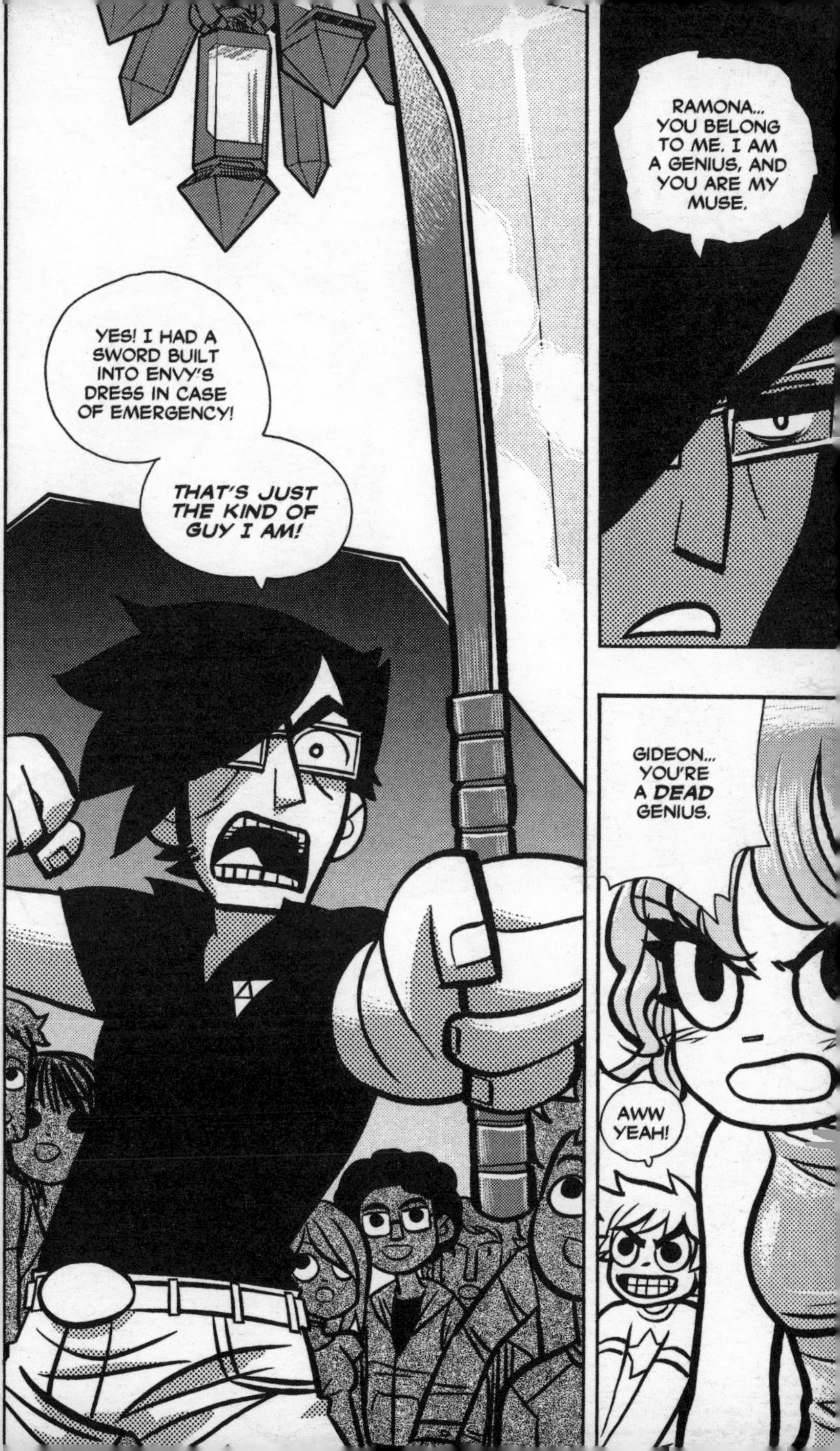
YES! I HAD A SWORD BUILT INTO ENVY'S DRESS IN CASE OF EMERGENCY!
THAT'S JUST THE KIND OF GUY I AM!
RAMONA... YOU BELONG TO ME. I AM A GENIUS, AND YOU ARE MY MUSE.
GIDEON... YOU'RE A *DEAD* GENIUS.
AWW YEAH!

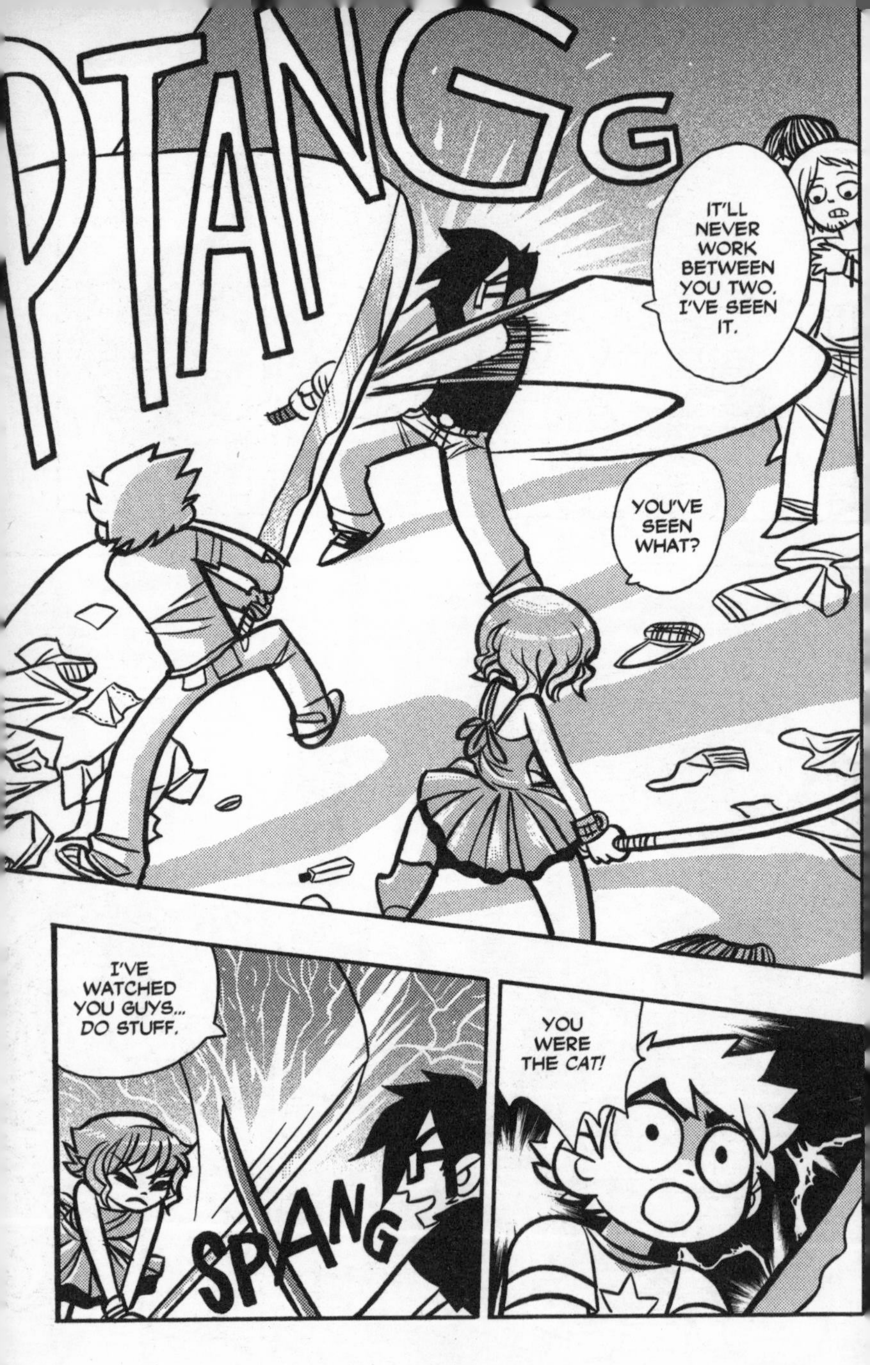
PTANGG
IT'LL NEVER WORK BETWEEN YOU TWO. I'VE SEEN IT.
YOU'VE SEEN WHAT?
I'VE WATCHED YOU GUYS... DO STUFF.
SPANG
YOU WERE THE CAT!

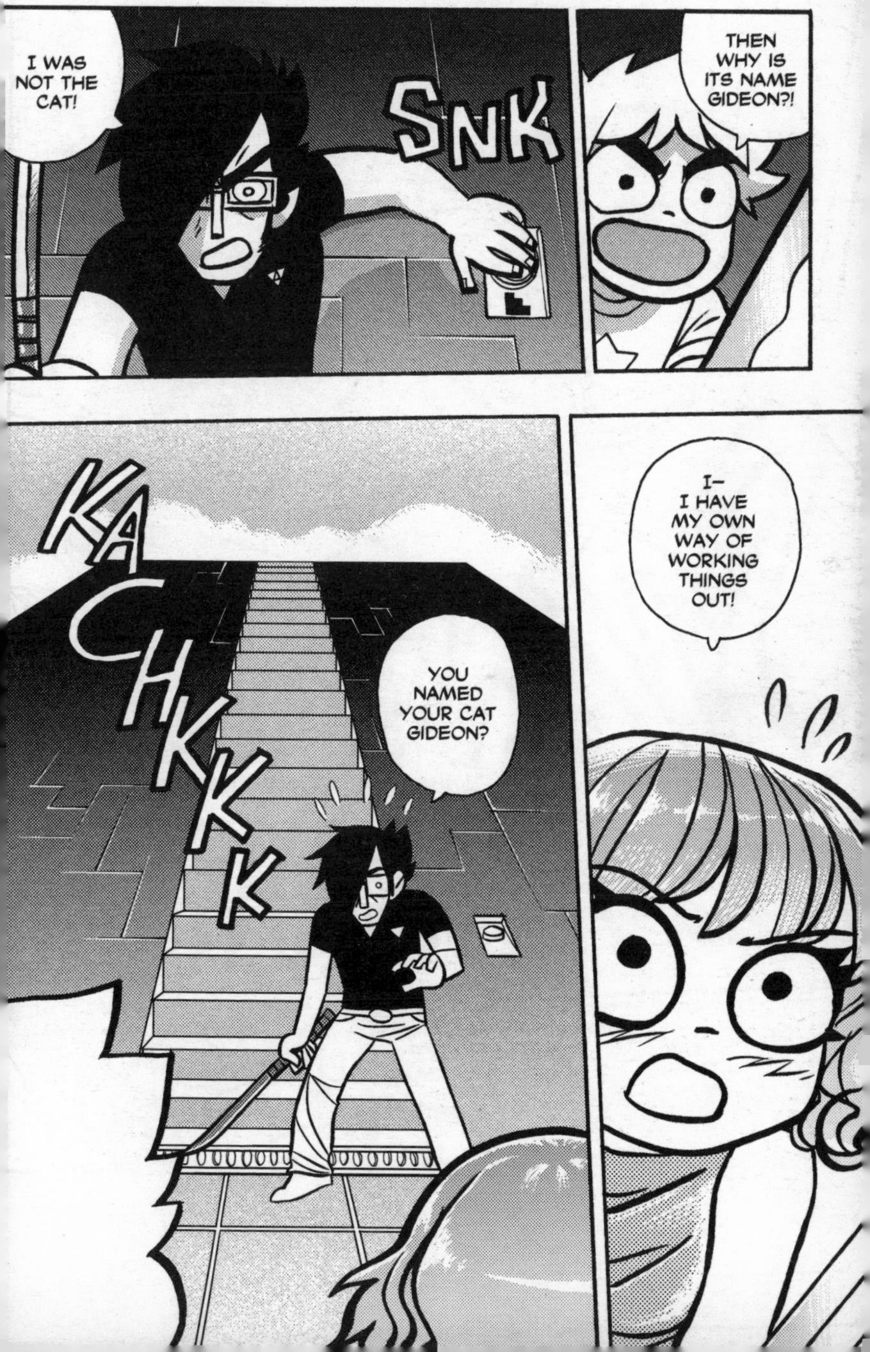

I WAS NOT THE CAT!
SNK
THEN WHY IS ITS NAME GIDEON?!
KACHKKK
YOU NAMED YOUR CAT GIDEON?
I– I HAVE MY OWN WAY OF WORKING THINGS OUT!

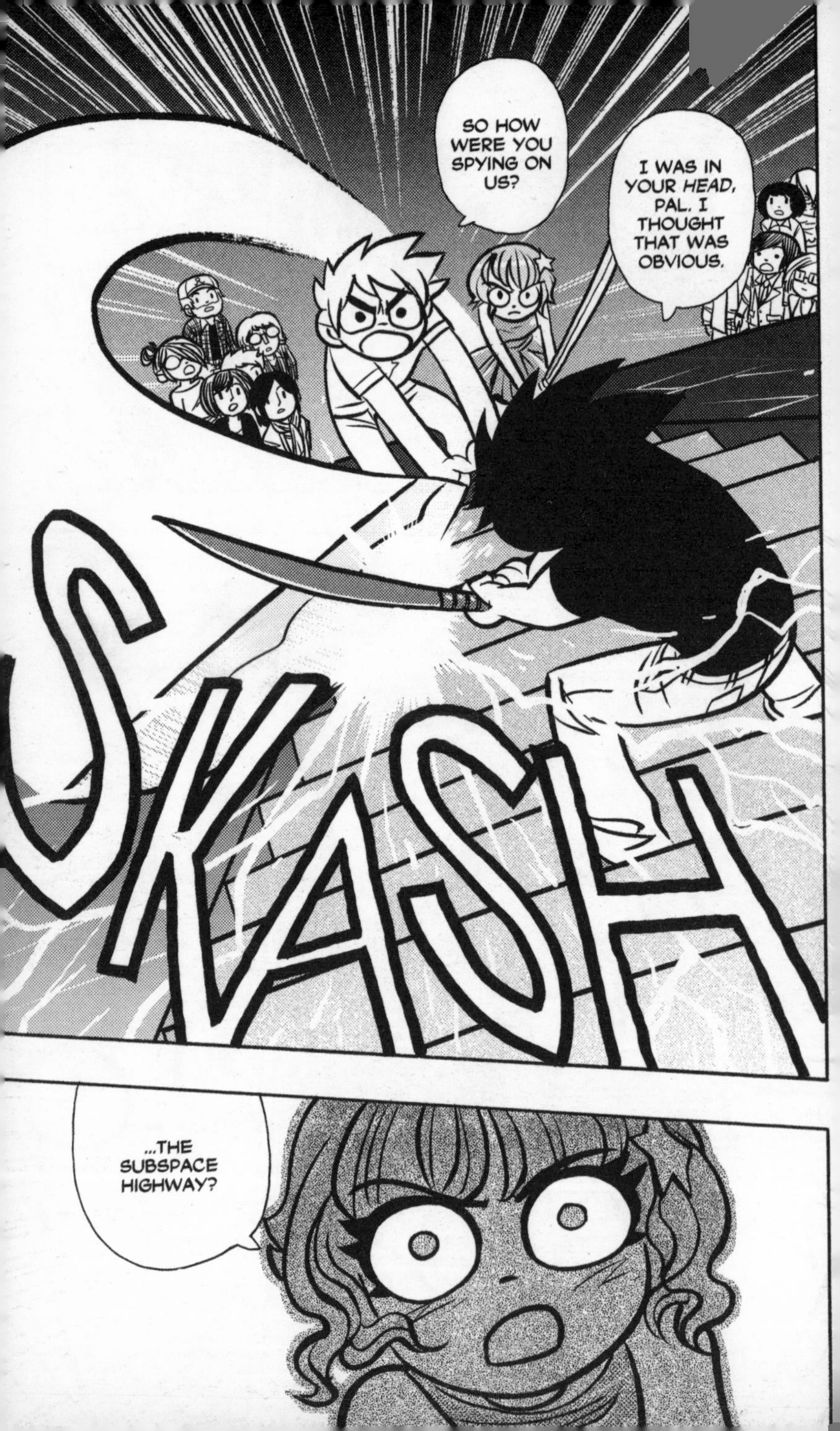
SO HOW WERE YOU SPYING ON US?
I WAS IN YOUR *HEAD*, PAL. I THOUGHT THAT WAS OBVIOUS.
SKASH
...THE SUBSPACE HIGHWAY?

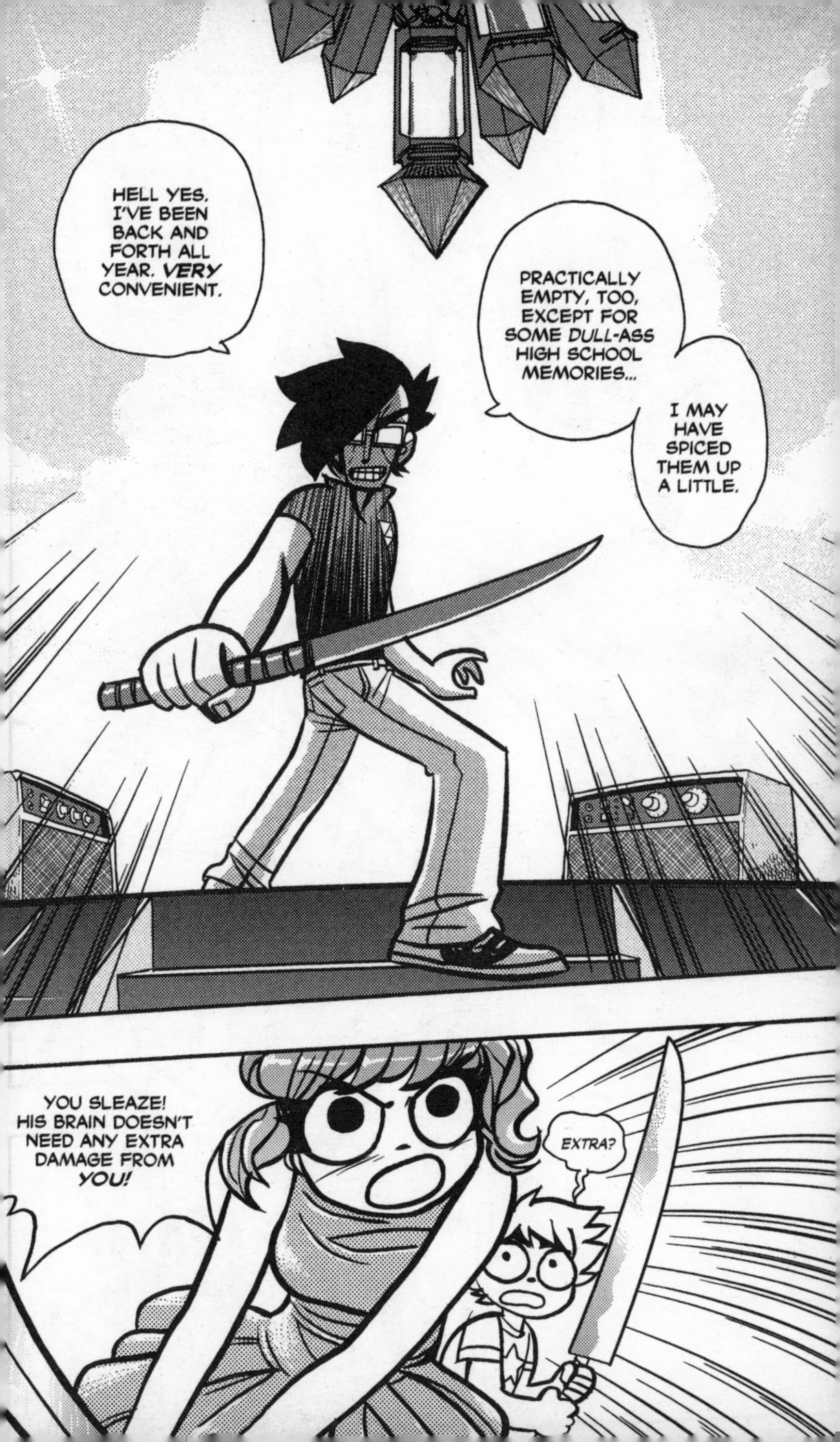
HELL YES. I'VE BEEN BACK AND FORTH ALL YEAR. VERY CONVENIENT.
PRACTICALLY EMPTY, TOO, EXCEPT FOR SOME DULL-ASS HIGH SCHOOL MEMORIES...
I MAY HAVE SPICED THEM UP A LITTLE.
YOU SLEAZE! HIS BRAIN DOESN'T NEED ANY EXTRA DAMAGE FROM YOU!
EXTRA?

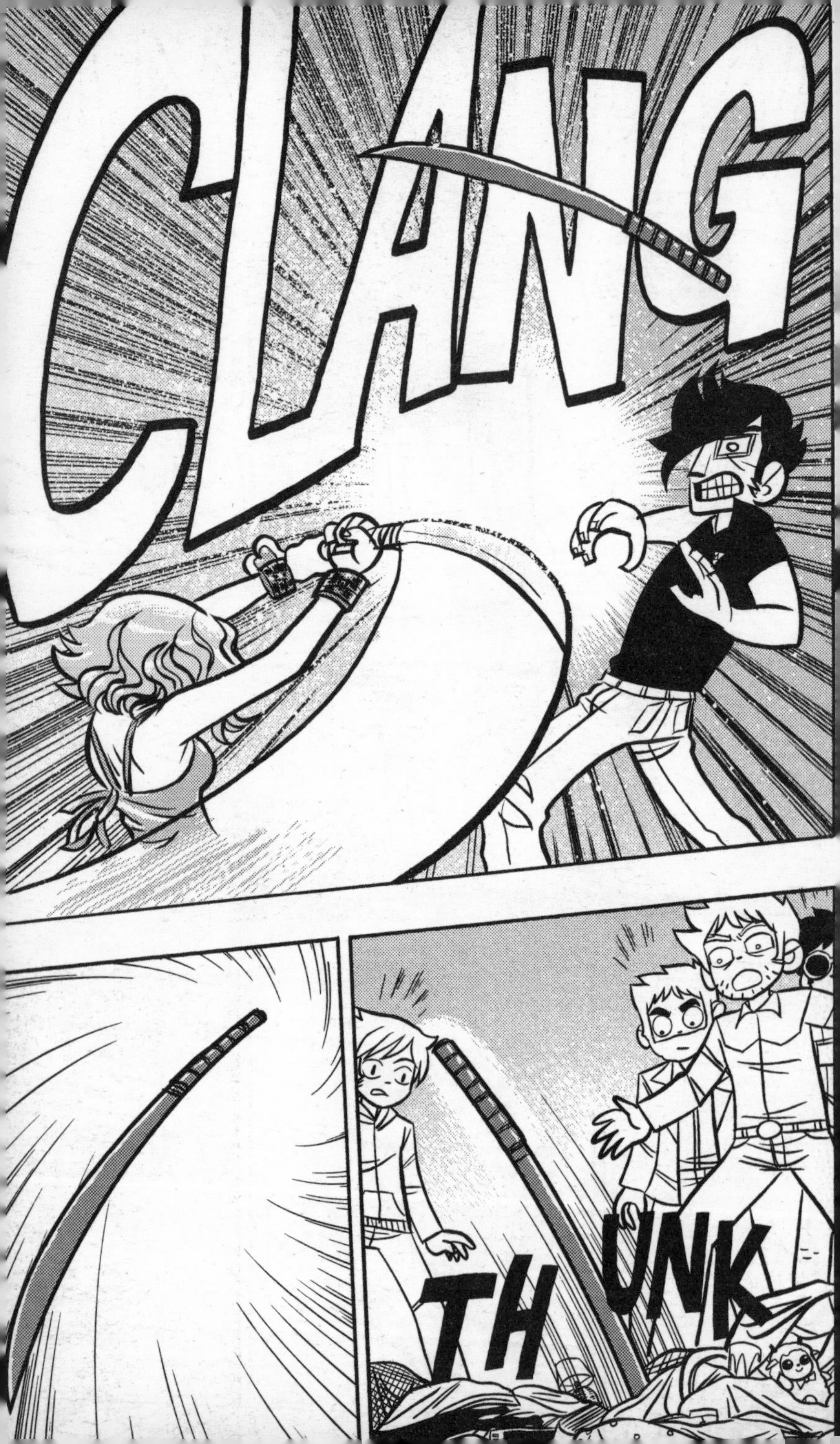
CLANG
THUNK

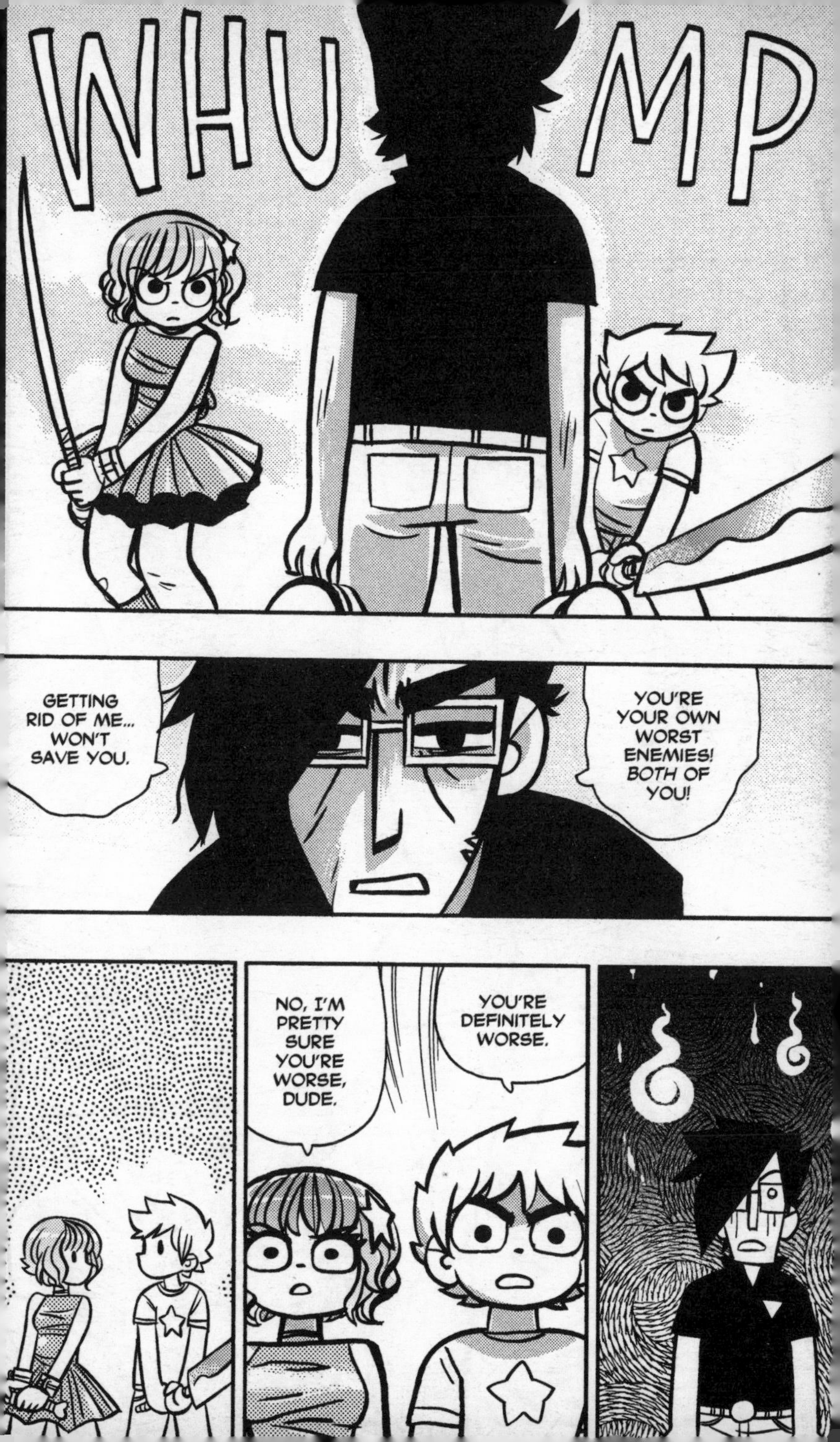
WHUMP
GETTING RID OF ME... WON'T SAVE YOU.
YOU'RE YOUR OWN WORST ENEMIES! BOTH OF YOU!
NO, I'M PRETTY SURE YOU'RE WORSE, DUDE.
YOU'RE DEFINITELY WORSE.

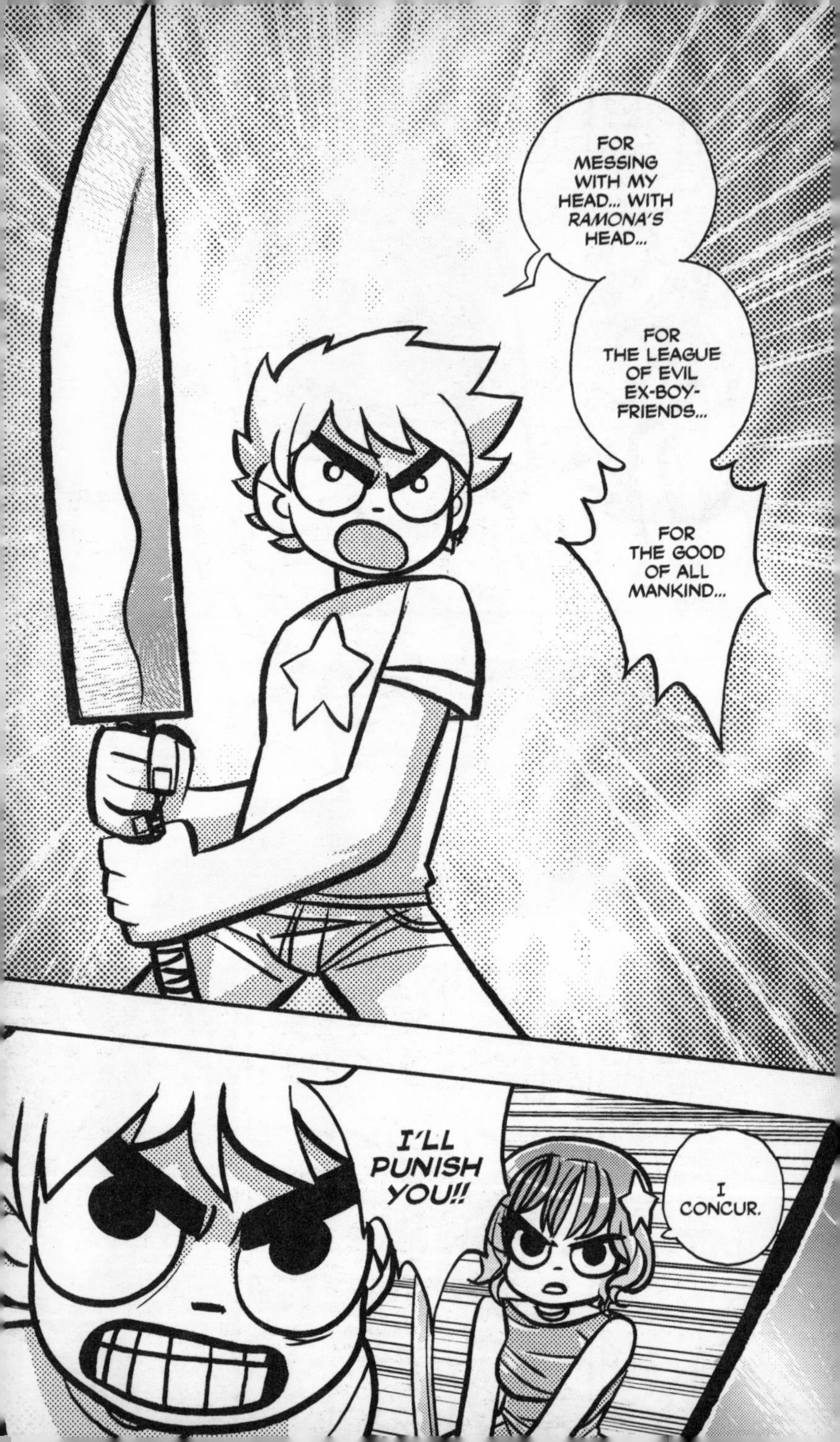
FOR MESSING WITH MY HEAD... WITH *RAMONA'S* HEAD...
FOR THE LEAGUE OF EVIL EX-BOY-FRIENDS...
FOR THE GOOD OF ALL MANKIND...
I'LL PUNISH YOU!!
I CONCUR.

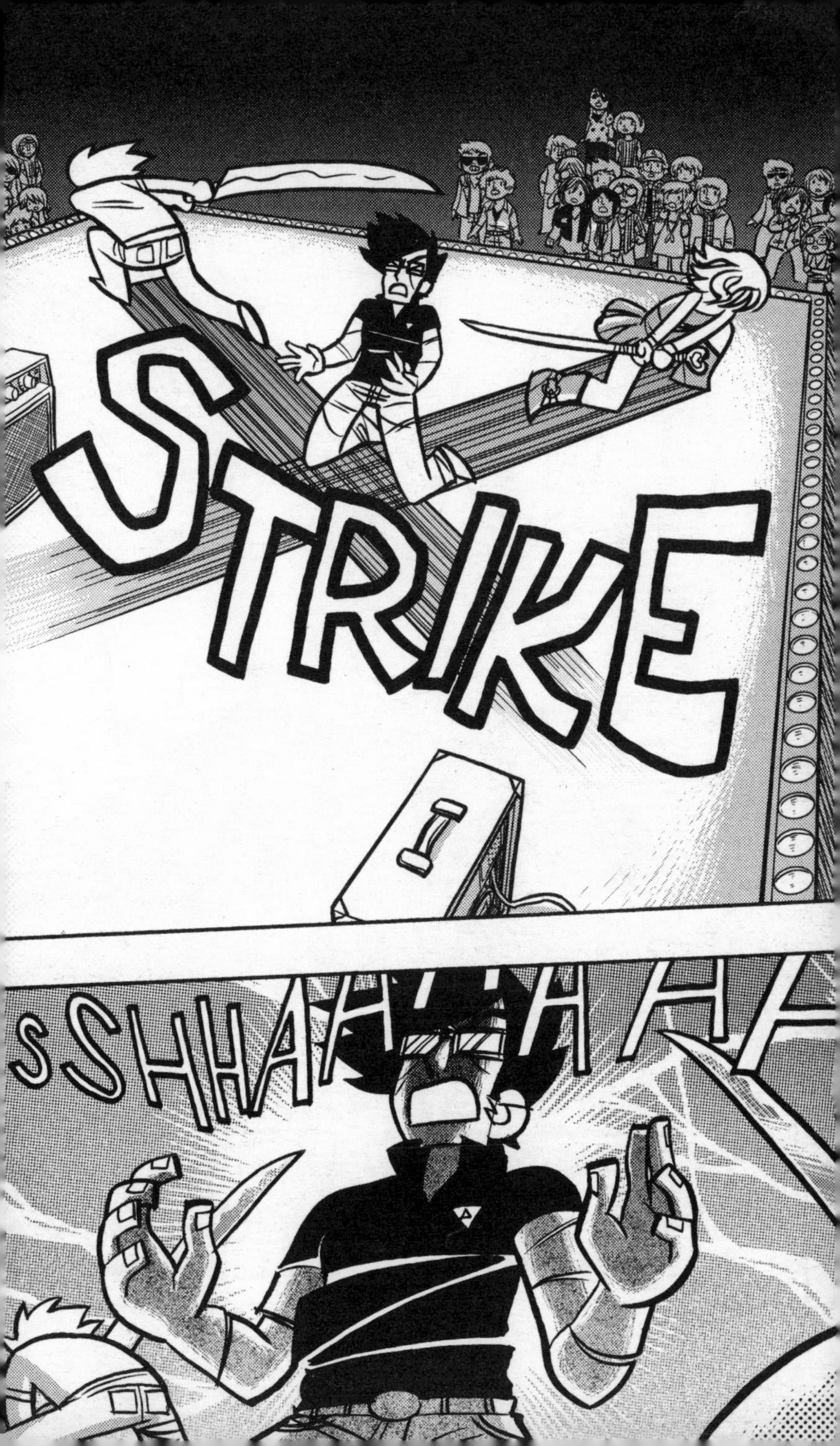
STRIKE
sSHHAAAAAA

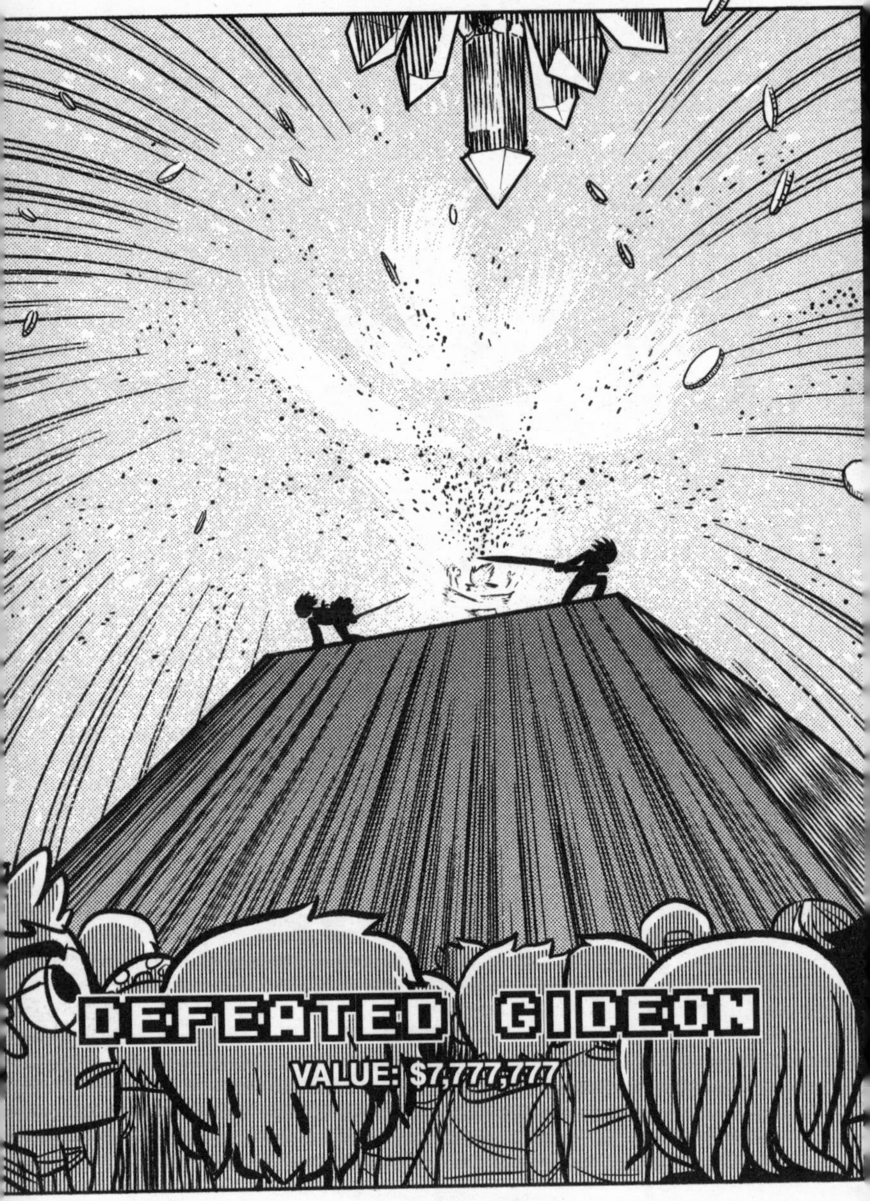
DEFEATED GIDEON
VALUE: $7,777,777

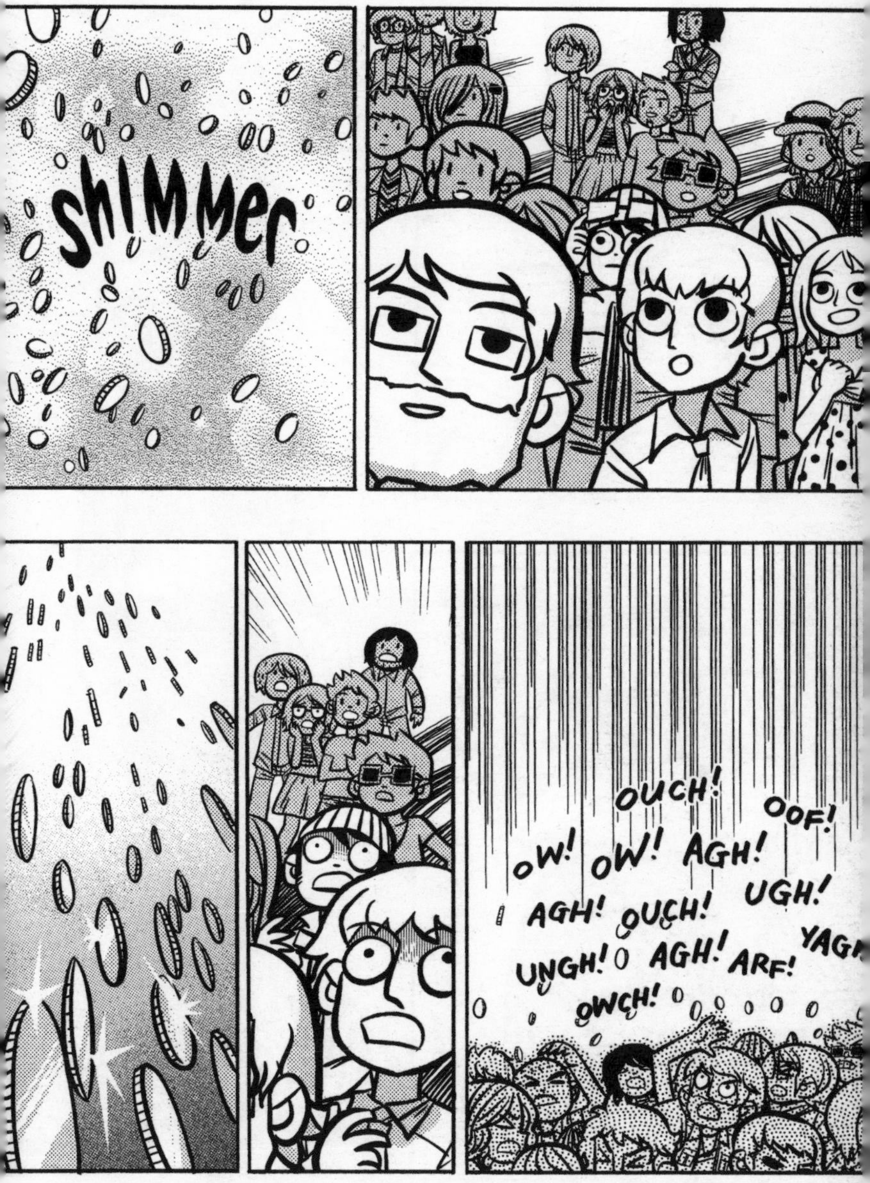
SHIMMER
OUCH!
OOF!
OW! OW! AGH!
AGH! OUCH! UGH!
UNGH! AGH! ARF!
OWCH!

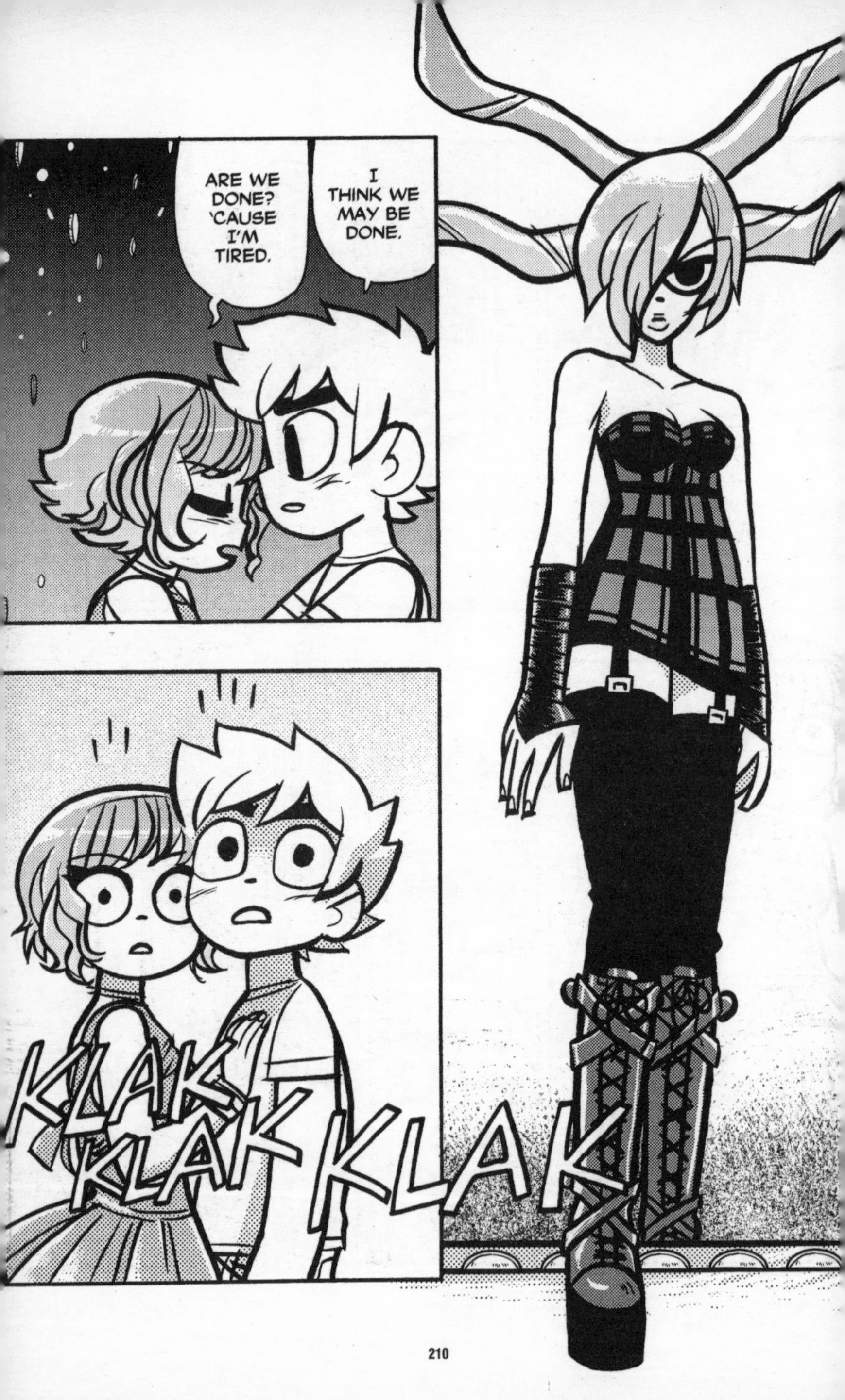
ARE WE DONE? 'CAUSE I'M TIRED.
I THINK WE MAY BE DONE.
KLAK
KLAK KLAK KLAK

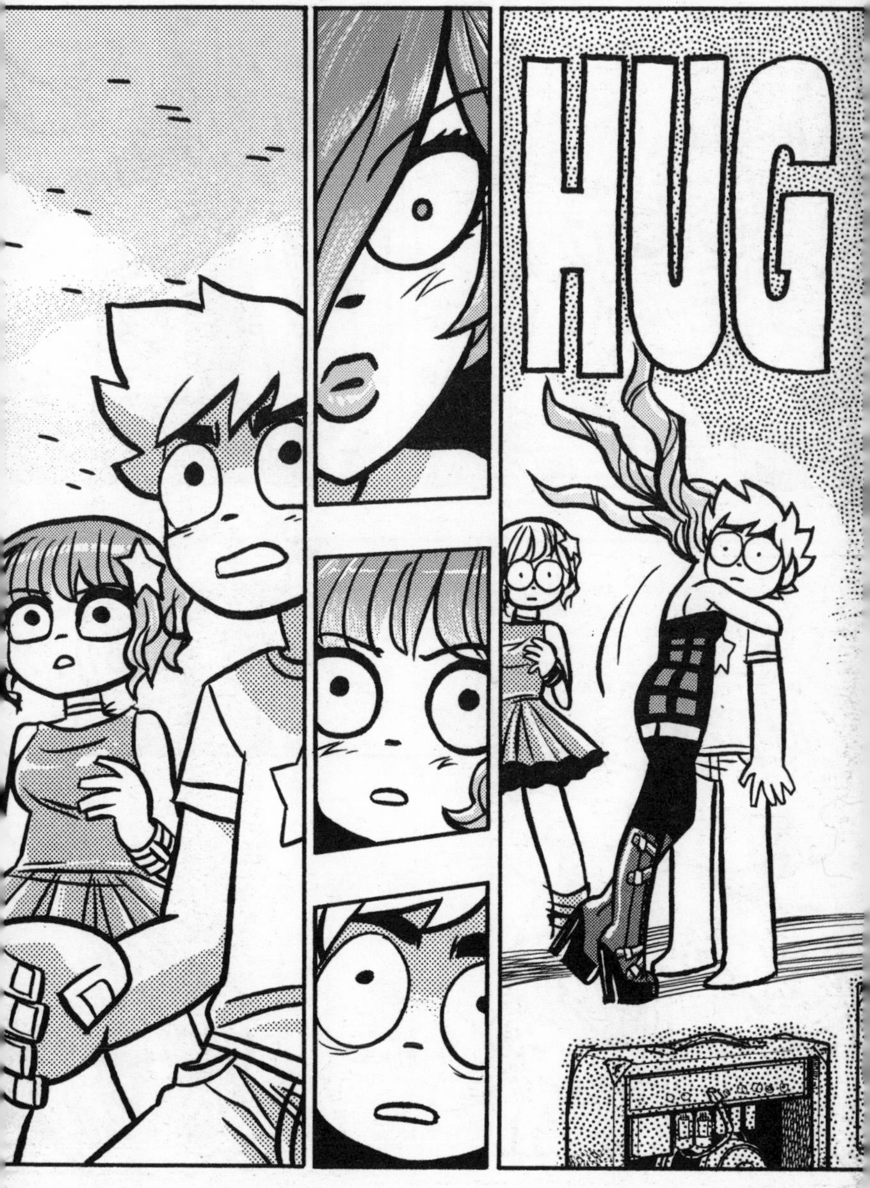
HUG

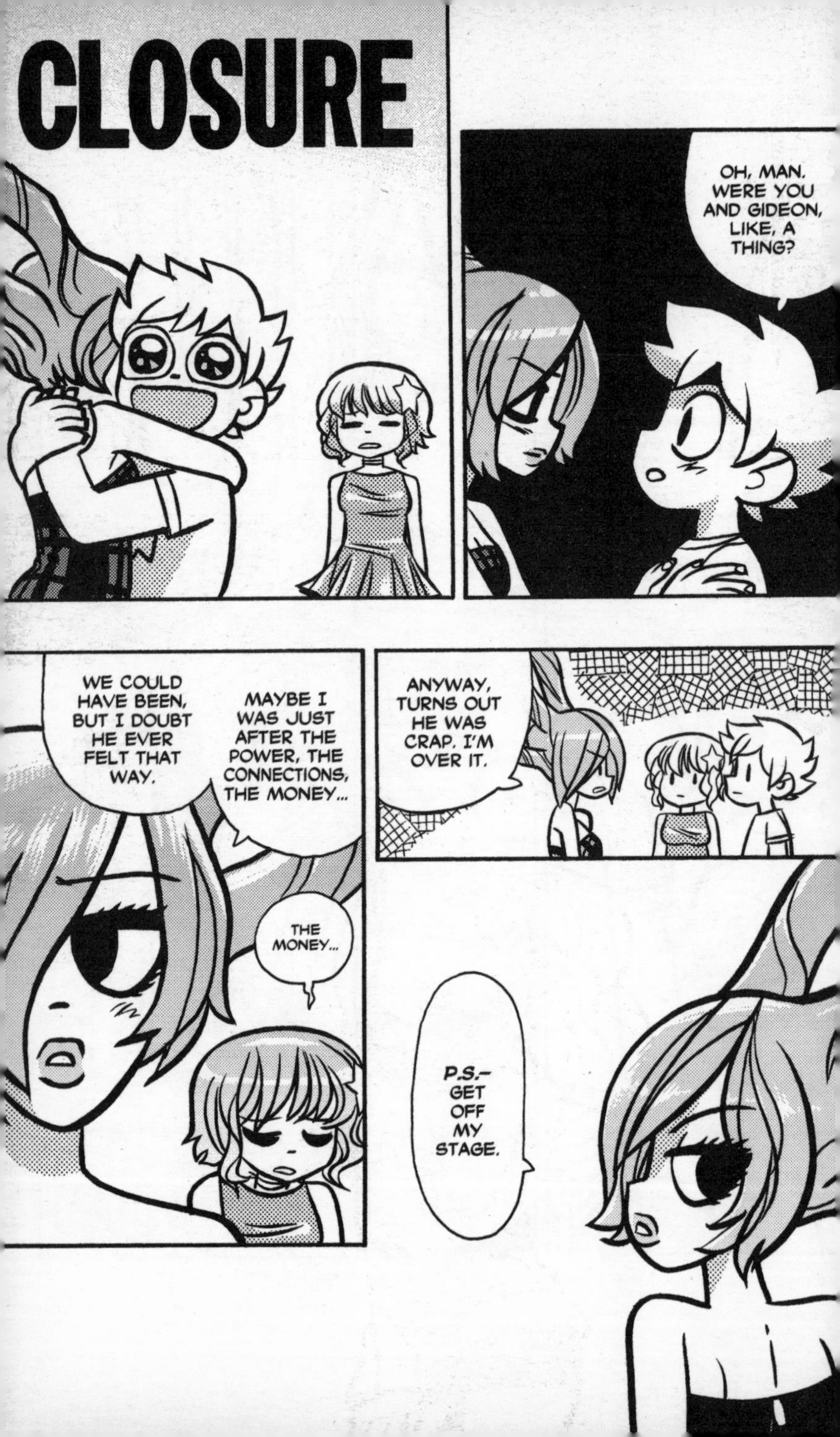
CLOSURE
OH, MAN. WERE YOU AND GIDEON, LIKE, A THING?
WE COULD HAVE BEEN, BUT I DOUBT HE EVER FELT THAT WAY.
MAYBE I WAS JUST AFTER THE POWER, THE CONNECTIONS, THE MONEY...
THE MONEY...
ANYWAY, TURNS OUT HE WAS CRAP. I'M OVER IT.
P.S.- GET OFF MY STAGE.

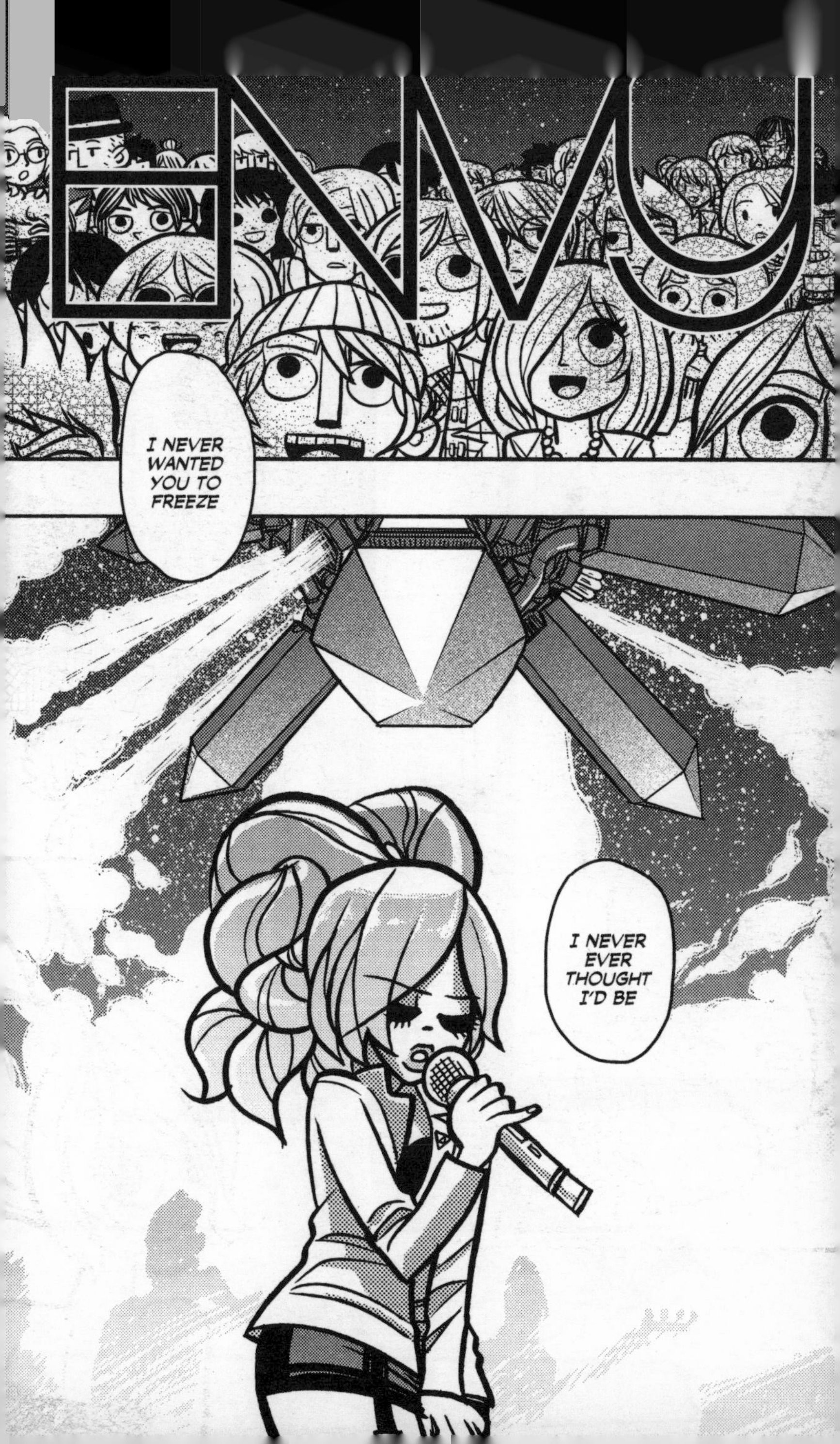
I NEVER WANTED YOU TO FREEZE
I NEVER EVER THOUGHT I'D BE

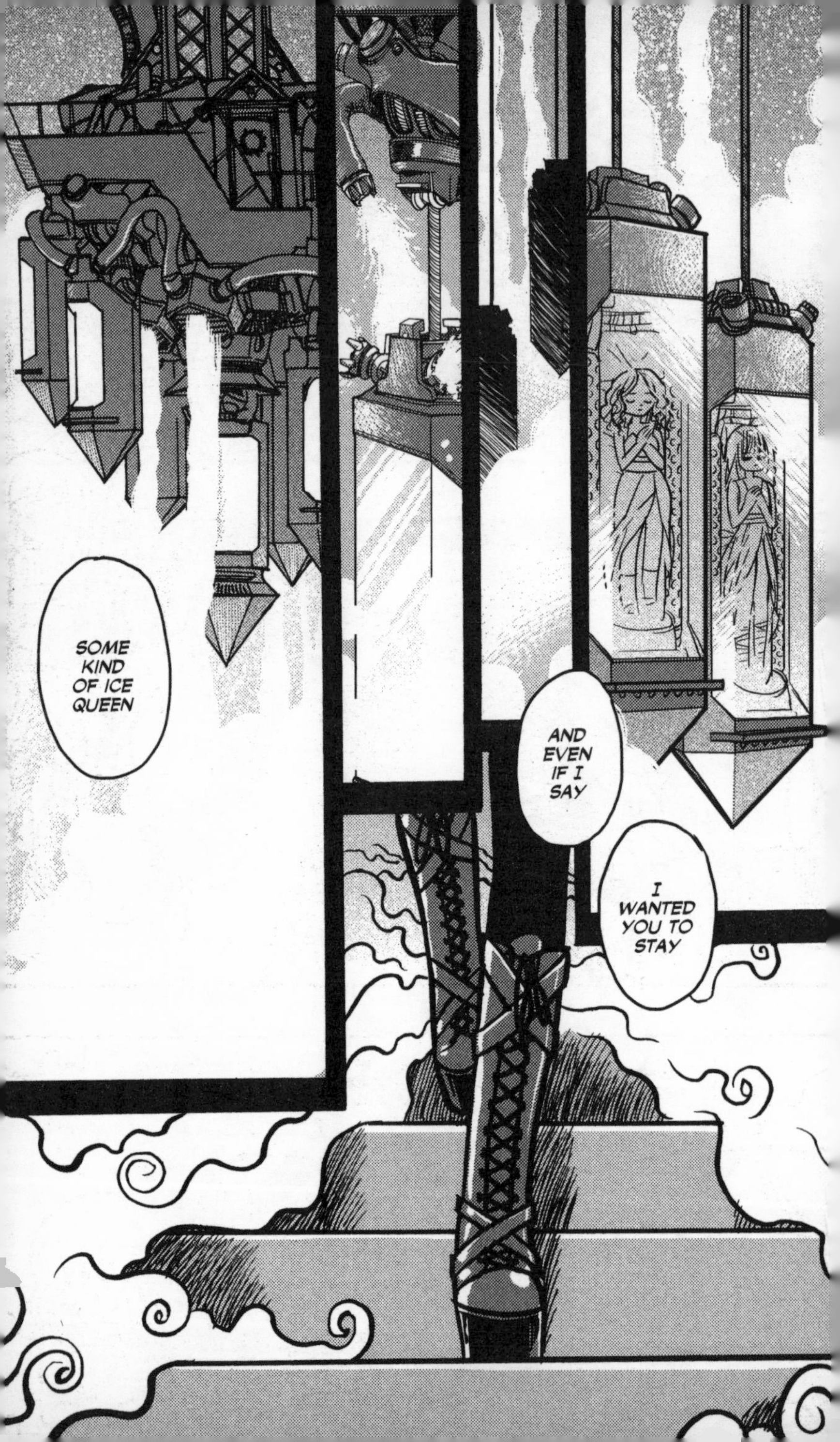
SOME KIND OF ICE QUEEN
AND EVEN IF I SAY
I WANTED YOU TO STAY

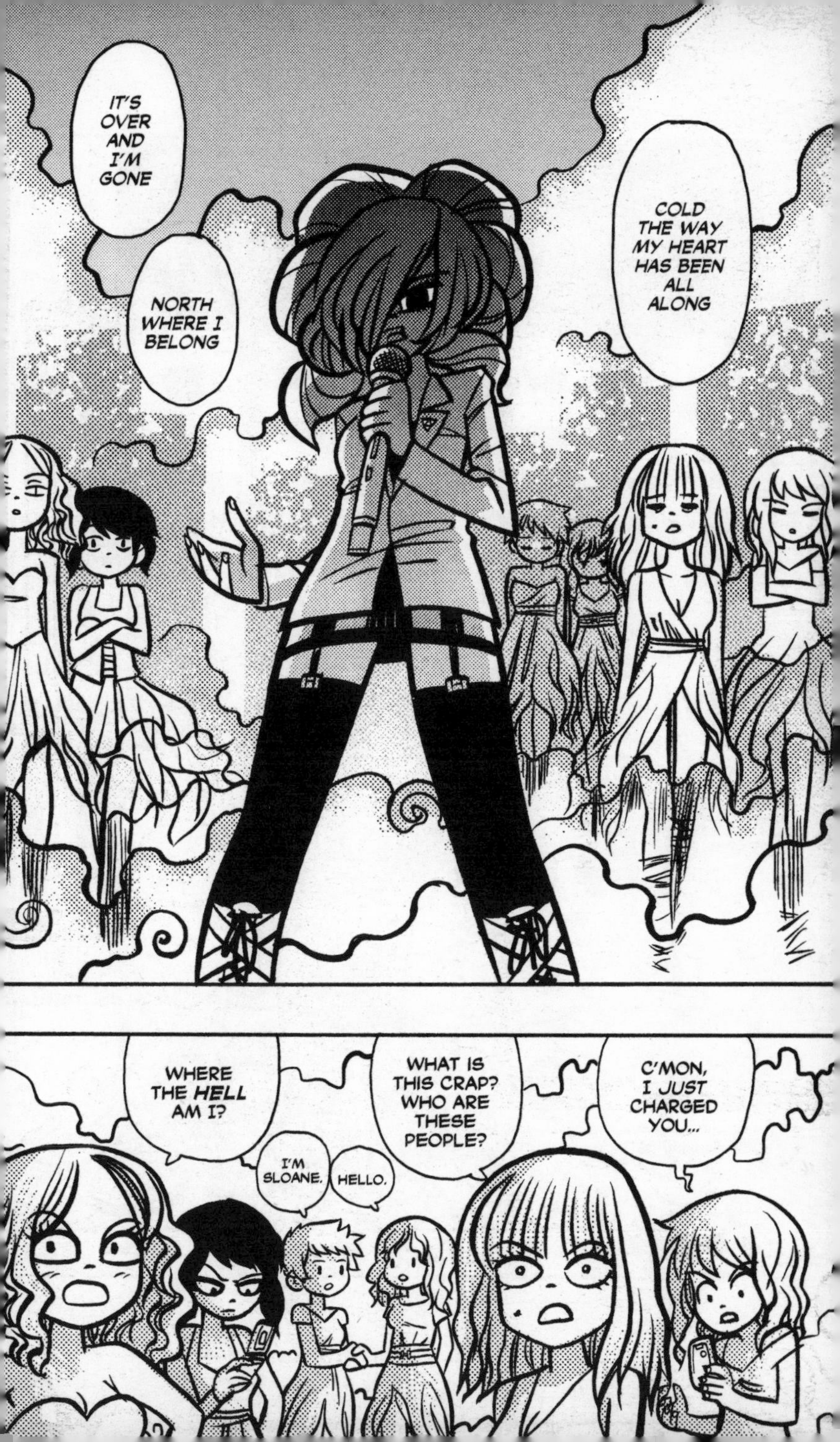
IT'S OVER AND I'M GONE
NORTH WHERE I BELONG
COLD THE WAY MY HEART HAS BEEN ALL ALONG
WHERE THE *HELL* AM I?
WHAT IS THIS CRAP? WHO ARE THESE PEOPLE?
C'MON, I JUST CHARGED YOU...
I'M SLOANE.
HELLO.

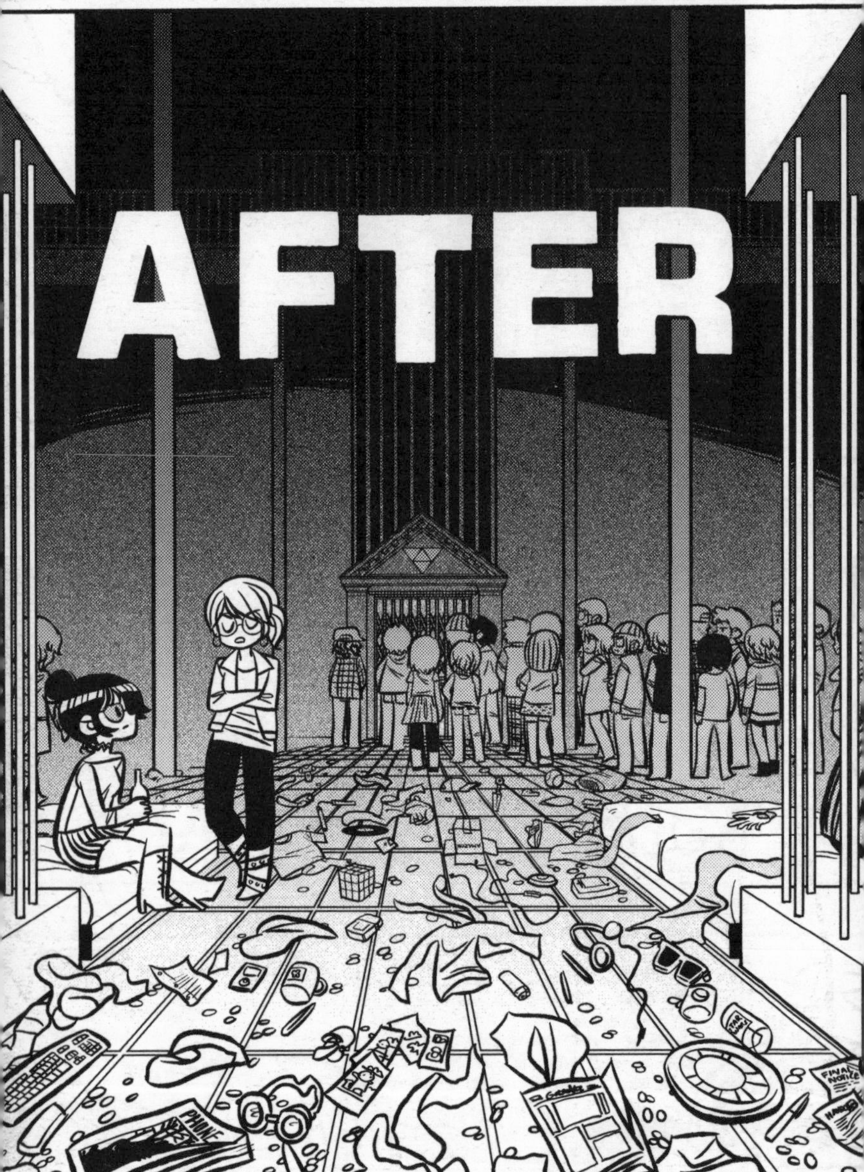
AFTER
PHONE
FINAL NOTICE

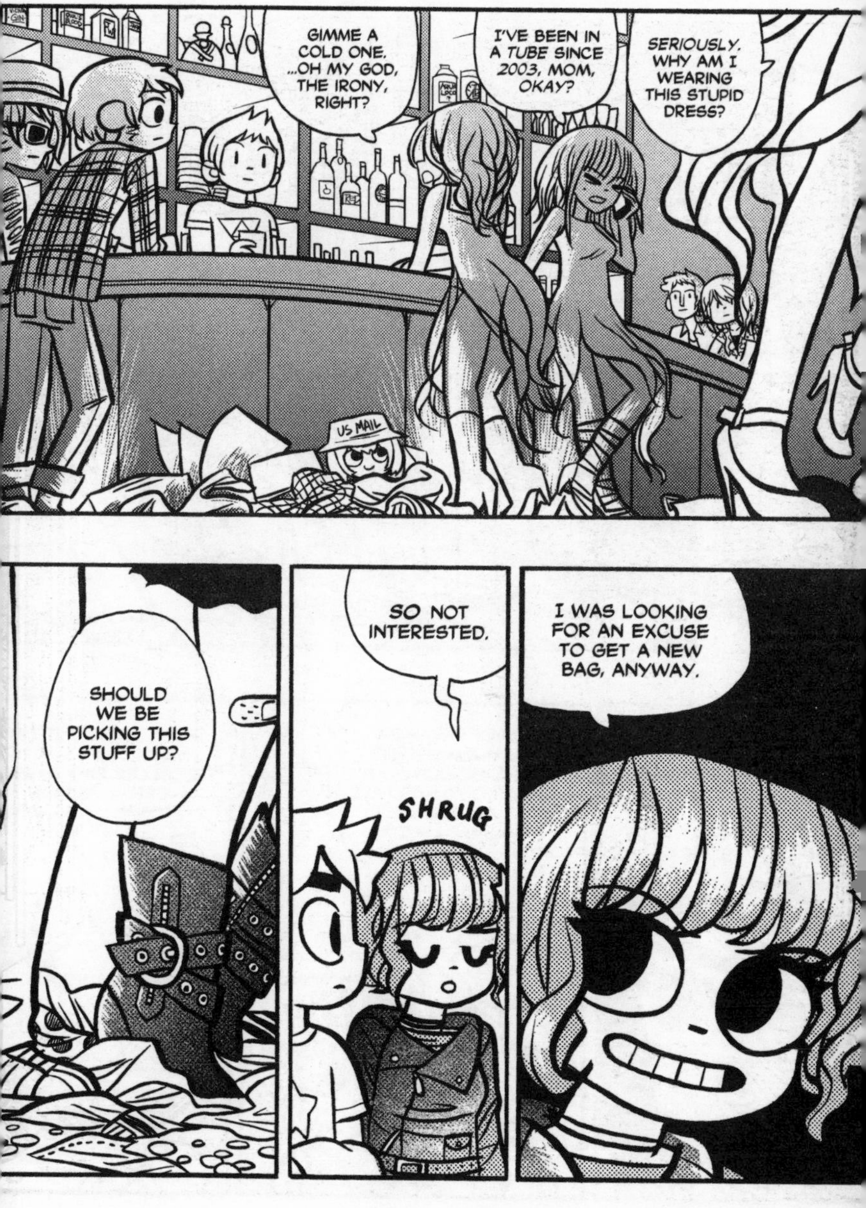
GIMME A COLD ONE. ...OH MY GOD, THE IRONY, RIGHT?
I'VE BEEN IN A TUBE SINCE 2003, MOM, OKAY?
SERIOUSLY. WHY AM I WEARING THIS STUPID DRESS?
US MAIL
SHOULD WE BE PICKING THIS STUFF UP?
SO NOT INTERESTED.
SHRUG
I WAS LOOKING FOR AN EXCUSE TO GET A NEW BAG, ANYWAY.

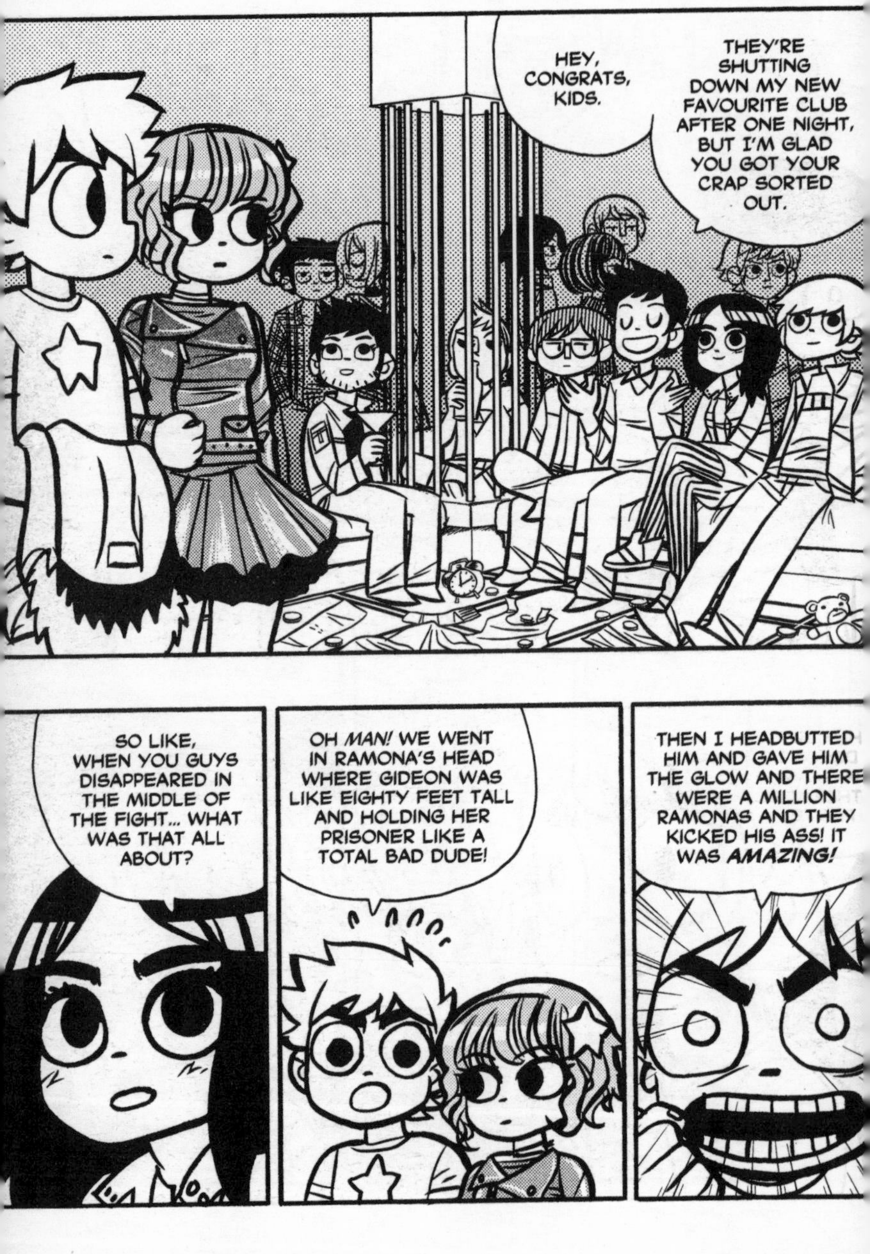
HEY, CONGRATS, KIDS.
THEY'RE SHUTTING DOWN MY NEW FAVOURITE CLUB AFTER ONE NIGHT, BUT I'M GLAD YOU GOT YOUR CRAP SORTED OUT.
SO LIKE, WHEN YOU GUYS DISAPPEARED IN THE MIDDLE OF THE FIGHT... WHAT WAS THAT ALL ABOUT?
OH *MAN!* WE WENT IN RAMONA'S HEAD WHERE GIDEON WAS LIKE EIGHTY FEET TALL AND HOLDING HER PRISONER LIKE A TOTAL BAD DUDE!
THEN I HEADBUTTED HIM AND GAVE HIM THE GLOW AND THERE WERE A MILLION RAMONAS AND THEY KICKED HIS ASS! IT WAS *AMAZING!*

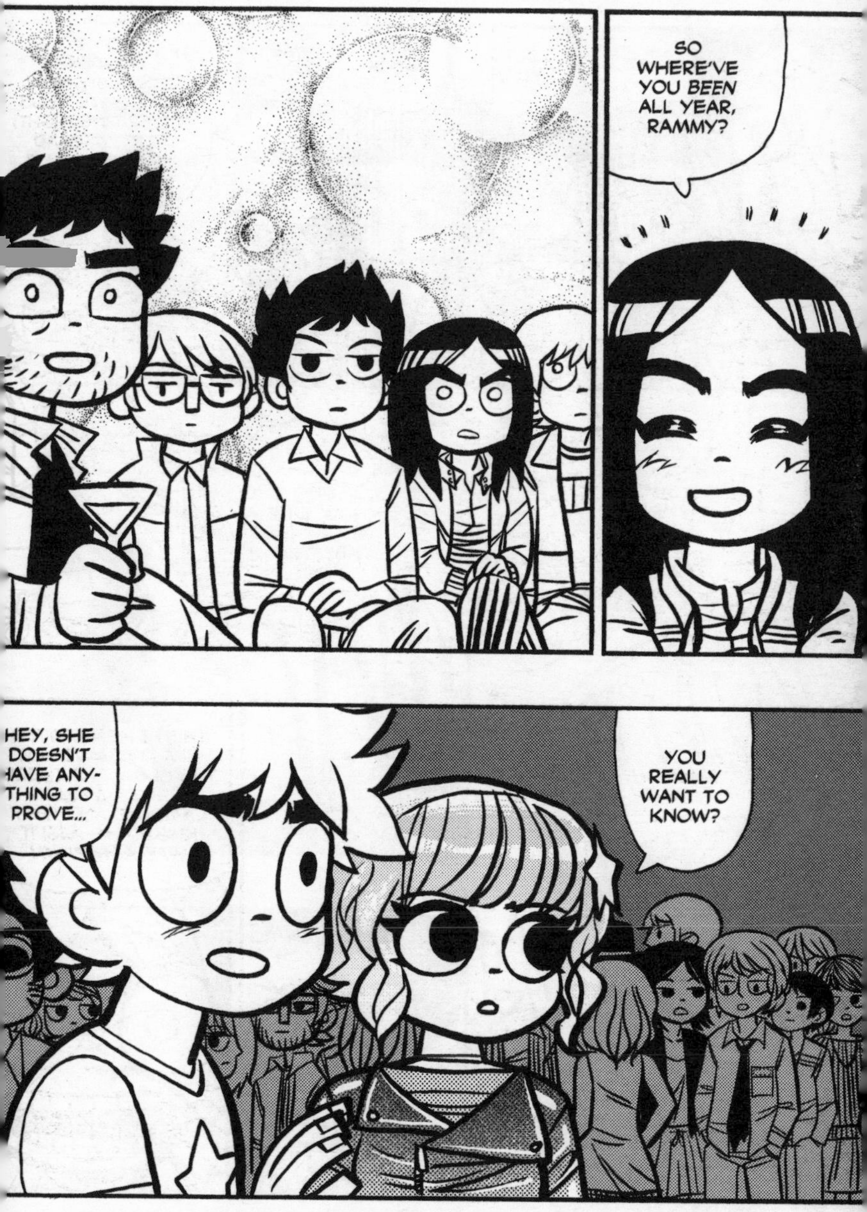
SO WHERE'VE YOU *BEEN* ALL YEAR, RAMMY?
HEY, SHE DOESN'T HAVE ANY-THING TO PROVE...
YOU REALLY WANT TO KNOW?

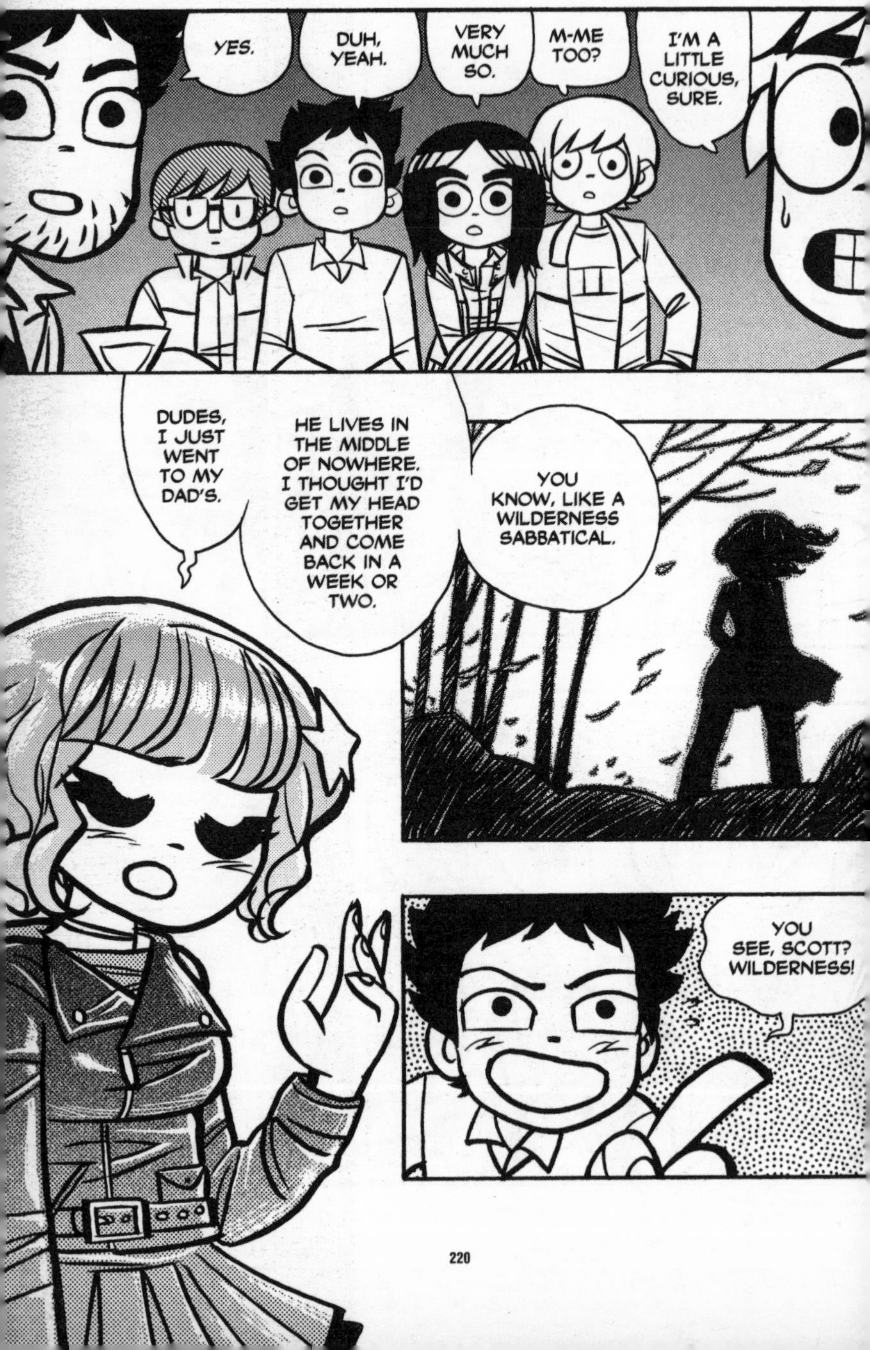
YES.
DUH, YEAH.
VERY MUCH SO.
M-ME TOO?
I'M A LITTLE CURIOUS, SURE.
DUDES, I JUST WENT TO MY DAD'S.
HE LIVES IN THE MIDDLE OF NOWHERE. I THOUGHT I'D GET MY HEAD TOGETHER AND COME BACK IN A WEEK OR TWO.
YOU KNOW, LIKE A WILDERNESS SABBATICAL.
YOU SEE, SCOTT? WILDERNESS!

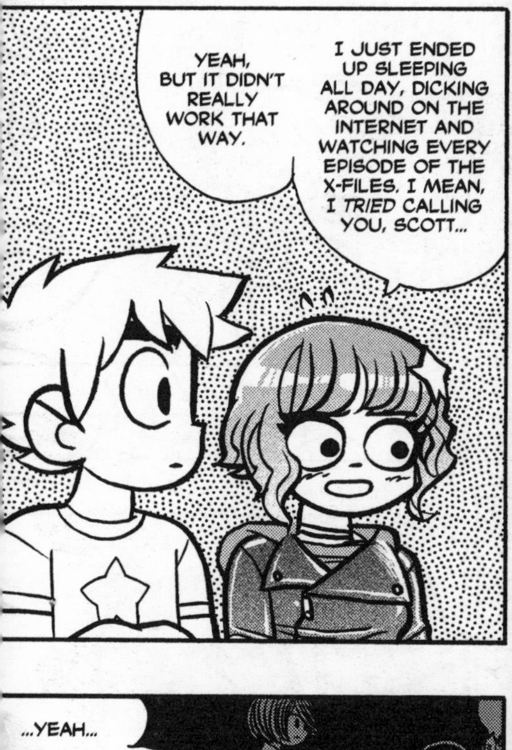
YEAH, BUT IT DIDN'T REALLY WORK THAT WAY.
I JUST ENDED UP SLEEPING ALL DAY, DICKING AROUND ON THE INTERNET AND WATCHING EVERY EPISODE OF THE X-FILES. I MEAN, I *TRIED* CALLING YOU, SCOTT...
...YEAH...
...MAYBE YOU TWO WERE MEANT TO BE.
JUST CALL ME FOR THE WEDDING.

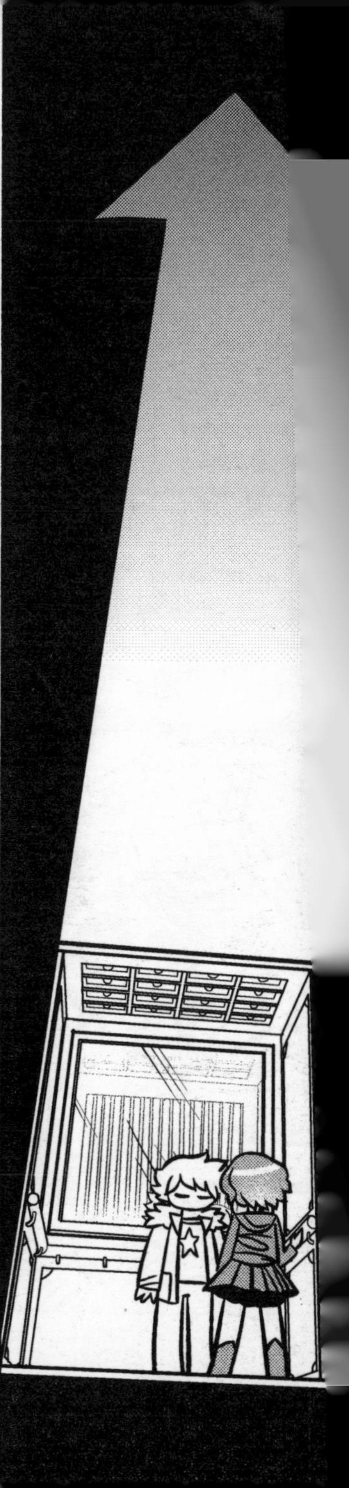

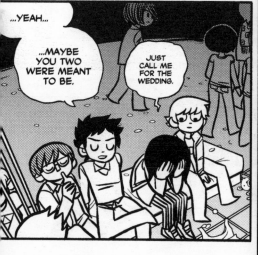

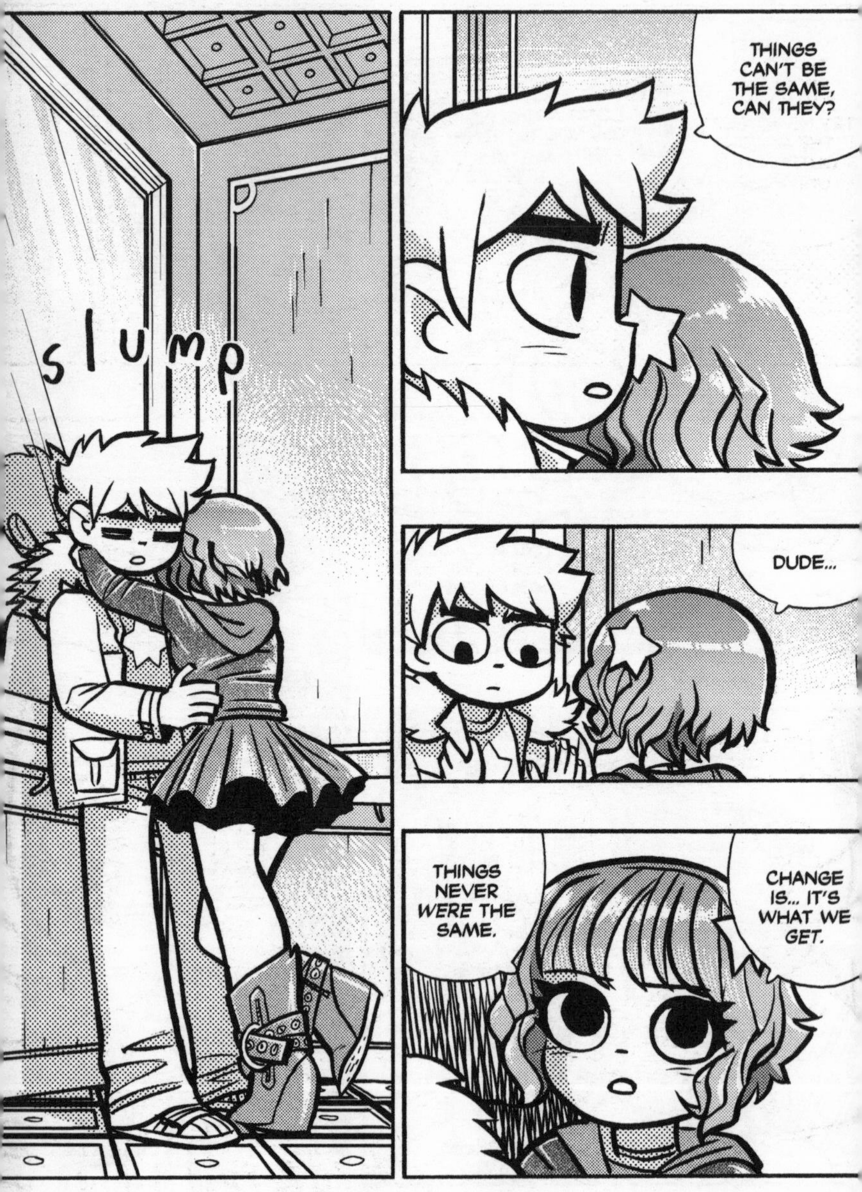
SLUMP
THINGS CAN'T BE THE SAME, CAN THEY?
DUDE...
THINGS NEVER WERE THE SAME.
CHANGE IS... IT'S WHAT WE GET.

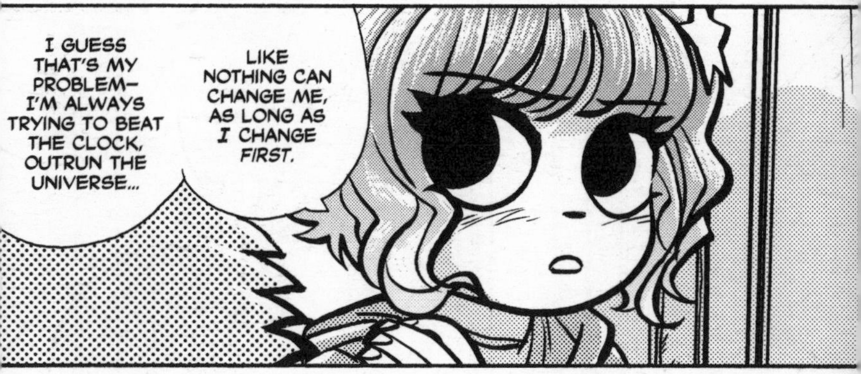
I GUESS THAT'S MY PROBLEM— I'M ALWAYS TRYING TO BEAT THE CLOCK, OUTRUN THE UNIVERSE...
LIKE NOTHING CAN CHANGE ME, AS LONG AS *I* CHANGE *FIRST*.

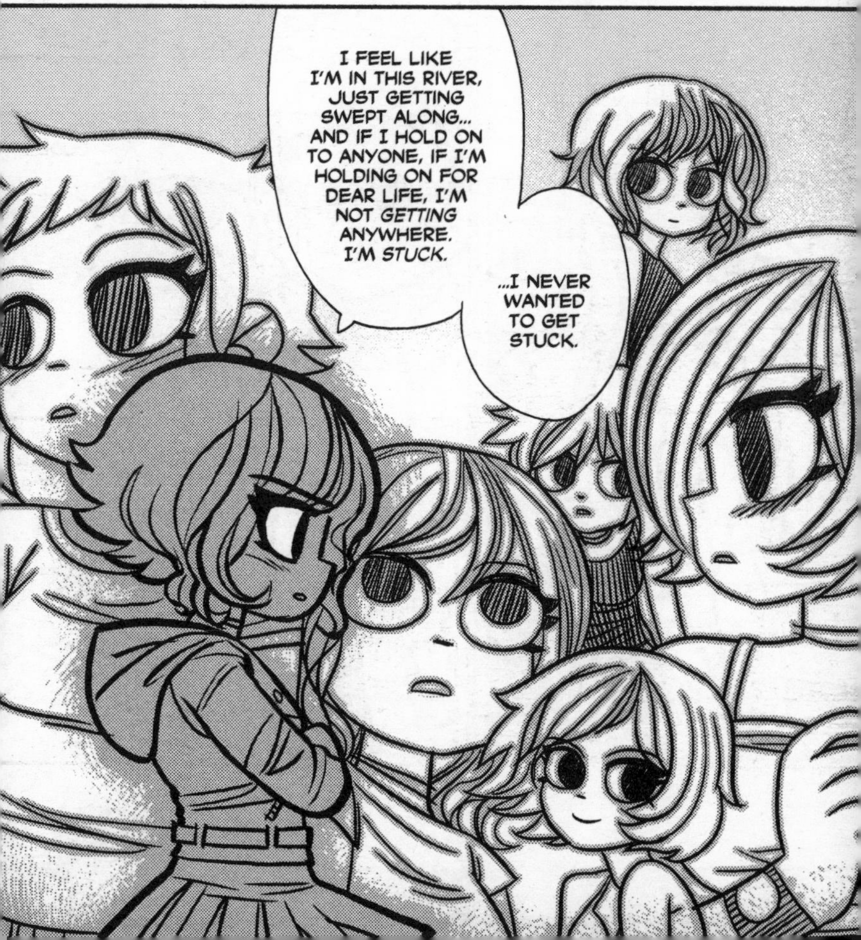
I FEEL LIKE I'M IN THIS RIVER, JUST GETTING SWEPT ALONG... AND IF I HOLD ON TO ANYONE, IF I'M HOLDING ON FOR DEAR LIFE, I'M NOT *GETTING* ANYWHERE. I'M *STUCK*.
...I NEVER WANTED TO GET STUCK.

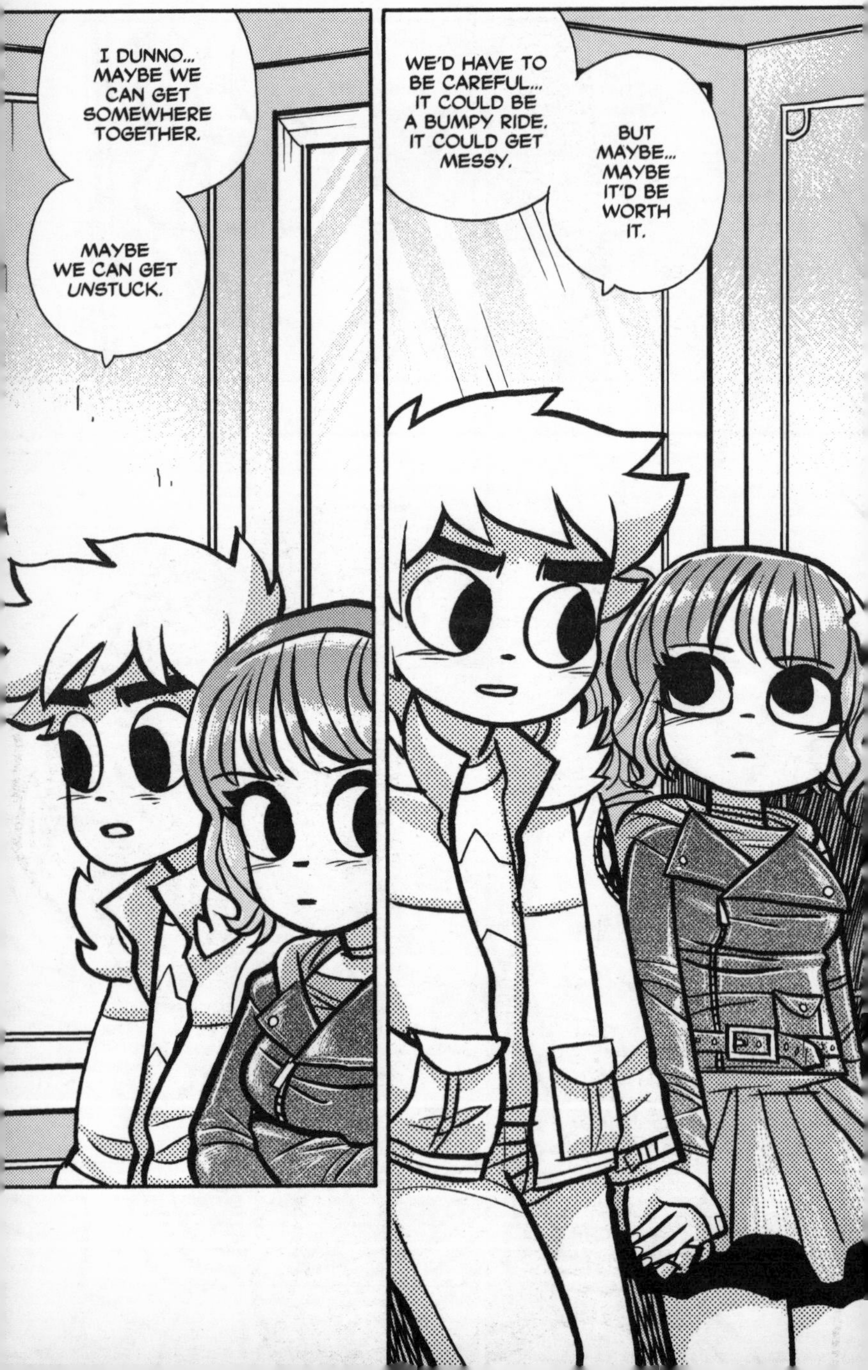

I DUNNO... MAYBE WE CAN GET SOMEWHERE TOGETHER.
MAYBE WE CAN GET *UNSTUCK.*
WE'D HAVE TO BE CAREFUL... IT COULD BE A BUMPY RIDE. IT COULD GET MESSY.
BUT MAYBE... MAYBE IT'D BE WORTH IT.

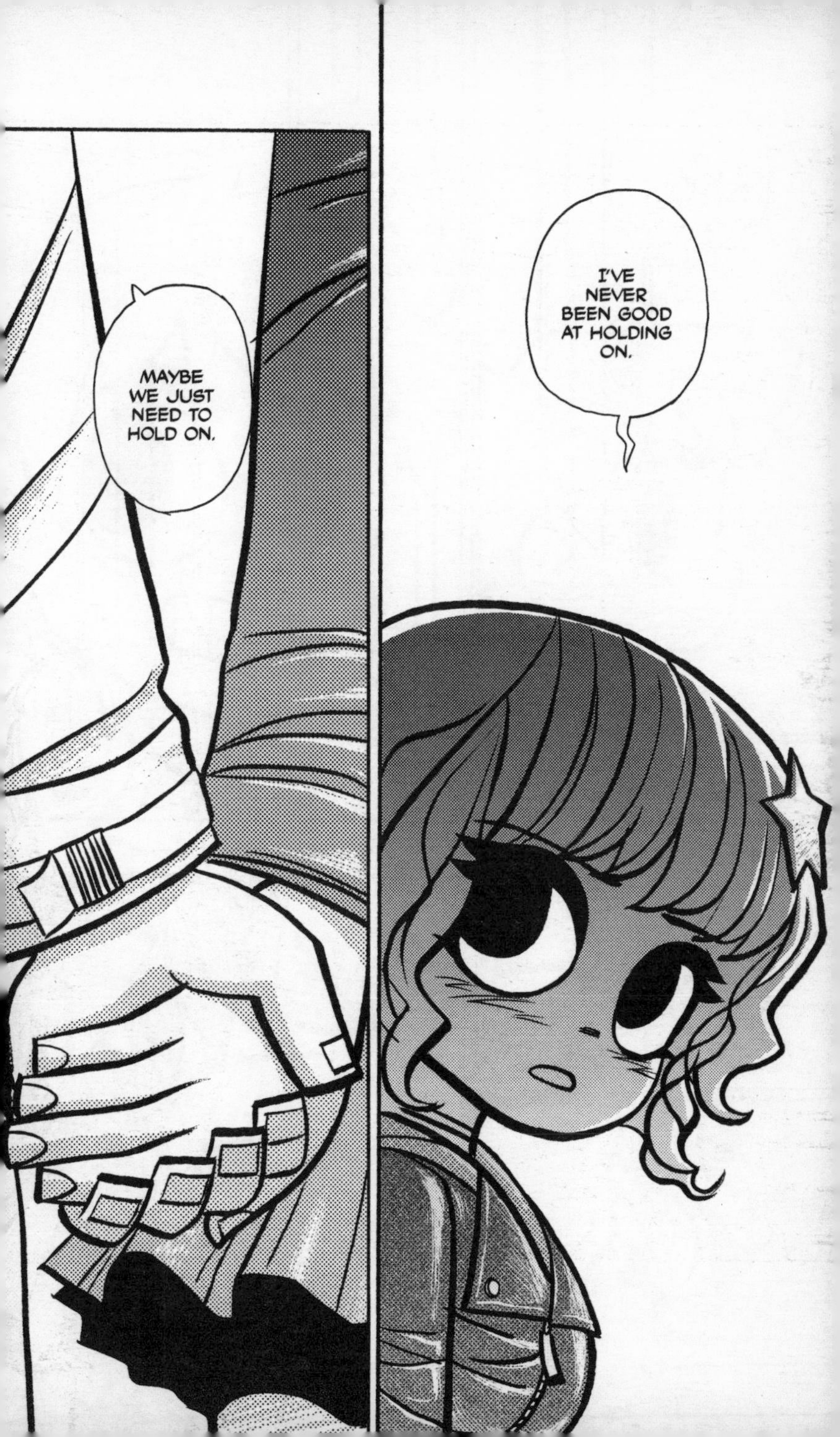
MAYBE WE JUST NEED TO HOLD ON.
I'VE NEVER BEEN GOOD AT HOLDING ON.

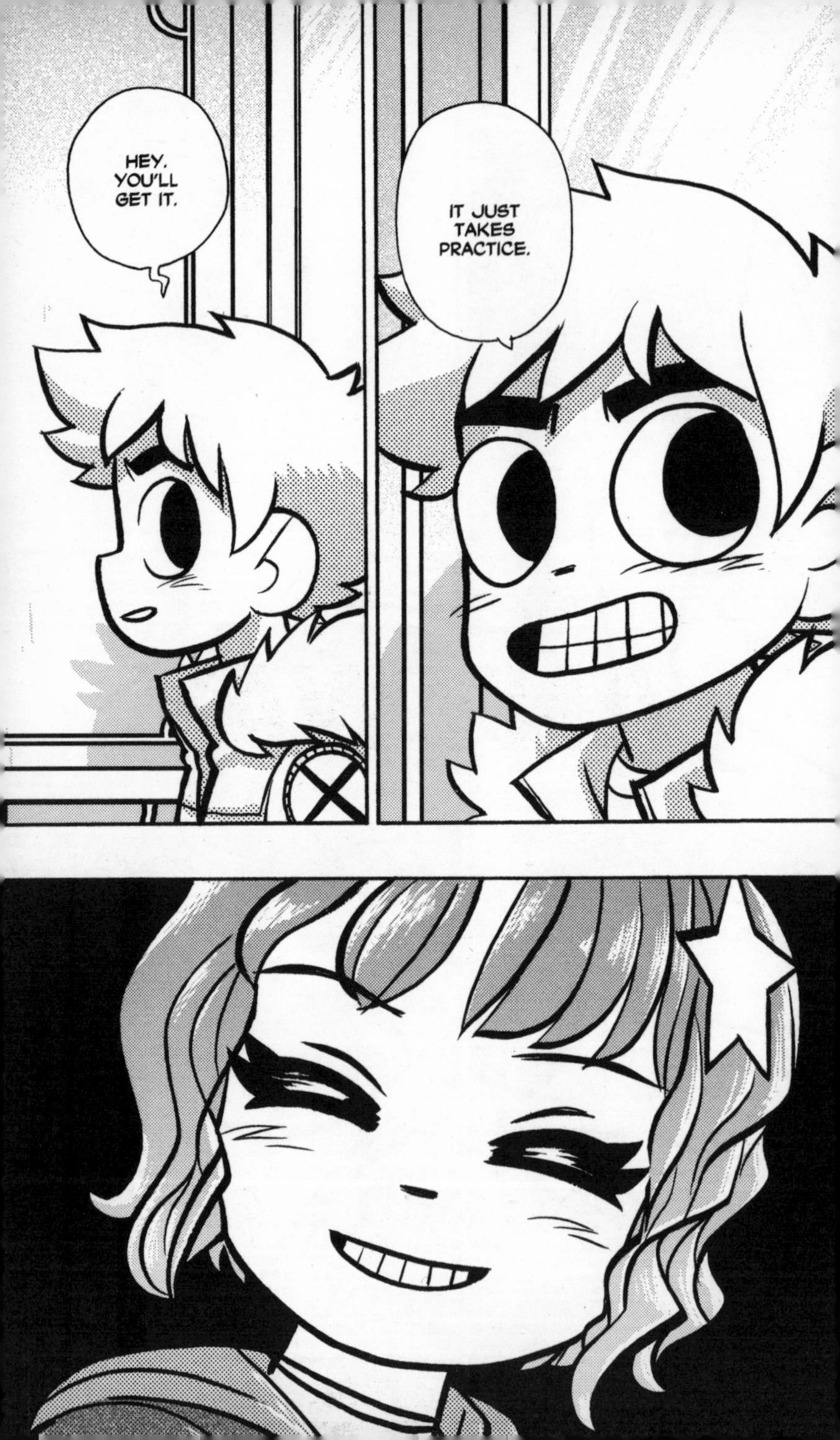
HEY. YOU'LL GET IT.
IT JUST TAKES PRACTICE.

SO
ANYWAY

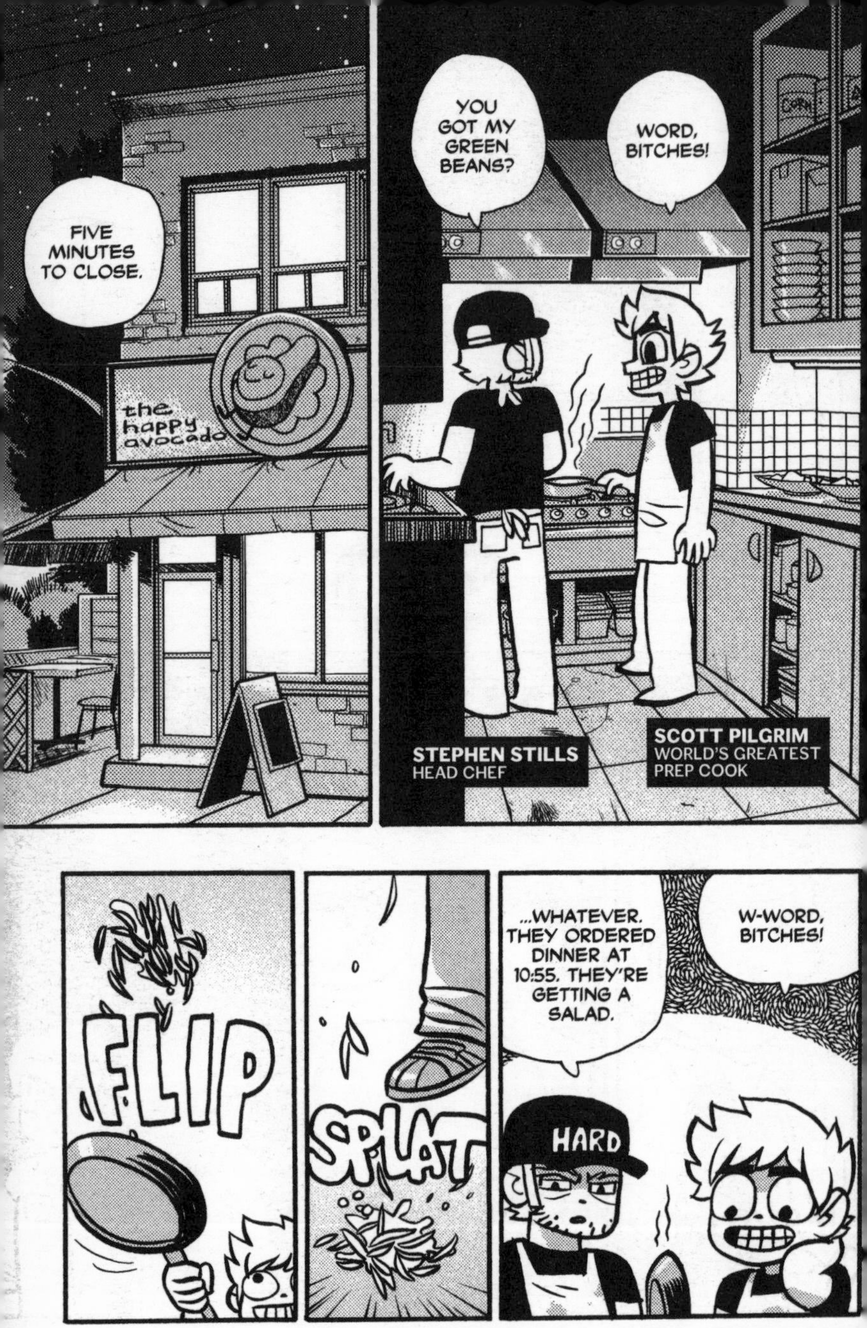
FIVE MINUTES TO CLOSE.
the happy avocado
YOU GOT MY GREEN BEANS?
WORD, BITCHES!
STEPHEN STILLS
HEAD CHEF
SCOTT PILGRIM
WORLD'S GREATEST PREP COOK
FLIP
SPLAT
...WHATEVER. THEY ORDERED DINNER AT 10:55. THEY'RE GETTING A SALAD.
W-WORD, BITCHES!
HARD

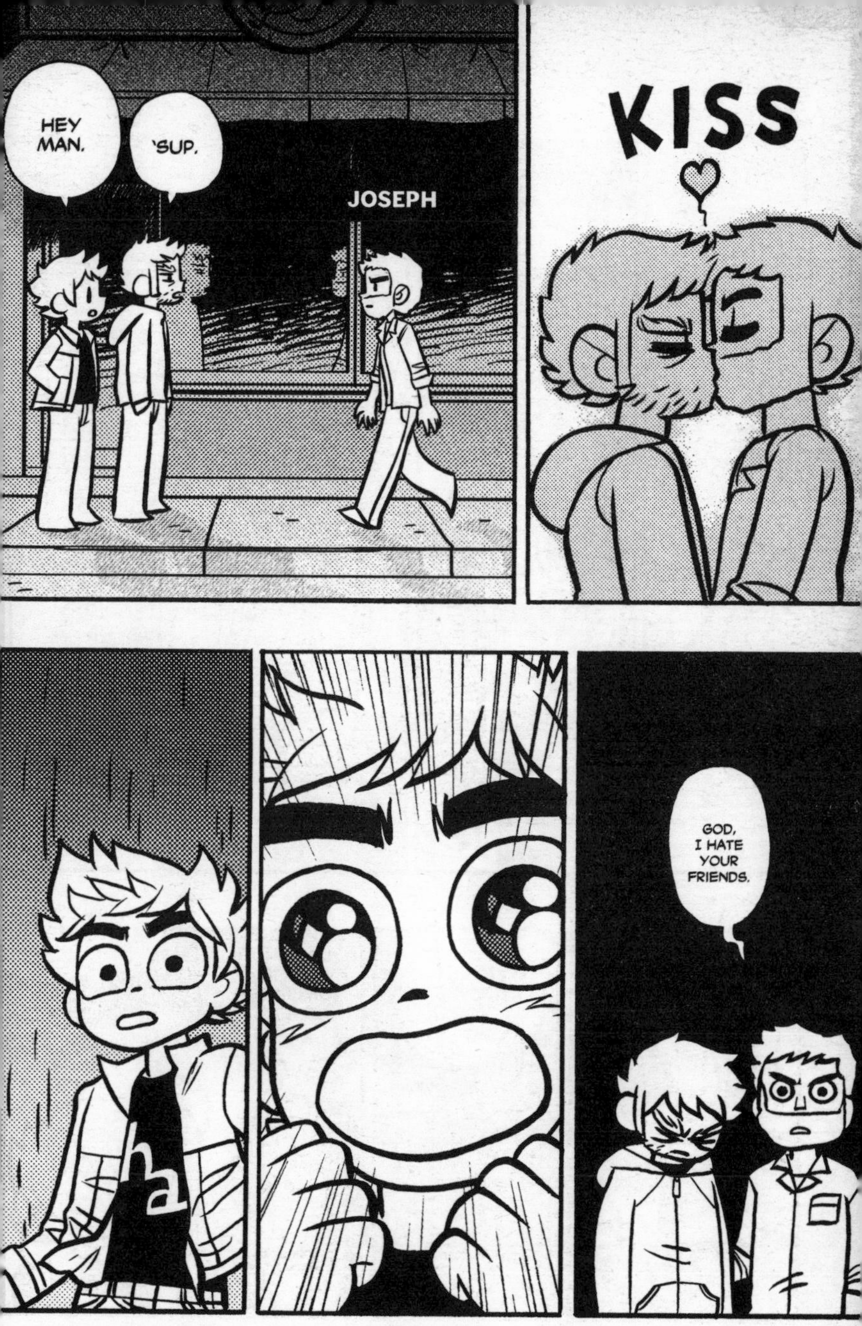
HEY MAN.
'SUP.
JOSEPH
KISS
GOD, I HATE YOUR FRIENDS.

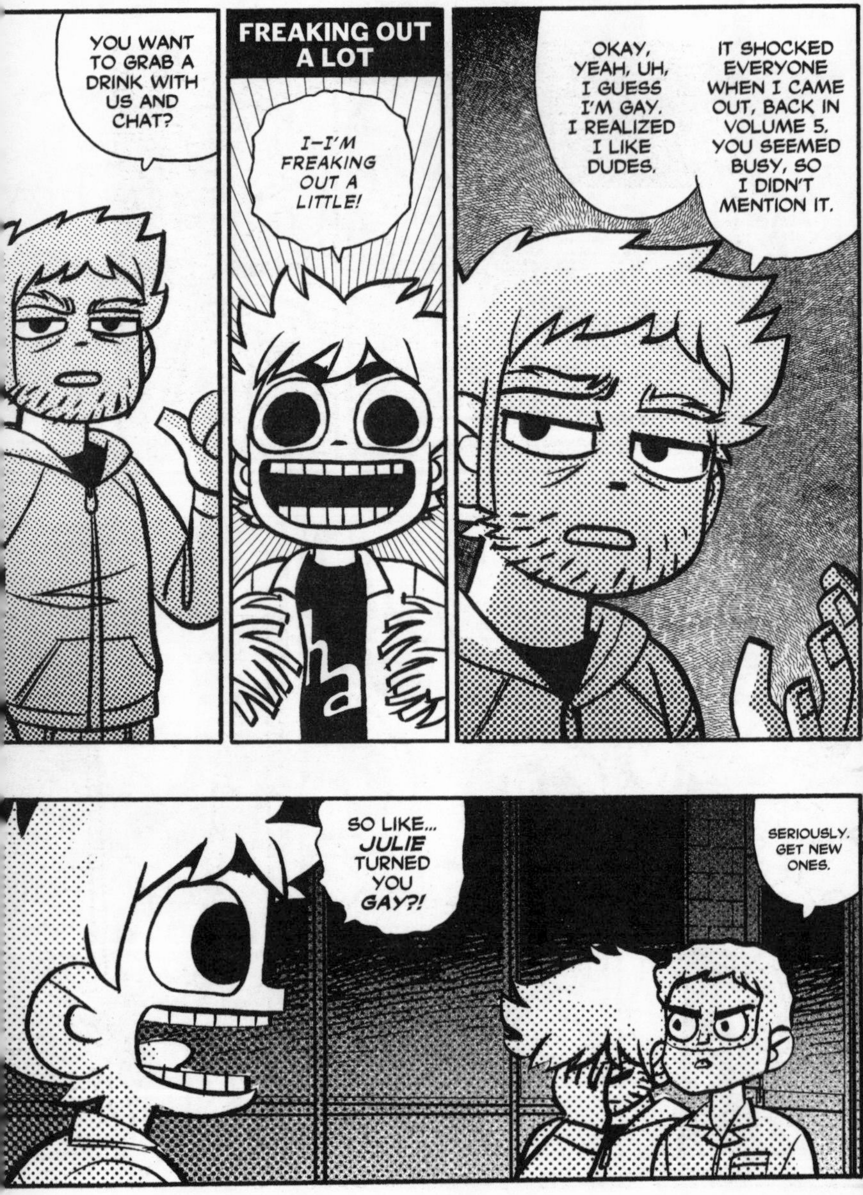
YOU WANT TO GRAB A DRINK WITH US AND CHAT?
FREAKING OUT A LOT
I-I'M FREAKING OUT A LITTLE!
OKAY, YEAH, UH, I GUESS I'M GAY. I REALIZED I LIKE DUDES.
IT SHOCKED EVERYONE WHEN I CAME OUT, BACK IN VOLUME 5. YOU SEEMED BUSY, SO I DIDN'T MENTION IT.
SO LIKE... *JULIE* TURNED YOU *GAY?!*
SERIOUSLY. GET NEW ONES.

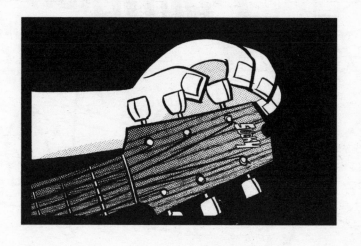

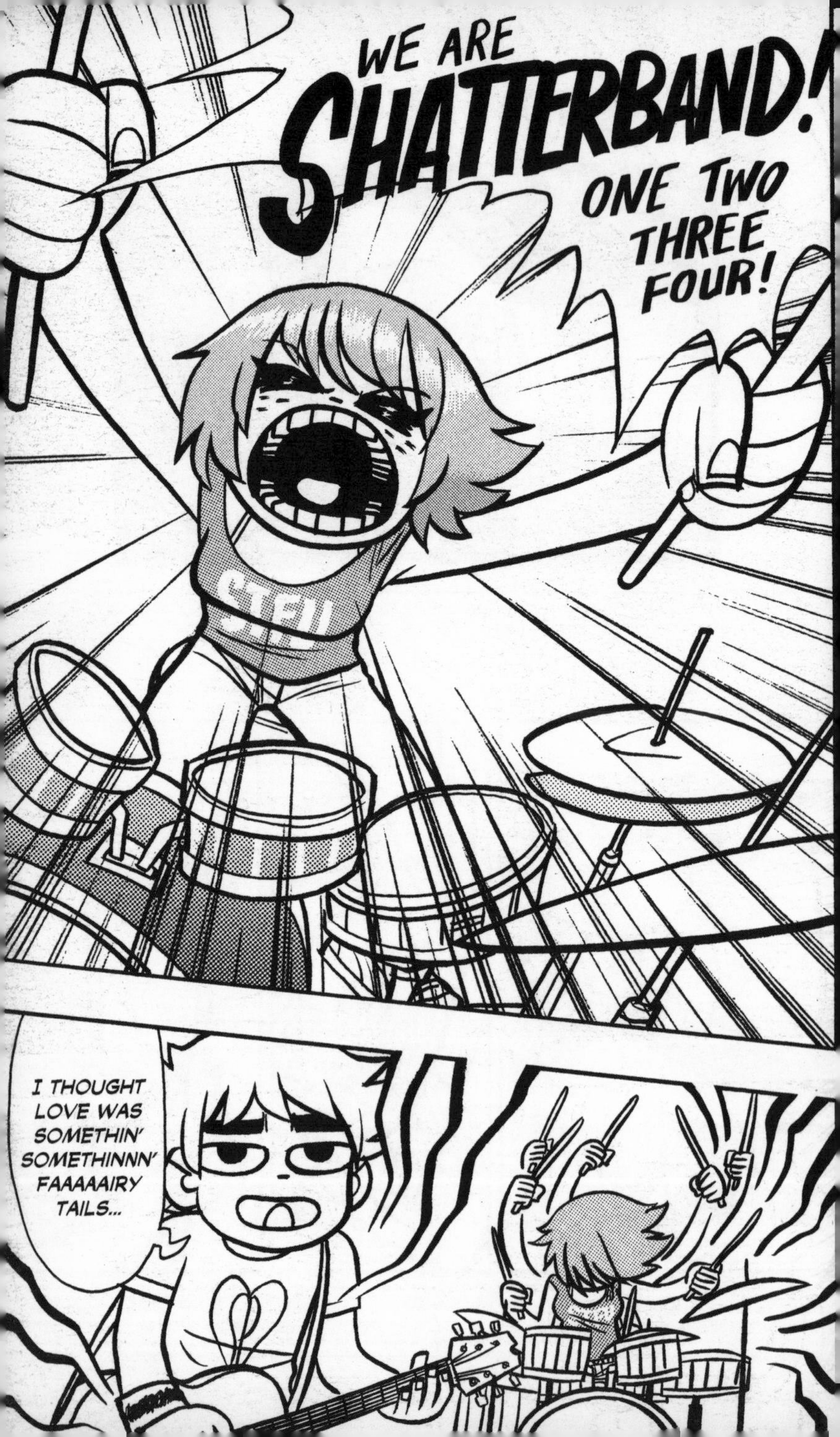
WE ARE SHATTERBAND!
ONE TWO THREE FOUR!
STELL
I THOUGHT LOVE WAS SOMETHIN' SOMETHINNN' FAAAAAIRY TAILS...

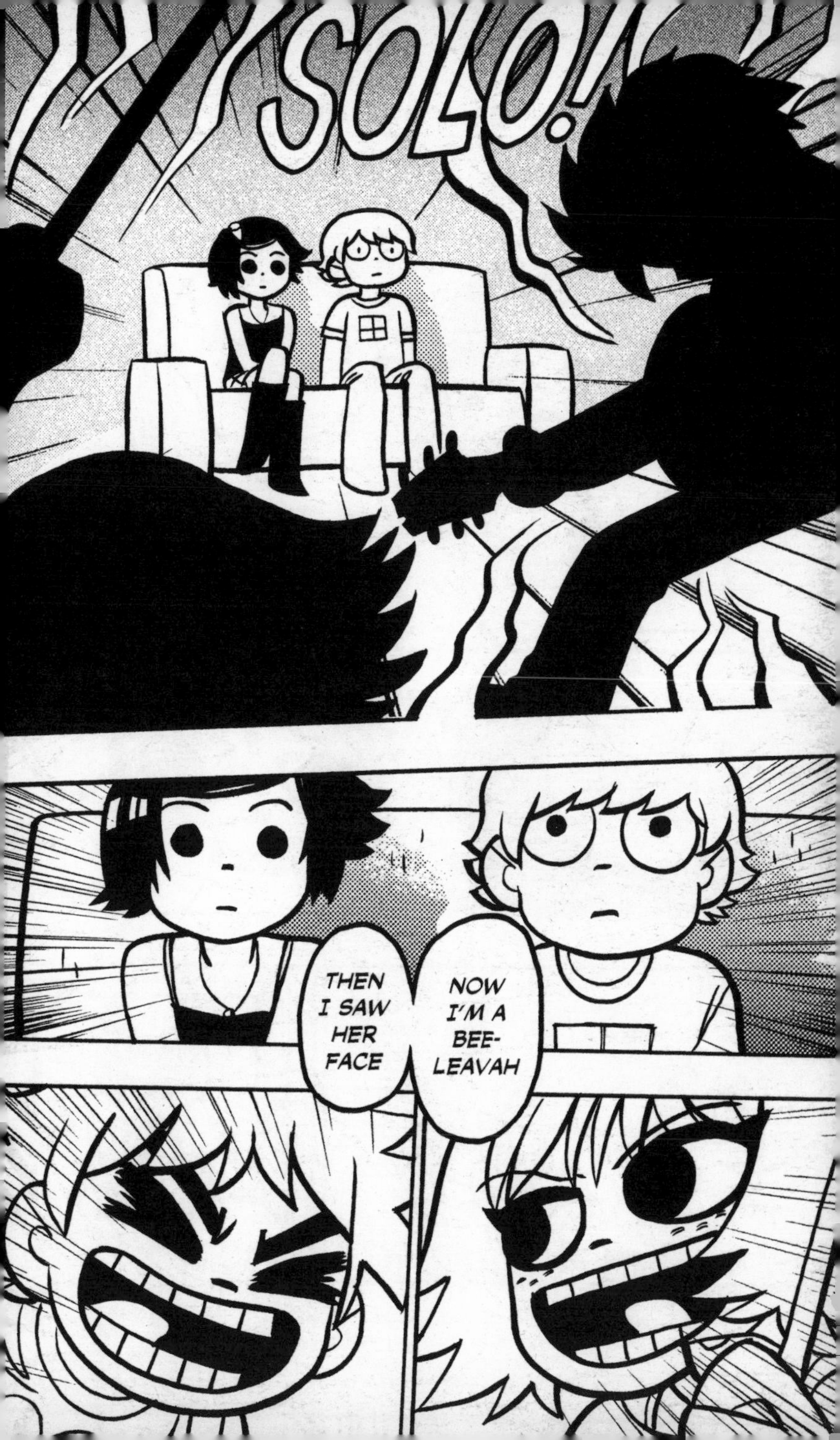
SOLO!
THEN I SAW HER FACE
NOW I'M A BEE-LEAVAH

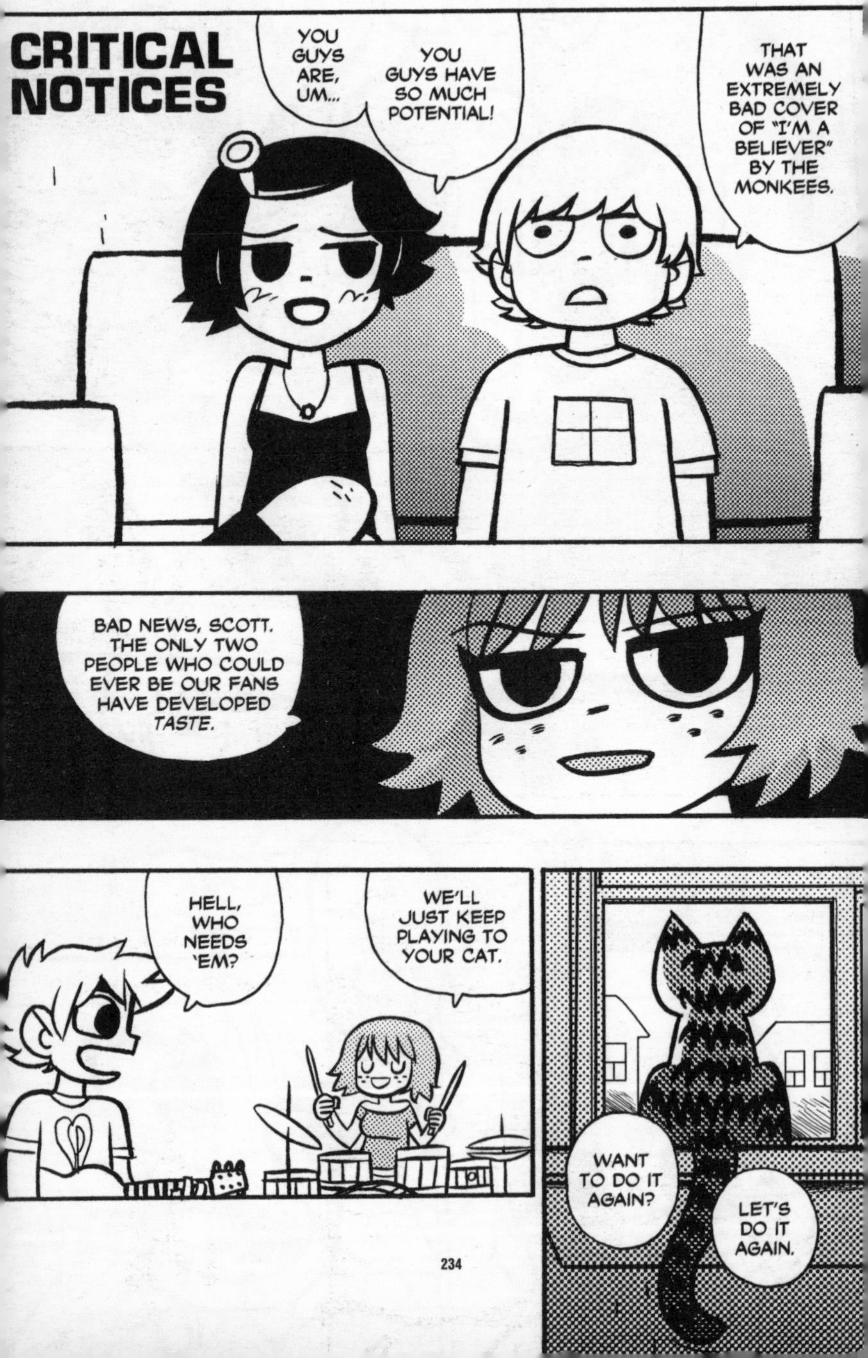
CRITICAL NOTICES
YOU GUYS ARE, UM...
YOU GUYS HAVE SO MUCH POTENTIAL!
THAT WAS AN EXTREMELY BAD COVER OF "I'M A BELIEVER" BY THE MONKEES.
BAD NEWS, SCOTT. THE ONLY TWO PEOPLE WHO COULD EVER BE OUR FANS HAVE DEVELOPED *TASTE*.
HELL, WHO NEEDS 'EM?
WE'LL JUST KEEP PLAYING TO YOUR CAT.
WANT TO DO IT AGAIN?
LET'S DO IT AGAIN.

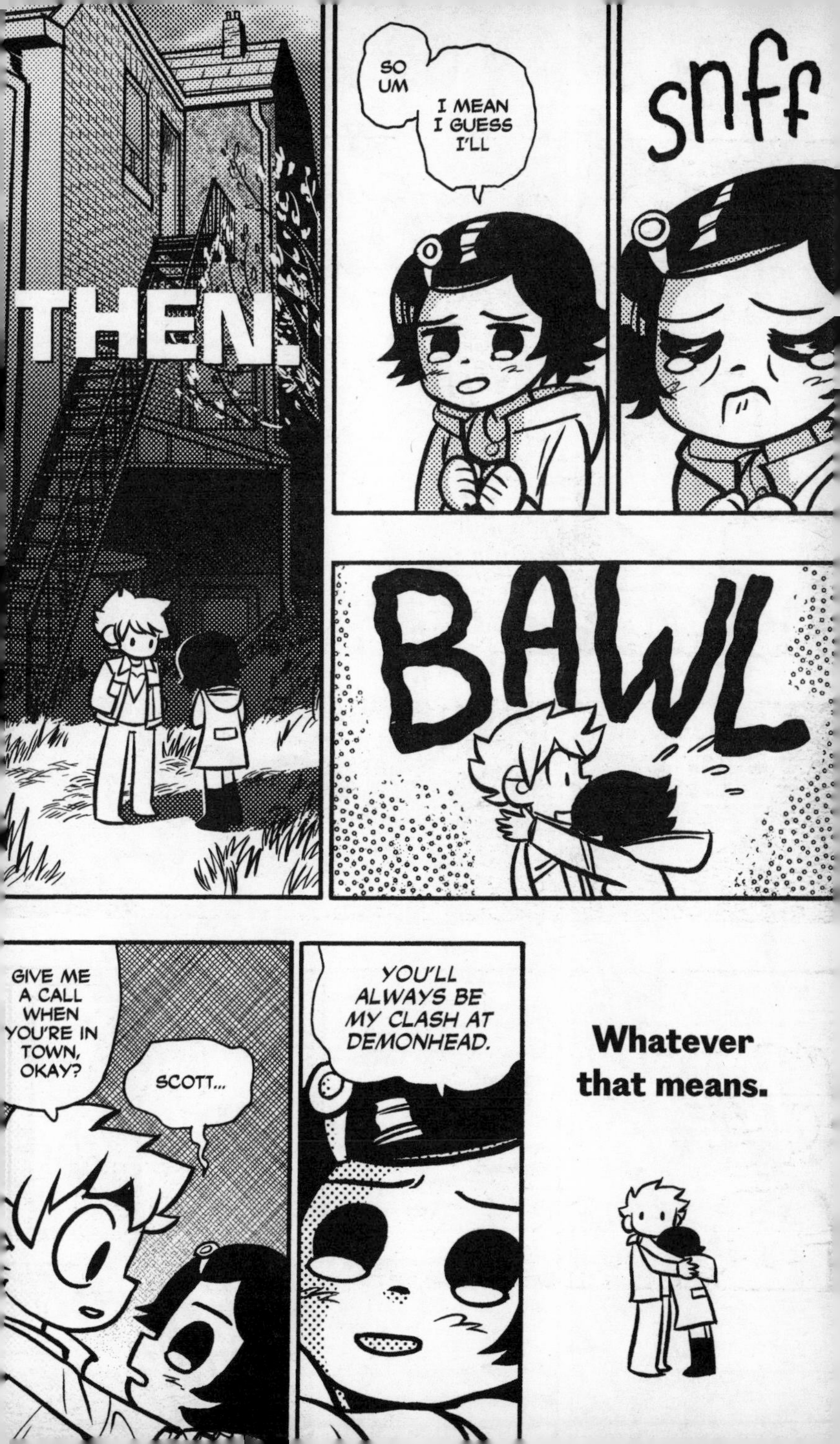
THEN.
SO UM
I MEAN I GUESS I'LL
snff
BAWL
GIVE ME A CALL WHEN YOU'RE IN TOWN, OKAY?
SCOTT...
YOU'LL ALWAYS BE MY CLASH AT DEMONHEAD.
Whatever that means.

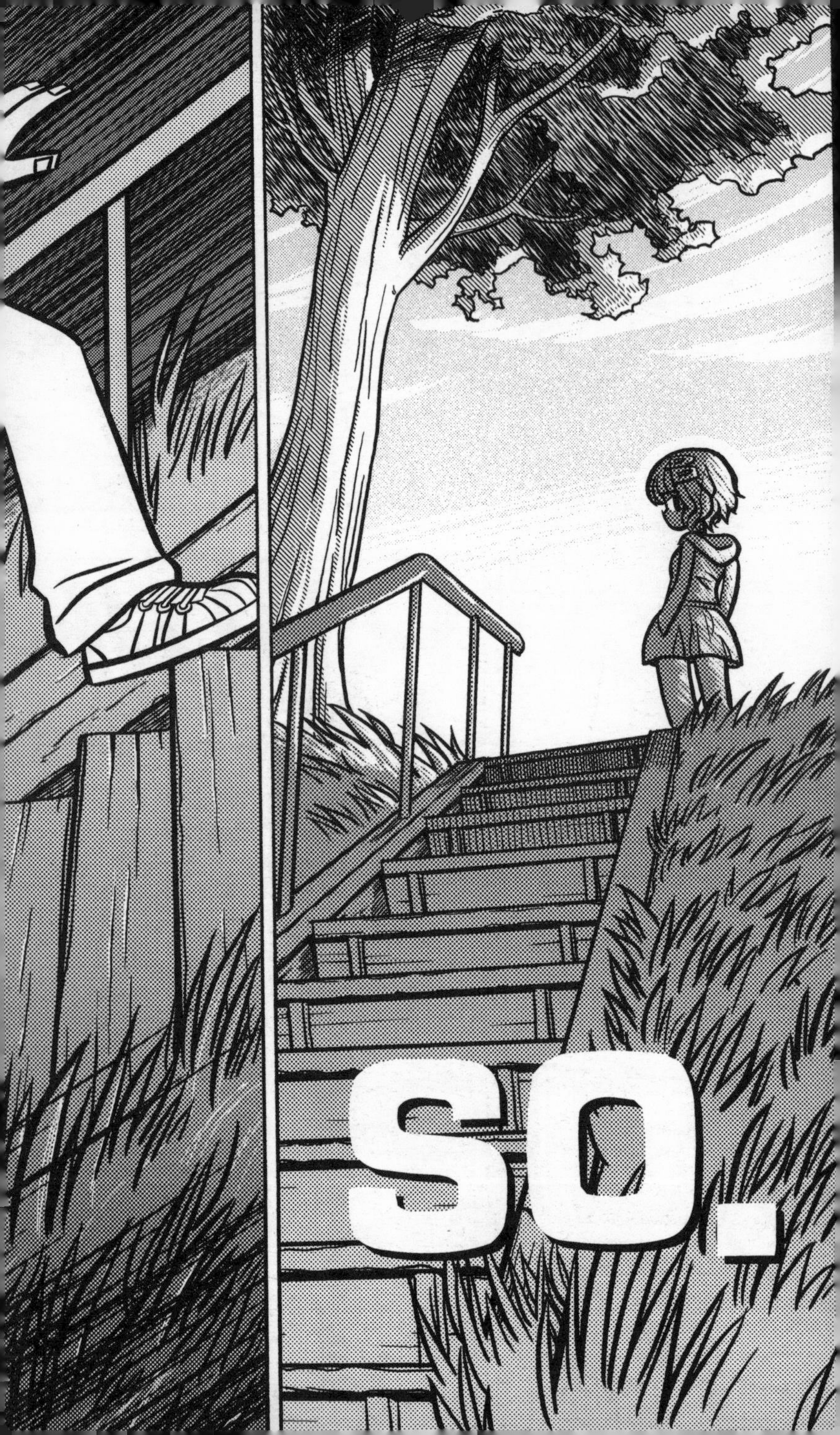
SO.

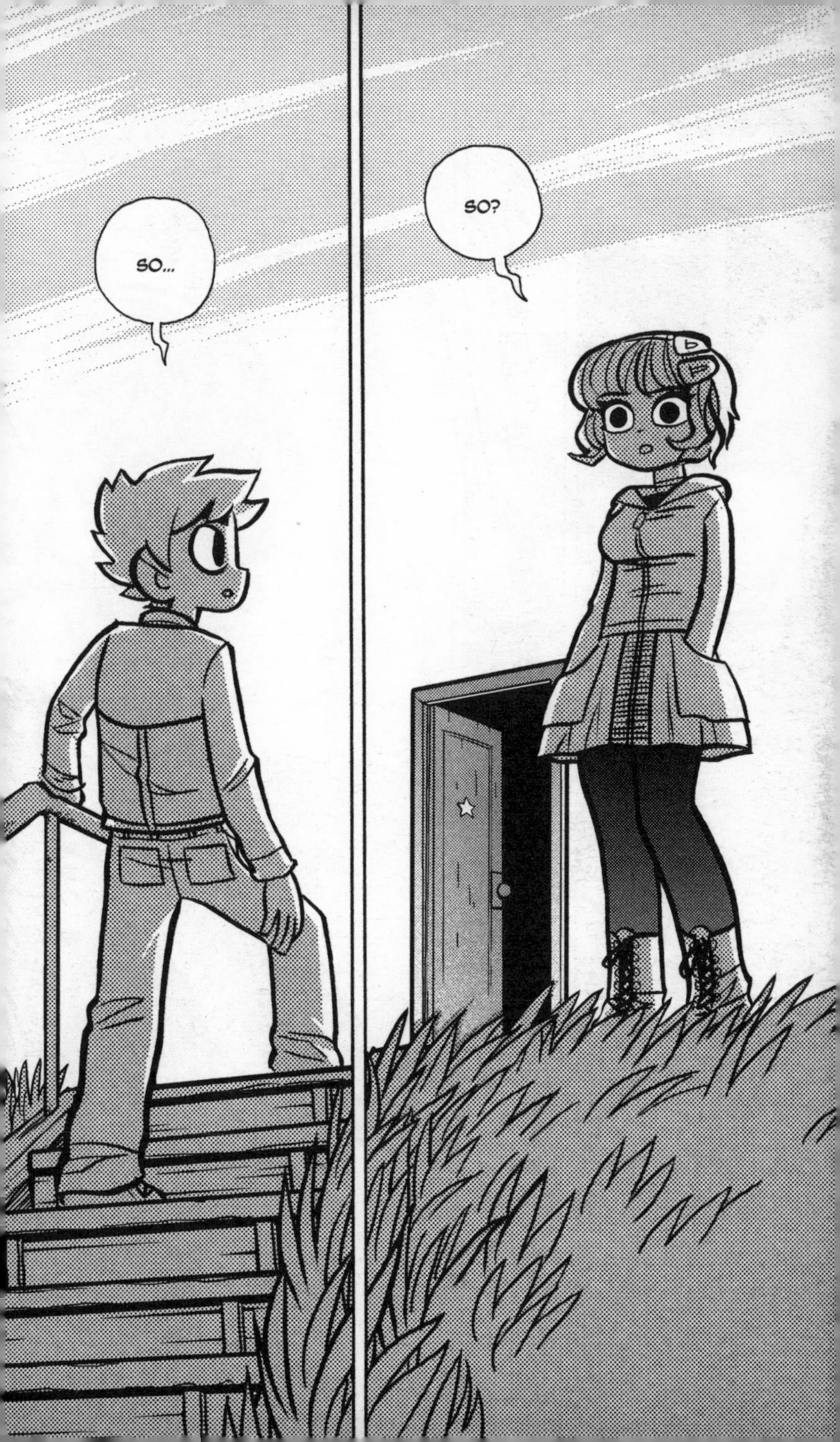
SO...
SO?

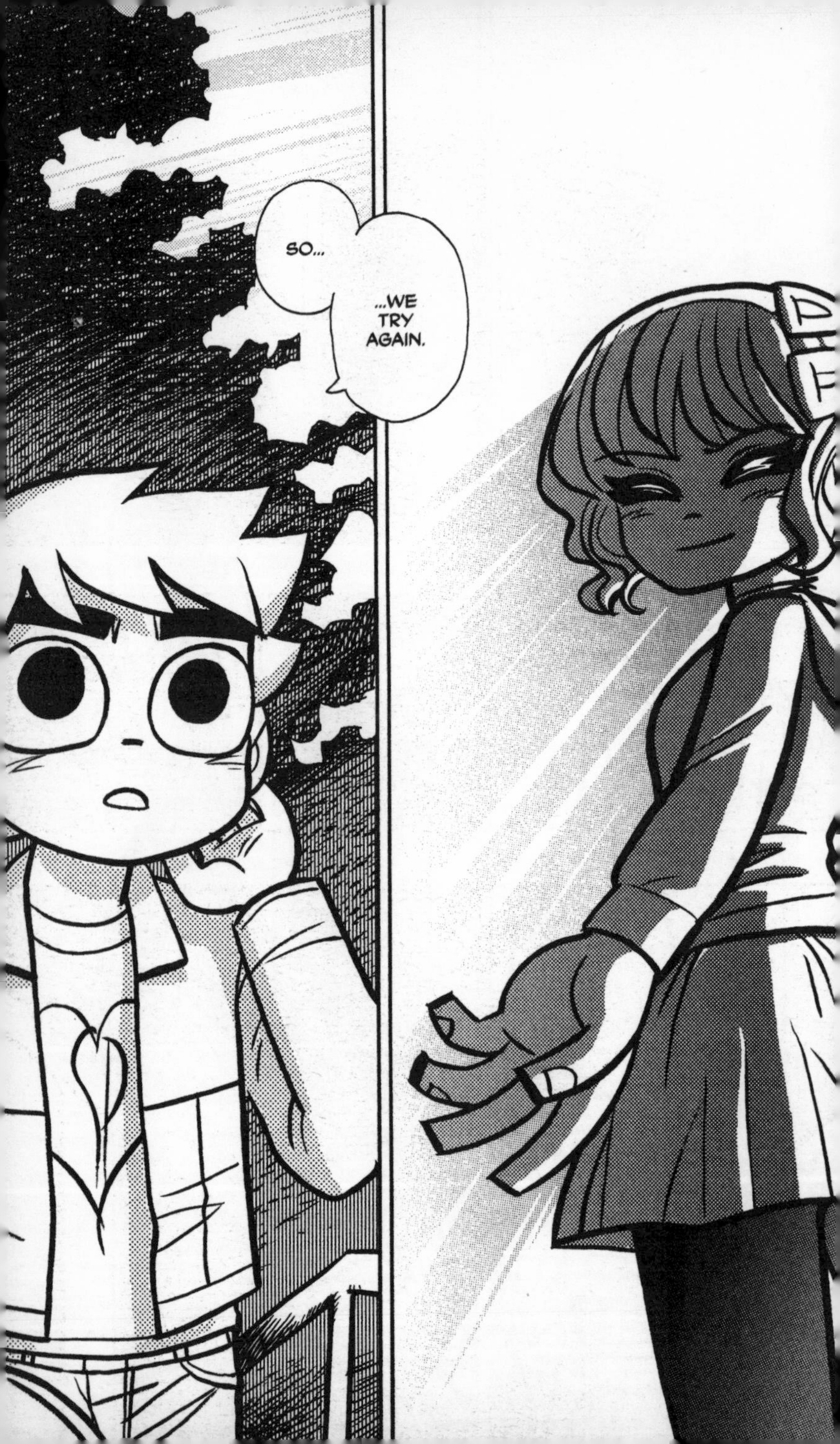
SO...
...WE TRY AGAIN.

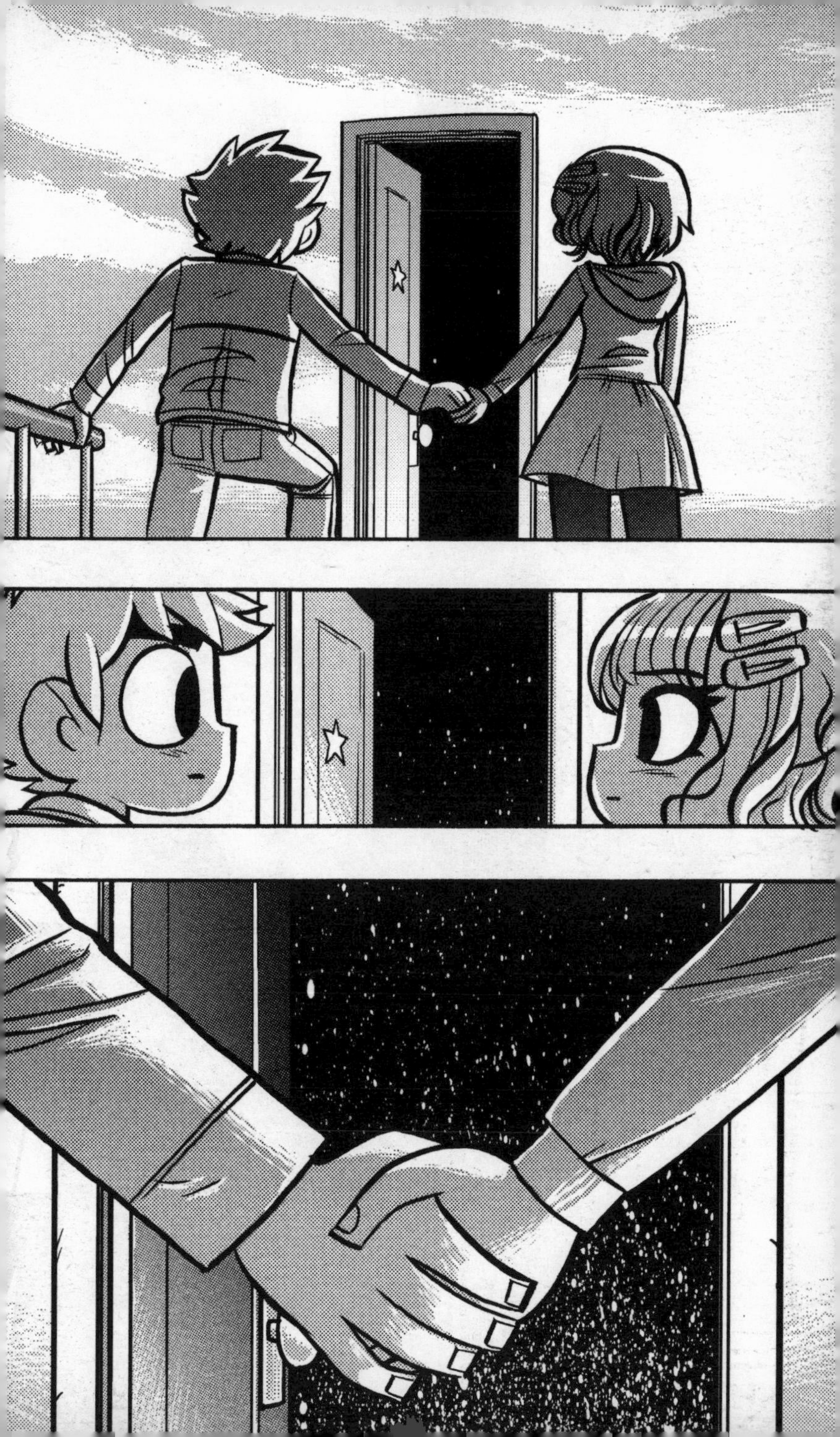

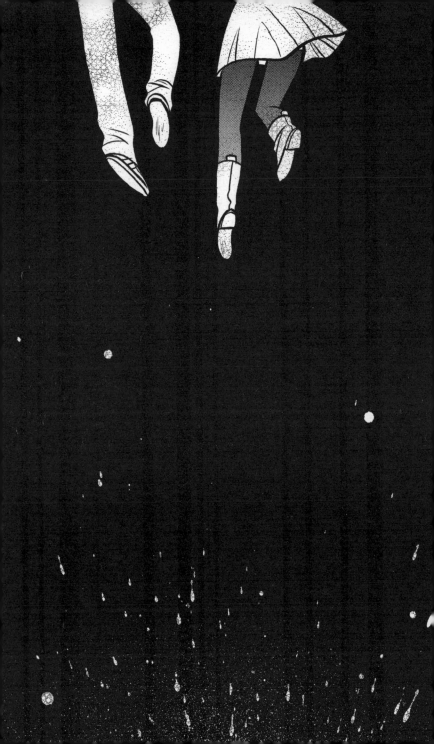

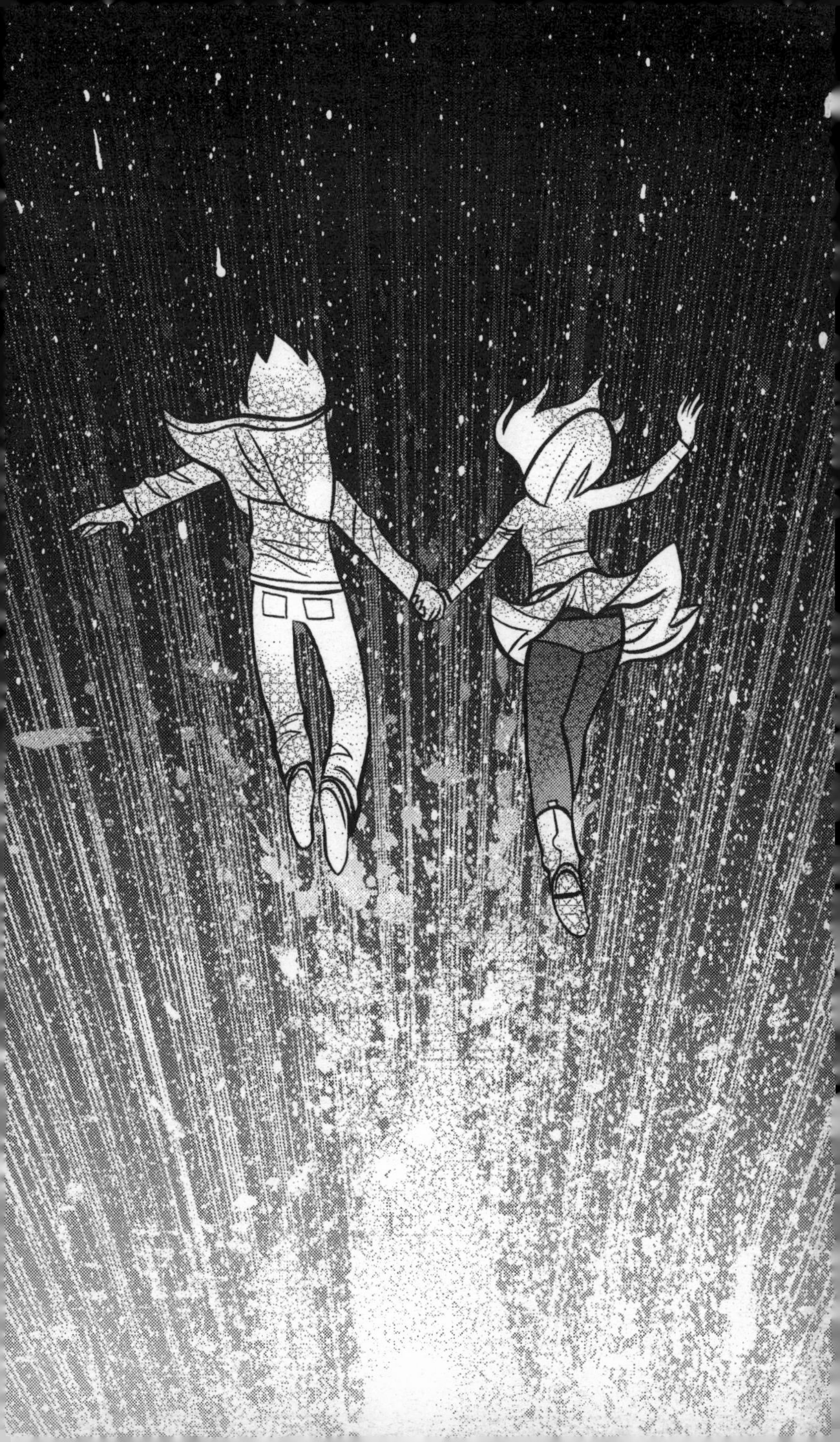

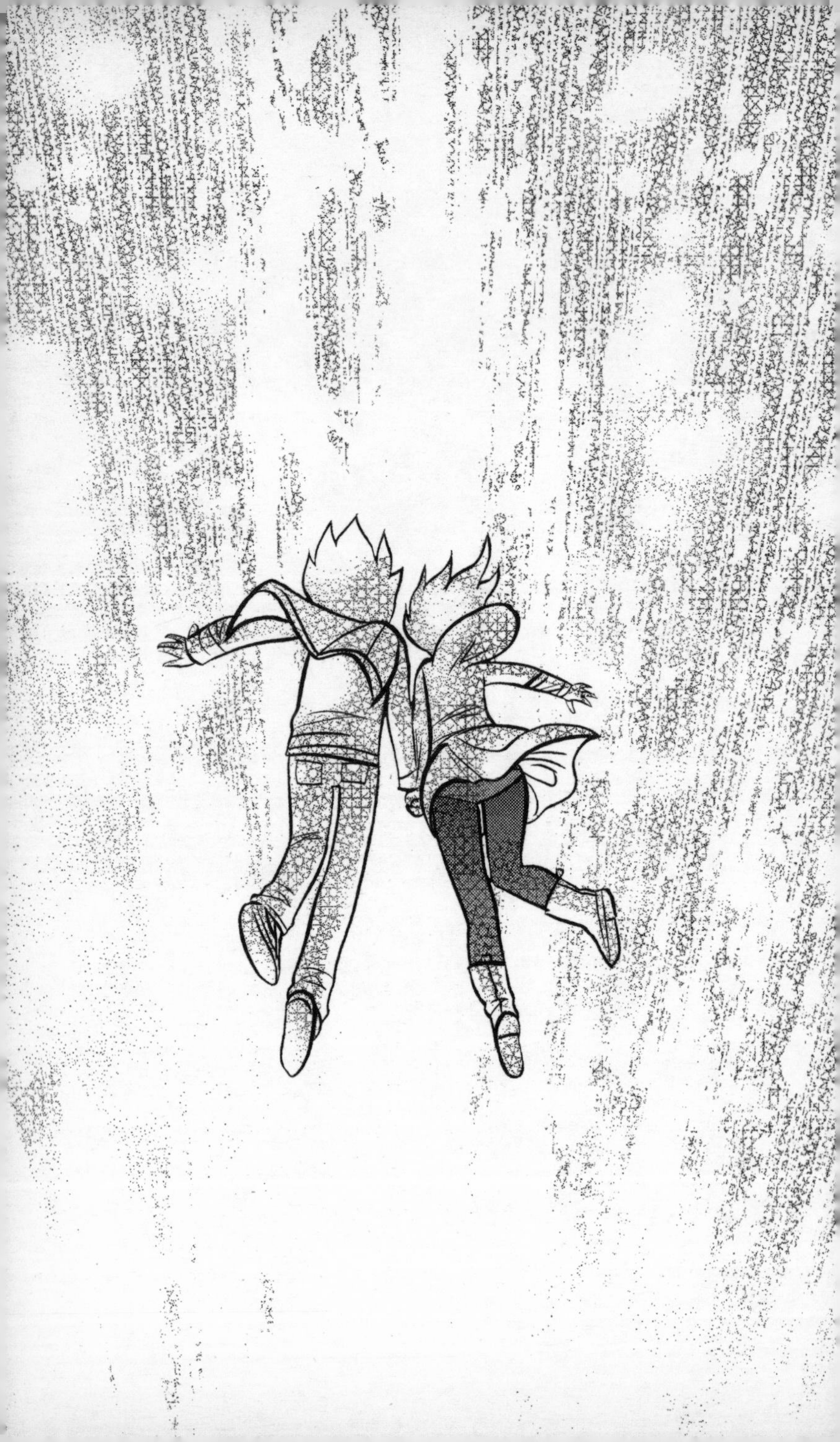

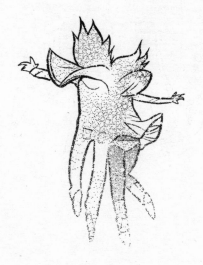

CREATED BY

BRYAN LEE O'MALLEY
(CREATOR — 31 YEARS OLD)

Wrote and drew the book, despite everything.

This book and all the others and the past six years and the other years are all dedicated to Hope Larson.

Thank you and goodnight.

Albums that got me through this:
The Cardigans - *Super Extra Gravity;* Annie - *Don't Stop;* Neko Case - *Middle Cyclone;* Gorillaz - *Plastic Beach;* LCD Soundsystem - *This Is Happening;* Sleigh Bells - *Treats;* Pavement - *Quarantine the Past;* and Spoon - *Transference.*

JOHN KANTZ
Screentone, background art (28 years old) Artist, Legends From Darkwood. Designed Gideon's cryogenic apparatus. www.jackmo.com

AARON ANCHETA
Crowd scenes, inking assist (20 years old) Student at the University of Arizona. This is his first published work. Drew a lot of Ramonas. www.aancheta.com